Reggae
Wisdom

REGGAE

WISDOM

Proverbs
in Jamaican Music

Sw. Anand Prahlad

University Press of Mississippi
Jackson

www.upress.state.ms.us

09 08 07 06 05 04 03 02 01   4 3 2 1
∞

Photographs from the collection of the author

Library of Congress Cataloging-in-Publication
Data

Prahlad, Sw. Anand.
    Reggae wisdom : proverbs in Jamaican
  music / Sw. Anand Prahlad.
      p.   cm.
    Includes bibliographical references (p.),
  discography (p.), and index.
    ISBN 1-57806-319-1 (cloth : alk.
  paper)—ISBN 1-57806-320-5 (paper : alk.
  paper)
    1. Reggae music—Texts.   2. Proverbs,
  Jamaican—History and criticism.   I. Title.
  ML3532.P73   2001
  782.421646′0268—dc21   00-044911

British Library Cataloging-in-Publication Data
available

To my wife, LuAnne; my son, Nick; my guide, Osho; and warriorpriests Joseph Hill, Burning Spear (Winston Rodney), Keith Porter, Winston "Pipe" Matthews, Lloyd "Bread" McDonald, Bob Marley, and Bunny Wailer

Contents

Acknowledgments

My thanks for this work must go first to the countless Jamaican artists and communities responsible for the evolution of roots reggae. This includes the many unsung artists whose names we may never know, Rastafari visionaries and community workers, and those who have gained a measure of notoriety in the record business. To those whose voices and sounds have been like lights in the darkness of the postmodern, neocolonial world, I offer "much respect." I thank artists such as Bob Marley, the Wailers, Culture, U-Roy, the Itals, Justin Hinds and the Dominoes, the Gladiators, the Mighty Diamonds, I-Roy, the Abyssinians, Leonard Dillon and the Ethiopians, Bunny Wailer, the Congos, Burning Spear, Dennis Brown, Freddie McGregor, Danny Red, the Wailing Souls, the Meditations, Yabby U, Peter Tosh, Mutabaruka, Steel Pulse, Prince Far I, Donovan, Hugh Mundell, Lee Scratch Perry, Roman Stewart, Johnny Osborn, Judy Mowatt, Sister Carol, Sister Nancy, the Melodians, Delroy Wilson, Ken Booth, Black Uhuru, the Pioneers, Gregory Isaacs, Arema, Don Carlos, the Heptones, Augustus Pablo, Thunderball, Alpha and Omega, Count Ossie and the Mystic Revelation of Rastafari, Jacob Miller, I-Jah Man, Linval Thompson, Cornell Cambell,

Mikey Dread, Ras Michael and the Sons and Daughters of Negus, I-shan People, Carlton Patterson, Larry Marshall, Jah Lloyd, Pablo Moses, the Rastafarians, Joe Higgs, Peter Broggs, Ras Levi and the Family of Rastafari, Alton Ellis, Johnny Clark, Bob Andy, Frankie Paul, the Viceroys, Sugar Minott, Jr. Byles, Luky Dube, Alpha Blonde, and the many players of instruments. And a special thanks to the deejays and promoters, young and old, who have ensured that reggae sounds reach the hearts of fans internationally. In this regard, I thank especially Roger Steffens and Hank Holmes for their *Reggae Beat* radio program that aired in Santa Monica, California, in the 1980s, contributing greately to my reggae education.

The support of friends and family has been invaluable during the years of research and writing of this manuscript. I thank my wife, LuAnne, for the endless support she has given me in the various phases of this project, including her perseverence during the countless hours I spent in the library and crouched in front of a computer terminal. Her companionship and assistance in the field were invaluable, and I am especially grateful for her recording and photographic skills. I thank her for the unwavering love and friendship that saw me through a project about which I often felt I had "bitten off more than I could chew." I thank also those other lights of my life, my son Nicholas, my mother, and my siblings, whose love has helped to sustain me and without whom I would not have had the strength and focus to complete this work. I am grateful as well to fellow folklorist and friend, Elaine Lawless, for her continued encouragement and belief in my work, and for the many conversations and ideas, not only about this particular work but about folkloristic concerns in general. I thank folklorists and scholars Daryl C. Dance, Alan Dundes, Wolfgang Mieder, and Shirley Arora for their continued support and encouragement.

I owe a special debt to a former student, Tiffany Grahm, who volunteered to help with my research and uncovered many of the references cited here. She was a tireless and enthusiastic assistant to whom I am deeply grateful. I thank also Julia Timphony and Pippa Letsky for the generous and careful proofreading of the manuscript, and Sharon Fisher and Vickie Thorp for the many times they have helped with typing and photocopying. My thanks also goes to the many students and colleagues at the University of Missouri, Columbia, whose good vibes helped to create an environment in which the creative inspiration for this work could blossom. Finally, I am indebted to the

University of Missouri Research Council and Research Board for several grants that helped to support my fieldwork in Jamaica.

Grateful acknowledgement is made for the use of portions of the following:

1. CULTURE
"Jah Rastafari," by Joseph Hill, copyright 1979. Virgin Music Ltd. Used by permission. All rights reserved.
"Outcast," by Joseph Hill, copyright 1997. Tafari Music, ASCAP. Used by permission. All rights reserved.
"Alone in the Wilderness," by Joseph Hill, copyright 1977. Joe Gibbs Music, BMI. Used by permission. All rights reserved.
"Play Skillfully," by Joseph Hill, copyright 1981. Joe Gibbs Music, BMI. Used by permission. All rights reserved.
"Callie Weed Song," by Joseph Hill, copyright 1981. Joe Gibbs Music, BMI. Used by permission. All rights reserved.
"Frying Pan," by Joseph Hill, copyright 1989. Shanachie Records, Inc. Used by permission. All rights reserved.
"Iron Sharpen Iron," by Joseph Hill, copyright 1981. Joe Gibbs Music, BMI. Used by permission. All rights reserved.
"Hand a Bowl," by Joseph Hill, copyright 1989. Tafari Music, ASCAP. Used by permission. All rights reserved.
"Weeping and Wailing," by Joseph Hill, copyright 1981. Joe Gibbs Music, BMI. Used by permission. All rights reserved.
"A Double Tribute to the O.M.," by Joseph Hill, copyright 1982. Cultural Foundations: Poli-Rhythm Ltd. Used by permission. All rights reserved.
"Walk with Jah," by Joseph Hill, copyright 1997. Tafari Music, ASCAP. Used by permission. All rights reserved.
"Have E Have E," by Joseph Hill, copyright 1999. Tafari Music, ASCAP. Used by permission. All rights reserved.
"Be Honest," by Joseph Hill, copyright 1991. Shanachie Records, Inc. Used by permission. All rights reserved.

2. MIKEY DREAD
"My Religion," by Mikey Dread, copyright 1991. Dread at the Controls Publishing, ASCAP. Used by permission. All rights reserved.

7. BOB MARLEY

"Forever Loving Jah," by Bob Marley, copyright 1980. Bob Marley Music Ltd./ Almo Music Corp., ASCAP. Used by permission. All rights reserved.

"Small Axe," by Bob Marley, copyright 1973. Tuff Gong Music Ltd., ASCAP. Used by permission. All rights reserved.

"Revolution," by Bob Marley, copyright 1978. Bob Marley Music Ltd./Almo Music Corp., ASCAP. Used by permission. All rights reserved.

"She's Gone," by Bob Marley, copyright 1978. Bob Marley Music Ltd./Almo Music Corp., ASCAP. Used by permission. All rights reserved.

8. LARRY MARSHALL

"Heavy Heavy Load," by Larry Marshall, copyright 1992. Poli- Rhythm Ltd. Used by permission. All rights reserved.

"Throw Me Corn," by Larry Marshall, copyright 1992. Kings Music Records, Inc. Used by permission. All rights reserved.

"Nanny Goat," by Larry Marshall, copyright 1992. Kings Music Records, Inc. Used by permission. All rights reserved.

9. MICHAEL PROPHET

"Hear I Prayer," by Michael Prophet, copyright 1980. Grove Music, MCPS. Used by permission. All rights reserved.

10. MAX ROMEO

"Smile Out of Style," by Lee Perry, copyright 1976. Island Music, BMI. Used by permission. All rights reserved.

11. THE WAILING SOULS

"Stop Red Eye," by the Wailing Souls, copyright 1990. Used by permission. All rights reserved.

"Who Lives It," by the Wailing Souls, copyright 1982. Shanachie Records Corp. Used by permission. All rights reserved.

"Old Broom," by the Wailing Souls, copyright 1990. Shanachie Records Corp. Used by permission. All rights reserved.

"Run Dem Down," by the Wiling Souls, copyright 1982. Shanachie Records Corp. Used by permission. All rights reserved.

"Fire Coal," by the Wailing Souls, copyright 1999. Used by permission. All rights reserved.

12. BURNING SPEAR

"Slavery Days," by Winston Rodney, copyright 1975. Island Music, BMI. Used by permission. All rights reserved.

Introduction

In the early 1970s, while attending an African literature conference in Austin, Texas, I heard Bob Marley for the first time. I remember vividly lying in bed, balmy Texas air blowing in the window, and along with it the scents of Mexican cooking and the distant sounds of salsa and Tex-Mex border music. The host with whom I was staying put *Natty Dread* on the turntable, and by the time the bass line of "Lively Up Yourself" had circled back I was permanently hooked. I was overwhelmed by the familiarity of this music I had never heard before. I felt as if it had always been in the recesses of my soul, waiting to be ignited. This music unlatched the door to a cage in my heart where scents and sense and rhythms of Africa, Caribbean sunshine, and forgotten spirits had been kept secret, and let them all loose to soar.

From that moment forward, reggae became a food, a nourishment, a meditation, a heartbeat that helped keep me centered as I followed the path away from home, deeper and deeper into the white American world. At this time, I was a junior at Virginia Commonwealth University in Richmond, majoring in English. I had accepted that a university education was necessary in order to acquire a measure of respect and comfort in American society. At the same time, I realized that very little of the material that I would be introduced to would resonate with who I was, where I came from, or where I envisioned my spiritual self to be going. In the years that followed, reggae would become the cultural/spiritual/political force that helped me to "hang together" and not to succumb to the schizophrenia that looms like a shadow over so many of us who are first-generation, fresh off the plantation, and trying to navigate the waters of American higher educational institutions.

I have loved reggae as I have loved no other music. Not even the blues. I love its brashness, its audacity, its tones, its harmonies, its chords. I love its infectious beat, its spiritual strength and insistence on telling the truth in as raw and naked a fashion as possible. I love its spiritual militance: I believe it is the most militant music of the twentieth century. I love its eloquent articulation of a neo-African cultural space and time. I love how it embodies an utter refusal to surrender to the rat race, to Western ideology. How adamant it is to maintain an African-based rhythm, speed, and philosophical orientation, slow and meditative, reflective and wisdom seeking. I love its clarity of vision, its commitment to reexamining old myths and creating new ones. And I love that one of the fundamental elements in reggae is the use of proverbs.

I will always remember sitting in my family's living room in Virginia, listening to the Wailing Souls and hearing my great- grandmother echo a proverb from the song that was playing. "**New brooms only sweep clean**," she said, smiling. "**New brooms only sweep clean**. Now that's a good one." I had not even realized she was listening. But nothing could have demonstrated more profoundly the connection between reggae and the world I grew up in, with elderly black people who adored the well-spoken metaphor, who lived by contemplation and musing, and tried, as much as possible, to live by wisdom. People for whom culture meant the remembrance of stories, the accumulation of lessons, the codes whereby these are communicated, and the wisdom to interpret them; people much like those in the hills of Jamaica.

For most of the time from my introduction to reggae until now, I have not "studied" the proverbs found in the lyrics, at least not in the academic sense. I have lived them, just as someone "churchical" might live with the preacher's sermons, or a zen disciple live with his master's words. I have continually contemplated their meanings and used them as tools to guide my thoughts and actions as I wrestled with the challenges of an academic career and the complexities of modern American life. And so I am writing not only as a folklorist but also as a member of the international reggae community, a group of people around the globe who look to this music for its joy, wisdom, and strength. I am also writing as a musician who has played reggae in various nonprofessional capacities over the past twenty years. As such, I have written this book not just for academicians but for all the "singers and players of instruments" who have helped to create reggae, and for my fellow travelers who have, to some extent, relied upon reggae for sustenance.

I first began collecting proverbs from reggae lyrics around 1990, when I was completing my dissertation on African American proverbs. The following year, I had the opportunity to interview members of the Itals about the proverbs in their songs, which led to an article, "Proverbs of the Itals Reggae Group" (1995). In 1992, I traveled to Jamaica for the first time for the purpose of documenting proverbs as they are used in everyday speech and comparing this usage to the way they are used in the lyrics of a selected group of singers. My plans were to interview different artists about their proverbs—among them, Culture, the Wailing Souls, Bunny Wailer, the Itals, Jimmy Cliff, and Justin Hinds. I eventually came to the realization that a book attempting a thorough discussion of this many artists would be too lengthy and that only a limited number of readers would be interested in the particularities of each artist's lyrics.

So I moved toward a study of proverbs relative to the rhetorical strategies of roots reggae. This includes an understanding of narrative personas used by reggae singers, as well as the cultural traditions and social circumstances out of which these voices emerged. The dominant influence on roots reggae has been Rastafari philosophy and ritual; however, this cannot be fully appreciated unless considered in its historical and cultural context. Thus chapter 1 is devoted to a discussion of critical aspects of the Rastafari religion, including key elements of ideology, rituals, and components of the Rastafari speech community and sociolinguistic symbols and coding. In chapter 2 I explore in depth the nature of the major narrative persona in roots reggae, the warrior/ priest, which evolved out of the historical matrix of other African Jamaican religious and political movements. I also explore in this chapter the rhetorical influences and strategies characterizing roots reggae lyrics and music. Included in this survey are not only proverbs but other traditional genres such as folk songs, children's rhymes and games, boasts, toasts, sermons, Biblical texts, and religious songs (such as spirituals and Sankeys). In the interest of establishing the aesthetic parameters of reggae discourse, I furthermore consider the impact of these various genres on the lyrical structure of reggae.

For those well versed in reggae, these two chapters may seem unnecessary or old hat; however, their content is essential to the main concern of the study—the uses and meanings of proverbs. In fact, one of the challenges of writing the book was to become cognizant of what background information a reader might need in order fully to appreciate proverb application in reggae discourse. I begin with the assumption that many readers will be knowledgeable concerning proverbs but relatively uninformed about elements of Jamaican culture that give some of the proverbs their distinctiveness within reggae.

Since my major goal is to explicate proverb meaning in reggae, a discussion of proverbs in Jamaican society seems essential. There are a number of impressive field studies of Jamaican proverbs but none that discuss the proverbs of particular persons as they are used in context. Hence, chapter 3 is a discussion of proverbial speech acts collected during my fieldwork in different parts of Jamaica. I discuss proverbs from the Jamaican media and informants. My primary informant was a Rastafari who lived in the mountains east of Negril, and considerable space is devoted to my interactions with him in which he used and explained the meanings of proverbs.

This study represents a departure from convention, in part because I am concerned with the contextual analysis of proverbs in a popular medium. While articles have been written on proverbs in popular music (Mieder 1988, Folsom 1993c, Taft 1994), as yet no full-length study has been devoted to this topic, and to my knowledge my essay on proverbs used by the Itals is the only explication of proverbs in reggae. In general, folklorists have shied away from the study of folklore situated in electronic media. Hampered by archaic notions about what constitutes folklore and the ofttimes suspect distinctions between it and popular culture, folklorists often push the realities of the contemporary technological society aside and persist in focusing on "pure" expressions. In essence, these distinctions between folk, popular, and elite culture hinge on romantic perceptions of time and a nostalgic longing for a simplicity that has all but vanished from the face of the planet. Reggae is, unquestionably, folk music in the purest sense of the word. In this study, I embrace every facet of reggae as a context for the proverbs under discussion. This includes the cover art of record albums; promotional materials; the nuts and bolts of the recording industry; the pulse of the electricity that surges through giant speakers at concerts; the name brand and tenor of electric instruments, receivers, and amplifiers; radios, turntables, and stereos; and stage props. The proverbs *live* in an electronic environment and, to be fully appreciated, must be explored within that context.

Chapters 4, 5, and 6 are theoretical analyses of proverbs from the songs of various artists. In chapter 4 I examine proverbial speech in roots reggae in general. I propose theoretical models, note relationships between structural elements and proverb use, and explore how rhetorical strategies of the warrior/priest persona influence the meanings of proverbs that are used. Chapter 5 focuses on the proverbs of Keith Porter of the Itals, the most prolific proverb master in roots reggae. I examine the most prevalent structural model of Ital songs, which is comparable to the lack/lack liquidated motifemic plot discussed by Dundes (1965) in his analysis of Native American folktales. The idea of "oracular" proverb clusters, comparable to the verses recited by Ifá diviners, is also proposed. The final chapter is an explication of proverbs in the context of Bob Marley's songs. Special focus is given to Marley's propensity to raise everyday objects to the level of cultural symbols, laden with aesthetic and political meanings.

A final goal of this book is to further the appreciation for the lyrical and musical genius of roots reggae artists. The creators of roots music conceptualized it as a spiritual, medicinal force, containing certain essential "ingredients." It relies heavily on African musical sensibilities, evolving out of traditions found among African Jamaican groups such as the Maroons and the Kromantees. I am not concerned in this project with all different kinds of reggae. "Roots reggae" refers to both the form and the content of the genre; both aspects are anchored in neo-African traditions. For example, the music employs African-derived rhythms and uses instruments such as cowbells that are grounded in African musical aesthetics. The lyrics reflect spiritual and social concerns, usually from the perspective of Rastafari ideology. Overall, the songs serve functions of social critique and deconstruction, inspiration, and guidance and are based upon the idea of meditation as a precursory ritual to social action. Of the types of reggae, roots contains by far the largest concentration of proverbs.

As I write this, the face of reggae has changed dramatically from what it was during the late 1970s and 1980s, when roots reggae was the dominant form of the music. During that period, this type of reggae dominated the Jamaican airways and was in demand on Jamaican stages. One could catch roots groups such as the Wailing Souls, Burning Spear, Culture, the Itals, the Meditations, and Bunny Wailer regularly in a variety of venues in urban centers around the

United States. There was in northern California, where I was living at the time, a sizable community of Rastas and numerous local roots reggae bands that played weekly in different clubs around the Bay Area. There were groundings among groups of Rastas in which anyone seriously interested in the religion could participate. The Rastafari presence, along with that of other spiritual groups, colored the cultural and psychic landscape.

But this was a special moment in time. Slowly the Rasta communities became less visible, and many Jamaicans moved away. Roots reggae bands were booked with less frequency. For many it had been a fad and it was time to move on to the next exotic movement. Things were changing in the country, and a particular brand of conservatism that swept across the nation blew into the corners of even the most progressive cities. And in Jamaica, things were also changing, as the American dream infiltrated the consciousness of many people, providing a panacea of hope. In 1991, when I traveled around Jamaica, I was always surrounded by reggae music, either roots or the dancehall of the then popular Shabba Ranks. I heard reggae in the airport, taxicabs, hotel lobbies, restaurants, along the street, on buses. Reggae was clearly the Jamaican music of choice. Upon my return in 1998, I seldom heard reggae. Taxicab drivers were listening to Spice Girls, Celine Dion, African American hip-hop, rap, and gospel. Only one driver either tuned to a radio station playing reggae or played a reggae cassette. The same was true of most shops and restaurants.

The next generation of reggae singers plunged headlong into a new style—dancehall and/or ragga—characterized by borrowings from African American digitized rap, including lyrics and dances centering on the sexually provocative (referred to as "slackness"). To an extent, this period was a response to the foreign embrace of roots reggae and a watering down of the music, a degree of stagnation, and a trend of artists directing their energies more to foreign than to Jamaican audiences. Dancehall represented a search for a more purely Jamaican aesthetic than could be found in much roots reggae of the 90s, and for a music that would speak directly to the next generation of Jamaican listeners. As some scholars note (Bilby 1995; Chang and Chen 1998, 64) this search led to a more sparse, digitalized sound, but it also often employed African-derived rhythms more ancient than Nyabinghi. Although in recent years there has been a movement by many dancehall artists back to more "conscious," "cultural" music, changes in Jamaican society make it practically impossible for the phenomenon that occurred with artists such as Bob Marley ever to happen again. Thus, gone is the era that some call "the golden age of reggae," a moment in history when social, cultural, and political forces converged to ignite a proliferation of culturally, spiritually, and artistically inspired lyrics and music that may never be duplicated.

Fortunately, many roots artists and master proverb users are still actively recording and touring, including the Itals, Culture, the Wailing Souls, Burning Spear, the Meditations, the Abyssinians, the Gladiators, the Congos, and Bunny Wailer. Unfortunately, one cannot always assume that their most recent works are as rootsy or inspired as their earlier recordings. Whatever disposition one takes toward the continual evolution of Jamaican music, one cannot dismiss the reality of subcultures around the globe united by their love of Rasta reggae. As my discussion will indicate, these are subcultures that love the spiritual "vibe" of the music as well as the sermonic and religiously based structures and aesthetics of this type of reggae. Ironically, one stands a better chance of seeing these artists perform abroad than in Jamaica.

While some writers are highly critical of roots artists for catering to foreign tastes (Chang and Chen 1998, Regis 1994), such criticisms overlook compelling facets of this dilemma. First, artists such as Culture and Burning Spear are still producing music firmly grounded in Jamaican roots reggae. It is not so much that they have abandoned Jamaican audiences, but they have resisted the impulse to change their styles to keep up with the current Jamaican trends. Rather, they remain committed to the ideology that produced roots reggae in the first place, and some are quite adamant about this. Culture argues that reggae should be a music observing specific cultural ideas of decorum. He sings in criticism of dancehall, "You can't even play it for the children in the house" ("Selector," *Three Sides*).[1] Burning Spear sings in a similar vein, "We want back the roots in the music / We want back the history in the music / we want back the culture in the music!" ("Appointment with His Majesty," *Appointment with His Majesty*). Hence, it is more accurate to suggest that segments of the Jamaican population have lost interest in some of these artists, and in the philosophy they represent. To put it another way, despite the eventual respect accorded Rastas in Jamaica, the movement has remained marginalized and its philosophies do not represent the sentiments of most Jamaicans. Another issue confronting roots artists is that Jamaican fans or devotees have no financial base upon which to operate performance venues facilitating more opportunities for roots bands to perform regularly in Jamaica. The reality is that these artists, like everyone else, have to make a living. The tragedy is not so much the impact of foreign interests on roots reggae but a poverty- stricken economy that cannot support a full range of cultural forms.

Beyond the fact that proverbs are more prevalent in roots than in other styles, this is the type of reggae I personally prefer. Change and Chen (1998, 64) write that: " 'Classic' reggae in Jamaica today is like rock and roll in America—acknowledged as the tradition's foundation, but also yesterday's music, what daddy and mommy used to listen to." But mommy and daddy are joined by a worldwide network of listeners for whom this period of music simply fulfills a need that later periods do not. One might compare these aficionados to listeners who prefer Bach, Charlie Parker, Billie Holiday, Muddy Waters, or Frank Sinatra. For them the music is timeless, making the notion of current trends irrelevant. For some it is a spriritual fountain, for others not. Because of my bias in this regard, I have listened almost exclusively to roots reggae and have not surveyed either dancehall or ragga for proverb use.

It is my conviction that roots music will someday be appreciated by a larger world audience. I believe that in time more people will recognize the genius of these works and marvel that a figure like Bob Marley was not nominated for such honors as the Nobel Peace Prize, validating the enormity of his contribution to the betterment of human kind. Of course, racism is a barrier to this wider recognition. But history offers abundant examples in which once maligned and misunderstood Black music forms eventually receive greater attention and appreciation. For instance, it has now become fashionable for American intellectuals and professionals to support jazz, a music that was once considered primitive, exotic, too linked to "the other" for "decent" people to patronize. I contend that while the musical structures of reggae may not be as complex as those of jazz, the subtleties of rhythm and the intelligence that courses through the music rivals that of any genre. That intellect can only become accessible to those willing to stretch themselves, to work at deciphering the verbal and musical codes, which in many instances is no easy task for non-Jamaicans. However, the rewards can be quite sublime, in fact, as transcendent as those evoked by any great art. Moreover, reggae has captured more poignantly than any contemporary art form the prevailing pulse of the colonized; consequently, anyone interested in better understanding New World African or "Third World" philosophy has to engage reggae. What better doorway to enter this rich and powerful, eclectic world of sound and sense than through the magical wisdom of proverbs?

**Reggae
Wisdom**

THE ORIGINAL MAN

Culture and Ideology; A Contextual Frame

Do you remember the days of slavery?
Do you remember the days of slavery?
Do you remember?
Do you remember?

Burning Spear, "Slavery Days," *Marcus Garvey*

I'm the original man,
straight from creation,
the original man.

Andrew Tosh, "Original Man," *Original Man*

A contextual study of proverbs in reggae is challenging for a number of reasons. The most obvious is that one has to rely primarily on textual fragments lifted from the musical and performative contexts in which the proverbs live. There is no completely satisfactory way to treat oralic discourse in the textual media of print. In my previous study of African American proverbs in context (1996), I extended the argument made by others (Kirshenblatt-Gimblett 1981, Jordan 1982, Levy and Zumwalt 1990) that proverbs "mean" only in context; that there is no singularly "correct" interpretation for any proverb but instead multiple meanings generated by different speakers/hearers in varying situations. In an attempt to account for this multiplicity of interpretations, I theorized four levels of meaning that operate simultaneously when proverbs are used. Those levels are the *grammatical,* the *social,* the *situational,* and the *symbolic.* In short, the *grammatical* meaning is the literal translation of the proverb. The *social* is the meaning generally understood within a particular group. The *situational* meaning refers to how the proverb is used rhetorically in any given instance. Finally, the *symbolic* meaning suggests the personal associative images and meanings that a speaker or listener brings to a given proverb speech act as a result of past experiences with the proverb.

Looking at proverbs in reggae poses different kinds of problems from those I encountered in my study of African American proverbs. There are no person-to-person speech acts, per se, but rather recordings—and in some cases live performances—of songs in which proverbs are used. The proverb lives as a part of a performed sound event in which the actual speaker is not so significant as the persona being employed in the song. Thus the levels of proverb meaning are more restricted in this study. I am concerned only occasionally, for instance, with the *symbolic* associations that proverbs might hold for particular speakers or listeners. Nor am I very concerned with *situational* meanings, for in the case of recordings there is no specific interactional situation about which to refer. The *social* level of meaning, however, becomes a major focus of my concern. Undoubtedly each listener will give the proverbs slightly different nuances of interpretation, an assumption that is made by the songwriters who are often deliberately vague to elicit multiple interpretations. At the same time, however, songwriters are also hopeful that an awareness of their ideological perspectives will inform the listeners' interpretations.

A concentration on the *social* level of meaning necessitates a thorough exploration of the worldview of the group from which the speakers come—in this case African Jamaican Rastafari. While I wish to avoid the common practice of narrowly viewing proverbs as reflections of group "values," it is important to understand the cultural and historical factors that shape the perspectives and concerns of the artists whose lyrics are under discussion. Otherwise, one cannot fully appreciate the distinct uses of proverbs within reggae compared with their uses within other song traditions. For example,

Folsom (1993c) notes that the proverbs **Everything that glitters is not gold, Absence makes the heart grow fonder, Still waters run deep, An ounce of prevention is worth a pound of cure, Where there's a will there's a way,** and **A rolling stone gathers no moss** are found in American country music. Taft (1994) and Prahlad (1996) examine a plethora of proverbial expressions found in African American blues music, including **You reap what you sow, A rolling stone gathers no moss, You never miss your water until your well runs dry, The blacker the berry the sweeter the juice, Don't bite the hand that feeds you, Seeing is believing, Don't burn your bridges behind you,** and **To jump from the frying pan into the fire.** As it turns out, all of these proverbs are also used in reggae; but, as one would expect, there they carry different shades of meaning. To a large extent the differences result from the radically distinct worldviews informing blues, country music, and reggae.

An examination of the cultural context out of which these songs arise is also essential to understanding the aesthetic dimensions of the lyrics, including poetic devices, timing, innovations in syntax, and relationships to musical elements. Because Jamaica has retained such a strong African heritage, its proverbial speech is more African-influenced than parallel speech behavior among African Americans. Numerous scholars have written on the general importance of proverbial speech across the continent of Africa (e.g., Finnegan 1970; Christensen 1958; Messenger 1959; Oledzki 1979; Crepeau 1978; Yankah 1989a, 1989b), where it is said by the Yoruba that "Proverbs are the horses of speech; if communication is lost, we use proverbs to find it" (Priebe 1971, 26). Even more scholars have studied specific applications of proverbs within particular African groups. For instance, Evans-Pritchard (1963a, 4) and Finnegan (1970, 424) both discuss the uses of proverbs among the Azande as a part of *sanza*, or veiled insult. Yankah has written the most on contextualized uses of proverbs, discussing aesthetic dimensions of them among the Akan (1989).

A number of studies provide information on the uses of proverbs in African song traditions. Knappert's exegesis (1997) of Swahili proverbs in songs is a glimpse into a fascinating tradition of proverbs in Islamic poetry and song, covering a wide range of areas, including work, love, marriage, hymns, epics, and political song. Ogede's insightful essay on proverbs in the praise songs of the Igede (1993) provides an intimate look at the use of proverbs by an African bard, Michah Ichegbeh. Among other things, we learn from these articles about the strong African tradition of proverb use in song as forms of social critique and to boost the spirits of warriors. But what distinguishes Jamaican proverbial speech from that of the above-mentioned groups on the African continent? Furthermore, what aesthetic influences do the beliefs and practices of Rastafari add to Jamaican proverb use? How do other influences such as biblical, American, African American, and British enter into this sociolinguistic equation? To what extent does the medium of popular music affect the encoding and decoding of reggae proverbs? And finally, how are these influences realized in the proverbial language of reggae discourse? For answers to these questions, we must begin with an investigation of the cultural and ideological context from which reggae discourse arises.

The Proverbs

In Michael Taft's essay on proverbs in blues lyrics, he concludes that although proverbs are not uncommon in blues, they are relatively infrequent. He only found about twenty-five proverbs, thirty-six proverbial comparisons, and fifteen proverbial expressions in several thousand blues texts. I have not undertaken the same kind of statistical survey of reggae, nor have I listened extensively to all types of reggae music. My survey does suggest, however, that proverbs are frequently found in a certain kind of reggae and, more specifically, that the lyrics of particular artists are especially rich in proverbial expressions. These artists include Culture, Bob Marley, the Itals, the Wailing Souls, and to a lesser degree Peter Tosh, Bunny Wailer, and Justin Hinds and the Dominoes.

We might conclude from this, therefore, that such artists are proverb masters (Prahlad 1996) and that it is their mastery of proverbial speech more than the genre of reggae itself that accounts for the proliferation of proverbial items in their works. It must certainly be more than coincidence, however, that these artists share ideological orientations, reached the height of their artistry around the same time period of reggae's development, and all play "roots" reggae. Undoubtedly, there is some connection between the emergence of proverb masters and these other factors. The generally recognized periods of Jamaican popular music are ska, rock steady, reggae, dancehall, and ragga. Although some critics refer to all of these periods as "reggae," each period is, in fact, marked by distinct musical and lyrical elements. The category of "roots" was most prominent during the rock steady and reggae periods. The roots category refers to reggae that is inspired by Rastafari ideology (as well as musical and lyrical aesthetics). This includes a conscious effort to celebrate various African-influenced cultural elements, including but not limited to verbal expressions. Reasons for the prevalent use of proverbs in this type of reggae will become apparent as this study unfolds.

In addition to "traditional" proverbs—those that have already been documented in a previous collection—I am also concerned with so-called invented expressions in this study—hence, with the issue of proverbiality as well as with proverbs proper. Within the context of reggae discourse, phrases are used effectively as proverbs even though they may have no established traditionality prior to the lyrics of a particular song. Several factors facilitate this. Many of the proverbs used in reggae discourse are Jamaican and are thus unfamiliar to a large percentage of the foreign reggae audience. Therefore, foreign audiences are commonly confronted with expressions that sound proverbial but of which they have no previous knowledge. Why should such listeners respond any differently to invented expressions than to those that are, in fact, traditional? Rather, it is more likely that invented expressions can succeed rhetorically because they *sound* proverbial, and within the context of a song the rhetoric of sound is paramount. Arora (1994) has demonstrated in her study of Hispanic proverbs and speakers that listeners often assume proverbiality based on the sound of an expression. My study of blues lyrics also indicated that proverbs were often found with accompanying lines that sounded proverbial (1996, 81–90). It would prove negligent to ignore examples of invented proverbs in reggae discourse, especially if the aesthetic rhetoric of the lyrics is a main concern.

Ideological Influences in Reggae

The lyrics and rhetorical strategies of reggae reflect a wide range of influences. Proverbs, for instance, which sparkle like diamonds among other precious stones, are one of many traditional genres that find their way into this music. In order to understand the role proverbs play, however, the connection between them and other genres must be explored; at the same time, we have to survey the general and specific cultural contexts out of which these oral traditions emerge. Such an examination of Jamaican traditions is particularly complex, as it includes elements from the rich and diverse African heritages represented in different parts of the country; a variety of religious and secular folk groups, dialects, and performance styles; a dense fabric of mythology, legend, ritual, and belief; and a charged history of political and social movements that have had no small impact on the aesthetics of proverb use. In fact, I will only have time briefly to mention these components, which are extensive enough to require multiple volumes to give them the scrutiny they deserve. The dominant worldview influencing the construction of roots reggae is, of course, Rastafari. Hence, this chapter is concerned with the ideology of this mystical religion in the historical context of Jamaican society and, specifically, with those elements that have the most profound impact on reggae discourse. Narrative personas and the diverse rhetorical genres that comprise reggae will be explored in the next chapter.

Before the advent of Rastafari influence in reggae, the lyrics and music were less rhetorically complex. Early reggae was dominated by lyrical trends borrowed from American rhythm and blues and from soul music. With the development of ska and rock steady, we see the inclusion of more purely Jamaican aesthetics. It was not until reggae artists began their conversion to Rastafari, however, that elements of African Jamaican culture moved to the forefront as symbols of identity and pride, and as markers of aesthetic standards. One can compare this period in Jamaican music to the Black Arts Movement in African American poetry. Beginning with the Black Arts Movement, African American poets rejected English standards of poetry, turning instead to their own oral traditions to define the parameters of their aesthetics. While earlier poets, such as Langston Hughes, Sterling Brown, and James Weldon Johnson, may have occasionally relied upon oral traditions, most poets began doing so after the Black Arts Movement. Hence, the African American poetic aesthetic was permanently changed. My discussion of reggae, then, begins with a comparable period of dramatic change in the way in which Jamaican reggae was conceptualized.

One of Rastafari's most significant contributions to reggae was the impact on the narrative personas used by singers in their lyrics, lives, and performances. The spread of Rastafari eventually heralded a new age of consciousness, an era in which many Jamaicans—not only reggae artists—would experience a fundamental transformation of identity. With this new identity came forms of self-presentation, a new voice, and an altered relationship to elements of Jamaican and African culture. The role that the music played in society and the nature of the audience also changed. Prior to 1945, for example, "the radio stations of Jamaica continuously played the music of white America—Elvis Presley, Pat Boone, Doris Day and Neil Sedaka" (Campbell 1987, 126), and early singers aspired to an aesthetic for popular and "worthwhile" music that was based upon European and American aesthetics.

The introduction of Rastafari elements into Jamaican music coincided with the emergence of ska and the tradition of "sound systems." Sound systems developed in the mid 1950s as a reactionary response to the neocolonial control of Jamaican airways. In fact, many people had no access to radios because they could not afford to buy them. Sound systems brought people together in large yards, in Kingston and rural areas, where "the music of Jamaica and black America could be played without restraint" (Campbell 1987, 127), where they could dance, party, and have a good time. The name "sound system" referred to the powerful, large sound systems (amplifiers, turntables, and speakers) that the deejays used and that were the heart of these gatherings. Deejays such as Duke Reid and Clement Seymour Dodd competed with each other for the best sounds and largest crowds, beginning a tradition that remains an integral part of the Jamaican music scene today. Jones writes: "To date the sound [system] remains the principal context of musical activity for a large proportion of the black working class, and one of the main institutions through which reggae's audience is able to exert some control over the music, by demanding danceable and relevant music" (1988, 30). In many ways, sound systems are comparable to secret nocturnal meetings held by slaves in bush arbors (hidden meeting sites) or other out-of-the-way places. These meetings allowed slaves the opportunity to sing, dance, and worship in the manner they preferred, but which was forbidden by slaveowners. Sound systems were a continuation of a tradition of resistance that characterized every slave and neocolonial settlement of Africans in the Western world.

During the period of the late 1950s and early 1960s, the Rastafari influence in Jamaican music emerged, alongside songs that addressed social problems. This period is marked by the Folks Brothers, "Oh Carolina," which featured the burro drumming of Count Ossie, "the renown Rastafarian elder and percussionist" (Barrow 1993, 32). Campbell writes:

The drumming of *O Carolina* heralded a new era of music, for the songs sung by the Rastafari which extolled Ethiopia and Africa were developed within the confines of the sound systems which vied with each other for supporters. Socio-religious and political songs echoed and reverberated across the gullies from the sound systems, with *By the Rivers of Babylon, Let the Power Fall on I, and the Macabs Version* played along with the classic instrumental records called *Man in the Street, Schooling the Duke, Far East,* and other music of joy, consistent with the pride of achieving the status of political independence. (127)

So while the majority of singers continued to base their lyrics and perform-ance styles on American soul and rhythm and blues, the seeds for a new musi-cal direction had begun to send shoots up from the soil. The guiding concept of a song was still as a form of entertainment; however, a dramatic shift in this as well as in the concept of audience, as indicated by the emergence of sound systems, was in progress. Much to the dismay and discomfort of the Jamaican elite, singers began composing in the dialect of the ghetto and ad-dressing the masses at the lower end of the social ladder: the people of the ghetto, the Dungles,[1] and the rural parishes and shantytowns.

The new identity that began to take root among Jamaican artists included elements from a plethora of sources. The combination of these influences rep-resents a complex synthesis of traditional Jamaican, African, African Ameri-can, African Caribbean, European, and biblical components, as well as many constituents that cannot be divorced from their associations with local and international popular culture, such as allusions to American film. While some of these elements may have been of relatively new historical origins, the prin-ciples whereby the synthesis or creolization of these diverse ingredients was organized have roots in the historical experience of Africans in the New World and, more specifically, in Jamaican culture and history. I have argued else-where that the three major personas in roots reggae are the priest, the rude-boy, and the epic hero (Prahlad 1995). While I would like to modify these here, I will first examine the roots of these narrative personas that led to sig-nificant aspects of their philosophical orientation, aesthetic guidelines, and performance styles.

Rastafari, Resistance, and Revolt

Certainly the most dominant factors bearing on the philosophical and rhetor-ical tenor of roots reggae is Rastafari. The religion itself evolved as a culmina-tion of a diverse set of influences and events. Its origins are sometimes cited as the crowning of King Haile Selassie in Ethiopia in 1930, which precipitated the teaching of a new religion by a number of former Garveyites, including Leonard Howell, Archibald Dunkley, Robert Hinds, and Joseph Hibbert. However, seeds of Rastafari were planted in the soil of the slave trade and the subsequent colonization of Jamaica and other Caribbean islands. This single event in Western history set the stage for the dehumanizing and oppressive conditions under which not only Jamaicans but other survivors of the African

Diaspora would suffer the atrocities of plantation life and struggle for generations in the crucible of poverty, fractured identity, and social and economic disenfranchisement. In this crucible, religious worldview would become one of the most significant avenues of resistance, subversion, and empowerment. It is perhaps no coincidence that Rastafari began in Jamaica, an island that has been "credited with one of the highest rates of slave revolts and conspiracies in the history of any slave society," or that Jamaica "was one of the few slave colonies where an enslaving power was forced into a treaty of accommodation with maroons" (Chevannes 1998, 1).

Long before the emergence of Rastafari, there existed a strong tradition of successful resistance to colonialism on the island of Jamaica; the island on which "the African element of this creole culture was stronger and more prominent than in any other New World slave system" (Jones 1988, 4). That resistance can be seen most prominently in the history of the Maroons, who formed free communities in the Jamaican hills as early as 1738, sixty-six years before Haiti gained its independence and almost one hundred years prior to the official abolition of slavery in Jamaica. One of the first groups of Maroons evolved in 1655 from a group of slaves who were left by Spaniards to the British following the British defeat of Spain. The slaves fled to the hills where they engaged in a lengthy war with the British. Other groups of Maroons included slaves brought from the Koromantyn slave castle on the coast of what is now Ghana, referred to in the New World as "Coromantees" or "Kromantis." The Coromantees were mainly Ashanti and Fanti people, and it is from this group that the legendary fighters Cudjoe, Johnny, Accompong, Cofi, Acheampong Nanny, and Quaco derived. These figures, like many of the Maroon fighters, were well trained in guerilla warfare before coming to Jamaica, which undoubtedly helped them to survive and eventually win their freedom. After almost forty-five years of mostly defeats at the hands of Maroon forces, the British eventually conceded, declaring peace and granting freedom to the Maroons (Barrett 1988, 26–38). Of utmost importance is the fact that the Maroons—unlike many transplanted Africans in the New World—were able to maintain their African languages, customs, and worldview.

Resistance and revolt did not end with the Maroons. It continued throughout the slavery period; the period from 1865 to 1962, during which Jamaica was an independent nation of the British Commonwealth; and in the decades since the island became truly independent. It is significant that several of the most notable leaders of revolts have been associated with religious groups, and religious ideas played key roles in these rebellions. Jones notes: "A closer examination of Jamaican religious traditions, however, reveals a complex fusion of 'spiritual' and secular themes, and a strong 'present-world' orientation, which helps to explain why, throughout Jamaican history, resistance and political unrest have consistently manifested themselves in religious terms. . . . The colonialists, for their part, knew only too well that upsurges in religious activity amongst the black masses were invariably preludes to rebellion and armed revolt" (13). Sam Sharpe, who inspired the famous Rebellion of 1831–32, one of the most extensive in Jamaican history, was a charismatic minister of the Native Baptist Church. Much of the groundwork for the revolt was conducted in prayer meetings (Barrett 1988, 41). As with many slave insurrections, biblical texts served as the authority and justification for many uprisings.

George William Gordon was another key African Jamaican who fought for Black liberation. He became a member of the House of Assembly, and later a magistrate, but was also a minister of the Native Baptist Church and a radical political activist. Although he was not directly responsible for the Morant Bay Rebellion of 1865, his connections to it are evident. His ongoing attacks on the British government in speeches, sermons, and political debates helped to create a climate for rebellion. He was also a close friend of the man who actually planned the revolt, Paul Bogle.

Bogle was a Black Baptist preacher baptized by Gordon who also relied, at least in part, on biblical theology as authority for his commitments. Although the Morant Bay Rebellion was crushed by the British militia (with the help of the Maroons who, since their independence, had chosen to aid the colonialists in maintaining the status quo of slavery), and Bogle and Gordon were tried and hung, the rebellion helped to bring about the end of legalized slavery in Jamaica (Barrett 1988, 51–62).

The same resistance to colonial rule and worldview is also evident in the earlier African-influenced religions, such as Myalism, Kumina, Pocomania, Obeah, Convince, and Revivalist, although these may not have directly given rise to revolts. Much of the resistance lies in the insistence on defining one's own cultural and spiritual self, and maintaining autonomous worldviews. While the specific practices of these religions vary, most of them share certain core, African-derived characteristics—for example, rituals involving a pantheon of spirits, sacred dancing, drumming and chanting, symbols recognizing the powers of earthly elements, possession, and multiple concepts of the soul. While these religions relied upon aspects of African worldview, they also incorporated elements of Christianity. Of course, these were reworked and inverted to support the liberation ideology of African Jamaicans. For instance, the leaders of a number of these groups are referred to as "shepherds" or "shepherdesses," drawing upon biblical terminology and concepts (Barrett 1988, 22). There are also correlations drawn between the Israelites and enslaved Africans, just as there have been by New World Africans throughout the Diaspora. Motifs such as "the evening/morning train," "Zion," "the dragon," "going home," and "the river Jordan," as well as the Old Testament heroic figures such as Daniel, Moses, Shaddrack, Meeshack, Abednego, Samson, David, and Elijah existed in the religious traditions of Jamaica well before Rastafari, appearing in genres such as spirituals and sermons.

Rastafari continues the tradition of resistance that has characterized the spirit of African Jamaican culture from the beginning. Many writing about the religion have regarded it as unique and exotic; however, almost all of its elements have historical precedents in Jamaican traditions. For example, the concept of maroonage is reflected in the behaviors and attitudes of Rastas. In 1940 Leonard Howell established Pinnacle, the first Rasta commune, in the Parish of St. Catherine. It was here that the roots for Rasta philosophy and rituals were developed, including Nyabinghi drumming and dancing, ceremonial ganja smoking, and ideas of self-sufficiency and living in harmony with nature. Jah Bones (1984) writes: "Repatriation meant everything to the Rastas at Pinnacle and since as someone was stopping their just movements to Africa then the next best thing was to maroon oneself in an Africa within Jamaica which was what Pinnacle represented to the brethren and sistrins. Pinnacle was run on lines which made it resemble a State within a State" (1984). As with earlier Maroon settlements, the Jamaican ruling class grew fearful of the Pinnacle commune, and the Rasta movement it nurtured and, in 1954, sent in troops to tear it down. As a result, large numbers of Rastas resettled in Kingston, setting up small groups and continuing to spread the religion. But maroonage is only one example illustrating how closely connected Rastafari is to Jamaican history and culture. In the following brief discussion, I explore some of the key ideological aspects of Rastafari and particularly those that have most impacted reggae discourse, suggesting their relationship to Jamaican folkways, historical movements, and other African Jamaican religious groups.

Anciency

A fundamental concept among Rastas is the idea of *anciency*. According to their theology, they are the "original man," the "first from creation." Many facets of the religion grow out of—or directly relate to—this motif, including dreadlocks, the importance of the Bible, the concept of *ital*, the idea of repatriation, and the centrality of prophecy. The idea of anciency implies purity, righteousness, and a natural state in which human beings are in touch with their full intuitive powers and innate intelligence, where they are in harmony with the natural world. Owens writes:

They look longingly into the past and see there a more desirable way of living, free from the encumbrances of modern existence. They speak often of adhering to the 'ancient' way, there alone is found true righteousness. . . .

The brethren strive to live as if in the era which followed the dawn of creation, when the world was uncontaminated by the ways of men. (1976, 150–51)

And as one Rasta states: "Others may think I-n-I mad; others may think I-n-I uncivilized, but it is ancient living that I-n-I live here" (Owens 1976, 151).

One facet of this ideological complex is the idea of *ital*, which, like most elements of this religion, has roots in traditional Jamaican culture. Homiak notes: "Ideas associating food with ideas about purity and pollution as well as with spiritual and physical fortification were already well fixed within the African-Jamaican milieu encountered by I'tesvar brethren" (1998, 143). While *ital* refers specifically to a natural, organic vegetarian diet, it embodies much more than that. It is an all-encompassing ideology centering on the idea of the "natural man." The dietary elements of this philosophy emphasize not only vegetarianism but especially unprocessed foods, most notably raw fruits and vegetables. Homiak has suggested the implicit focus on nature versus culture in the Rastafari elevation of raw foods over processed or even cooked meals, which is consistent with the effort to live as closely as possible to the "original man."

Ital living has included at different times among various groups of Rastas the promotion of the plainest garb possible, bare feet, and the use of all natural food implements, such as gourds and bowls made of coconut shells. The attitude toward naturality extends to such practices as dreadlocks and facial hair, and the aesthetic that eschews razors or clippers. Dreadlocks, which are in obvious binary opposition to shaved or manicured hair, are an extension of this principle, as are beliefs that Western forms of birth control are bad (unnatural). At the heart of the concept of *ital* is a concern with purity of body and spirit, a steadfast belief that whatever is natural is better, and the accompanying faith that one derives power and strength from the natural forces imminent in plant and mineral life.

Knowing

Another powerful concept among Rastas is *knowing*, which stands in binary opposition to *believing*. **One should *know* and not *believe*,** the Rasta proverb goes. To believe implies a false knowledge. Believers are those who have been brainwashed by Western institutions that distort history by omitting the African's contribution and misrepresent religious ideas in order continually to subjugate the oppressed. Believers have been told that there is a God and heaven beyond the physical reality of earth, and this belief prevents them from actually living in the here and now, from experiencing, from *knowing livity* (life, spiritual aliveness). It creates docility, self hatred, and confusion. Knowing can be likened to enlightenment in Zen or other Eastern spiritual traditions. There is an emphasis on an inward spiritual search that leads eventually to an epiphany and is often marked by visions. McFarlane compares Rasta knowing to "Plato's notion that knowledge resides in the soul and is 'teased' in conversation and introspection" (1998, 119). Owens (1976) notes:

The truth which the Rastafarians know—not just believe—has been discovered by each of them after personal searching of their own experience, examination of the scriptural prophecies, prolonged reasoning sessions with other brethren, and endless hours of meditation under the stimulus of the sacred herbs. . . . Like the very ganja which provides the inspiration for acknowledgement, the knowledge about Rastafari grows in secret and secluded places. . . . The Rastafarian brethren recognise themselves as the chosen purveyors of this hidden wisdom to the remnants in the West. (90)

The critical difference between Rasta knowing and Eastern enlightenment is that Rasta knowledge is culturally based. There is an emphasis placed on culture as a key component of identity, selfhood, and spirituality. It is believed that the essence of African culture is its humaneness and spirituality, which contrasts with the inhumanity of European-based, Western culture or the heathen. One knows, for example, what it means to be black in the Western world. One knows that one is African and that the history of the West is the brainwashing of Africans and others by European conquerors. One knows that God is a man, Emperor Haile Selassi of Ethiopia. This knowing, however, is not something acquired from external sources but an essence that resides in every human being, waiting to realized. Thus, one does not become a Rastafari, one comes to a realization that this is, in fact, one's inner essence. One wakes up to the reality of who one is.

African Nationalism

The centrality of Africa in Rastafari thought is related as well to the concepts of *knowing* and *anciency*; however, it cannot be explained solely on these bases. As the cradle of civilization, Africa certainly connects to the idea of the "original man," but its significance is just as dependent upon threads of black nationalism, historical unfoldings such as Emperor Haile Selassi's successful defense against European colonization, and biblical interpretations. To add to these factors, Ethiopianism has historically been present in Jamaica, surfacing in 1784 when George Liele founded the Ethiopian Baptist Church (Barrett 1988, 74). The church, like many other Jamaican religions, included neo-African forms of worship and Christian elements. It became one of the most popular denominations, largely because it provided an opportunity for "grassroots resistance to oppression" (Barrett 1988, 76). Hutton and Murrell writes that "the Ethiopianist tendency in black people's struggle against European domination dates back to the epoch of the antislavery resistance movement, when Ethiopia (Africa) became a symbol of hope for black liberation and return to the homeland" (1998, 39). Ethiopianism reached its zenith with Marcus Garvey's back-to-Africa movement in the early 1920s. Numerous components of Garvey's philosophy were highly influential not only among Rastafari but within other religious groups throughout the Diaspora—the Nation of Islam in the United States, for example. For instance, Garvey preached that Africa was the birthplace of humanity, God was black, and the black races were culturally superior. But not only did his focus on Ethiopia become a cornerstone element of Rastafari, his rhetorical style did as well. Garvey was a charismatic speaker and writer who chose the discursive style of Old Testament prophets.

The primary ideas of Rastafari revolve around Africa and are validated by biblical texts. God, or Jah, is incarnated in the person of King Selassi of Ethiopia, who traces his lineage back to the line of King Solomon. Rastas are fond of citing passages from the Bible that support their perspective that biblical folk were Africans. These include, for instance, the first chapter of the Songs of Solomon: "I am black, but comely, O ye daughters of Jerusalem, as the tents of Kedar, as the curtains of Solomon" (1:5); and "Look not upon me, because I am black, because the sun hath looked upon me" (1:6). Other passages include Lamentations 4:8, 5:10; Joel 2:8; Job 30:30; Psalms 119:83; Jeremiah 14:2; and Revelation 1:14. The height of early civilization, it is felt, was reached in Africa, as evidenced by African spirituality. Hence, repatriation to Africa has from the beginning been a major Rastafari theme.

Essentially, Rastafari is an Afro-centric ideology and, along with the Nation of Islam in the United States, perhaps the most radical expression of Afro-centrism in the twentieth century. It delights in and elevates selected components of African culture, drawing upon elements of Garveyism and extolling Garvey as the first prophet of the movement. It was Garvey who first encouraged the address of prayers and songs to the God of Ethiopia, and the national anthem for the Garvey Movement was adopted by Rastas.[2] The warrior element, which is a strong metaphorical component of Rastafari, was lifted from images of African fighters, specifically the Mau Mau of Kenya and the Nyabinghi. Omo Kenyatta, who organized the Mau Mau, was heralded as a hero, and this group, known to many as terrorists, was regarded as freedom fighters by Rastas (Chevannes 1998, 92, Savishinsky 1998, 133). Ethiopian-related symbols central to the Rastafari religion are so numerous that one could write a book on them. Key symbols include the deification and worship of King Selassie, also called Ras Tafari; the numerous biblical passages that allude to Ethiopia; the symbol of the Lion (Selassi was called the conquering Lion of Judah); and the colors of the Ethiopian flag (Savishinsky 1998, 134 35)—red, gold, and green—and sacralization of this previously political and nationalistic symbol.

More critical than the particular symbols, however, is the acute Rastafari awareness that the essence of Africanness is diametrically opposed to Western, European-based thinking and ways of being. Critical binary oppositions reflecting the conflict between Africa and the West include spiritual/materialistic, communal/individualistic, natural/artificial, intuitive/rational, open to humanity/closed, and loving/hateful. At the heart of Rastafari philosophy is the matrix of cultural memory; at the core of that matrix is the memory of slavery. Stripped bare of the canonical rationalizations and propagandistic depictions of Western history, Rastafari theology focuses on the simple truths that African societies were ravaged and Africans brutally enslaved and forced into centuries of labor that built the empires of the Western world. When slavery was legally ended, Africans and their descendants became victims of neglect, racism, genocide, and other forms of political and social oppression. The African body and soul is situated within this historical context and the reflections such as those of the enslaved writer Olaudah Equiano remain at the forefront of Rastafari consciousness:

The closeness of the place, and the heat of the climate added to the number in the ship, which was so crowded that each had scarcely room to turn himself, almost suffocated us. This produced copious perspiration, a variety of loathsome smells and brought a sickness amongst the slaves, of which many died, thus falling victims to the improvident avarice, as I may call it, of their purchase. This wretched situation was again aggravated by the gulling of the chains, now become insupportable, and the filth of the tubs into which the children often fell and were almost suffocated. The shrieks of the women and the groans of the dying reduced the whole to a scene of horror almost inconceivable. (Campbell 1987, 14)

Although the rhetoric of Rastafari poses good against evil, there is an underlying sense not of Adamic innocence but of the pain felt by Abel when his brother rose up and slew him. Beneath the anger and philosophical attempts to come to terms with the horror of slavery are the recurring questions, Why? How could you do this to your brother? And the incessant torment of no reply.

The Bible as Sacred Text

The Rastafari relationship to the Bible is a complex one. The Bible is undoubtedly a sacred text, from which inspiration, guidance, and knowledge are gained, as well as validation for rituals and ideology. It is problematized, however, because the first Bible was allegedly written on stone in Amharic (the ancient Ethiopian language) by and about black people but translated by Europeans. These Europeans distorted and truncated the original texts in order to "conceal from blacks their true identity" (Owens 1976, 30), further brainwash them, and justify their own false claims as rulers of the earth. Rastas are fully aware of the extent to which the Western Christian power base has used the Bible in campaigns of colonization, indoctrination, and oppression. Hence, Rastas rely on their inner wisdom for deciphering what is truly being conveyed by biblical passages and depend on the guidance from their spiritual communication with Haile Selassi. To assert that Rastas have a very active interpretive approach to the Bible in no way insinuates a lack of genuine love and reverence for it. Indeed, they study it continually, are inspired by its visions and poetry, and are fond of quoting substantial passages among themselves and to non-Rastas.

Of the biblical concepts that have influenced Rastafari, the tradition of prophecy has to be among the most significant. There is also precedence for this among earlier Jamaican religions. Some of the major communications by possessed individuals in the rituals of Pocomania and Revivalist groups are predictions of events to come (Barrett 1988, 24). Among Revivalists, ancient biblical prophets such as "Jeremiah and Ezekiel, and angels such as Michael and Gabriel, and other archangels often appear in their services as real figures" (Barrett 1988, 26). The idea of reincarnated prophets has been so ingrained in Jamaican thought that, in 1972, Michael Manley won the seat of prime minister in a landslide by exploiting this motif. Taking on the role of a Revivalist shepherd, he called himself Joshua and carried a shepherd's staff (Campbell 1987, 137)!

The salience of this ideological motif cannot be overemphasized. Although it has roots in Afro-Jamaican religious ideology prior to Rastafari, its prominence among Rastas is one of the distinguishing features of this religion. In other African-derived religions, figures such as the shepherd or "obeah-man" served as the central healer whose power represented the strongest site of resistance to colonial values and worldview. A part of their power grew out of their ability to communicate with spirits and be effective channels between the human and spirit realms. Even in religions that incorporated more elements of Western Christianity (Revivalism, for example) there is still the idea of a leader or main healer, with preachers taking this role. Rastafari, however, is practically antihierarchical. There is the sense that every Rastafari is a priest/healer/prophet for the rest of the world. As Owens notes, "The Rastafarians do not hesitate to compare themselves with John the Baptist and cast themselves in a role very similar to his" (1976, 45). One of Owens's informants states: "We the prophets are in the wilderness telling the people of he that is to come, and now he is fulfil!" (45). Thus, to be Rastafari *is* to be the Hebrew prophets of this historical period, for, as one Rasta put it, "We are those who shall right all wrongs and bring ease to the suffering bodies and peace to all people" (Owens 1976, 48–49).

Also closely connected to the Bible is the Rastafari perception of time. The Bible is taken as an accurate account of human history, beginning with Genesis and ending with Revelation; the plight of Africans in the New World is located within the context of that historical framework. This leads Rastas, as Owens perceptibly observes, to "sit and read the newspaper in one hand, as it were, and the Bible in the other. They search out the manifold correlations between contemporary events and the sacred recorded history" (1976, 37). It is through the lens of biblical prophecy that world events are viewed and interpreted and upon which visions of the future are based. Rastas live in and experience the world in sacred time, which, as Levine has demonstrated when discussing early African Americans (1978, see chapter 1), is more expansive than the mainstream American, secular view of time and history. From this experiential perspective, the Bible is a living entity, and every moment of life is imbued with prophetic significance. No other role, then, is so momentous as that of the prophet. It is no small wonder that one of the events that gave rise to Rastafari was Marcus Garvey's "prophecies" that a king would be crowned in Ethiopia. The central role that Garvey plays in Rastafari mythology is testimony not only to the importance of the Pan-Africanist element of Rastafari orientation but also to the predisposition toward prophecy as a rhetorical nexus in the ongoing struggle for liberation.

The Bible also lends Rastafari an immediacy born out of an apocalyptic vision. It aids in the validation of their reality and contributes to the experience of life in mythological time. Levine paraphrases Eliade's discussion of sacred time:

For people in traditional societies religion is a means of extending the world spatially upward so that communication with the other world becomes ritually possible, and extending it temporally backward so that the paradigmatic acts of the gods and mythical predecessors can be continually re-enacted and indefinitely recoverable. By creating sacred time and space, Man can perpetually live in the presence of his gods, can hold on to the certainty that within one's own lifetime "rebirth" is continually possible, and can impose order on the chaos of the universe. (31–32)

Unquestionably, Rastas live in sacred time, which grants each act—individual, social, national, international, or cosmic—an intensity of meaning it could not otherwise have. While traditional Christianity, like many religions, teaches that sacred time begins at some point after physical death, Rastafari teaches that the here and now is sacred. It is simply a matter of whether one is able to experience it as such. Rastas insist that divinity and spirit must exist within the material realm. Hence, God must be a man with whom other men and women can interact, not some invisible spirit somewhere in the sky. So human drama takes place in mythological time, which is magical, powerful, and poetic. McFarlane writes that "Jah's children do not seek to escape the ravages of time; they attempt to make an opening in time for the introduction of eternity" (1998, 109).

Chanting Down Babylon: Word/Sound/Power

One of the most central tenets of Rastafari is the conviction to "Chant Down Babylon," which refers to destroying the "forces of evil arrayed against God and the righteous" (Edmonds 1998a, 25). However, as numerous authors remind us, the forces of evil are "not metaphysical entities; rather, they are human attitudes and activities that are out of touch with the divine-natural order and that oppress, exploit, and kill" (Edmonds 1998a, 25). Chanting down Babylon includes making sounds that mystically undermine evil forces as well as educating, organizing, and rhetorizing for effective change. One of the most essential elements of this Rastafari practice is the philosophy of *word/sound/power*. This is an African-derived orientation that imbues sound with agency, with the power to manifest in the material world. It is essentially the same concept sometimes referred to as *Nommo* and is discussed in depth in Jahn's *Muntu*. In this worldview, all of existence is conceptualized as vibrations. For lack of better words, the concept adds a fourth dimension to the three-dimensional reality as perceived by Westerners. While this fourth dimension may be invisible to the human eye, it is no less real than those that can be seen. Moreover, even what is visible is deceptive, because it is not "solid" in the usual sense but a density comprised of vibrations. The nature of matter *is* vibrational.

Nommo is the word/power that gives all things agency, the force that brings "things" into existence and sets them into motion.[3] As Jahn describes it: "Thus all activities of men, and all the movement in nature, rest on the word, on the productive power of the word, which is water and heat and seed and Nommo, that is, life force itself" (1990, 126). "The force, responsibility, and commitment of the word, and the awareness that the word alone alters the world; these are characteristics of African culture" (133). The Rastafari innovation on this concept is minimal: it extends the realm of this force not only to include the word (which suggests speech, orality, and the constraints of a language system) but to encompass all sound. Therefore music or other sounds apart from spoken or thought language take on the power of nommo.

The ramifications of this ideology are tremendous, and one cannot comprehend the world from a Rastafari perspective without delving into this perceptual sphere. Nor will one ultimately be able to appreciate either the lyrical or the instrumental elements of roots reggae until one can approach the songs with an awareness that this fundamental outlook informs every facet of this genre. As we will see in the following discussion, Rastafari speech, rituals, and ceremonies rest upon the principle of *word/sound/power*.

Dread Talk

The attitudes toward sound mentioned above are realized in the development of Rastafari language, sometimes referred to as "Dread talk." The impetus for Dread talk is the overwhelmingly strong conviction that words produce effect in the material world and should thus be used with utmost care and awareness. Not a single sound should be uttered that is inconsistent with the corporeal world one is attempting to create. Furthermore, words should not lie but be accurate reflections of material and social reality. Otherwise, there is a potential for one to become lost in false perceptions, in the labyrinth of deceptive sounds characteristic of Babylon and, worse, unwittingly to contribute to the oppressive reality endorsed by the neocolonial system. Scholars studying Dread talk are in agreement that few groups display the intensity of concern with particularities of speech that the Rastas do (Homiak 1998; Barrett 1988; Yawney 1979; Owens 1976; Pollard 1982a, 1982b, 1980).

Indications are that Rasta talk originated in the late 1950s among a group of young Dreadlocks in a camp on Paradise Street in Kingston (Homiak 1998). This language has a number of characteristics, the most commonly recognized being the proliferation of "I-words." Homiak argues that this feature is related to an aesthetic that privileges the idea of vision (the association between "I" and "Eye"). He states, "Through this device Rastas derived the appreciation that the most positive force is 'perception,' realized both physically and metaphysically through the 'I/Eye' " (162).

Another element bearing on the development of I-words is the Rasta view that a person is inseparable from God. Therefore, Rastas speak of themselves as "I n I" or as "I," insinuating their connection to God, "the I." This reflects the feeling that there is nothing other than God, who encompasses the individual as well as everything else in creation. Yawney notes: "The concept of *I and I* both reaffirms the identity of the individual as an individual, while at the same time stressing his union with other beings and the forces of life. This is a paradoxical concept that represents the simultaneous recognition and overcoming of the opposites embodied in I and you, self and other. Coupled with this is the elimination of the sound *you* from the vocabulary" (1979, 171).

She goes on to quote an informant on the subject: "Who is you? There is no you. There is only I and I. I is you, I is God, God is I. God is you but there is no you, because you is I. So I and I is God. It's the same God in all of I and I" (171). Bunny Wailer's lyrics attest to this idea: "In the beginning there was only one concept / and that's the concept of I" ("Armagideon," *Blackheart Man*). Homiak writes: "What I think is noteworthy is that the 'I' morpheme performs one of the most important functions of ritual metaphors. It signifies a 'return to the whole' . . . it is about source, authenticity, primordiality, and completion. All of the related symbolism and interlocked codes with which this dialect originated serve, within a specific historical discourse (e.g., Ethiopianism, the Bible), to support this function" (1998, 173). The sacred sound *I* "is combined in a number of ways to create word variations. It is often substituted for the sound *you* or for key syllables in words" (Yawney 1979, 171). Thus words such as "children," "natural," "heights," "vibration," "angelic," and "meditation," become "Idren," "Ital," "Ites," "Iration," "Igelic," and "Itation."

Other innovations include further experiments with "I" words to better accommodate Rasta worldview. For example, "I'hivity" is used instead of "activity," indicating that this is a positively viewed state, in contrast to inactivity, which would be called in Dread talk "lowvity" (Homiak 1998, 164). Another example is the change from "I-man free" to "I-rie." One of Homiak's informants states: "In those ages [1959–61] yuh have man saying 'I-man free.' I-n-I in de I-gelic House now tek dat sound and seh, *Irie!* So it just become a creativity within de I-rits dat I-mple and I-mple could full-first a language. Dat sound now gone throughout de whole creation to show de sound is positive" (168). In fact, "Irie" has become so common a term in Jamaican society and throughout the parts of world in which reggae has made an impact, that one can find it on postcards, in cartoons, and on the lips of tourists along most Jamaican beaches. Its significance, among Rastas, however, is related to the premium placed on personal freedom and individuality, and on the state of being okay, at peace and in harmony with the universe. The complexity of the term includes its use as a simple greeting, qualifier of the terms of a relationship, and much more. As some of Homiak's informants suggest: "Yuh can write a book out of I-rie" (168).

Another category of words in Rasta talk evolves out the impulse to correlate linguistically the verbal signifier to the way in which its effect is realized in the physical world. Pharmacies (Pharma-sees) are considered an element of colonial, materialistic shortsightedness, and in direct opposition to more natural folk healing practices. So "pharmacy" becomes "pharma-blind." "Understanding" is associated with being oppressed, because of the *sound* "under." So it is changed to "overstanding," which implies that one is on top and thus has a positive *sound*. Likewise, "oppressor" is changed because "op" (up) is a positive *sound* but prefaces a negative word. The Rasta term "down-pressor" captures more accurately what the term really signifies.

A final tendency is the substitution of "y" for the beginning consonants of many words. This leads to the construction of words such as "yood," "yot," "yound," "Y-ungo," and "Y-anti" for "food," "pot," "sound," "Congo," and "Shanti." "Y" constructions are sometimes used in combination with "I" to form phrases or words like "I-yah-yound" for "higher sound" or "I-jah sound"; or "I-yadda Yool" for "the Fullness of the Father" (Homiak 1998, 163). For example, a communicative passage might go as follows: "*See-knots-see-I, I-yah Kongo, I-yah-Yinghi-I!. . . One Yantifull I-I-yound!*—those art words dat Headful I-on and I create—even up to *I-rie I-tes*. . . . Well after a time now we had to leave Wareika Hill to penetrate all dem *I-tesvar I-ses I-yasta Y-ool-I I-yantiful-I* into Back-o-Wall to form a group. Dat was de *I-gelic House*" (Homiak 1998, 162). This can be loosely translated as: "Selassi I, I am Congo, I am Binghi! One beautiful sound! Those are words that Headful I-on [a person's name] and I created, even I-rie I-tes [free flowing heights, a meditative space]. Well, eventually we had to leave Wareika Hill and concentrate all of our beautiful, Ashanti, Rastafari praises at Back-o-Wall [a place in Kingston] to form a group. That group was the Angelic House."

While the extreme form of Dread talk developed by the radical group of young Rastas at the Camp on Wareika Hill in the late 1950s has not persisted in its entirety, elements of it have been widely diffused among Rastas internationally. Moreover, the philosophy behind the language bears special attention. Homiak and others note quite accurately the social significance of this development. First, it is a strategy for signifying on and deconstructing the dominant European-derived vernacular and, symbolically, the worldview and social system inherent in that language. Second, it represents an "attempt to decolonize and repatriate Black people's consciousness from 'mental slavery'" (Homiak 1998, 163) and to aid in the construction of a new ideology and paradigm of identity. Third, the language functions to reinforce social boundaries between Rastas, a group devoted to cultural/spiritual resistance, and all other groups within Jamaican society.[4]

Hence, in Rasta ideology word-sound has agency and, as vibrations, has the power to affect the material and psychic worlds (both being types of vibration). Even human beings are, as Homiak refers to it, "living sound, the Word incarnate" (175). Consequently, the importance of using speech precisely and wisely is immense among Rastafari. It is not far-fetched to suggest, then, that Dread talk as it is conceived by Rastas is an inherently sacred and magical language and, along with music and dance, functions as a tool for healing. Even the language has roots in traditional Jamaican culture. Scholars have linked it to Jamaican creole or patois (Pollard 1980), "African-derived dialect, archaic in Jamaican speech," and Bongo talk, "a dialect sometimes used in the recitation of Anansi stories" (Homiak 1998, 163). Although eschewed by Rastas, Jamaican creole has often served subversive and political ends. Furthermore, the idea of inherent power in words is embedded in Jamaican folk thought, although it may not be consciously articulated. Bilby notes the pervasive Africanness of Jamaican language: "Any American or British English speaker who has listened carefully to spoken Jamaican Creole, or 'patois,' knows that its unintelligibility has much to do with its unfamiliar rhythms. . . . It is perhaps at this deep level—in language and movement style, for instance, where behavior is so ingrained that it is often unconscious and seems almost innate—that the African heritage in Jamaica has had its most profound and enduring impact" (1985, 143).

Ritual Sound

Chevannes notes that the two chief rituals among Rastafari are reasonings and the "binghi" (1998, 17), both of which hinge on the concept of word/sound/power, which assumes the power of sounds to effect change in the corporeal world. In some instances these changes might be creative and, in others, destructive. In their references to "chanting down Babylon," Rastas reflect the ideology that actual sounds can literally and figuratively help to deconstruct the towers of Western colonial powers. It is no accident that the story of Joshua blowing his trumpet and causing the walls of Jerico to crumble is a favored one.

"Reasonings" or "groundings" (Edmonds 1998, 335–36) are small informal gatherings in which a group of brethren share the smoking of ganja, the holy sacrament, and engage in philosophical discussions. It is through reasoning sessions that the knowledge, aesthetics, and philosophy of Rastafari concerning political, social, personal, and metaphysical issues are expounded upon and further developed. Reasonings are dynamic organic processes that reveal the ever-emergent nature of the Rastafari worldview. It is also in these contexts that the language is further honed and scrutinized. Pulis observes, "For Bongo, and all Rastafarians, language is an arena, a site of political struggle and personal transformation" (1993, 291). Pulis is one of the few researchers who presents a transcribed segment of a reasoning session, in this case between himself and a Rastafari named Bongo. The extreme importance placed on using the correct words is evident in Bongo's responses to some of Pulis's comments. In the following excerpt, Bongo takes exception to Pulis's use of the term "consciousness," because the sound "con" implies deceit. He further critiques Pulis's use of "but," and the idea that Rastas "drop" certain words from their vocabulary.

> (BONGO): "I-n-I [Rastafarians]," he interjected, "no deal wit no KON-sciousness [pronounced with an emphasis on KON], I [Bongo] deal wit trut, rights, WIZ-MON, na KON no one, Jah seh, 'Him dat have ear. . . . HEAR! Him dat have eyes. . . . SEE!' I-n-I no KON no one, if dem wan see, dem mus jus open dem selves an dem see."
>
> (PULIS): "Well, I didn't mean KON, but . . . "
>
> (BONGO): "WELL, ha! dat fa water, BUT-TA, ha! dat fa bread, mon, dem na UP-FULL sounds, I-n-I no deal wit dem," he interjected once again, as he smiled and shrugged his shoulders.
>
> (PULIS): "So," I asked, responding to his criticism and his shift or change in the conversation to language, "you drop out certain words."
>
> (BONGO): "I not seh I-n-I DROP dem, cause, if dem bust [are spoken], dem must bust. I na bust sounds dat deal wit down-press-ion or kon-sciousness, cause, how I lif-up, if I reason down, I-n-I deal with UP-press-I, I-sciousness, dem sounds UP-FULL, deal wit livity [life] not death. I-n-I no KON no one, jus words, sounds, power, bradda, words, sounds, power," he declared. (290)

Carole Yawney also discusses Rasta reasoning, noting the varieties of discursive strategies she observed in these rituals. As her discussion verifies, reasoning sessions are events of cooperative creativity, each one having its own discursive tenor. There are no set guidelines. Instead, these sessions are characterized by inspirational interactions that take on a meditative quality, the brethren prompting each other "on to higher and higher *I-ghts*, each in turn accreting layer upon layer of meaning until a satisfactory overview is reached" (1979, 170). "This is a critical point if we are to understand how the Rastafarians go about sacralizing their existence together. For them reasoning is not meant to *entertain* (though it may well be entertaining), but to *elucidate*. It is intended to shed new light upon their condition, to unveil truth and help the wisdom flow. For this reason the activity is treated as sacred, requiring ritual and symbolic demarcations to set it apart from the ambient babble" (174). Because reasonings are inherently spiritual rituals, concerned with inducing meditative, inspirational states of consciousness, it is therefore critical to use *I-ance*, or Dread talk; English is considered inadequate and counterproductive to the goals of reasonings. Reasonings, moreover, become a performative arena for experiments in creating new sounds and symbols, however, always with the intent to apply the subjective and metaphysical realities of Rasta to issues in the larger world.

Yawney gives an example of a reasoning that might begin with the idea "that the Pope is the head of the Mafia" (172) (a common assumption among Rastas). In such a session, comparisons between the Catholic Church and the Mafia would be reasoned out, including the assumed connection between Europeans in general and Romans, who are considered the descendants of Babylon. The negative critique of Italians, descended from the Romans and indicted twice over because of their invasion of Ethiopia in 1935, would consume a part of the session. The subtle and obvious connections between the Roman Catholic Church, which is viewed as an agent of colonialism made rich by the profits of slavery, and the Mafia, which profits as well through corruption and crime, would be extensively explored (170–74). The session might end when this topic has been fully explored, which would take several hours, or it might continue, moving to a new, albeit related, topic.

Nyabinghi

Chevannes notes the Nyabinghi, or binghi,[5] as the other main Rastafari ritual and describes it as "a dance held on special occasions throughout the year, to mark the coronation of His Imperial Majesty (2 November); His Majesty's ceremonial birthday (6 January); His Majesty's visit to Jamaica (25 April), His Majesty's personal birthday (23 July), Emancipation for Slavery (1 August) and Marcus Garvey's birthday (17 August)" (Chevannes 1998, 17).[6] These occasions would bring together hundreds of Rastas from different parts of Jamaica, who would camp in "tents and makeshift lodgings" (17–18) for several days. Binghis are also known as "I-ssemblies" [Assemblies], "Nyabinghi conventions," and "Nyabinghi I" (Edmonds 1998b, 356). At such occasions, Rastas play drums, chant, and dance. As rituals of word/sound/power, not only are they celebratory and inspirational, but they function symbolically to deconstruct and undermine the "downpressive" system (17).

The three chief elements of these ceremonies all have derivations in older Jamaican traditions; however, they are marked with distinctive meanings and performative styles. Nyabinghi drumming is decidedly African, or, as Bilby refers to it, "neo-African" (1985), evolving out of Burro and Kumina traditions. Unlike the Maroon traditions that were brought to Jamaica during the slave trade, Kumina traditions were "introduced to the island by 'voluntary' post-Emancipation African labourers from Central Africa who came to work the plantations on contract roughly between 1840 and 1865" (133). The influence of Kumina "cults" permeates the culture in the eastern regions of the island and includes a complex of religious and secular rituals and ceremonies, as well as a strong African-derived musical tradition. Bilby writes that "Kumina music remains a part of the fabric of daily life, as characteristic of the landscape as the rows of sugar cane, or the aroma of burning palm leaves and white rum" (133). The Kumina presence is also found in the form of bands that sometimes play at marketplaces, at gambling tournaments, and on other secular occasions. Kumina religious ceremonies, like those of the Maroons and other groups, employed drumming in rituals designed to contact ancestral and other spirits, much as drumming functions in Haitian Vodou and most other African-derived religions.

As Nyabinghi drumming was developing in the 1950s, there was an infusion of influence from Kumina and Burro, brought to West Kingston by rural migrants. According to Bilby and others (see Reckord 1998) who have studied the Nyabinghi tradition, this influence was absorbed by Nyabinghi drummers:

From these Buru-Kumina hybrids, urban Rastafarian musicians, who had previously been without drums, took what they needed in order to create their own new dance-drumming style, which they christened Nyabinghi. The three-part drum ensemble of Buru—the bass, funde, and repeater (or pita)—was retained in modified form in Nyabinghi, but the music played on it was neither Buru nor Kumina, combining as it did elements of both. It was this new fusion that was later brought to the recording studios of Kingston by the Rastafarian master drummer, Count Ossie, and a large number of others who followed in his footsteps. (Bilby 1985, 146)

Influences of Kumina also passed into Rastafari tradition from its earliest leader, Leonard Howell, who had been immersed in Kumina before becoming a Rastafari prophet. In the settlement at Pinnacle, "Howell used Kumina drumming, dance, and the Kongo-based 'African Country' language in his ceremonies" (147).

At Nyabinghi meetings such as those mentioned above, as well as at smaller, less formal gatherings, drumming is a constant sound: the heartbeat rhythm of the bass drum, which sometimes sounds as if the foundations of Babylon are audibly crumbling; the tighter skin of the funde, just behind the beat of the bass, syncopating; and the higher voice of the repeater, or kete, narrating stories. The drumming goes on all night into the wee hours of the morning, along with chanting, smoking, praying, singing, and dancing. Barrett's description of a meeting contains useful information:

All around the camp the air was thick with smoke from the holy herb. . . . The drums kept a haunting beat while the cultists sang songs such as:

There is no night in Zion, there is no night there
Ras Tafari is the light, we need no candle light
Hallelujah there is no night there . . .

One tune continued as long as an hour and without a break; another was started and continued on and on throughout the evening until the drummer was exhausted. His place was then taken by another and the singing and drumming continued. Many songs were new creations of the movement, but a great many had been adopted from the native religion and Christian hymns, using Rastafarian tempo and words when necessary. (123)

Again, the philosophical tenor of these gatherings is simultaneously to achieve higher states of spiritual consciousness (I-ya I-ights, or higher heights), deeper states of meditation, and collectively to create an enormous concentration of word/sound/power that will speed the collapse of Babylon. This is ideologically comparable to the collective chanting of mantras or meditations in Eastern traditions, which are said to create concentrations of positive energy, of light that dispels some of the negative and dark energy hovering around the planet.

Thus far no scholar has really focused on Nyabinghi dancing. I have not been able to find photographs or more than brief narrative allusions to it. I am therefore left to my own nonscientific observations. Rastas would be horrified by the comparison of their dancing to ceremonial movements of other groups involving spirit possession, for they are adamant in their criticism of religions with this African-derived characteristic. Paradoxically, some of these elements are for Rastas associated with being under colonial rule. There is also the criticism that these religious components are ineffective in dealing with the contemporary, neocolonial reality of African Jamaicans. Hence, the practical necessity among Rastas to purge themselves of elements inherited from earlier Jamaican religious traditions, and especially those that are seen as either politically ineffective or inconsistent with a monotheistic, biblical orientation. Even scholars have failed to note the common threads between Nyabinghi and other religions on the basis of these Rasta-referenced, ideological differences. Alleyne writes, for instance: "Whereas Africa remains very high among Rastafarians at the level of ideological consciousness, there isn't very much of African continuity in the system of religious belief and religious behavior" (1988, 103).

To the contrary, as one sets the rhetoric of Rastafari aside, one can see in the movements of Nyabinghi dancers elements of African dance also present among other religious groups of Jamaica and the Diaspora. And although the concept of spirit possession is foreign and abhorrent to Rastas, dancers often move as if in deep trance, inhabited by some invisible spiritual force. Their dance, like that of Vodou, Kromanti Play rituals, or John Canoe, contains components of drama and theater.[7] The countenance and posture of dancers, however, is imbued with something distinct, a spirit of pride and defiance reflecting the newly acquired sense of self arising from Rastafari social critique. One of the movements in Nyabinghi dancing resembles a lion prancing like a horse. Another movement involves the body arching backward, head thrown back, like the yoga pose called "Cobra," while the hips rock forward and the knee lifts, like a soldier's marching to battle. There is the foot raised and slapped, first one, then the other, as the Zulu of South Africa do in their gum-boot dance. And there is the treading, stepping lightly, in a bounce, upward and back, right foot crossed over left to the side, then back, arms swinging or stretched outward, body always moving regally as Babylon is trodden down. The essence of the dance is narrative in motion, as the events at the center of Rastafari ideology are paralinguistically enacted.

One can also observe in these dances the philosophical orientation of Rastas that infuses them with the sacred power to transform social and material realities. In this way, they are connected to African and neo-African traditions that are not only medicinal and magical in nature but reminiscent of such phenomena as the Native American ghost dances, which were also practiced to give warriors magical assistance in battling colonial powers. The motif of healing underlies all of these rituals. It entails transforming the consciousness of individuals whose illness is rooted in the brainwashing and racism of the colonial and neocolonial system. As such, groundings or binghis are no less ceremonial healing rituals than are Vodou, Santeria, Revivalist, Kumina, Baptist, or other New World African religious rites. The healing motif also involves eradicating the source of the illness. In this case that source is a system of thought, symbolized by the Babylon reference and manifested in countless inhumane and Eurocentric social policies. Cures include not only ceremonial rites but attitudinal and behavioral adjustments, as well as foodways, prayers, chants, and ingestion of the holy sacrament (ganja), which purifies and dispels the Babylonian cloud over the eyes and permits insightful and clear vision.

Rastafari and Roots Reggae

The connections between Rastafari and roots reggae are manifest on a number of levels. One can view roots reggae as an extension of Rastafari inasmuch as it became the chief vehicle for the spread of this doctrine and orientation in Jamaica and abroad. The term "roots reggae" in fact suggests that the form and content of the music are saturated with Rastafari sensibilities, aesthetics, ideology, and perspectives. These elements certainly influence the use of proverbial expressions. Singers and musicians who "awoke" to their Rastafari essence became ministers and ambassadors of the faith. While, on the one hand, the utter embrace of the record industry and activities that are clearly a part of popular culture may seem to be entirely inconsistent with the monastic tendencies of Rastafari, on the other, we can view it as a continuity of certain elements of the religion. The monastic nature of early Rastafari communities is best illustrated by the I-gelic House of Wareika Hill in Kingston, which was most active from 1960 to 1964. Members of this community viewed "the Hill" as a place for spiritual retreat and meditation and lived in a similar manner to monks of other religions, rejecting material comforts, items associated with the killing of animals, and indulgences of the flesh.

However, even Rastas from this community evangelized, or prophesied. Dressed in crocus bags and bare feet, they walked through parts of Kingston spreading the gospel of Rastafari, sometimes orally, at other times simply allowing their intimidating appearances alone to speak. Indeed, there have always been a heightened social conscience among Rastas and an active concern with influencing social policies. The idea of ital, for instance, is linked to a recognition that the Jamaican government, in alliance with governments abroad, is responsible for the poor diet and health care of Jamaicans. Instead of developing educational and agricultural programs that would take advantage of the abundance of natural foods available, the government has led Jamaicans to depend on imported foods and, more recently, American fast food chains (Campbell 1987, 122). A component of ital is the rejection of political policies that disempower and undermine the well-being of Jamaicans. Thus, the spiritual dimension is not divorced from the social and political.

The social/political agendas of Rastas have sometimes been overlooked, in part because of their own rhetoric, which emphasizes that they are *not* political. Watson, for example, in writing about Rastafari and Black Muslims, states: "Religion *per se* is not their major attraction. Both are social protests which move on a semi-religious vehicle, with emphasis on social action geared to transforming their objective life situations. They are nationalistic, and nationalism is political; their foci move from one plane to another—from one based on the quest for religious experience to one grounded in a struggle for readjusting the status systems of their respective societies to accord with an ideal concept of society" (1973, 199). But what Watson fails to grasp is that this is, in fact, a main distinction between African and European religions. African religions have as their focus external behavior, not internal states, social and community action, not private pacts with the deity (Mbiti 1970, 2). The idea that religion is separate from social action and behavior is largely a Western concept.

When one looks at the history of Rastafari in the Caribbean and in other parts of the world, it becomes abundantly clear that the movement is intricately linked to political advocacy and social programs (see Turner 1991). What better way to advance the philosophy and social agendas of Rastafari than through the recording industry? No other avenue would grant the degree of public exposure available through the different forms of media connected with record making. In fact, it is in a sense the perfect situation, as Babylonian technology is subverted in the war against the Empire in much the same way as military arms are used by guerrillas fighting against the very governments that manufactured the weapons in the first place. In the case of reggae, the technology is transformed to carry the kind of subversive messages that the artists wish to convey, to produce the word/sound/power grounded in Rastafari principles and aesthetics that can "heal the nations." Because many Jamaican artists had already experienced exploitative situations with producers and studio owners, they were not blind to the dangers of the recording industry. They were aware that the experiment to use the recording context was laden with contradictions and possible failures. Bob Marley reflects the questioning that many artists must have experienced: "Can we free the people with music?" ("Trenchtown Rock," *Confrontation*).

One of the most difficult challenges these craftsman faced was to create a new definition of the recording artist. Whereas those in this line of work had previously been perceived as entertainers, these reggae maestros were defining themselves as priests and prophets. Among the techniques used to subvert the recording context are the development of the warrior/priest persona and the inclusion of multiple traditional Jamaican folklore genres—topics that will be discussed in more depth in the next chapter.

JAH MESSAGE TO PREACH

Personas and Rhetorical Aesthetics

I have Jah message to preach
and I have Jah people to teach

Mikey Dread, "My Religion," *Best Sellers*

Jah set I-n-I as a watchman
around Babylonian walls
Yeah-eh, children of Israel.
I-n-I shall never hold I peace
While wrong is going on
Day or night.
Bust down Babylon gates
Prepare ye the way.
Prepare ye the way for Jah people.

Culture, "Jah Rastafari," *International Herb*

Although reggae began as a popular form of Jamaican music, roots reggae goes well beyond the conventional expectations of the "pop" genre. The creators of roots reggae hailed from a generation of urban youth attracted to the doctrines and teachings of Rastafari; and most of these pioneers subsequently became Rastas themselves. Artists such as Bob Marley, Peter Tosh, Bunny Wailer, the Wailing Souls, Culture, the Abyssinians, Burning Spear, the Itals, I-Jah Man, the Congos, Prince Fari, I-Roy, U-Roy, the Meditations, Leonard Dillon and the Ethiopians, the Gladiators, and many others saw themselves, and were perceived by Jamaican and international audiences, principally as messengers of Rastafari. The role of messenger was taken to another level, however, by most of these artists who, in keeping with Rastafari philosophy, viewed themselves as prophets and priests (Prahlad 1995). With the combined influences of liberation movements at home and abroad the priest became merged with the "warrior," resulting in a warrior/priest persona that dominates roots reggae lyrics. In this chapter we will discuss the characteristics of this persona and specific rhetorical strategies used by it, and explore the rhetorical and stylistic features of reggae songs and music, performance styles, and audiences.

The warrior/priest persona encompasses multiple facets and incorporates a number of significant identities such as healer, oracle, prophet, and spiritual advisor. Most often the distinctions between these roles are minimal, and the roles commonly merge within the same song. There are times, however, when singers clearly emphasize one identity more than the others. For example, the prophet's focus may be to provide glimpses into the future or to draw correlations among past, present, and future events. At other times, the narrative voice may speak as if it has been asked advice about a particular problem. On other occasions, it is the healer who is highlighted, as the cure to a particular illness is considered. Very often these subtle shades of difference are important to the encoding of proverbs and other phrases.

In addition to these identities, there are several other distinct secondary voices that contribute to the warrior/priest persona. One is the educator or teacher. The teacher focuses on specific areas of history and culture that have been distorted by the texts found in colonial school systems or in other forms of hegemonic propaganda. Reggae priests teach, for instance, that Christopher Columbus was a pirate who, like other colonial explorers, helped to wipe out the indigenous native population and assisted in the enslavement of Africans. In fact, "explorers" are called "pirates" in the teachings of reggae priests. Burning Spear sings: "Christopher Columbus was a damn-blasted liar! / What about the Arawak Indians who were down here before him?" ("Christopher

Columbus," *Hail H.I.M.*). A Culture song opens with the lines, "Yes mi brother Winston Rodney. Christopher Columbus, we catch him. Hold him vampire!" The song continues:

Them never want Christopher Columbus ina Italy
Then tell me how come him down in a West Indies land a bother with?
Them never want Christopher Columbus ina Rome.
Then how come he come down here to ravish my home?

("Outcast," *Trust Me*)

Some of the lessons in these songs take the form of stories about Jamaican heroes. One of the best examples is Culture's "Innocent Blood," a chilling sermon that depicts the Babylon system as vampirelike, feeding off the blood and essence of black people. The song retells the story of freedom fighters George William Gordon and Paul Bogle, who were hung by the colonial government.

In a previous discussion, I considered the rudeboy as a separate persona in roots reggae (Prahlad 1995), but I would like to modify this assertion. Continued research leads me to view the rudeboy as an aspect of the warrior/priest persona. The rudeboy phenomenon developed as a result of Jamaican urban migration, which created a subculture of unemployed youths in Kingston ghettos. The rudeboy symbolized an attitudinal and behavioral response to the problems of ghetto life and the disdain with which more affluent Jamaicans looked upon those who lived in poor areas. The rudeboy posture is defiant, tough, rebellious, and sometimes lawless, the term itself having its roots in traditional Caribbean vernacular and referring to "bad" or ill-mannered young men (Abrahams 1983, 111, 164). Its relationship to reggae mirrors that of Trinidadian street gangs and steel drum music, or African American gangs and gangsta rap. The world of rudeboys encompasses rhetorical genres similar to those found among African American inner-city males—for instance, rapping, boasting, signifying, and toasting (Abrahams 1963; Mitchell-Kernan 1972a, 1972b; Kochman 1970).

This urban hip element is crucial in roots reggae discourse. Rowe notes one connection between rudeboys and Rastas: "The open defiance and opposition to the state linked the rudeboy phenomenon to the Rastafari movement, where rudie tendend to seek refuge when fleeing from the authorities" (1998, 78). Many roots artists identified themselves as rudeboys, or "rudies," before becoming Rastas, most notably Bob Marley and the Wailers, whose early recording careers were as rudeboys. Songs by such artists often addressed others within their subculture, as in Marley's first recording, "Simmer Down." The Wailers were no strangers to physical confrontations; and skirmishes in which Marley reportedly always came out on top formed a part of the lore that surrounded him and contributed to the respect he commanded from his peers. The tough, streetwise youth known as "Tuff Gong" would forever remain a component of the warrior/priest persona that developed later. I have chosen to view the rudeboy as a component of the warrior/priest rather than as a distinctly separate persona, largely because it became subsumed in this larger narrative voice at the moment that reggae artists were transformed into Rastafari.

Another component of the warrior/priest is paradoxical: the Epic Hero/everyday man. This secondary voice is embodied by the title "Natty Dread," a heroic figure engaged in the struggle for political freedom and spiritual ascension since creation. The original man/woman was "Natty Dread." The Israelites were "Natty Dread." Jesus, as Rastas are wont to say, was a "Natty Dread": "Never gonna see a bald head Jesus yet," Bunny Wailer sings (*Liberation*). The slaves were "Natty Dreads." Hence, Natty Dread embodies the struggles and trials of Africans in the Western Hemisphere but also of ancient wise people who, because of their wisdom and spirituality, were likewise persecuted. Reggae has successfully mythologized this heroic figure, testifying to his/her trials and triumphs through song and ritual enactments performed on stage before international audiences. Of these compositions, one of the most compelling is Bob Marley's "Natty Dread" (*Natty Dread*), which chronicles the historical and heroic qualities of this figure.

The song also indicates why I have called this figure Epic Hero/everyday man. For not only are the epic aspects highlighted but artists insist on the everyday nature of this character. He lives the same life as every other oppressed person, walks the same streets, rides the same buses, and so on, and is separated only by the quality of his consciousness. Because of his knowledge of history, he has a different perspective and awareness of the situation in which he finds himself. He may suffer the same material inconveniences, but his thoughts are not bound by or influenced by the Babylonian "shit-stem" (system). He is the inheritor of an ancient spirituality and wisdom. Since this knowledge is implicitly linked to their Rastafari identity, the Epic Hero is bound to the priest.

While reggae has sometimes been compared to rock music by critics, it is, in fact, more accurately likened to African American gospel—not the gospel of large choirs and sophisticated choral arrangements but the tradition of small quartets that shared fundamental performance styles with older blues singers. It is religious music drawing upon lyrical traditions going back to slavery and incorporating elements of African and New World Western musical heritages. The promotion of roots artists as warrior/priests becomes evident at every possible level of reggae, including speech, album cover art, lyrics, music, and live performances. The development of this persona represents a tentative marriage between the personal convictions of artists dedicated to their roles as emissaries, visionaries, and healers, and the interests of those within the music industry such as producers and promoters who seized upon such images as sales gimmicks.

Some have asserted, in fact, that the presentations of reggae singers were largely the work of foreign business interests. Regis (1994), for instance, credits the American consumer influence with the entire complex of lyrical and musical orientation of Jamaican reggae, beginning in the mid-1970s. The prominence of ganja as a symbol used by promotional conglomerates to sell reggae to young whites in Europe and America (Regis 1994; Jones 1988, 71) provides a representative example. However, a survey of the album covers and lyrical content for records produced and marketed in Jamaica by artists such as Culture, Bunny Wailer, and I-Roy reveals a consistency of Rastafari themes and symbols, some of which were *continued* as foreign promoters entered the reggae business. The interpretations of these symbols depend on the consumers' knowledge base. Thus the affinity felt by fad-conscious white youths does not prevent a deeper reading by more cultural-sensitive consumers. I maintain that: (1) the personas of roots reggae artists were largely their own creations; (2) those personas are firmly rooted in African Jamaican culture; (3) thousands of reggae fans around the world went beyond the superficial marketing strategies of record promoters to educate themselves to the true substance of reggae, lyrically and musically; and (4) live performances of reggae artists, the reggae club scenes, and reggae radio shows have provided education about the rhetorical and philosophical dimensions of roots reggae.

Let us consider a few examples from reggae songs and album cover art reflecting the advancement of the warrior/priest persona. On the back cover of Augustus Pablo's LP *Earth Rightful Ruler* is essentially a synthesis of prayer and praises, and a small sermon.

This album was created through the powers of his Majesty Emperor Haile Selassie I for He inspired I and taught I to play I harps unto him and his sons and daughters over the creation. Oh Jah, all I ask for is life, health and strength, wisdom and understanding. Some see this music as Lovers Rock or Dub Music, well I and I see it as Jah Rastafari Haile Selassie I. Work to call I and I brothers and sisters from the four corners of the earth: so you see no matter how long it takes all have to bow and give praise unto I father who rules creation in righteousness. Jah Rastafari Haile Selassi I—Selah. (1978)

In the center of the front cover is a large picture of King Selassi wearing a gold crown. The upper part of his body is garbed in an elaborate regal robe. Behind his image horizontal bands of color appear: green at the top, gold in the middle, and red at the bottom. In the upper left corner is the star of David and, in the upper right corner, the image of a black lion with a scepter, against a background circle of red, green, and gold. Above Selassi's picture are the words "Emperor Haile Selassie I" and, above that, at the very top, "Earth Rightful Ruler." Among the many distinctive features of the cover is the complete absence of the artist's name. Only his legal name, H. Swaby, appears in small print among the names of other "players of instruments" and as songwriter next to each song. Among the credits is "Produced by: Jah Rastafari—Haile Selassie I (original). Co-Produced by: Augustus Pablo (Levi)."

On the back cover appear two pictures, side by side, taking up two-thirds of the cover space. The photos, framed by bands of green, gold, and red, are separated from each other by a band of gold between two bands of red. On the right is a photo of Augustus Pablo, seated outside, playing the melodica, completely absorbed in his music. On the left is an Ethiopian drawing of a king, seated on a throne, playing a harp. Behind him is another figure holding a sword in one hand and an umbrella (to shade the king) in the other.

The cumulative effect of the cover presentation embodies and promotes a Rastafari worldview. The specific artist is less significant than the deity whom he serves and for whom he is prophesying. The "musicians," however, are considered much more than this term typically implies; they are reincarnations of ancient souls carrying on a spiritual tradition and fulfilling prophecies. Ultimately, the album purports not simply to entertain but to illuminate, edify, and minister. Consider some of the song titles: "Earth Rightful Ruler," "King Alpha and Queen Omega," "Jah Love Endureth," "Rastafari Tradition," "City of David," "Zion Hill," and "Israel School Yard."

The cover of Bunny Wailer's seminal *Blackheart Man* utilizes similar motifs to Augustus Pablo's *Earth's Rightful Ruler.* The background of the cover is black. Two figures, His Majesty and a dreadlocked lion, are in black and gold, and the same two images appear on the back cover. At the top of the front and back covers is the title "Blackheart Man," in textured black and gold to suggest dreadlocks. There are few other albums that explore and elucidate Rasta roots, mythology, and ideology more thoroughly than this one. A part of its genius is the integration of personalized poetry and multiple facets of the warrior/priest persona. All of the songs deal with Rastafari themes and reflect Rasta worldview. The title song, "Blackheart Man," refers to the derogatory Jamaican legend about Rastas. The "Blackheart Man" is comparable to the bogeyman of American folklore. In one of the most beautifully poetic songs in reggae, Wailer chronicles the path from being told stories in childhood about the "Blackheart Man" to his later conversion to Rasta, from "Check out the Blackheart Man, little children / don't you go near him" to "It's the Blackheart Man, he is the wonder of the city!" In "Reincarnated Souls," Wailer sings declarations of Rasta identity and entreaties to the multitudes to seek wisdom and truth.

We are reincarnated souls
from that time
Living on earth

In the beginning was one concept
and that concept was the I.

Other artists reflect similar points of view in their compositions, demeanors, and album covers. The cover of Peter Tosh's *Mystic Man* for example, shows a side view of Tosh's face, his hands raised as if in prayer. The titles of the albums *Mystic Man* and *Bush Doctor* insinuate the role of healer and prophet that Tosh adopted. On "Recruiting Soldiers" (*Mystic Man*) he sings:

I'm recruiting soldiers
For Jah army
Recruiting soldiers,
For Jah time is near.

Culture's famous LP *Two Sevens Clash* can be seen as an annal for Rastafari theology and mythology and as a personal testament to one person's baptism into this religion. It includes motifs of the search, isolation in the wilderness, and the consummate moment of illumination. "Calling Rasta for I" is an intense evocation of the deity. "I'm alone in the wilderness" is a testimonial to the process of becoming a prophet, in the mold of Old Testament prophecy.

I'm alone in the wilderness,
With Jah Almighty I.
I'm alone in the wilderness
with only Jah to vindicate for I and I and I

When I'm alone
Jah be my help all day
and all night when I'm way down in these desert.
I say a prayer
and yes it answer . . .

(*Two Sevens Clash*)

"I'm not ashamed" is a declaration of pride in wearing dreadlocks. Other titles are almost self-explanatory to those familiar with Rastafari theology—for example, "Get Ready to Ride the Lion to Zion," "Natty Dread Taking Over," and "See Them a Come." "Black Starliner Must Come" refers to the legendary ships that will take Jamaicans back to Africa (the name derived from the ships that Garvey planned to use for repatriating African Americans). "Jah Pretty Face" is a jewel of a song, reflecting the intimacy with which Rastas often speak of His Majesty, and the rapture they experience contemplating the meeting with Him.

I and I want to see
King Rastafari,
to look into Jah
pretty pretty face.
To walk the streets of glory
Shining around Jah throne.

Cause we are going home,
going home
to see King Rastafari!

The song continues with a traditional chant, elaborating on Rasta mythology. Joseph Hill, the lead vocalist and composer for Culture, is known for lyrics and music that remain anchored in traditional Rastafari and Revivalist chants and music.

Rasta have the root of David
Halle-lu Jah.
Rasta have the root of David,
Halle-lu Jah
Chant it out!

Reggae artists have occasionally compared their works to the prophetic books of the Bible, alluding to each album as a new chapter in their "book." These oral traditions have helped to structure Rasta mythology internationally. Within this context, the songs are not only sermonic but often function rhetorically as reasoning sessions, in which particular topics are elucidated. As such, they provide forums for the continued theorizing about and elaboration on various aspects of Rasta ideology. Besides the elaborative voices of the warrior/priests, however, songs in this tradition invite the same kind of active response that face-to-face reasonings do. A part of their function encourages the listeners to engage the process of thinking about and formulating their own philosophical positions on the subjects addressed.

Some of the most instructive "chapters" have been created by Joseph Hill of Culture. Hill's ability to render Rasta philosophy in beautifully crafted poetry is surpassed by none. His visions are deep and often highly esoteric, and give us unending dimensions for exploring the depths of Rastafari theology. Although scholars have argued, for instance, that dreadlocks are a phallic symbol (Chevannes 1998), Hill sings: "Put on your wedding garments, which are your nats / And prepare to meet the king ("Ethiopians Waan Guh Home," *International Herb*), which suggests a feminine role. The Dreadlock is depicted here as a bride of Jah, just as Catholic priests are wed to Christ. In his lovely eclectic images, Hill illuminates the role of music and, thus, of reggae artists and their connection to biblical legacy. In a sonnet to reggae musicians, he sings:

Play skillfully,
On your harps, my brothers, my brothers
Play skillfully,
On your harp.
King David was the first musician
And he played for the whole inhabitants of Israel, give thanks
And if I should rise up forward and say
music, sweet dub music,
what should the wicked have in their minds to say?

(Chorus)

When David was a boy he slew Goliath,
with only a sling and stone and music in the background.
Children of Israel once they crossed the Red Sea, yeah
Music was what they took and helped over
so that is the reason why we got to play,
rise and praise Jah . . .

(Chorus)

("Play Skillfully," *More Culture*)

In another song on the same album, Hill reveals ganja as a source of wisdom for King Solomon, biblical ancestor of present-day Rastas:

Just like a seed
Planted on Solomon grave
It was I
Brought down here in slave eh eh eh
eh eh eh eh eh smell so sweet, yeah
Callie weed song,
Jah knows.

("Callie Weed Song," *More Culture*)

These artists provide poetic insights into the mythology, rituals, and world-views of Rastas that are unavailable elsewhere, unless one is able to spend time in a Rasta community. Because songs are poeticized, in conjunction with music that carries with it a profound, hypnotic, and compelling "vibe" also filled with Rastafari energy, they are highly effective. They communicate subtle details and ideas that become ever more plentiful as the listener becomes more attuned to Rasta vision and the rhetorical nuances employed by the artists. Most important to my discussion here, the artists validate the warrior/priest persona that, in turn, adds authority to their discourse.

No other singer adopted the role of warrior/priest as profoundly as Bob Marley, and the lyrical allusions to this role are found throughout his repertoire. In "So Much Things to Say," he insinuates his place in the mythological arena, alongside Moses, Job, Garvey, and Jesus:

But I never forget, no way,
They crucify Jesus Christ.
I never forget, no way,

They sold Marcus Garvey's rights.
I never forget, no way,
They turn their back on poor Moses and Job.
So don't you forget, no way
Who you are and where you stand in the struggle. . . .

I and I no come to fight flesh and blood,
But spiritual wickedness in high and low places.
So while they fight we down
Stand firm and give Jah thanks and praises.

The warrior component of this persona is also evident in cover art and lyrics. The most glaring example is Winston Rodney's reggae name, "Burning Spear," derived from the Kenyan president Omo Kenyatta. The cover of Spear's *Marcus Garvey* LP consists of a black-and-white image of African warriors holding spears in their hands. Across the bottom of the cover are chain links, broken in the middle by the words *Marcus Garvey*. The cover of Culture's *Culture in Dub* presents a drawing by Tony Walsh that includes, among others, these same motifs. A row of African women joined by chains stand with a slave ship behind them. An African warrior with a spear and shield appears on the right side of the cover, and behind her is a shaman.

Donovan reiterates this motif on his LP *Banzani*. On the front cover is a photo of the artist's upper body, bare chested, adorned in a beaded African necklace, holding a spear. On the back cover, more of the artist's body is shown. This time he is in motion, as if about to throw the spear. He is wearing the kind of skirt traditionally worn by various African tribes, and in his belt are what seem to be a machete and a knife. "Banzani" (which is translated on the cover as "own soldier") begins with a military trumpet and snatches of a military snare drum, and is woven around the motif of modern-day warriors—soldiers. The opening lines are spoken as a commander might utter them: "Soldier, report for duty!" The chorus goes as follows:

I'm my own soldier
I don't bow down to Satan's order.
I a' my own soldier
I'm on this mission
and it will be for my master

Bob Marley's *Confrontation* also employs these motifs, both on its cover art and in the lyrics of numerous songs. The cover depicts Marley dressed in

Ethiopian garb riding a white horse, which is also arrayed in Ethiopian colors. Marley's horse rears up as Marley pierces the heart of a giant dragon (Satan) with a long lance, similar to those used by knights in medieval Europe. The album cover folds open to a two-page drawing "adapted from a traditional Ethiopian painting depicting the battle of Adowa, 1896." The drawing shows Selassi and his army in the decisive battle against the Italians. The first song on the LP, "Chant Down Babylon," serves as a call to the righteous to "chant down Babylon one more time," using reggae music as the weapon. The second song utilizes the legendary American motif of Buffalo Soldiers,[1] transforming the motif into a mythological one:

Buffalo Soldier, Dreadlock Rasta
In the heart of America
Stolen from Africa, brought to America
Fighting on arrival, fighting for survival.

("Buffalo Soldiers," *Confrontation*)

And on the third song, listeners are encouraged to "Jump Nyabinghi," to dance the sacred dance that will bring Babylon walls tumbling down:

It remind I of the days in Jericho
When we trodding down Jericho walls.
These are the days when we trod through Babylon
Gonna trod until Babylon falls . . .
Jump, Jump, Jump Nyabinghi!

("Jump Nyabinghi," *Confrontation*)

It is not surprising that the warrior would be such an important part of the major roots reggae persona, given Selassi's dual role as religious head and military leader, combined with the guiding metaphor of spiritual war derived from the Bible and images of African warriors that helped inspire the Rastafari movement from the beginning. The military motifs surrounding Selassi's reign have made a major impact on Rastas. Khaki or green military fatigues has been a favored style of subversive dress among many reggae artists.

Another rhetorical marker of the warrior/priest persona is the frequent use of biblical phrases in reggae lyrics. Some of the recurring lines include the following, which are usually combined into a single stanza: **The lips of the righteous, teach many / But fools die for want of wisdom / The rich man's wealth is in his city / The righteous wealth is in His Holy Place**. Another favored couplet is: **Destruction of the poor is in their poverty / Destruction of the soul is vanity.** Other lines include **Only a fool lean upon his own misunderstanding / And what has been hidden from the wise and the prudent, shall be revealed to the babe and the suckling,** and **The stone that the builders refuse shall be the head cornerstone.** By weaving these phrases into their lyrics, artists further validate the biblical authority of their statements and, by association, their role as chosen spokesmen and visionaries for Jah.

Segments of traditional Rastafari liturgical quotes and prayers, based on Bible verses, are also common on album covers and within the lyrics of songs. On the back cover of Hugh Mundell's *Time and Place,* for example, is the text of Psalm 98, verses 1–9, and on the Melodians' *Irie Feeling,* Psalm 11. On Gregory Isaacs's *Lonely Lover* are the first two verses of the second chapter of The Song of Solomon: "I am the rose of Sharon, and the lilys of the valleys," "As the lilys among the thorns, so is my love among the daughters." Danny Dread's *Hit Me with Music* cover contains the following prayer: "and a special thanks to our Lord and Savior Jesus Christ, who has this day revealed to us in the personality of His Imperial Majesty (H.I.M.) Haile Selassi." And Peter Broggs includes on his LP cover *Rastafari Liveth* a similar prayer: "I give thanks unto Jah Rastafari, Selassie I, for the people who made this album possible." The inscription at the bottom of Marley's *Rastaman Vibration* is in this tradition. Titled "The Blessing of Joseph," it draws lines from Genesis 49:22–24, Revelation 19:16, and Deuteronomy 33:16. These include, for instance, "Joseph is a fruitful bough, even a fruitful bough by a well; whose branches run over the wall"; "But his bow abode in strength, and the arms of his hands were made strong by the hands of the mighty God of Jacob." In cases such as this one, the verses support the singer's claim to a particular biblical incarnation. The idea of being a reincarnation of specific biblical figures or linked to particular tribes is found not only with Marley but with a number of other artists. Culture, for instance, insinuates his association with Elijah in a tune on *Lion Rock.*

Biblically inspired texts are also integral to oral performances, in which they are chanted before or during songs. An artist might open a concert, for example, with "Behold, how good and pleasant it is for I-n-I to come together in I-nity in the presence of His Imperial Majesty, JAH," to which the audience would respond formulaically with: "RASTAFAR-I!" The singer might go on from there for several minutes more, giving thanks and praises, sometimes with no musical accompaniment, and at other times with Nyabinghi drumming playing softly in the background. Thus the ensuing performance is contextualized as a religious, ceremonial occasion. Forms of address used by roots reggae artists also give clues to the warrior/priest persona. For example, Bob Marley frequently indicated this role by addressing the audience as "O Children," as an aside between lines of his songs. The phrase implies that the audience is his flock and he is the visionary/prophet.

However pronounced the role of priest may be in the lyrics, it is even more obvious in live performances, in which intense enactments of healing sessions, sermonizing, and prophesying are the norm. Imagine first the performance space as a temple, in which such stimuli as the scents of incense, the burning of the holy sacraments, the pervasiveness of a communal spirit, and often the lowering of the lights are not so different from such elements characterizing sacred ceremonies of other religions. Burning Spear is well known for going into deep trance during his performances, filled with the spirit of Jah, and communicating that presence to the audience. Bob Marley was famous for his stage props: large banners of King Haile Selassi; the red, gold, and green; symbols such as the lion; and the pictures of Selassi that he held high over his head while sermonizing. He is just as famous for his ritualized performances that included Nyabinghi dancing, prophetic and evangelical gestures and facial expressions, and enactments of the warrior/priest trodding down Babylon.

It is instructive to contrast the performance styles of diverse African American ministers such as Dr. Martin Luther King, Malcolm X, and Reverend C. L. Franklin with traditional Jamaican preachers of various denominations and with Bob Marley. Marley is clearly closer to Franklin and the so-called fire-and-brimstone-style Jamaican preachers, who come out of the evangelical mode. Franklin's animated sermons built slowly to the intense rhythmical chanting and singing style referred to as "whooping" (Franklin and Titon 1989, 43). His performance incorporated waving of the hands, stooping, stomping, jumping, walking rhythmically back and forth, hand claps, and a host of dramatic facial gestures.

Marley's style also incorporated all of these elements, but with a completely different flavor. First, his movements were to a different beat, a different rhythm. His face ran the gamut from the sorrow and pain of the first Africans dragged from their homeland, the frustration of being held down by Babylon institutions, the ebullient pride of awakening to Rastafari knowledge, the anger/determination to chant down Babylon, to the ecstasy of contemplating a moment in Jah sight. In many ways, to view a Marley performance was to observe a ritual reenactment of the history of Africans in the Western world. He stepped deeply in the spirit of African warriors. He jumped Nyabinghi, his dreadlocks flailing about him like a mystical aura, like a giant leaving a path of smashed castles and government buildings in his wake. He pranced, like a lion, moved his hips slowly in a twinkle of laughter. He summoned the spirits, stirred up the lightning and thunder, made love to the earth and the wind.

One of the most memorable moments in a Marley performance was during the One Love Peace Concert in Jamaica in 1978. The purpose of the concert was to help heal the rifts between warring political parties and among rival street gangs. During this concert, heads of rival street gangs were brought on stage by reggae warrior/priest Jacob Miller, and the heads of the political parties—Michael Manley and Edward Seaga—were brought on stage by Marley and cajoled into joining hands. Among the many very special moments of that concert was one that happened during Marley's "Natty Dread." For a brief period, he stopped singing, as if too filled with the spirit to utter words. Instead, he dramatically mimed the entire stanza and chorus, as if in deep trance, his characteristically outstretched hand showering the audience with invisible rays of energy, then pointing here and there, his eyes closed, his head shaking, his body possessed with spirit and the music. And in the background, the music played the bridge:

Don't care what the world say
I-n-I never go astray
Just like a bright and sunny day
We're gonna have things our way
Oh Natty Natty Natty Natty
Natty Dread one thousand miles away from home.

A number of singers go further in their performances, becoming like Vodou priests or Pentecostal preachers who step down from the pulpit to "lay on hands." They move among the audience, continuing to raise the pitch of their ecstasy. At a concert in Columbia, Missouri, I observed Joseph Hill of Culture during the final song moving along the edge of the stage. The volume of the music lowered, as he sang/whispered into the mic, his dreadlocks falling forward around his face. He bent down, reached out, and took the hands of individuals in the audience, one by one, as the concert was transformed into a religious healing ceremony.

A poster advertising a reggae show, and recognizing roots artists as educators and warriors: "Mikey Dread and 'I' Chele in association with Musik Beat and the Musikal Tabernacle present . . . Inspector Willie, U-Roy (The Teacher), (Principal) Charlie Chaplin, (Colonel) Josie Wales . . . Special Guest, Sanchez." (Courtesy of LuAnne Roth)

The Rhetoric of the Music: Healing, Trance, Meditation

The lyrics of reggae cannot be considered separate from the music, which embodies the mission of roots messengers, sometimes even more completely than the words of the song. Jones (1988) makes an interesting observation in this regard, about the initial appeal of reggae to European listeners whom he studied.

As initial foci of attraction, and sources of pleasure, the lyrics of reggae were often secondary to the music's non-verbal sounds. For while all showed some understanding of reggae's lyrical discourses, it was the music's different rhythmic emphasis and formal principles, its bass, off-beat and polyrhythms, which initially captured their interest. . . . As I argued earlier, for the vast majority of white listeners the music's initial appeal was not dependent on its lyrics making literal sense, but on the capacity of its rhythms and vocal and instrumental sounds to hold other kinds of meaning and pleasure. (153)

A typical reggae ensemble includes, in addition to singers, a drummer, a bassist, lead and rhythm guitarists, a keyboardist, at least one percussionist, and often a horn section consisting of saxophone, trombone, and trumpet. The music centers around the bass and drum, with the bass playing a melody line and the drummer playing on the offbeat, referred to as a "one drop."

Reggae drumming is based on the Rastafari or Nyabinghi "heartbeat" drumming. Nyabinghi ensembles consist of three drums, the bass, funde, and repeater, or kete. The bass drum plays on the one and three beats, simulating the rhythm of a human heartbeat, the supposed heartbeat of the universe, a concept akin to the "Ommm" mantra of Eastern meditation. The funde is struck a half-beat behind the bass, creating a syncopated polyrhythm. Atop the voices of these two, the kete improvises, reciting the epic of Natty Dread, dancing, crying, rejoicing, recounting every trial and tribulation. The reggae bass line weaves in and out of the drumbeat, lyrically, militantly, persistently, like a Nyabinghi dancer during grounation or other Rastafari ceremonies. The drum is ever marching forward, insistent, determined, tireless. One can hear the thud of walls tumbling, wood and bone smashed, whipped flesh rising to deliver blows, earthquakes, thunder and lightning. Sometimes the drums play snatches of military snares, signifying on European armies, declaring the strength of Jah's army, and smiling toward Armageddon. Bilby notes the cultural depth of sounds found in reggae drumming: "Traces of John Canoe, Kumina, and mento phrasing can be heard in the rolls and carefully-placed accents of reggae trap drummers" (1985, 144).

Thus the foundation of roots reggae is an innovative, sacred, ceremonial music, laden with philosophical connotations (see Jones 1988, ch. 1; Bilby 1985, 1995). In fact, one could say that the best roots music represents reenactments of Rastafari ceremonies. The rhythm guitar and keyboards fill in the afterbeat, loping just behind (or just ahead of, depending on one's perceptual standpoint) the drumbeat, creating a syncopated, hypnotic effect. Bubbling, cool, and dangerous. Skanking, deceptively aloof. The horns, like fabric, add layers of warmth, and perhaps more than other instruments, set the tone, like colors on a canvas. Sometimes playful, sometimes somber, sometimes ironically bittersweet, but always grand, royal, and shimmering with dignity. One can hear echoes of humor, pathos, and sarcasm, sometimes stridently pronounced, other times whispered, almost under the breath while looking in the opposite direction. Atop the instruments are the vocal harmonies.

Reggae does not just espouse a particular message but is in and of itself an experience of a specific vision. It is word/sound/power, a dynamic interaction not only with the neocolonial world of ideas but with the lived reality of sound and motion in neocolonial societies. It is a sound force, blasting from mammoth speakers at Half Way Tree, or stereos, radios, or jukeboxes in bars, pool halls, shops, and taxis; colliding and interfacing with the rush of neocolonial machines and engines: automobiles, buses, trucks, air conditioners, and fans. Talking back to the concrete, metallic reality of urban life. It is chiseled sound, sculpted electricity; the buzz, snapping, popping, roaring, crashing, seething sound in a neocolonial jungle. Sound by the sea. Sound by the river. Sound inna tenement. Sound pounding in the thighs of someone peddling a bicycle on busy Kingston streets. Sound bouncing off the walls of a shanty. Bass swelling and driving through walls, through floorboards, through metal and glass, through bones, through Hitachi, Sanyo, General Electric speakers. All to the sarcastic have-a-good-time-laid-back beat bubbling over caustic rage, and deejays scatting "Murder!"

Envisioned as word/sound/power, it is healing, inciting, awakening, tearing down "the walls of Jericho," the temples of Babylon. These musicians *are* David, playing songs on his harp to Jah. They are Joshua blowing the trumpets to tear down the walls of Jericho. And this is trance music, capable of inducing states of meditation, of healing and liberation. Lyrics often reflect these philosophical tenets; for example, Burning Spear testifies to the medicinal properties of roots reggae:

Reggae physician
play I some reggae music.
What went wrong
you want a reggae physician?
Reggae physician
give I some meditation.

("Reggae Physician," *Appointment*)

Roots reggae artists are quite adamant that reggae is music designed for sacred healing. Bob Marley sings in "Trenchtown":

One good thing about music,
When it hits you, you feel no pain.
Can we heal the people with music
With music,
with music, music, oh music?

(*Confrontation*)

It is a neo-African beat played upon instruments held like surgical tools: kete, funde, bass drum, bell/gong, iron. Hammering the body/spirit. Molding and reshaping the body/spirit into the postures of proud, holy warriors. Teaching through dance. Healing through dance. Lending the energy a flavor. Danny Dread sings:

Hit me with music
Culture music
Roots rock reggae music.
Every time I hear the reggae music
I have to take a dip.
I have to move my hips.

("Hit Me with Music," *Hit Me with Music*)

The word/sound/power of the music not only heals, it creates a unique dwelling place, a spiritual city that transcends time and space, a city of consciousness. "We're building a city," Burning Spear sings.

But like the goddess Shiva, word/sound/power is simultaneously a creative and destructive force, for the emergence of the new world depends on the collapse of the old. Reggae sounds are not only implements of healing but a major arsenal of Rastafari prophets. Nowhere is this sentiment better expressed than in Gregory Isaac's "Kill Them with Music." The song opens with a deceptively soothing and melodic instrumental phrase, during which Isaacs speaks, "Victory!" In contrast to the almost happy tone of the music, the theme is a serious one, exemplifying *ritual dissonance*, an element of reggae I will discuss in more depth further along. The song also illustrates a fairly common rhetorical strategy in reggae: allusions to American film for critical and humorous effect. In most such cases, such allusions are reinterpreted to highlight differences between Rastafari and Babylonian worldview. "License to Kill," for instance, is the title of a James Bond film.

You put me through great tribulation, yeah.
I'm like the rock of salvation.
Now the prophecy fulfill, yeah.
Jah gave me a license to kill.
I'm gonna kill them with music.
I know they can't escape it.
I'm gonna kill them with music, yeah.
It's my only weapon and I got to use it.

("Kill Them with Music," *Pardon Me*)

The Song Structure

The term that best describes roots reggae song structure is eclectic. One cannot speak of a typical stanza structure as one can, for instance, when talking about blues music; in fact, reggae lyrics are characterized by liberal poetic license. Generally speaking, lyrics range from simple, seemingly trite repetitive phrases to stanzas that approach the sophistication and complexity of more formal written poetry. The songwriting of artists who use proverbs most often is more akin to works by American popular singers who compose their lyrics than to blues singers who might build their songs by basically integrating traditional stanzas.

While quatrains are common, they are not the rule. To the contrary, each artist seems to base his or her lyrical structures on different rhetorical influences. One can see influences of calypso couplets but (more important) the longer lyrical units of meanings found in calypso, sometimes upward to twenty-five lines. The calypsos is a topical song that "derives its essential substance from African songs of complaint, social comment and recrimination" (Courlander 1976, 101). Folk songs and mentos are other influences. For instance, Barrington Levy's "Shine Eye Girl" (*The Best Of*) is an adaptation of an old folk song, with most of the lyrics intact (Chevannes 1998, 105–6; Dance 1985, 190–91). Spirituals, hymns, Revivalist and Rastafari chants are also obvious influences on lyrical structure and content. Quite a number of songs are basically Rastafari hymns, especially songs by artists such as Leonard Dillon and the Ethiopians, and by Culture. Even more frequently, songs employ entire stanzas that are hymns, single lines taken from Rastafari singing, or new words set to traditional Rasta tunes.

The compositions of Bob Marley and of Keith Porter of the Itals exemplify the most complex reggae lyrical structure. These songs often remind one of sermons or oratorical speeches. Quatrains, even couplets, are sometimes used, but just as often the structure deviates from these formalized patterns. Burning Spear's songs are combinations of chanted words, phrases, and sung lines, idiosyncratically repeated to the background of bass heavy rhythms that lift the listener into trance. His approach is comparable to jazz scatting, in which the voice is an instrument, weaving in and out of the ongoing melody and beat. Culture relies heavily on Rastafari phrases, melodies, and harmonies, approaching his song structure in a very fluid manner. As Bilby observes of Culture, "The melodic, harmonic, and rhythmic influence of traditional Afro-

Protestant Revival music is certainly there as well" (1985, 144). Culture's style evokes that of the storyteller, who alternately sings, chants, and talks, sometimes stringing lines together in a way that would be virtually impossible for anyone else to duplicate. In fact, most of these singers interject so many critical lines, by talking in between stanzas or during choruses sung by backup singers, that it is a challenge to transcribe accurately the verbal texts of many songs. The texture of roots music is often quite dense, with multiple levels of vocals occurring simultaneously. We find the vocal sounds of trios working in eclectically alternating patterns of call and response, interweaving spoken and sung lines with two- and three-part vocal harmonies.

Children's rhymes and taunts also find their way into reggae lyrics and music. The most common illustration of this is the use of phrases similar to the taunt "Na na na na na," which is used among children to tease or make fun of someone, often indicating a one-upmanship on another. Such a phrase is found in the Wailing Souls' "Stop Red Eye" (*The Best Of*) and Bob Marley's "Them Belly Full" (*Natty Dread*). Another excellent example is Jacob Miller's "Tenement Yard" (*Tougher*), which is essentially a protest against confinement and restrictions placed on Rastas by the Jamaican government. The taunting is reflected in the exaggerated vibrato vocal style, which mockingly repeats certain phrases: "Dem a watchee watchee watchee, Dem a sus a sus a sus a sus." The entire tone of the song, however, is sarcastic, using the style of children's taunts to signify on those who feel they have to "keep an eye" on Rasta. The effect of such phrases is to create a tension in the songs, similar to the tension created by instrumental segments that counterpose playful tones against the profound seriousness, even rage, underlying the actual message of the song. It is this kind of tension I refer to as *ritualized dissonance.*

While attending the Ethiopian Orthodox Church on Maxfield Avenue in Kingston, I noted what sounded to the ear of an outsider as strangely discordant. During several parts of the service, the clergy were singing/chanting in a vocal style derived from northern Africa; the choir was singing in a style more akin to Baptist or Revivalist; the drumming accompanying the singing was Rasta Nyabinghi style; and the congregation was singing in a style that much like the Baptist church back in Virginia where I grew up—all simultaneously. It struck me as an excellent example of the typical creolized experience of sound that characterizes Jamaica and other parts of the Caribbean. Barrett takes the analysis of disjuncture a step further, correlating it to tensions within the society. He suggests quite astutely that "anyone who listens to Rastafarian music, be it the ritual Nyabingi or the popular reggae, will detect in the lower beats deep structural dissonance which mirrors the social conflicts within the society" (1988, 167). He argues further that there is also present a search for "consonance," a resolution to the conflicts, and discusses the evolution of Rastafari as a possible avenue for such a resolution within Jamaican society.

I wish to add to Barrett's observations and suggest that dissonance becomes ritualized in reggae as a means of consciously negotiating social tensions. As such, ritualized dissonance became one of the musical/lyrical strategies characterizing reggae, which facilitated social critique. Compared to rap or ragga, the ritualized dissonance of roots reggae is very subtle and, in the music of certain artists, muted to the point of silence. The dissonance occurs largely in tonal and inflectional incongruities between lyrical and musical sounds and grammatical meaning. For example, in the previously mentioned Gregory Isaacs song, "Kill Them with Music," musical phrases are lighthearted and playful at the same time that the vocal message is threateningly serious. The Wailing Souls exemplify a roots group that makes constant use of this strategy. The song "Stop Red Eye" is a good illustration. The song is sung almost in the melody of a children's game, incorporating sounds from a playground; however, its message is a sermon on the greed and evil of slave traders and subsequent generations of neocolonial oppressors. As we continue our discussion of oral genres influencing reggae song, it will become clear that ritualized dissonance complicates the use of whatever genres might appear in a given composition.

Nursery rhymes and phrases from other children's lore are also found in reggae lyrics. As with other elements, they may be used to create tensions within songs but they might just as well be simply an artful demonstration of verbal play. I-Roy's "Love and Unity" is a classic song containing lines from nursery rhymes. The song begins "Gather round little children" and alternates between lines actually addressing and giving advice to children and speaking to adults. Central messages of the song include the power of reggae (rockers) and the virtues of listening and dancing to it:

Never be like humpty dumpty
who had a great fall.

Says that the mouse ran up the clock
the clock struck one
the mouse come down

children gather 'round,
no need to worry, rockers style.

("Love and Unity," *African Herbsman*)

The allusions to Mother Goose continue.

Baby bow wow wow wow wow wow wow
show you how to milk that cow.

Little bo peep has lost her sheep
and don't know where to find them
Leave her alone and she will come home
dragging her tail behind her.

Two further examples include the Wailing Souls' "Sticky Stay We Play" (*Best Of*), which is taken from a children's game, and Justin Hinds and the Dominoes' "Dip and Fall Back," based upon a children's ring play game. In Hinds's beautiful rock-steady composition, messages of social unity and even sexual pleasure come together with his characteristically soulful, church-tinged vocals and music, all woven around lines from a children's game.

Dip and fall back yeah
Dip and fall back
That's what the game [music] say.
Make no use for fussing and fighting
all come from the same fountain.
There is so many kinds in the fountain,
which one will the fountain bless?
There is a black girl, in the ring,
Tra la la la la la la la

And she loves sugar and I love plum,
she loves sugar and I love plum . . .

Sugar in the morning, sugar in the evening . . .

(*Jezebel*)

The Deejay Tradition

Of all genres of reggae, the deejay tradition is perhaps the richest in traditional oral forms, and in many regards, deejays such as I-Roy, U-Roy, Big Youth, and Prince Fari have had more license than other reggae poets. The deejay style developed in connection with sound systems and is a more open mode in which poets rap, chant, talk, and toast to the sound tracks and "dubs" of recordings made by other artists. "Dub" is a musical form that developed in the 1960s: "Dub originated through sound engineers experimenting with the separation of different tracks and instruments in the studio. Through the use of echo, reverb and phasing, and by means of skilful tape-editing, the dub engineer was able to transform the music in endlessly different ways" (Jones 1988, 24). By the 1970s, a dub or "version" of the A-side became the staple B-side of most reggae 45rpm singles. The further development of sixteen- and twenty-four-track recording equipment facilitated a more complex kind of dub, leading to a completely new art form. Engineers and artists began using dub techniques to modify and accentuate song meanings, a process that can produce endless transformations of the same song. Entire dub albums began to appear, some of them dub versions of already-issued albums by particular artists. In other cases artists became known for their creative dub work: Vivian "Yabby You" Jackson, and Augustus Pablo, for example. A typical dub relies primarily on the drum and bass, with segments and fragments of other instruments and vocals echoing in at selected moments.

The deejaying style has, for all practical purposes, no limitations on lyrical structure. Deejays invented what is popularly known now in rap music as "sampling" (see Rose 1994, 73, 78–79), drawing upon segments of previously recorded (or oralized) discourse and weaving these into the song. At times, this tradition exemplified the most obvious ritualized dissonance in reggae music, as segments of discourse that might seem completely incongruous were placed in close proximity. On the other hand, the technique is reminiscent of the cubistic element of African sculpture and appliqué and thus has obvious, ancient cultural roots. The "sampling" aspect of the deejay style is also evident in deejays' reliance upon already produced sound tracks. Deejays might take a popular Bob Marley tune as the basis for a composition, then build their version around a particular line or phrase from the original song, modifying its meaning through transformation of context, and "sampling" lines and phrases from many other sources. One can also see that this tradition is the musical equivalent of "signifying" on selected texts (Rose 1994, 78–79; Gates 1988).

Deejaying differs from other styles of reggae performance in the degree to which it is improvisational. Deejays tend to have stock phrases they rely upon, and even specific sets of phrases that are chanted to particular musical songs.

However, their performance of these songs is a dynamic process, involving a give and take between musicians and deejays, as instrumentalists accent the spoken words in different ways and the deejays build upon various musical phrases that might catch their ears. There are also completely improvised lyrics, sometimes addressing something going on in the club that night or in the current local or national news. Bilby mentions not only the demanding art of deejay style but some of the cultural sources for lyrics: "Not only do Deejays make the appreciation of rhythm through verbal improvisation an end in itself, but they constantly draw directly from traditional sources, quoting proverbs or snatches of ring-play tunes, digging songs, mentos, or even cult songs" (1985, 144).

The deejay tradition makes apparent another important aspect of reggae lyrical structure: its sound import. As Bilby's comments indicate, this genre is rooted in sound aesthetics. Deejays such as Big Youth and I-Roy employ a wide range of mimetic sounds as a component of their art. These include—but are not limited to—whoops, yells, grunts, animal and machine voices, each inflectionally coded to suggest and critique performance and interactional contexts found in Jamaican society (such as church, lovemaking, on-the-job interactions, and so on). As such, this is an extremely sound-sensitive genre, in which the medium of communicative competence is sound-based and tonal—hence, very Africanized. Meaning relies on tonality and inflection and, while words do not lose their commonly ascribed meanings, those meanings become subordinate to the sound meaning projected in the deejay discourse.

Deejays are not as restricted by the idea of stanzas and can string long lines of prose together, alternately with shorter ones, drawing from every possible source of discourse available in Jamaican society. They tend to rely heavily on rhyming couplets, many of which are inspired by the rhyming traditions of "the street," such as the dozens. In fact, Jamaican deejaying was the forerunner of African American rap. In the song discussed above, I-Roy uses lines of nursery rhymes to give advice, in much the same way that proverbs are used in reggae lyrics. "Never be like humpty dumpty" conveys the value that it is unhealthy to just sit around, being a watcher. Instead, one should give one's self up to the beat of life: get up and dance, surrender to the healing power of reggae. Dispersed throughout the song are messages reflecting a Rastafari ideology. For example: "Only salvation last forever / so baby, you got to be clever," and "Lick up the chalice [ganja pipe] / and throw away your malice."

Boasting associated with the rudeboy is another prevalent rhetorical device used in roots reggae. Consider Peter Tosh's "Steppin Razor" or "I Am the Toughest":

If you want to live,
treat me good.
I'm like a steppin' razor
don't you watch my size
I'm dangerous.

("Steppin Razor," *Equal Rights*)

Anything you can do
I can do it better,
I'm the toughest.
I can what you can't do
you never try to do what I do,
I'm the toughest.

("I Am the Toughest," *Bush Doctor*)

Other times boasting is directly related to sound system wars, in which deejays attempted to best each other and brag about their musical prowess, as in for example, Bunny Wailer's "Rule Dance Hall" (*Rule Dance Hall*). Most often, however, boasts are made in the name of Rastafari and merge with less ego-centered concerns. There is an element of boasting in the Itals' "Don't Wake the Lion," as they sing, "Don't wake the Lion / for he will eat you / eat you to the edge of the bone" (*Early Recordings*).

Of course, biblical texts play a significant role in reggae lyrical structure. First, as we have mentioned, entire passages from the Bible are often quoted as lines of songs. But less apparent is the influence of biblical texts on syntax and vocabulary. For example, such words as "countenance," "thy," "thee," and "shall" are common, as are inverted syntactical phrases. All of these influence the length and meter of lines, and therefore the structure of stanzas. We can turn to Bunny Wailer's "Wanted Children" (*Protest*) by way of illustration. The first stanza is as follows:

Now didn't jah create the earth
And to the waters did he give birth
He divided the waters from the land
rivers for land, and seas for sand.
Then he said, let there be light.
And he made the darkness bright

Greater lights to rule by day
Lesser lights to rule by night.

As the song continues, other lines from the Bible are used, for example, "And to man and woman he gave all dominion / To all creatures that live on creation." The language of the verse is permeated with biblical vocabulary; and the second line reflects a syntactical inversion derived from biblical syntax.

The Use of Proverbs

It is understandable why proverbs would become such an important genre in this narrative tradition. Wisdom is one of the most essential characteristics of the warrior/priest, who embodies Rastafari worldview and accepts the role of contemporary social/spiritual guide. No other genre connotes wisdom and communicates anciency so effectively as does the proverb (Taylor 1950a, 1950b; Abrahams 1968a, 1968b). The proverb is also an effective rhetorical device for inducing reflective or meditative states of mind. As noted by numerous scholars (Prahlad 1994, Abrahams 1968a), the nature of the proverb is to disrupt the "normal" flow of thought or conversation, creating a reflective space. This is accomplished in part through the proverb's poetic qualities, such as metaphor, alliteration, and the use of images. It is also achieved through the proverb's cultural association with things that are "deep" and profound. The proverb can be effective in this way, even if the listener is unfamiliar with a given expression. As Arora demonstrated in her study of Mexican proverbs (1994), listeners can identify when a phrase "sounds like" a proverb, even if they have never heard the expression. If one of the goals of reggae is to lead listeners to the inward search necessary to gain knowledge, no other genre would seem so perfect as the proverb.

Proverbs are well suited for reggae discourse for a number of other reasons. As noted for proverbs used in other genres of song, their brevity makes it easy to fit them into the lyrics (Mieder 1988; Folsom 1993b, 1993c). Often proverbs are used as substitutes for parables, as a way of telling an entire story in as few words as possible. Other times they are used in conjunction with actual parables, to emphasize the main point. Two other paradoxical characteristics of proverbs make them a perfect genre for reggae discourse. On the one hand proverbs can be cultural markers, symbolizing the weltanschauung of a given group, in this case Jamaican Rastafari. Cultural promotion and affirmation are key goals of this music. Using proverbs such as **Iron sharpeneth iron, The half has never been told,** and **No cup no mash no coffee no throw away,** celebrates Rasta and traditional African Jamaica culture. On the other hand, the universal appeal of many proverbs creates a connection with international audiences. In this regard, such expressions as **What goes around comes around, Man cannot live by bread alone,** and **Still waters run deep** are familiar enough to most listeners internationally to permit individuals their own interpretations.

Proverbs are known for their function in making didactic comments. Given that reggae discourse is very concerned with giving advice, with preaching, as it were, proverbs are the most logical genre one can imagine for this context. In some cases reggae artists are castigating Babylon, pointing out its greed, treachery, and inhumaneness. Culture sings, for example, "Babylon, **You jump from the frying pan / jump ina fire**" (*Nuff Crises*). At other times, the behavior under censure is that of other Rastas or New World Africans, as illustrated by "**Crab walk too much, yes him lose his claw, now,**" from the Wailing Souls' "Who Lives It" (*Fire House Rock*). "**If you're gonna dig a pit, I tell you my brother, don't dig one always dig two,**" sings Culture in "Iron Sharpeneth Iron," and Peter Tosh warns, "**If you live in a glass house / don't throw stones** / If you can't take blows, brother / don't throw blows" ("Glass House," *Mama Africa*). Similar assertions are found throughout reggae lyrics, for example, Bob Marley's

Like one of my friends say
from a reggae riddim [rhythm]
**Don't jump in the water,
if you can't swim.**"

("Misty Morning," *Kaya*)

Proverbs also allow reggae poets to reflect the strong sense of community that is so integral to Jamaican culture. This is accomplished with the use of introductory formulas that paint pictures of speakers within the community. For instance, a proverbial line echoes throughout "War" by the Wailing Souls: "Grandma says, **Penny wise and pound foolish,** see them" (*The Very Best*). Although the proverb is used to comment on the behavior of world leaders and governments, echoes of its performance and the contextual associations surrounding that use in a traditional Jamaican community reverberate. We can imagine grandma talking to those around her, and with a little knowledge of Jamaican culture and social dynamics, we can reconstruct commonly witnessed scenes in our minds. Those scenes are permeated with a community ethos and strong familial and social bonds. A previously mentioned Wailing Souls song further exemplifies this proverbial function:

Your mama say, you better stay at home.
Cause that's what happen when you try to roam.
Crab walk too much him lose him claw, now.

Although there is no introductory formula used here, the stanza structure leads us to connect the proverb to the parental admonitions that precede it. This provides, as in the example before it, an illustration of how the proverb can evoke associations of interactional dynamics within a traditional Jamaican community, becoming a marker for the values that characterize those neighborhoods. This function is especially prominent in songs by the Wailing Souls, who introduce us to a number of characters in Jamaican communities— "Tom Sprang," for example (*Inchpinchers*).

Proverbs are well suited for reggae not only because of functional elements but also because of their poetic qualities. We have noted the centrality of sound as an aesthetic standard in reggae discourse. It is important to keep in mind that in this tradition the proverb is sung, shouted, or chanted and becomes another musical voice in the tapestry of reggae sounds. In addition to *sounding* wise and ancient, proverbs contain poetic, musical features. Rhyme is one element that leads to such reggae couplets as "**It's not all that glitter is gold / half the story has never been told.**" Rhythm and meter are others, producing such couplets as "**Never burn your bridges behind you / Never bite the hand that feeds you.**" Proverbs often occur in relationship to specific musical phrases within songs and are sometimes used to establish that subsequent musical lines should be taken as proverbial. Thus proverbs are played by instruments as well as sung vocally, a common practice in African cultures (Finnegan 1970). One can often hear bass lines "speak" proverbs, drums pound proverbs, guitars skank proverbs, horns blow proverbs, and keyboards bubble proverbs. This is most apparent in dubs, in which the vocal singing of proverbs may be edited out. A listener familiar with the original version of the song will recognize that the music is playing the melody of the sung proverb.

On other occasions, proverbs become chanted leitmotifs in songs, serving as vocalized segments to which the artists can return and make the focus of their emotional intensity. This is comparable to a blues or rock guitarist, or even a reggae percussionist, playing the same note over and over as a way to work the audience into a frenzy. I witnessed such an example in a Big Youth performance at the Grand Emporium in Kansas City, Missouri, January 1998. Big Youth began the concert with an extended invocation, a prayer, followed by chants of "JAH! Rastafari!" Throughout the "service," he chanted liturgies and prayers, at one point orating an entire book of Psalms. During one song, he kept returning to the proverb, **A hungry man is an angry man**, chanting it intensely. During one segment of the song, he leaned backward, his body half dancing, half trembling, a shamanic figure in trance, chanting over and over, "**A hungry man is an angry man.**" The performance of the proverb communicated all of the frustration, rage, and compassion he felt contemplating the present and historical situation of colonized people in Jamaica and throughout the globe. The proverb became, in this performance, a sound weapon, an energy, a force conjured and flung forth from the ceremonial flame of the band's musical groove.

The proverb walks over to you
and opens up a space inside.
It finds a tumor
and cuts it out.
It rubs soothing salve
in the wound
and sends you on your way
with a melody
and a mission.

The proverb taps you on your shoulder
and momentarily
stops your breath.
It falls down
from your head to your heart
gets into your feet
and makes you jump
Nyabinghi.

The proverb makes you nod.
It makes you laugh.
It makes you shake your head
in wonder.
How we brought it over.
Yes Jah.
Come on and chant it over.

Audiences and Communities

As I argue that roots reggae artists use the personas of warrior/priests, it is necessary to examine the audiences, fans, students, followers, and congregations of the music. The initial audience for most roots reggae artists was made up of Jamaicans. Certainly in the early days, reggae was conceptualized as a music primarily meeting the needs of the Jamaican listener. Distribution of recordings were limited to local people and the idea of touring internationally was just that, an idea. It was not long before this scenario changed, however, and distribution extended to Great Britain, and then to the United States. So a number of different communities at home and abroad comprised the reggae audience. These included—but were not limited to—Rastas in Jamaica, the Caribbean, and other parts of the world; those who might be serious fans of reggae, listening closely to the lyrics for insights, but who would not identify themselves as Rastas, also at home and abroad; and more casual listeners, who may or may not have paid very close attention to the lyrics.

Roots reggae celebrates and validates Rasta vision and worldview, and expounds upon Rasta philosophy. It has been, since its conception, the chief vehicle for spreading the Rastafari gospel abroad—although, as Hepner notes, reggae is not the only cultural force involved in the growth of Rastafari (1998, 213). But it has been through the medium of reggae that thousands living in countries outside of Jamaica have been initiated into the mysteries of Rastafari. While there are certainly many listeners who have the most superficial understanding of Rasta philosophy, there are also international communities of Rastas, many of whose members have learned as much through reggae lyrics as they have from contact with Jamaican-born Rasta emissaries, and many who are earnestly devoted to the most authentic principles of the religion.

Savishinsky's essay (1994) is one of the best summaries of the spread of reggae and Rastafari internationally. But it also considers several other significant aspects of this phenomenon. One is the extent to which Rastafari has been embraced throughout the world, largely because of its potential to provide a positive and progressive religious, cultural, and political framework for other groups (or individuals) who have also been victims of colonial/neocolonial oppression. The movement has become more and more associated not simply with ideas but with political and social activism leading to enormous changes and advancements for poor and historically voiceless masses. According to Savishinsky; "It can be argued that the Rastafarian movement represents one of the most visible, potent, and progressive pan-regional cultural forces at work in the Caribbean today" (263).

The same can be said of Rastafari abroad, where it has steadily crossed class and racial lines. Savishinsky provides many such examples. For instance, a group of middle-class whites in Miami over twenty years ago formed the Ethiopian Zion Coptic Church, and "have been carrying on an international campaign to legalize cannabis while simultaneously expounding their stridently anti-communist 'Rasta' philosophy" (264). In 1979, the television program *60 Minutes* did a feature on the group. Many Native American groups of the Southwest have embraced Rastafari, and for a number of years reggae concerts were held annually on reservations. The political connections between the historical situation of Native Americans and Africans is evident: both had their cultures ravaged and displaced by colonial powers. But there is also another link. Rastafari is similar to Native American revitalization movements, the Peyote Cult in particular. This movement "relied heavily on indigenous interpretations of the Old Testament, preached a form of pan-Indianism (where Rastas preach pan-Africanism), prohibited the use of alcohol, and held a drug (peyote) to be the only remedy for the social, physical, and psychological ills introduced into their societies by the white man" (264–65).

Unfortunately, there is a such a "lacuna in the literature on Rastafari in the United States" (Hepner 1998, 200), that it is impossible to provide any kind of comprehensive picture. Hepner notes settlement patterns of Caribbean immigrants to the United States and the corresponding sites of Rastafari communities, predominantly in New York City and Miami. "The growth and presence of Rastafarians in the United States followed the waves of Caribbean migration to North America in the 1900s, especially since the 1960s and 1970s. The high concentrations of Caribbean Americans in New York City and Miami now make these metropolitan centers the largest 'Caribbean' cities in the world to date. In fact, parts of Miami and Brooklyn have so many Jamaicans the neighborhoods are referred to, colloquially, as 'Kingston 21' and 'Little Jamaica' respectively" (199). One could find, as early as the 1970s in the these cities, Rastafari organizations and institutions such as churches and various associations. As one might expect, there has been consistent "hostility experienced by immigrant U.S. Rastas at the hands of the law-enforcement agents and the corporeate media" (200), creating a popular image of Rastas as bloodthirsty, drug-dealing cultists. Because of these all-out assaults by U.S. officials, "by the mid-1980s, more than two thousand Rastafarians were be-

hind bars in New York's state correctional facilities, and scores more lan-
guished in state and federal prisons around the country" (203). Such realities
make clear the practical need for songs of inspiration, hope, and cultural affirmation and the importance of warrior/priests to these communities.

For further evidence that Rastafari-influenced communities—and specifically, reggae-centered communities—have strong roots in the United States,
one need turn only to magazines such as *Reggae* or the *Beat*, the proliferation
of reggae shows on radio stations across the country and the communities
they serve, the multitude of annual festivals such as "Reggae on the River"
held in northern California every August, and the ongoing concerts by touring
artists, for evidence that the communities in the United States are substantial.
Most major cities that I know of in the United States have at least one club
that books reggae regularly, and many clubs have at least one day of each
week devoted to reggae music. In areas such as northern California, there are
numerous such clubs and even venues devoted entirely to reggae and world-
beat. My experiences suggest that there tends to be a core community of people who support these reggae outlets. Thumbing through a booklet produced
for the Kansas City annual reggae festival of 1998, I counted advertisements
for no less than thirty-eight festivals happening around the country. While
many of these were in different parts of California, there were also festivals in
Texas, Chicago, Arizona, Ohio, New Orleans, Belize, Hawaii, Washington,
D.C., New Mexico, Michigan, Minnesota, Vermont, Oregon, Washington,
Rhode Island, and Colorado. Also of interest is the international organization
Reggae Ambassadors Worldwide (RAW), which is devoted to the growth of
reggae and to forming links between people worldwide who are committed to
the music and its philosophies. RAW has been holding annual conferences
since 1992, and its members include reggae artists, deejays, managers, promoters, producers, vendors, shops, distributors, photographers, travel agents, ar-
chivists, and fans (Allie-I 1998, 50–51). RAW joins a number of other reggae
organizations with web sites on the internet. Such developments point to the
burgeoning institutionalization of this movement in the United States.

Rastafari has been a growing presence in European urban centers since the
1970s, led by large numbers of immigrants from Africa and the Caribbean.
Rastas come not only from African and West Indian ethnic groups, however,
but also from working, middle- and upper-class whites who, each in their own
way, feel some affinity with Rastafari symbols and philosophy. Cities such as
London, Birmingham, Paris, and Amsterdam have become known as havens

for Rastas (see Van Dijk 1998) and scenes for reggae in much the same way that Paris was, for example, for African American artists and musicians during the 1920s and 1930s. Friends traveling in Russia, Yugoslavia, the Ukraine, Thailand, Japan, Korea, Cambodia, and Germany have told me stories of small reggae enclaves they happened upon and of fans who have memorized the lyrics of Bob Marley's songs. And like Rastafari communities in the Caribbean, those in Europe have moved beyond the purely ideological and mystical to take leading roles in social and political activism. Savishinsky reports that large numbers of "Surinamese in the Netherlands have adopted the beliefs, practices, music, and dress of Rastafarians in an attempt to forge a distinct 'black' identity for themselves in their alien (predominantly white) European home" (267). He also writes that Amsterdam "harbors the largest population of white Rastafarians I have yet come across" (267).

Jones's study of whites involved in the reggae scene affirms the presence of Rasta communities in Great Britain, and the enormous impact that they have had on many young Europeans (1988). He discusses the involvement of fans from their early adolescence and discovers that, for many, their initial interest in the music deepens and extends to an interest in Jamaican and African culture, and Rastafari, as they grow older. During this process, they grapple with the militancy of reggae that implicates them as white Britons; with the discrimination and abuse of white peers and family, resulting from their association with black people; and with the suspicion and sometimes hostility of members of the Jamaican community toward them as outsiders. Of interest to our discussion is the extent to which they study and become well versed and fluent in reggae discourse. This fluency allows them to apply many of the symbols and theoretical ideas to aspects of their own lives, and to hold conversations and reasonings using lines from Rastafari tradition and reggae songs. As one informant stated: "It's like if someone come up to me and said, like, 'Africa for the Africans, and you're not an African so bat out [get lost],' I could always find something in the song to argue them down, like 'they don't want to see us live together' [from Marley's "Top Rankin," *Survival*] or 'stop the fussing and fighting' . . . you know, there's always another side to it" (Jones 1988, 191). So in the process of being socialized to Rasta and reggae ideology, these fans are educated to African and New World African history, worldview, and forms of cultural expression, such as proverbs.

The continent of Africa has also experienced tremendous influence from Rastafari. It is a well-known fact that in the 1970s Emperor Selassi gave land to Jamaican Rastas who wanted to repatriate to Africa. This community of Rastas, called Shashemane, has continued to grow and has created interest among Ethiopian urban youths. But the movement has also taken root in East, West, and South Africa (Savishinsky 1994, 268–70; Bergman 1985; Zindi 1985). Marley's famous concert in Zimbabwe in 1980 paved the way for other prominent reggae performers and helped to promote Rastafari throughout Africa. By the 1990s, roots reggae groups from Africa began to emerge and become prominent on the international music scene, all promoting Rastafari philosophies— for example, Lucky Dube, the Mandators, Alpha Blondy, and Majek Fashek.

Contemporary Rasta communities are found all over the continent. Terisa Turner writes that Rasta communities in East Africa have strong ties to those in "London, Lagos, Caribbean and elsewhere" (1991, 82). According to her, "The new Rasta of East Africa consists of dozens of autonomous groups which above all provide for survival. They combine study, artistic creation, childcare, economic activities, community service and politics. . . . Political reggae is of central importance. Marley's lyrics and those of other artists are studied carefully in Saturday afternoon 'reasonings' in slum yards. Marley's teachings are virtual primers for those seeking to develop their capacity to speak English" (82). She notes strong reggae followings and Rastas in Nairobi and Rwanda. Rastafari and reggae are also among the subcultures of South Africa. During a month I spent in Durban, South Africa, in 1997 I encountered a number of Rastas. I attended a reggae club, where a large crowd danced to reggae records into the early morning hours. Just as significantly, I was constantly greeted everywhere I went with great enthusiasm by people who assumed that because I had dreadlocks I was a Rasta. People either yelled "Bob Marley!," mistook me for Lucky Dube, or stopped me to share Rasta greetings and reasonings. At times this was awkward and overwhelming, for, with one or two exceptions, all of the people I met spoke only Zulu.

Rastafari communities can also be found in South and Latin America and throughout the Pacific (see Van Dijk 1998). There are documented settlements on islands such as Samoa, Panape, Tonga Fiji, Australia, and New Zealand, and, ironically, there is more research conducted on Rasta communities in the Pacific than in the United States. Hawkeswood's anthropological study of Rasta communities in New Zealand (1983) is one of the most serious works on Rastafari outside of Jamaica that exist to date.

The chief conduit for the spread of Rastafari internationally has been reggae music. As Savishinsky suggests: "For whereas many who have written about Rastafari claim it to have acted as a major source, inspiration, and catalyst in the creation of reggae, nearly *all* acknowledge the fact that reggae has functioned, and in many instances continues to function, as the principal medium through which people the world over have acquired their knowledge and awareness of Rastafari (the lyrics of Jamaican reggae songs having been dominated since the early 1970's by Rastafarian themes, imagery, and symbolism)" (1994, 260). Thus in our consideration of Rastafari communities throughout the world, we must simultaneously be concerned with reggae music as a gospel and cultural vein that has, in many cases, led in part to the development of these subcultures and that, in all cases, provides them with spiritual sustenance, guidance, education, and inspiration. One can take for granted that all of the communities mentioned above share a devotion to reggae. Hence, it is no exaggeration to speak of roots reggae lyricists as priests. In fact, these artists serve very real and identifiable communities who, since reggae and Rastafari began to spread in the 1970s, have looked to these figures to initiate and educate them into the mysteries and philosophies of the religion, as well as to guide their thinking and behavior on social and political fronts.

As Hawkeswood discovered working among New Zealand Rastas, and as is probably the case in such communities throughout the world, "Listening to reggae may be likened to a form of homework for aspiring Rastas here, as most obtain the greatest degree of knowledge about the movement through their contacts with this music and the Rasta-based messages it espouses" (1983, 272). And of Africa, Savishinsky writes: "Eighty percent of the Rastas I interviewed in Ghana and 66 percent of those in Senegal—where a small Rastafarian community has been functioning for over a decade on the island of Gorée—admitted that their initial interest in Rastafari came about as a direct result of their prior exposure to reggae. And in the vast majority of cases it was the music of Bob Marley that made the most intense and lasting impression" (1994, 269). Obviously, varying degrees of devotion to Rastafari can be found among reggae devotees worldwide, as can different levels of interest in learning about Jamaican culture. In fact, there is a wide range of commitment even to particular practices among diverse groups of Rastas, and an openness to individual interpretation is one of the cornerstone facets of the religion. Savishinky lists six factors he believes have contributed to the spread of Rastafari, and these have a bearing on reggae lyrics and ultimately on proverb performances and interpretations. They include: (1) the emphasis on the Bible; (2) the focus on natural, healthy living; (3) "condemnation of . . . injustice . . . in colonial and neo-colonial societies"; (4) encouragement to colonized people to "take pride in their ancestral heritage"; (5) the "decentralized nature of the movement, which gives adherents everywhere the freedom . . . to select and interpret specific aspects . . . in a way that is best suited to their own need"; and (6) links "between the movement and various aspects of contemporary transnational popular culture—namely music, drugs, and fashion" (274).

This last factor encompasses a complex of forces bearing on the artistry, production, and dissemination of the music—for instance, the recording industry, promotional trends, and the proliferation of electronic technology to the far corners of the earth. It supports Regis's argument that foreigners latched onto specific elements of reggae, and that their taste in turn helped to shape the personas of the singers and also their music (1994). This argument rests on the notion that popular forms—and specifically those that have as their foundation authentic ethnic rituals, religions, and so on—reflect the cultural domination of these ethnic groups by Western powers. This dynamic is not new, however, and has characterized the relationship of black musicians to the recording industry from the very beginning. It gives rise to significant questions. To what extent, for example, is the dominant persona in reggae a media-influenced creation? Several assumptions underlie my treatment of this persona, the artists, and their work. One is that they are aware of the conflicts between the urges and demands of the industry, and their own ideologies and goals. Another is that they actively negotiate these conflicts and work to subvert the industry's philosophical tenets whenever possible. And third, in most cases the lyrics of roots reggae artists reflect genuine concerns and sentiments that are, in fact, more aligned with their own cultural, social, and political agendas than with the expectations or ideational orientation of foreign consumers.

2.2 Billboards advertising reggae shows, along with other commercial ventures and commodities, Negril, 1998.

NO CUP NO MASH

Proverbs in Jamaican Society

In beginning a study of proverbs in reggae music, a consideration of proverbs in Jamaican society in general is necessary. It is important to know, for example, when reggae artists are using proverbs common among Jamaicans, and when and in what ways the forms or meanings of these are altered. Answering such questions depends on a knowledge of which proverbs are in use and what their *social*—and possibly, some of their *situational*—meanings might be.

The prevalence of proverbs in Jamaican society has been noted by scholars; and numerous collections of Jamaican proverbs exist (Beckwith 1925; Bates 1896; Grant 1917; Cundall 1910; Frank 1921; Anderson and Cundall 1927; Morris-Brown 1993; Watson 1991). As yet, however, there are no book-length studies of Jamaican proverbs. No folklorist or other scholar has gone out and conducted extensive interviews, probing the meanings of particular proverbs, beyond eliciting simple paraphrases. Collections by Jamaican authors have tended toward arguments of national character and cultural reappraisal. For example, Watson (1991) writes in the preface to his *Jamaican Sayings,* "This volume is conceived as a small but important contribution to the ongoing process of cultural and historical reappraisal and synthesis taking place in the lives of Caribbean peoples" (xii). Watson's collection is based in part on field trips that were "experienced as intense interaction and total immersion . . . into the ordinary folk life of Jamaicans, mostly but not exclusively, in the rural regions of the country" (23). He found, for example, "seventy- and eighty-year-old rural people whose daily conversations, social criticisms, and even storytelling were replete with the witticism of Sayings" (23). Such sayings were supplemented with proverbs from other collections, such as Beckwith's to form *Jamaican Sayings*. Although Watson mentions the importance of context to proverb meaning, he does not include descriptions of interactions in which proverbs were used or names of speakers who used them.

A similar work to Watson's is Morris-Brown's collection, *The Jamaica Handbook of Proverbs*. Morris-Brown notes that her work is "the result of many years of research, collection, and discussion involving encounters with Jamaicans from every parish in the island, and from virtually every walk of life ('one, one coco full basket')" (1993, xi). The strengths of this collection are Morris-Brown's immersion in her native Jamaican culture and the intimate, insider's knowledge of the proverbs. Like Watson, she ascribes to the proverb-as-reflection-of-cultural-values perspective and emphasizes the frequent use of proverbs by adults to children in Jamaican society. Proverbs in the collection are given in Jamaican patois, followed by a standard English translation, and a brief summary of the base meaning or explanation of the proverb. There are no contextualized accounts of speech events in which the proverbs are actually used, or informant information on whom they were collected from. There are, however, occasional examples of newspaper cartoons and advertisements in which a given proverb is used.

Beckwith collected from women students of the Bethlehem training school, asking them "to write out lists of old sayings" (1925, 5). She put these together with occasional proverbs given to her by "negro servants" and items from other collections, most notably Cundall and Anderson's. Some of these include brief but helpful explanations. Beckwith is aware that contexts influence proverb meanings; however, this does not lead her to explore further any of the explanations. She notes that "a saying may in another community take on a quite different shade of meaning" (6). She even mentions that some of her informants offered contextual examples of proverb applications, and some of these are included. Watson (1991) notes that his collection is based on fieldwork, but like others before him, he simply presents the proverbs with very generalized meanings.

Beckwith makes a number of other pertinent observations about Jamaican proverbs. According to her, a large number of proverbs address injustices and social problems such as hunger and poverty. She states: "I was chiefly impressed with the dark sense of wrong and the nursing by the weaker folk of injuries real or fancied inflicted by those upon whom they were impotent to avenge themselves" (1925, 6). Carolyn Cooper notes Beckwith's "limited understanding of the Jamaican psyche" (1993, 45), and especially her failure to comprehend the extent to which Jamaican speakers " 'teck bad tings mek joke,' " in other words, the humor inherent in many proverb applications. Instead, Cooper cites Finnegan's more comprehensive view of proverb function in African and neo-African cultures (1970). However, in spite of these criticisms, she grants that Beckwith's "description of the psychic consolation of the proverb, though limited in its general applicability" is accurate. This function then, although only one of many, establishes a strong cultural precedent for applying proverbs to social ills and as forms of resistance, before Rastafari or reggae. It alerts us that reggae artists were not inventing a rhetorical tradition but simply building upon one that already existed.

Another element touched upon by these and other writers is the difficulty posed by Jamaican patois. While technically classified as English, its rhythms, intonations, and pronunciations are as close to a foreign language as one can come and still be English. This dialect, spoken with varying degrees of thickness by most Jamaicans, is pretty unintelligible to the untrained ear. In general, Jamaicans sing their words; and their accents, consonant and vowel sounds, pitch, and timing are very foreign to American sensibilities. Several problems immediately confront the observer. The first is that of becoming a fluent enough listener to know what is being said. To identify proverbs, one must be conversant beyond a general intuitive understanding of what people are saying. The listener must be able to understand word for word what is being said. A second problem is that of being knowledgeable enough about Jamaican proverbs to know when one has been used. And a third problem arises when one attempts to write down the conversations and proverbs. To what extent should one attempt to write in patois, a dialect for which there is no standard written format?

Between Beckwith and Anderson and Cundall four sources of Jamaican proverbs are acknowledged. Beckwith mentions British and African sources.

Anderson and Cundall note four possible sites of origin: Africa, the West Indies, Europe, and "those that are frankly European proverbs expressed in negro language" (1927, 9). The necessity of separating European proverbs spoken in "standard English" from those spoken in Jamaican dialect escapes me and has nothing to do with origins. Furthermore, the large umbrella of "West Indies" is not very useful; it overlooks the disparities between language, dialect, and culture that would interfere with proverbs circulating freely among all peoples of the Caribbean. A more useful category of origin for my purposes is simply Jamaican, and even this can be further broken down into two categories: traditional Jamaican and Rastafari. Another source of proverbs is the Bible. This source is alluded to in passing by Anderson and Cundall but is considered somehow less valid than the others mentioned: "Many phrases, it will be noted, are more or less Biblical in character" (10). The placement of this statement in the essay suggests that the comment refers to the content of proverbs rather than to their origin. To the sources these authors mention we can add yet another: modern America. Thus, possible origins of proverbs used in reggae include African, English, biblical, American, traditional Jamaican, and Rastafari—as well as phrases invented by given lyricists.

It is important to my study to have not only sources for annotating Jamaican proverbs but some understanding of how these expressions are actually used in context. Unfortunately, as I have indicated, no scholars have explored in depth the different contextual meanings of Jamaican proverbs. Thus we have no information on specific proverb users. In order to obtain at least a minimal picture of proverb performances and to gain a more comprehensive picture of how proverbs are used in contemporary society, I conducted fieldwork in Jamaica. My first visit was for three weeks in 1994. During that time, I spent approximately a week in Kingston and the Blue Mountains, a week in the interior near Montego Bay, and a week in Negril. The second visit was for a month in 1998. On this visit, I spent approximately ten days in Kingston, three days in Port Antonio, five days in Ocho Rios, and seven days in Negril. Although I consulted libraries, cultural centers, and other organizations that might have either archives of proverbs or names of people who would be good informants, my major focus was on observing proverb performances and on meeting people to spend time with and to interview. The first part of the following discussion is a short survey of proverbs from the media, primarily television, radio, and newspapers. In the second part of the chapter, I provide examples of proverb speech acts I observed. The final section is an in-depth exploration of one proverb master who, as good fortune would have it, is a Rastafari. While I would like to have spent more time living among Jamaicans in rural and urban settings, observing more examples of proverb speech acts, time and resources simply did not permit me to do so.

Proverbs in the Media

Jamaican people are well aware of their penchant for using proverbs, and one can easily find small, locally produced collections that give the proverbs in patois and then provide standard English translations. In addition to these, locally published chapbooks and even dictionaries of Jamaican popular phrases are not uncommon. These humorously rendered publications are directed primarily toward tourists and can be found in hotel or other gift and souvenir shops (Thomas 1987, Cleary n.d., Chen 1994). Proverbs are sometimes found in newspaper articles, in the speech of television or radio commentators, on stickers, and carved onto wooden plaques. In the lobby of the Sunset Inn in New Kingston, for example, a wooden plaque on the wall read: **Cuss cuss no bore hole ah me kin will never hurt me.** Two popular local television commercials I saw in 1998 used the proverbs **Actions speak louder than words**, and **Boys will be boys.**

In two weeks' time I found eleven instances of proverbial expressions in the Jamaican newspapers the *Gleaner, EXS,* and the *Daily Observer.* Their uses ranged from lines in editorials to article headlines to quoted comments made by people involved in specific events being reported on. The proverbs from editorials usually commented on specific social issues and supported a given course of action. For example, in a plea for the water commission to be more proactive in fixing broken lines and pipes, the writer states, "We should bear in mind the words we used to hear while we grew up, '**Prevention is better than cure**'" (*Gleaner,* 26 Aug. 1998, p. A5). This same proverb is alluded to in the headline of a separate article, which argues that the Minister of Health is focused on preventative health care: "Junor advocates **Prevention over cure**" (*Gleaner,* 28 Aug. 1998, p. A9). In an editorial letter condemning the environmental problems stemming from the Kaiser Bauxite plant, a writer uses **One picture is worth a thousand words** (28 Aug. 1998, p. A5). His letter is a response to a previous article that praised the plant for creating job opportunities. In fact, the plant has been responsible for severe environmental damage and is rumored to be the cause of health problems in the communities surrounding it, such as a sharp rise in the numbers of deformed babies born to mothers in that region.

In at least one case, a judge cited a proverb as the authoritorial basis for his decision. A woman who was raped had her case dismissed by the judge, who stated unsympathetically, "**Big woman know what dem gettin into**" (*Gleaner*, 26 Aug. 1998). A popular romance story in *EXS* has one sister saying to the other, "**Blood is supposed to be thicker than water**, remember," (27–29 Aug. 1998, p. 27). Another editorial from the *Gleaner* is an entreaty for more jobs for young people. The writer states: "I am a young girl who believes in the words—'**By the sweat of your brow you shall eat bread.**' A lot of us young people are willing to sweat but there are no jobs" (27 Aug. 1998, p. A5). Several proverbial expressions are also applied to problems of education, which received enormous discussion in editorials and feature stories. In an essay titled "Education for Today and Beyond," the writer laments the deterioration of the moral and ethical fiber of Jamaican society: "In order to be competitive in this world, it is extremely important to 'aim high' and 'think big.' The saying goes '**Whatever one is doing, one should do it to be the best of one's ability**'" (*Gleaner*, 28 Aug. 1998, p. A8). The advertisement for the *Gleaner* is even rendered in proverbial expressions: "Every Sunday we **dish out** a **real spread**." In a final example, the headline for an article on a new U.S. FDA-approved product, Nu-Trim, is an allusion to the proverb **An apple a day keeps the doctor away.** Nu-Trim is touted as a "fat substitute" that will take the place of shortening in deserts such as cookies, cakes, and muffins. Hence the headline: "**Four cookies a day may keep the doctor away**" (*Gleaner*, 26 Aug. 1998, p. C7). It is evident from the use of proverbs in headlines that proverbial expressions continue to play an important role in Jamaican society.

I was also treated to several proverbs in a theatrical production I attended in Kingston: a play titled *Augus Mawnin* that was showing at the Little-Little Theater. The production, scripted by Barbara Gloudon and directed by Brian Heap, centered on a group of slaves who fled the plantation in anticipation of "Augus Mawnin," when slavery would legally end. The play, which was a synthesis of traditional Jamaican folk songs and reggae and poems by writers such as Dennis Scott, A. J. Seymour, and Lorna Goodison, included a number of proverbs. **Time longer than rope, and rope is running out** was used in reference to the approaching end of slavery. **Cleanliness is next to godliness** was used sarcastically to poke fun at the slaveowner's aesthetics and their dubious application to the lives of slaves. One of the characters used **Sweet nanny goat a go running belly**, during a segment reminiscing about a past experience. Because of the "folk" orientation of the play, it is not surprising that proverbs were used in it; however, this points to the general awareness of proverbs as a key cultural element among Jamaicans.

Proverbs in Everday Speech

Proverbs are, of course, still common in the everyday speech of Jamaicans. Many people with whom I spoke suggested proverbs are used most often by adults to children as a means of instruction and imparting values, a common practice in many societies (see Prahlad 1982; Prahlad 1996, pt. 2; Daniel 1973; Bornstein 1991; Hudson 1972; Kuhel 1991). Unfortunately, I was not able to spend sufficient time in a community to observe many such interactions. However, I did talk with many people about proverbs. In some cases I elicited the meanings of proverbs I had collected from reggae songs and, in other cases, I simply asked people about proverbs they might use. These conversations confirmed my theory that certain people tend to use proverbs regularly, while others seldom use them at all (Prahlad 1996). Many people with whom I spoke, for example, were familiar with a number of proverbs but did not

A plaque with a proverb in the lobby of a New Kingston hotel.

know their meanings or how to use them. I was fortunate to hear a number of proverbs used in conversations between adults and to spend considerable time with a man who is what I have termed a proverb master (Prahlad 1996, ch. 4), that is, someone who has reflected deeply on proverbs, who uses them frequently and masterfully in speech, and for whom this usage plays a significant role in his social identity. The remainder of this chapter is devoted to a discussion of these speakers and their proverb use.

The Indies Hotel

On my initial visit to Jamaica, I stayed the first few nights at the Indies Hotel in New Kingston. There I met a young man named Clive Frazer, who offered to show me around. I told him about my research and he took me to several nightclubs that played reggae, to bars with jukeboxes, and to Half Way Tree—an intersection where crowds of people gathered, awaiting buses, eating, or just hanging out, listening to stadium-sized speakers blare reggae from each corner of the large traffic circle. One of the clubs Frazer took me to was like an American disco and played exclusively dancehall music. The crowd was young and everyone dressed fashionably semiformal. Women wore expensive miniskirts or dresses, heels, and jewelry. Men wore equally flashy attire, occasionally even suits. I noticed that many people arrived in what would be considered, even by American standards, expensive cars. It was neither the kind of music nor the crowd in which I was most interested, but it provided me with a glimpse into one aspect of the Jamaican music scene. After a while, Frazer seemed to sense my discomfort and began talking about how beautiful some of the women were. At the same time, he noted, they were snobbish and pampered. "See, **Not everything that glitters is gold**," he said.

Rasta Inn

Maya Lodge is an alternative lodging site in the Blue Mountains outside of Kingston. It caters particularly to travelers interested in exploring the natural environment of Jamaica, hikers, campers, and people who just want to get away from the congestion of the city. A good twenty minutes' hike up the mountain from the tents and A-framed cabins at Maya Lodge was "Rasta Inn," a small, isolated hut without toilet or lights and with only a spigot in the yard for water. Because of budgetary concerns, I stayed in "Rasta Inn,"

Rasta Inn, at Maya Lodge, in the Blue Mountains, August 1992. (Courtesy of the author)

coming down periodically to the main lodge for meals and company. There I met Carolyn, a young Jamaican woman who cleaned, and Tony, a middle-aged man who also helped out around the place. The two were always joking and teasing one another and, during my stay of about four days, I overheard an exchange between them in which they both used proverbs. On one occasion, Tony was pretending to court Carolyn, teasing her and jokingly confessing his love and promising his true devotion. In the verbal banter that went back and forth for almost ten minutes, Carolyn said, while sweeping, "Yeah, **A promise is a comfort to a fool**." A little further along in the conversation, Tony switched rhetorical strategies, pretending that Carolyn was putting him off because of an interest in me. "You oughtta know, **New brooms sweep clean but old broom know the corners**. You oughtta remember that while you no talking to me now," he said. Carolyn blushed and went after Tony with the broom, as he laughed and ran off. I pretended, as I sometimes did for convenience sake, that I barely understood patois and, thus, had not understood what transpired.

Montego Bay

I stayed at a beautiful guest house in the Montego Bay area for three days. It was miles away from the downtown and the beach, which I found overwhelming, due to the combination of higglers, hustlers, and hordes of European tourists. While lodging there I became friends with a Jamaican man, Huntley George Angus, who was in charge of the guest house. We had many conversations about the problems that Jamaicans faced and the possible solutions to some of those issues. He was greatly concerned with problems such as poor education, poor health, and poverty. We also talked quite often about reggae, as he was an avid fan of cultural or roots reggae and passed along the latest rumors about this or that artist. When I was leaving, he asked me to remember him and to send him some books of poetry or other interesting literature so that we could stay connected and continue to learn from one another. With a firm handshake and a smile, he said, "Yeah mon, **cause Iron sharpeneth iron**." "True, true," I replied, and loaded my bags into the taxi, headed for Negril.

Taxis

It is no coincidence that the majority of proverbs I collected from Jamaican speakers came from taxicab drivers. My second trip to Jamaica was entirely self-funded and careful budgeting was a necessity. My field methodology was to lodge in inexpensive but moderately comfortable guest houses or hotels and make excursions into the surrounding communities, hoping to meet people or, at the very least, overhear proverbs. I was dissuaded from taking public buses on the basis of bad experiences I had on my first trip to the island. In the four years since the first trip, it seemed that the public transportation system had lapsed even further into decline, a fact that was not lost on Jamaicans, as there were frequent articles in the paper about the horrendous conditions of the buses. Some of the complaints included overcrowding, absence of schedules, and reckless drivers. As a foreigner, I had endured misinformation about routes, breakdowns, harassment, and attempted theft on my first trip. Having come with my wife and twelve-year-old son on my subsequent visit, the prospect of getting around on buses was tantamount to a nightmare. My wife's ethnicity—European American—was also a factor. Jamaica is, for all intents and purposes, a black country; and although one sees light-complexioned and white Jamaicans, one rarely sees them on public buses or walking.

To save money and to have more potential contact with Jamaican people, we often walked. However, the sun was unusually hot, a phenomenon many people attributed to El Niño. The second week of our stay, both my wife and son suffered from mild heat strokes, which alerted us to one danger that walking posed and led us to think more favorably about taking taxis. But there are important things a non-Jamaican may not know about taxis in Jamaica. First, as the tour book tells us: "What passes for a taxi in Jamaica varies from the gleaming white vans of the **Jamaican Union of Travelers Association** (JUTA), the official—and very expensive—carriers, to beaten-up old **Ladas** that crawl along the island's roads. Officially licensed taxis carry red number plates with 'PP' or 'PPV' on them, but there are a number of rogue taxis. . . . The authorities advise against using the rogues but, obviously, it's up to you whether you trust the guy or not" (Thomas and Vaitilingam 1997, 19). Second, official or not, taxis have no meters, and prices for each ride have to be negotiated before one gets in or allows the driver to put one's belongings in (there are standard fares for the more upscale, pricey taxis such as JUTA). A suffering economy and the scarcity of employment opportunities has led to a situation in which there are, as one speaker put it, **Dog more than bone**, that is, there are many more enterprising drivers than customers needing taxis. On one occasion, we negotiated a price, for instance, of $150 Jamaican (around $4 U.S.) for a ride from our guest house to the Bob Marley Museum. The initial negotiation with a different taxi driver for the return trip began with his request for $300 Jamaican. We were quoted a fare of $600 Jamaican for a ride from Tinson Pen Airport in Kingston to The Gardens Hotel on Linguinea Avenue, when we had paid only $250 Jamaican for the ride from the hotel to the airport. After a heated but failed negotiation with one driver had ended, another driver standing nearby offered to take us for $350. Fares are also affected by whether one does the negotiation oneself or can find a local Jamaican to make one's arrangements. As they say in the United States, "the hustle is always on" with taxicab drivers.

Once the fare has been negotiated and one is settled into the car, however, one cannot simply relax and enjoy the ride. One source states: "Jamaicans are notoriously bad drivers, with male drivers often dangerously macho and impatient. . . . Many drivers think nothing of overtaking a line of ten or more cars even if they can't see what's coming." (Thomas and Vaitilingam 1997, 18). Another source agrees: "Many Jamaican drivers rank high among the world's rudest and least cautious drivers. Jamaica has the third highest fatality rate for drivers in the world—behind Ethiopia and India—with a staggering 343 fatalities per 100,000 cars (compared to 26 per 100,000 in the US, and 22 in the UK)" (Baker 1996, 109). A ride in a Jamaican taxi is often akin to a ride on an American amusement park "ride" designed to bring one face-to-face with fear and terror. Drivers seem to take great pride in seeing how close they can come to other vehicles or pedestrians without actually hitting them.

In the folkways of Jamaican driving, the horn substitutes for brakes and common sense. In fact, a requirement for drivers seems to be fluency in a language I call "horn-talk." Horns are beeping and blaring constantly in a rapid Morse-code-like language, spoken to all nearby vehicles, whether in sight or anticipated; to pedestrians; to people in houses along the way; and to presences of which only drivers seem to be aware. Among the many stories that my family later laughed about is the one about the driver who took us from Port Antonio to Ocho Rios. Along the ride there were many long stretches of straight empty road, with endless fields of sugarcane, bananas, or other foliage engulfing us. Even on those long stretches, the driver continued to dot-dot dot-dot-dot-dot out his horn Morse code. Even when there was not a car, a bus, a person, a cow, or a goat for miles.[1]

Typically, we emerged from the taxis as one might from a time machine: trembling, weak-kneed, nauseous, having confronted the specter of our death or mutilation one more time. For my wife, who suffers from motion sickness, the long rides were especially grueling, as we were snatched from side to side as the car raced full throttle around narrow curve after narrow curve, accelerated far beyond safe speeds down hills, and came to screeching halts inches from the front or rear bumpers of trucks, buses, or other cars, sometimes having to drive in reverse for short distances on hills or around curves where there was not enough room for two vehicles to pass. When asked why he felt so strongly about sitting by the rear door rather than in the middle of the seat, my son replied that he felt he would be less likely to fly through the front windshield in the event of an accident. And, should another taxi catch afire, as one of those that we took in Ocho Rios did, it would be easier to get out.

So taxicabs played a significant role in our lives, beyond simply getting us from here to there. On one hand, they were small spheres of safety, insulation between us and the harshness of life on the streets of Jamaica. If being in Jamaica in the first place constituted a liminal reality, then traveling in taxicabs would have been superliminal. In a very real sense, the taxi was the only barrier between our survival and possible annihilation. What would have happened to us, for example, had we attempted to walk through downtown Kingston? Quite possibly, nothing; but, quite possibly, we would have been easy prey for thieves, or worse. And besides, it is not so much the reality of what might have happened if we had tried to traverse certain territory on foot and unaccompanied, but the fear of what might happen. At the same time that the taxis were our protection or our buffer, they only provided a tentative security, at best. Owing to the insensitivity of many drivers, their driving habits, and the unreliability of many car engines, the taxis posed significant threats even as they shielded us.

Out of this context came the paradoxical relationships that we founded with drivers. They were the people with whom we invariably had the most opportunities to engage in conversation and to develop relationships on a first-name basis. They were the people in whom, by nature of circumstances, we placed our trust. But the same social forces that made it problematic to form close relationships with other Jamaicans were also at work in the case of drivers. Their primary concern was, of course, making a living. And so in many instances what we first interpreted as invitations for friendship later turned out to be motivated by entrepreneurial zeal. The basic fact that we were Americans, and the monetary implications of this fact to Jamaicans struggling to survive in a failing economy, complicated most social relations between us and them. This complexity made it impossible ever to be sure whether a Jamaican might be genuinely interested in our friendship or our research, or driven by the prospect of obtaining some form of monetary compensation.

Relationships were further complicated by my appearance. Having long, thick dreadlocks, I was assumed to be a Rastafari. This engendered an automatic respect from most Jamaicans, as many people feel a great deal of admiration for the spiritual and political contributions of Rastas. Thus, most Jamaicans greeted me in the traditional manner of greeting Rastafari, and in many instances I was accorded special consideration and courtesies. At times, however, such acknowledgment seemed to be part of the rhetorical strategies of negotiation and manipulation and, ultimately, made it that much more difficult to assess what was really going on in any given interaction.

The Mad Driver of Negril

On my first trip to Jamaica, I lodged at a guest house on the west end called Addis Kokeb. From there into town where I shopped was approximately six miles, and so I usually hailed a taxi, especially if I was bringing back several bags of groceries. On one occasion a taxi stopped for me, and I sat in the back seat, leaving the door open while I negotiated the price. However, the driver, who was already carrying two other passengers, impatiently pulled off, my legs hanging out of the car and the door still open. He ignored my yells for him to stop and let me out and continued, the too-narrow road winding snakelike downhill into the town. Finally we came to a screeching halt in front of the post office and market. When I refused to pay the fare he demanded (which was considerably higher than he asked from the two Jamaican passengers, not to mention my protest at his rude and reckless behavior), a yelling contest by the side of the road ensued, drawing a crowd of curious bystanders and other taxi drivers who were parked nearby. During the exchange, in which he spouted derogatory comments about tourists, he also said a number of times "Don't be **Penny wise and pound foolish mon.**" The *situational* meaning of the proverb sank in much later when, heading back to the guest house with several bags of groceries, no taxicab would stop for me.

Chin

I cannot remember the first taxicab ride that we took with Chin, a young Jamaican man, around twenty-five years of age. Nor do I remember if his taxi was officially licensed or a "rogue" cab. But he drove with a care that many drivers did not, expressed a genuine concern for our welfare, and was a good conversationalist. We felt safe in his taxi, and so after the first ride, we tended to call him whenever we needed a ride somewhere in Kingston. On one occasion, he drove us to Michael Manley airport at four o'clock in the morning, waited three hours for us (my son flew back to the United States several weeks ahead of us, so he could start school), and took us back to the hotel. On the ride back, he stopped to say hello to one of the other drivers. He explained that he used to work for the company of taxis lined up at the airport, and this man was a friend from that time. "Up early this morning?" Chin yelled out to the other man, who was busy washing his taxi. Laughing, and obviously glad to see Chin, the man replied, "Jus a lickle car washing. Want belly full. Only way to full belly is to up early." To which Chin replied, "**Early bird gets the worm**," as they continued talking for another few minutes before we drove off.

After hearing Chin use the proverb, I asked him if he knew any others. He thought for a while, and then offered, **You can't stop bird from flying over your head, but you can stop him from building a nest**. He explained that the proverb was used by a woman in response to other women showing interest in her man. It was said to the man as a way of reminding him that, although he might have no control over other women flirting with him, he did have control over how he responded. Although not an overt threat, the proverb would be spoken with a threateningly serious tone.

The other two proverbs that he talked about were also given interpretations related to dynamics between a man and a woman. It became obvious that as a bachelor, Chin was especially concerned with relationships and dating, and the proverbs he offered and their interpretations reflected this. **Old fire stick easy to catch** is generally used to mean that two people who have once been lovers can easily rekindle their relationship. Chin's interpretation was consistent with this meaning. Specifically for him it meant that a man's current girlfriend does not want him to see a former girlfriend because they might end up getting back together. His interpretation of the other proverb, **They give you basket to carry water**, focuses on a similar theme. The *social* meaning of the proverb is that person A gives person B something that appears to be helpful when, in fact, it makes life more difficult than before. Chin relates the proverb to a situation in which a man might be dividing his time between several women. He appears to be totally dedicated to each one, and each one believes that he is monogamous. The proverb would be said about the man's deception. The difference in his interpretation and that of several other informants is that here it emphasizes a casual but ritualized dishonesty. Other interpretations focus on the deliberate malicious intent of one person to keep another down.

Driver from Ocho Rios to Kingston

The driver who carried us from Ocho Rios back to Kingston (a middle-aged man who identified himself as a Christian) was another wonderful conversationalist. One could even call him an entertainer, as he sang calypsos and ballads and told us stories and legends related to various sites we passed along the way. At one point the conversation turned to the police, whom he declared in no uncertain terms to be the biggest thieves and drug dealers of all. He alleged that the police were among the major distributors of ganja, cocaine, and other drugs, taking most of whatever was confiscated and smoking or reselling it. We asked if the police bothered to arrest the people from whom they took the

drugs, and the driver responded "**Sometimes you win, sometimes you lose.**
It all depends on the mood they're in."

Later on, our taxi was flagged down by the police for speeding, which gave
us an opportunity to observe a typical interaction between the police and
drivers. The driver protested that he was not speeding. (He wasn't. We had
been impressed that he observed speed limits and did not take any unnecessary or careless chances in passing other vehicles.) As the police viewed his
license and wrote the ticket, he stomped about, waving his hands, shouting
and cursing them in patois. "You're just a bunch of liars!" he shouted in their
faces, "Liars! Thieves!" We were frightened that he might be arrested, leaving
us in the middle of nowhere with no means to get the sixty miles or so back
to Kingston. Instead, the police (a man and a woman) continued to smile,
saying little, finished writing the ticket, and handed it to the driver. We asked
a number of people about such interactions later on and were told that Jamaicans can talk to the police any way they like because they know "what the
police are really doing," meaning the many forms of corruption and illegal
activities in which they are involved. For example, police might purchase
ganja from the same sources as many of the local citizens.

A typical Jamaican taxi, August 1998. (Courtesy of LuAnne Roth)

Delton Waite, Iaa (pronounced "I-ya"), the Proverb Master

We met Iaa as we were leaving a concert on the beach in Negril,[2] which is primarily a tourist town, described in the following manner by Thomas and Vaitilingam (1997):

Jamaica's shrine to permissive indulgence, **Negril** has metamorphosed from deserted fishing beach to full-blown resort town in less than two decades. . . . By the late 1970s, hippies had discovered a virgin paradise of palms and pristine sand, and the picture of beach camping ganja smoking and chemically enhanced sunsets set the tone for to-day's free-spirited attitude. Thanks to deliberately risqué resorts like the infamous **Hedonism II**, Negril is widely perceived as a place where inhibitions are lost and pleasures of the flesh rule. The traditional menu of ganja and reggae—Negril has a deserved reputation for its **live music**—draws a young crowd, but the north coast resort ethic has muscled in too—all inclusives pepper the coast. (248)

Iaa walked up to us and began talking, mistaking me for an African man whom he had given a ride to the night before. "Hey, Rastafari, didn't I give you lift to a hotel last night? Remember?" he asked. After he realized his mistake, he continued talking with us. He proclaimed that he was a mountain man who lived up in the hills and just came down to Negril sometimes to make a "lickle money." "**But dog more than bone**," he said. When I asked what the proverb meant, he explained, "It means the dog is hungry. People have it hard. It should be more bone, so it's plenty. People have to scrape. It's not good. So people will say it sometimes if you ask, 'How you doin?' You say, '**Dog more than bone**.' " With this, I could barely believe my luck. Not only did Iaa seem to be a possible proverb master, but he had a temperament and a "vibe" that seemed to connect with ours. He was articulate, dignified, and highly conscious of Jamaican and Rastafari culture. I asked him if he used proverbs like this often, and he said that he did, giving me a few other examples. "**Enough is enough**. Do you know that one?" he asked. I described my research project to him, inquiring if he would be willing to let me interview him. He seemed excited about the idea, walked us back to our hotel, and offered to come by the next day and talk more, and to take us into the hills to meet Rastafari elders. I wrote in my field notes that night: "A really cool and conscious brethren."

He dropped by the next day, just as we had planned, and we sat outside on the hotel porch and talked. Initially, I was reluctant to bring out the tape recorder, but eventually I did. It became apparent that he was willing to talk about proverbs, in fact, that he saw himself as our teacher. But he wanted the conversation to develop naturally and resisted any obvious interview questions. At some point, when it seemed relevant to the topic of conversation, he mentioned **Dog more than bone**, explaining it in more detail. He said that it was the low season for tourists, and so all of the people who relied on tourists for their business were now having a hard time. There were few tourists for the taxicabs, for instance, and so one could see multitudes of cars and drivers parked in the shade, desperate and competing for the handful of tourists who were now in Negril. This was just like having a lot of dogs competing for one or two bones.

During that same conversation he mentioned several other proverbs, relating them to the general theme of people struggling. The first was almost a response to **Dog more than bone**, saying that, in spite of the difficulty or harshness of life, one has to persevere, to maintain hope. "That's why we say, '**Man no dead no call him duppy.**'" In literal terms, "don't call a person a ghost if they're still alive." As long as there is life, there is hope. This might typically be said to lift the spirits of someone who is down and out, or to remind others not to give up on a person just because his life's circumstances are grim. There is always a chance the person might find a way out of poverty or misfortune.

He gave several others, including, **Seven times rise, seven times fall**, and **No cup no mash, coffee no throw away**. He explained that **Seven times rise, seven times fall** referred to the cyclical nature of life and could be used for consolation when things are bad, reminding one that things will eventually be good again. Beyond the conciliatory function of the proverb, it also encompasses the philosophical observation that life has ups and downs. Therefore, one should not be overly despairing when things are bad, nor overly confident when things are going well. The literal meaning he gave of **No cup no mash, coffee no throw away** is that one does not throw the coffee away as long as the cup is still intact. The general social meaning of the proverb is to not give up on a situation as long as there is the least possibility that something positive can be gained from it. The social meanings that he gave in this initial conversation were expounded upon in subsequent interactions when the proverbs were actually applied.

On Iaa's first visit he freely shared information about his life. Our "apartment" at Arthur's Golden Sunset, on Norman Manley Boulevard, was a modest one bedroom with a bathroom, and a kitchen shared with the adjoining apartment. There was a front balcony running the length of both apartments, with tables and chairs, where we sat, drinking juice and water. He told us that he had separated from his wife not long ago. Apparently she had committed a transgression with which he, in good conscience and as a Rasta, could not live. He had left her most of their possessions, including the house; and his son was also with her. Because of this separation, he was in a difficult period, struggling financially and still dealing with emotional wounds. The lifestyle that he adopted, out of necessity, was to spend time in Negril, driving a taxi and selling a few things here and there to make money, and then to go back home to the mountains for a few days at a time.

He hated Negril, referring to it often as Sodom, and spoke begrudgingly of the time that he had to spend there. Such common practices by tourists as partial or complete nudity on the beach, oral sex (taboo in traditional Jamaican society), rumored orgies, and the well-known "Rent-a-dread" business contributed to Iaa's opinion.[3] Most nights, he slept either in his car or in one of the many little wooden structures along the roadside, which were used in the daytime as souvenir stands. He was presently worried about the money necessary for the school-related expenses for his son, and for automobile registration and licensing. We did not realize then that these were as much statements about what he hoped to gain monetarily from our relationship as they were a simple sharing of life stories among people just getting to know each other. Nor could we have guessed then that the proverbs I was to collect would be used in the context of complex, ongoing negotiations for friendship, services, and money.

At some point in the conversation, Iaa asked if we wanted to smoke some ganja, and we went inside. While inviting anyone into our small space felt somewhat intrusive, we were relatively comfortable with his presence there. Once inside, we offered him the ganja that had been given to us a day earlier by another Rasta. In anticipation that he might want to smoke, we had rolled a joint (cigarette) quite clumsily, as we were rather naive about such rituals. He replied, suspiciously, after laughing at the joint, "**Well, seeing is believing**," and went on to explain what he meant by the proverb. Essentially, the *situational* meaning here was that only by inspecting the ganja first could he evaluate whether or not he would be willing to smoke a joint made from it. It implied a profound skepticism toward ingesting uninspected substances, a typical Rasta or "Italist" attitude.

So we began with a rather serious faux pas, even a transgression. In our efforts to be hospitable and culturally friendly, we had unwittingly insulted our guest. The Italist's insistence on a pure diet is presently heightened in Jamaica by the recent rise in cocaine, crack, and other synthetic drugs entering the country. Chemically treated ganja, initially produced to satisfy the taste of European and American tourists, has now become popular among many younger Jamaicans. Rumors also circulate about foreigners deliberately tainting foods with spittle, blood, or semen carrying AIDs or other infectious viruses. Thus, there are more reasons than ever to be cautious about the purity of what one consumes.

Seein' is believin'. Do you know why I say "**seein' is believin'**". Eh? It's the ganja. It's the ganja. I, I, I, I like to look. And to see. Because as old as I is,
any ganja
I'm gonna smoke,
I've got to see.
It's just my ability. From I was smoking ganja when   I was
12 year old, you know. Yeah, It's just my ability. You know?
Any ganja.
I have my best friend,
and I plant
my crop,
and he plant his crop,
I have to go
and say,
        "I need to taste
this plant"
        Yea.
He not gonna just, you know,
take ganja and give to me.
Unless, he had his crop,
and he had his special tree,
and he take a piece,
and he smoke, and it's a one in a million.
He say "ok my friend,
have to taste this." Yeah. Then I will. But I never, I *never* like do this, no friend never do like build me a joint. No.
No.
I like to *see*.
Quality.
Because. Yes, quality, if it's like what I regularly do, you

know. Not to say it . . . inside, but just to *see*
the quality.
(Opening the wrapped ganja.)

Oooh. (Disappointedly)
Brown stuff.

He stated that this ganja had been grown in the Morass, or marshland area
off the coast, and was therefore inferior. When we asked him for more information about ganja grown in this region, he used another proverb, explaining
its meaning. His explanations took the form of performances, as he took seriously his role as teacher/guide, explaining things in animated, poetic narratives that we came to love. He talked as much with his hands as with his
words, which rose and fell musically, for punctuation, emphasis, and effect.
He sang more than spoke the narratives. When he related conversations
within the narratives, he dramatized them, both with his voice and with gestures. His hands often drew picturegrams in the air, on the floor, or in his
own palm that illustrated the details of the narrative being told. In the narrative below, for instance, which he tells to embellish the proverb, the word
"No" in line 8 is spoken to convey sadness, and his facial expressions add to
the drama. "Yes," a few lines later, is equally dramatized. The proverb, which
is found in reggae, means generally that one cannot be blamed for one's ignorance. However, it often carries with it a critical judgment about the ignorant
party:

What you don't know
you just don't know. You know?
So, it's just like that.
That's why I tell you I like, always like to see what it's
like. Because, I saw my friend
with just like that [the ganja that we offered]
and I look
and I said "No . . ."
And I will saw my friend there
with some little tiny
little tiny [gesturing and squinting to dramatize the smallness of the ganja bud]
and I say "Yes!
I like." Not fertilized. But I look it's fertilized. So before I look, if I like this one, I will
just take a toke and say OK. Yeah you know? . . . It's the quality. That's why you have
to you know meet good people to get good stuff which is the farmer's choice. I
wouldn't say this is the farmer's choice. Because look, I'm in the wilderness, and I

gonna plant, like, a acre of crop. Like even here, not big, like the room here, I don't put no fertilizer. Special smoke. Farmer's choice.

Continuing, he told us that fertilizer was bad because it caused the crop to mature before its time. He compared it to the use of unsanitary feed for chickens:

It's really bad. Make it come early before time. Just
like the chickens, the white chickens, the fowl, the
chickens? Yeah. Yeah. No good. The sewer,
the sewer truck
come
draw
from the pit
the sewer pit
go
and they make
like the field,
the feed
to feed the chickens
then they eat.
So they get big and fat
off dat.
So, no way, yeah.
Because that's the way they come.
That's the way they brought up, yeah, you know. Yeah.
You know the rabbit you will have the rabbit. You you would
have to draw special feed for the rabbit? Well that's healthy
that's good. Yeah. Cause you know it's grass. Yeah. But like
like like from the shit pit.
To make
the field [feed]
for the cow
for the fowls
the chicken
it's like mess
to me.
That's why I tell you I ital from seven years. Yeah, And all
those things I put them aside.

At this point, sensing that the narrative had ended, I used the proverb to suggest that we intended no insult in offering the only ganja we had. Furthermore, we had no special knowledge about Jamaican ganja crop that would enable us to make sophisticated distinctions between one bud or another. Iaa responded with yet another proverb, which seemed to mean that our ignorance—and the resulting faux pas—were not entirely forgiven. Critical censure and judgment resonated in his voice. While we had an excuse for initial ignorance of cultural rituals, we had no excuse for being lackadaisical about learning. As implied by his earlier comment that we needed to get out and meet people in order to "get good stuff," he felt that knowledge about ganja and rituals surrounding it were essential cultural information. If we were really serious about our research, we should not have been so lax in our efforts to learn such things.

PRAHLAD: Well, **What you don't know, you just don't know.**
IAA: Just like that. [One of his favorite expressions.] And **You're never too old to learn.**

The next proverb came later in the conversation. We had talked about deejaying and different reggae artists that we like; foods; and other mind-altering substances, such as mushrooms and hash oil (which Iaa offered us but which we declined). When my wife was about to make lunch, she asked Iaa if he would like to eat. He responded by saying that he was a very picky eater and there were a number of things he would not consume. She asked if pasta with garlic and olive oil was a meal that he could eat.

IAA: My eating is very peculiar, you know.
PRAHLAD: Are you eating dairy?
IAA: Deery?
LUANNE AND PRAHLAD: Like cheese and milk . . .
IAA: Cheese? Well no. I eat cheese.
LUANNE: So if I make some pasta with onions and garlic, and olive oil and parmigiana cheese, that's something you can eat?
IAA: Garlic? . . . OK, well you could just go ahead and let me see, **Seein is believing.** [We all laugh] Yeah. Just go ahead and let me see it . . .
LUANNE: You can eat salt, right?
IAA: Yes
LUANNE: OK, anyway. . . I'll make it, and you can have some if you want to.
IAA: Yes. Yes. Yes.

While LuAnne was making lunch, I steered the conversation back to a proverb he had mentioned earlier, **No cup no mash, no coffee no throw away,** another expression used in reggae.

IAA: It's just a parable. It's like a parable. Yeah. Like, like you know? you know? you know? Like I would come, and I would tell you my tradition. What's happened to me. You know? And you would say "OK Iaa, **No cup no mash, no coffee don't throw away.**" Yeah. You know? Just a parable. Hah. And it's reality. Yeah. Just like that.

PRAHLAD: So it would be a way of saying don't get worried about all those things . . .

IAA: The past. Yeah, It would be like that. Like you say, "Oh don't worry about it. Don't worry about the past things."

PRAHLAD: So that's like **Seven rise and seven fall**?

IAA: Yeah, **Seven times rise and seven times fall**. Yeah. Yeah. Just like we say, **Mon no dead don't call him duppy.** Yeah.

PRAHLAD: So it might be bad, but it's gonna get better? So don't worry about it . . .

IAA: Yeah. Yeah. Yeah.

PRAHLAD: So even beyond that, it might get bad again at some point. Like it's bad now, but it'll get better. But even further down the road, it might get bad some other time, and then it might get better.

IAA: Get better. [spoken at the same time that I say "get better"] At another time. Cause that's life. **Life is one big road, with a lot of signs.**
Signs of love.
Signs of wonders.
Signs of joy.
Signs of peace.
Signs of beautiful.
Lots of signs.
One big road!
But it's many signs.
Life is one big road with a lot of signs.

PRAHLAD: That's a lot of food for thought.

IAA: Yeah, true true.

At this point Iaa raised the subject of his car insurance and, in talking about his situation, once again used the proverb **Dog more than bone.** During his speech, he asked about our transportation but went on to say that he was not talking about *our* situation but about *his.* Thus from the beginning, there was an ambiguity about how we, and possible monies that he would obtain from us, related to his immediate economic needs. This ambiguity, fueled by his mixed messages, hung like an ominous cloud over all of our interactions. Did he hope to be paid for the interviews? To make money by driving us places or selling us crafts? Any efforts on our part to clarify these issues were met with assurances that we should not worry, that there was, as the popular Jamaican expression goes (which had become by this point to us a red flag), "no problem."

I: I'm saying, like, like my car. License. Insurance. You know? Expect to go. Then I
  have to pay, you know? But I have like $10,000 for the insurance, but like the tax
  office . . . You you have your transport back home? Car? or eh?

P: You mean when we're going to the airport?

I: Oh no no no, I'm not speaking towards that. I'm speaking about my prerogative.
  My business. My *own* business. Not *your* business. About my car, you know? You
  know you have to insure your car. Fitness test, stuff like that. So I'm saying the
  time is coming shortly for my car to be overhauled, over. Time is coming up. So. I
  was saying that's why I say, I came down here from de mountain.

From Monday. And I don't go back home. You know? I just try to work. Yeah. And
to get some money, to go get the car straight towards the government. For this term,
you know? But it's just because of the matter of the car, and because I didn't meet no
accident. That's why insurance come down. If you meet accident? Then you have to
pay more money. But I meet no accident. But I have to get like $2,500 to go by the tax
office, to get to get the license, is 99. Now is 98. 89. Now is 89, the year, isn't it? . .
But to work on the road
to take people
it couldn't work.
Because it's
little much
just to gas
and to eat food.
Little much
take people
you know?
Which I had was to say this word
all the while
Dog more than bone.
Many taxi. Like you would have ten taxi. And it only three people. Only three people.
And it ten taxi. So what this other rest gonna do? What the seven gonna do? You
understand? . . . So it's what happenin now. It's only when time I take someone to the
airport. Or we take someone to the beach. You know? Or when we take someone to,
you know? Black river. To Wyatts Fall, and then they pay like $100 or $80. Then we
could say, OK, we make a $3,000, or a $2,000. That's how things could go, and good
could eat. But the tour bus. They doing all this. So we have to stay down all the while.
Well this is what happenin now. Is just some good people like you, who just say, "Oh,
this is the guy I'm supposed to spend my money with. I'm not gonna go with the big
guys out there and spend my money with him. This is the guy who sit and talk with
me. They comes I only give them money for the room and they do business with me,
they don't talk to me. I have to meet the guy on the street to talk to. But that's the guy
I should spend my money with, yeah." Lot's of people come here and do this. Cause

that's where you get the culture. And that makes sense where you spend your little earning. Be more joyful. That's the way it goes. Yeah. You know?

Soon after this part of the conversation, Iaa mentioned that he had some ganja in his car and went out to get it, so that we could "have a little taste of something different." When he returned, he used another proverb, **As a man thinketh, so is he**. I was never quite sure, though, how he was applying it. Was this a reference to the previous conversation, suggesting something about us? If so, was it a positive evaluation? Or was the proverb directed toward someone he had encountered on his way to or from the car?

If a man think
to do the right
he do the right
and if he think to do the wrong
he do the wrong.
You know?
So
a man thinketh
so is he
That's what when we're going to school and our friend try to bash at us, and we try to make things easier, we say, "yeah, **so a man thinketh, so is he**." We just told him dat. Yeah. Um humh.

As he began the ritual of sorting through the ganja buds, picking out little bits of stems, and tearing pieces into smaller bits to roll into a spliff, he talked about the different vibes induced by various kinds of ganja. "Now you're gonna taste the best quality. Yeah." He asked about some of the places we had traveled in Jamaica, for example Port Antony (Antonio). I hesitated to say that Port Antonio was the most unwelcoming town we had been in, only shaking my head. Iaa seemed to understand the implication, and said, "**Lonely road**. Narrow road. Less people. Small resort. When I say less people I mean like neighborhood, Jamaican people living far off one another. You know?" Although not a proverb, this phrase does recur in reggae lyrics, and his use of it helped me to understand its meaning more fully. Certainly it referred literally to the size of the road and density of population. But it also suggested an environment in which there were few conscious and positive people, and in which a conscious soul would feel isolated and have no social support.

We spoke next about my idea to bring a group of students to Jamaica. The more that I talked about students, the more Iaa seemed to understand the role my interviews with him might play in my teaching and writing. He seemed enthused by the opportunity for himself and others in his community to become representatives of Jamaican and/or Rastafari culture. He also made an offer for us to come and live at his house in the mountains for a week. This was in part a response to our earlier comment that we would probably be returning to the United States in a few days because we had basically run out of money. He stated that we could simply come and live in the mountains at his house, and not need to worry about money. That way we could experience more fully the culture and gain a deeper understanding of proverbs and other elements of Jamaican and Rastafari culture. In speaking, he used a variant of a biblical proverb, **Wisdom is better than silver and gold**, adjusting it to fit the topic at hand. Other researchers have mentioned the creative license with which Jamaican speakers approach proverbial expressions, freely innovating upon traditional items and inventing new ones. Beckwith writes: "but the process of 'composing,' as the people call it, is still going on, and some sayings have only a local recognition" (1925, 7). Anderson and Cundall verify this tendency: "But no collection of negro proverbs could hope to be exhaustive. As they improvise some verses to their songs as they sing, so the negroes improvise proverbs and proverbial sayings. For this reason one meets with two or three renderings of the same saying, and very often the same idea clothed in different words. Sometimes they are in direct opposition, as *Man mus' die, but wud neber die*, and *Wud mu' die, but man mus' lib*" (9). I assumed Iaa was familiar with the variant that began "**Wisdom . . .** " if for no other reason than it is prominent in Bob Marley's "Zion Train" and he seemed to be well versed in Marley's lyrics.

Alright now, you got your book, right? You got your book to write, right? Alright, that gonna be your work when you come up by our home. That gonna be your work. You gonna state it down. You know? When you go back you can rewind. And you can got it and you rewind and the children who you are with, who are with you. It's reality, yeah. So, when we go up, you know? Gotta make you get a good stock. Of these stuff. Cause I see, I see what it's like now. Like the ganja opened my mind, vibes you know and let me understand fully, you know? Yeah. So you're gonna get a book, you know? And you're gonna take a stock. Of what we're saying. And we're gonna go to places, and we gonna speak, and we're gonna speak, and you're gonna write about what we speakin about. Yeah. Tape gonna be there. Same way, you know? You're gonna get it on cassette. Then when you gone back home you have that stuff. It's from us. So just relax. Just relax. Just relax. You know? **Dedication is better than silver and gold**. You get me? Just like that.

We did relax, perhaps prematurely. We would find out later that Iaa's expectations regarding payment for his services were dramatically different from ours, leading to severely strained and uncomfortable relations. During the next little while, before eating, he talked about the importance of common sense, suggesting that some of the miscommunications we had described between us and Jamaicans resulted from our lack of common sense. He was emphatic that I understand the Jamaican way of thinking so I could explain it to students in my classes. This led to the use of yet another proverb, **Hardest head pickney dead in a sun hot**. As in some other instances, there was an ambiguity surrounding the timing of the proverb. Were we being skillfully and indirectly criticized? Was it our "hard heads" that were being alluded to? Or did the mention of students elicit a memory and an association of what he imagined teaching to involve?

IAA: **Hard head pickney dead in a sun hot**. That's what we Jamaicans say. What you would have to say "Hardest children died in sun now." That what you would have to say to them. That mean when your head is hard, when you stubborn, when you stubborn, you know? Hard to learn, you gonna die in seno [sun]. Cause you're too hard to learn. Yeah. You get that? That what gran what gran grandparents would say to their grandson, you know? To make they understand. And they say just dat, and they understand. So you have to say this two way, the American way, and the Jamaican way. To, you know? Yeah. Yeah. That mean they will try not to be hard head.

PRAHLAD: So they'll survive.

IAA: Yeah.
They will try
not to be hard
head. So
they will survive.

I inquired whether Jamaican children generally listened to the proverbial warnings of adults, stating one certainly cannot assume children in American culture will be respectful, much less reflective of what adults may say to them. Iaa responded that perhaps their rebelliousness is good. "Well maybe like how they ignore, it will be better. Because if they don't ignore they will be in the system deeper. Yeah. So it's better when they ignore. That mean they beat the system. Uhhmm. Uhhmm."

When I asked Iaa about the proverb **Rain a fall but the dutty tough**, he responded by singing the Bob Marley stanza containing the proverb, going on to explain it. His response illustrated better than any example I could have imagined, the interrelatedness of reggae lyric and Jamaican proverbial speech. Not only do roots reggae artists draw from the Jamaican oral traditions, but Jamaicans in turn draw upon the lyrics as a source for knowledge, inspiration, and innovation in proverb meaning. An earlier example, **Life is one big road with lots of signs**, demonstrates the same kind of relationship. The proverb is used in Bob Marley's "Wake Up and Live" but is not found in Jamaican proverb collections. Quite possibly it exemplifies an expression that was coined by an artist and passed into oral tradition. The second expression below, **Pot a cook . . .** , is also absent from collections. There is the possibility that it was first used in Marley's song and then became popular. Iaa's comment about the proverb as a sung expression is testimony to the ideology of word/sound/power. He sang the first six lines, in the tune of Marley's "Dem Belly Full."

The rain a fall
but the dutty tough.
Pot a cook but
the food no nough.
We gonna dance
reggae music, dance.
You know what I mean?
So you know, like, imagine
the rain falling,
but the dirt,
the dirt,
it's tough. Yeah.
It's a parable. Look.
The pot a cook
but the food no nough.
It's to the amount of us is there. And he [Bob Marley] saw.
The pot is cooking but the food is not enough.
Some going to starve. Yeah. See, it's a parable.
He [Marley] just sing it out. And who is around must listen!
And realize. Yeah. So it go . . .
Yeah mon.

Iaa asked if I had a Bob Marley tape back home, and if I listened carefully to the words. I answered that I did, and he responded, "So you don't follow, you follow? To listen is different than to do. OK. OK. So you have to do." This fit with some of his other comments, indicating his concept of proverbs as a lived part of culture, something that only came to life fully if one were willing to be attitudinally and behaviorally in sync with the entire cultural weltanschauung of which the proverb was only a fragment. While I could not "live" the words of the proverb, per se, I could allow the social, cultural, and economic reality of which the proverb spoke to become so much a part of me that my perspective would mirror that of Jamaicans. From Iaa's point of view, anything short of this could not be called a true understanding of the proverb.

The next day Iaa came by for a few hours and we talked at length about a number of issues; however, only one proverb was used. The conversation at one point turned to what it means to be a Rasta, and Iaa explained the significance of the red (ites), green, and gold. Red symbolizes the blood that was shed by Africans during the colonization of the continent, the slave trade, and subsequent centuries of slavery and neocolonialism. Green "is for the land," and gold "is for the riches they [colonizers] stole." We asked why some Rastas placed the red at the top, while others placed it at the bottom. Iaa explained that different groups of Rastas place more emphasis on different books of the Bible, reflecting their general attitudes toward other people. For instance, the groups who highlighted the Old Testament books in which war and revenge on one's enemies was a prominent feature were more likely to place the red at the bottom. "They trod in blood," Iaa said, "**Blood for blood.**" He, and certain other groups were more partial to Psalms and Ecclesiastes, because their messages were focused more on love, meditation, and prayer. These Rastas were "heartical"; that is, as he explained it, they responded to people based on their vibe, and would embrace anyone whose vibe was pure regardless of race or national origin. Such Rastas were more likely to place the red at the top.

We understood the proverbial expression more fully that night, when Iaa used it in response to an incident on the television. He had come by to accompany us to another concert on the beach, and we were watching the end of *The Edge* on the television. In the film two men are lost in the wilderness and are being stalked by a bear, who has already killed and eaten their partner. At one point, Anthony Hopkins decides that their only chance of survival is to make a stand and kill the bear. He dramatically slices his hand so that blood drips down, as a tribal warrior might before embarking on a hunt. "That's it," Iaa responded, "You see that? **Blood fe blood.** Just like that. Just like that."

We made plans to visit Iaa's home the next day. He suggested we go to bed early and told us he would be expecting to make $500 Jamaican for the journey up and back. We planned to meet again that night and go to one of the reggae concerts at the beach. (One of our primary reasons for being in Negril was to explore the reggae scene, for there was live music at one or more of the clubs every night.) In hindsight, we might have known from such offers as those to drive us to the club (which was, at most, a leisurely five-minute walk from our hotel) and home again, that Iaa saw us as most Jamaicans tended to: Americans with money. No matter what the friendship element amounted to, he hoped to get compensated for his time and services.

We suspected that his generosity in offering his house to us might also be economically motivated. On one hand, it was an appealing offer, as it would have given me a greater opportunity to understand many more facets of traditional Jamaican culture. On the other hand, we were nervous about being stranded so far away from anything familiar, and about health risks. We would not be able to continue exploration of the reggae scene, which Negril alone seemed to offer. And then there was the specter of unforeseen expenses. Before actually visiting Iaa's house, it was difficult to commit to such an arrangement, and simply "checking it out" was one of the main reasons for the next day's trip. For all of these reasons, Iaa's subtle suggestions—to throw caution to the wind and just go—made us all the more nervous. It took us a few minutes to realize that his parting comments reflected his eagerness for us to come to the mountains. "OK, I will come on, and we go to the show. And when we leave from the show, I take you here, from the show. You know. Yeah. Just like that. Or, if possible, if possible, from the show we lively, we drive home. From the show, we drive home and you just lay down and sleep. Gonna bathe in the fresh mineral in the morning. You can just go home and relax and sleep. No problem. Everything is just."

The next day we were up early to prepare for the trip to the mountains. We debated what equipment to take along, not clear if this was a research expedition or a friendly visit to Iaa's home. When he appeared at the door, LuAnne asked if he had had a good night. He responded by saying that he had been up most of the night. "**Enough is enough,**" he said, "but I didn't get enough sleep." With little fanfare, we settled into his small car and headed east out of Negril, into the mountains.

The Day in the Mountains

We ride on narrow roads through cane fields taller than we are. We ride through small towns, like Springfield, Delve Bridge, and Grange Hill. And there are people gathered at various stands and sites along the way. People walking. People riding bicycles. Men. Women. Children. School has just begun and there are schoolchildren walking in their uniforms. Cars. Taxis. Vans. Swerving in and out, the way they do, a hairline from violent disaster. The broken body of a child, cow, or goat. Shattered headlights. Naked water hose and carburetors. The horn talk. Coded conversations, blaring staccato musical notes of a telegraph. The set, though, is certainly not the Wild West American movie telegraph office. But the countryside of Jamaica. Of bread-fruit trees. Papaya trees. Akee trees. Ganja. Banana leaves. Curry. Bougainvil-lea. Mango trees, coconut trees, jelly and yam. A Gregory Isaacs tape is on the stereo, old Gregory. Iaa sings along. I sing along. Bumpy roads. Gullies of missing asphalt. Hills. The engine strains. Around curves, inches from tum-bling over the side of the mountain. Deep breaths.

We arrive at Iaa's in one piece, pull off the main road into a little dirt one. Iaa gets out, greets several people standing near a small one-room store across the gully road. Unpainted wood. Modest warped wood, as so many of the buildings in the country are. We get out, unsure where we are. Unsure whether to take our things with us or not. Soon a woman comes along, opens the door of the store. She speaks with Iaa. He buys a cigarette, turns, and walks up a water-worn path, stepping between red clay puddles; we follow behind. To his house, followed by a nameless dog. A house he built with the help of a few others. One big, open room, with a small stove, refrigerator, a table and chairs. A bannister-less green cement staircase going up the far wall to the second floor, to a loftlike bedroom with a closet, bathroom, and preci-pice or ledge outside the door: a balcony.

He just wanted to show us the house, to reiterate his offer to us to stay there for an extended week. We thought, naively then, that he meant the invi-tation as we might mean it back in the States. That is, we have a well-known habit of taking in guests for free. But Jamaica is not the States. And being in Jamaica makes one aware that the simplest things we take for granted as free, as givens, are actually paid for. Space. All the precious space we keep around ourselves. Time. The bounty of the enclosures we live in, the inventions we move about in. We had not come to understand the reality of most Jamaicans that makes it practically impossible for many of them ever to accept us on equal terms.

From there we ride a ways, upward-winding roads, higher into the mountains. We finally pull up in front of a bamboo fence at the corner of John's Lane, marked by a hand-painted sign with a jug atop it. We enter the yard of roaming chickens, where two children splash in a plastic tub, the little boy naked, somewhat younger than the girl. We meet Tiney, Iaa's girlfriend, who becomes a guide of sorts, telling us about the different plants. Together, they lead us down a hilly path toward "the River," and as we pass plants along the way, Tiney tells us about them, revealing a vast knowledge of plantlore. We pass the garden, which we mistake for a less-grown-over spread of the jungle. Even after it is pointed out, we still fail to grasp its significance at the time. Further down the trail, which winds around, dips, and rises again before dipping once more into Jamaican red clay, we come to "the River."

A woman who is bathing, but hidden by a clump of brush, calls to us to stop and wait until she is clothed. We wait, as Tiney goes ahead and joins the hidden voice. Sounds of water trickling over rocks. Iaa sucking on his joint, blowing white clouds of smoke into the clear blue sky. It's hot, and sweat trickles down our bodies. Soon the woman who had been bathing emerges out of the branches, and up the little footpath in front of us. Shyly. As if covering a

Iaa and Tiney in Tiney's backyard. (Courtesy of LuAnne Roth)

Tiney showing us dasheen and other garden herbs and plants in a small garden in her backyard. (Courtesy of LuAnne Roth)

shame, not seen but known anyway, her arms folded with towel and other personals across her chest. "Sexy girl," Iaa sweet-talks, softly. When Tiney returns, they tell us about "the River." It is pure, they say, fed from an underground spring higher up in the mountains. This river is their symbol of purity and health, we gather. We didn't know then, though, that much of this was a sales pitch, as one might make a commercial to make a product look so tantalizing that a consumer cannot say no. They mention, the first of numerous times, that we could sunbathe and read, or swim in the cool mineral waters. We were both thinking—as we looked at the shallow flow of water that rose no more than five or six inches above the bed of smooth pebbles, and was no wider than five feet across, flanked on either side by thick green plants—"*This is the river?*"

Tiney picks small branches of four kinds of ferns, telling us about each one. We start back up the hilly path, climbing slowly, reaching a side path to another bend in the creek and "falls." But we come upon an elderly man, naked, bathing with his catheter, having a difficult time. Three girls stand not far from him, watching. Beyond them is a pool of water fed by a very short fall about a yard high. One of the favorite bathing spots of the community, they tell us. Further along, we stop at the garden, where a man is chopping, pitching fat edible roots called "dasheen" into a pile, replanting the stalks. His machete slices cleanly through them and digs quick holes in the loose earth, as he carries on a conversation in patois with Iaa, without ever looking up. Tiney and Iaa point out the differences between plantain and banana trees, and between the different kinds of bananas. The short, fat, sugary ones. The longer ones we are more accustomed to. The kind that are boiled. The large green leaves flaps in the breeze. Other crops in the garden—which seems, to the untrained eye, mere weeds and trees—include okra, breadfruit, pineapple, ackee, yams, coconut, beans, peppers, mango, and ganja.

They explain to us the garden belongs to the entire community. Everyone helps to work in it, and everyone is free to eat from it. The foods sold at the roadside stand, twenty yards or so from Tiney's gate, are also from the garden, and people are free to make a little money for themselves by setting out some fruits and vegetables for travelers who might stop along the way. Some of those stopping are from neighboring communities, but there is always the hope that one of the excursion vans or buses from the hotels will happen to stop as they go by. We are unable to get all of the details about how the communal gardening worked—for instance, what percentage of their food do they get from the garden? But another proverb from a Bob Marley song is used and explained in this context. "**One one cocoa**" Iaa says, and he explains that the system extends to shopping etiquette in the marketplace. One should get a little from many different people, thereby supporting them and their communities, rather than filling up one's basket at any one vendor's table. As we continue on, Iaa mentions that the man in the garden is Tiney's brother, who will be making a traditional Jamaican meal for us later on.

Once back at Tiney's house, they show us more crops in the surrounding yard. A ganja tree. Avocados. Several varieties of the plant we call elephant ears, dasheen, whose roots are one of their staples. LuAnne and Tiney sit on the porch talking, while Iaa stretches out on a small bench, under a roof held up by four posts. I join him, lying on a refrigerator door that was there for that purpose. Our conversation turns to food, and Iaa mentions coconut jelly, which is, according to him, the main ingredient in Ital cooking. He chastises me for not knowing. He sets about cutting coconuts from the trees with his machete. He slices cleanly across the very end of the first one, then the second, and a third, handing one to each of us and keeping one for himself. We all

Iaa and the author hiking in the "jungle." (Courtesy of LuAnne Roth)

drink coconut milk, the watery, filling liquid from inside, slurping from the narrow holes made by the machete's slicing. Iaa is finished in a matter of minutes. I am done after ten minutes or so. LuAnne takes about twenty. I wonder about the mysterious water, where it comes from.

As we finish drinking, Iaa is cutting his and the children's coconuts into halves, carving spoons out of hardened coconut shell with only a few well-placed slashes of the machete. The children are already scooping coconut jelly, the inner white meat, tearing it into pieces among themselves and eagerly eating it. Iaa scoops his out and eats it in no time at all. When I finish my milk, he slices my coconut down the middle, scoops the jelly loose from the shell, and hands me the bowl of jelly. I eat, somewhat cautiously at first, but more vigorously as I grow accustomed to the raw texture and taste. I managed to squelch the nagging fears about illness resulting from the experience. LuAnne finally finishes her milk, and her coconut is also sliced, half of her jelly handed to the children and half to her. The shells are thrown into a pile and Iaa and Tiney explain to us that they use every part of the coconut. They drink or cook with the milk, eat or cook with the jelly, even making desserts from it at times. They use the fibrous inner shell to make brushes and save the hardened outer hull for firewood. I overhear Iaa describing his last few days to Tiney, as they speak affectionately among themselves, and his familiar proverb, **Dog more than bone.**

A little while later, Iaa leaves us and walks to a small roadside market stand, where he sits smoking and talking with the young man there. Tiney invites us on another walk, showing us a number of medicinal plants. Several kinds of mint. Herbs for bringing fever down. Herbs for upset stomach. She explains how bananas and coconut trees are planted in cycles so that there are always some at every stage in the growth toward ripeness, thus, some bearing at all times. Other crops are in season in various parishes at different times. For instance, the mango season has just ended in this area but may still be going on in other parishes. Their dirt, to some extent, determines what is in season. They eat a lot of avocado, pumpkin, okra, or whatever, when those vegetables are in season.

When we return from the walk, we join Iaa at the little roadside stand. He is purchasing ganja from the young man there. "**Lickle and long,**" he says, as he inspects the herb. "Better to have quality, and then it last longer. Only a lickle for good meditation. Better to have quality than quantity and just smoke up fast." The proverb triggers lines from an Itals song, "Wanti Wanti." Iaa suggests we drive further into the mountains and take a hike through the jungle. We head out, as Tiney leaves with another group of people to go to market

A roadside stand with fruits and sugarcane. (Courtesy of the author)

106 • Proverbs in Jamaican Society

in Sav-la-Mar. We stop along the way at several houses, and he yells out from the car, but in each case no one is home. He tells us, after several such visits, that he is in search of ganja. Finding none of the farmers whom he prefers to buy from at home, he heads further up the mountain, the sounds of Gregory Isaacs booming from the car stereo. We pull up on an infinitesimal shoulder, almost in a curve, and park, following Iaa down another hilly path, across a rickety bamboo bridge, and up another steep hill. He calls out to someone as we approach a small house, but again no one is home.

On a table in the yard, where chickens are clucking, are three pineapples and several other pieces of fruit. Iaa looks them over, leaves them, and leads us on another path through the jungle. He shows us a root they call curry, which, broken off, is moist and orange inside. The trail leads through a yam and bean grove, thick leaves engulfing arched bamboo trellises that rise four to five feet above our heads. A twenty-minute hike later, we come to another "river." Women and children are washing clothes downstream from us. Iaa talks about the purity of the water and invites us to step in. We learn that as far back as slavery, Jamaican people viewed the rivers and streams as medicinal. "They came to wash their bodies. Wash away pain. Wash away trouble. Wash away sickness. Just feel so good after bath in mineral water. So clean. New. Healed. Don't you want to get in? Wash?" We do, less than impressed again by the stream, even smaller than the previous one. Iaa invites me to bathe my locks, and I kneel, head down, while LuAnne scoops handfuls of cold water, pouring them onto my head, my baptism, as it were, in a Jamaican healing stream. For Iaa, an American Rasta come to be anointed in the magical waters. The water is cool and refreshing, a welcome relief from the suffocating heat. I cannot help but remember, though, the admonitions of the tourist book and the doctor back home to stay away from swimming in fresh water.

We hike back, and Iaa stops and chooses one of the pineapples from the table at the house we had passed on the way. We take off again, to Gregory Isaacs, making more stops along the way in search of ganja. When Iaa finally finds one of his sources home, we visit in the man's yard, sitting on rocks as he and Iaa converse in thick patois, catching up on relatives and so on. The man disappears and returns in minutes with an armful of ganja stalks, two to three feet long. Then begins the ritual of Iaa's inspection: smelling, looking closely at each bud, sampling the texture with his fingers. And the ritual of smoking: picking a bud, crumbling it into finer pieces, rolling it into a good-size joint, and finally lighting it. Time passes. The joint is passed. Talk comes easily. We are surprised when Iaa turns to me and asks, "So how much do you feel to give for the ganja?" I explain that I was prepared to give him money for the day's trip but cannot afford and do not need to buy ganja. More time passes. He asks the same question. I respond in the same way, a tension having entered the interaction. "Well, of the money you have for me, how much can you put toward the ganja?" he asks again. I make it clear that whatever I give him now means he gets less later, and finally hand him some money. He is clearly disappointed and can only come away with a few of the bundle of stalks.

Back at Tiney's house, he rolls and smokes one joint after another, offering us our own. With his machete, he skins the pineapple, giving each of us a piece. "**When in Rome, do as the Romans**," he says, encouraging us to relax, to experience life as he lives it. To eat and enjoy the pineapple. To smoke the joint we have laid to the side. "Just like that." The heavy sweet juice, like the coconut milk, is extremely filling. He tells me that several of the people we have met thought that we were brothers; the young man at the roadside market, for example, and the man from whom he bought the ganja. Their assumptions please him and affirm the sense of being on the same vibe that we have felt since meeting. After the pineapple is eaten, we walk back to "the River," LuAnne and I sitting and talking while Iaa bathes. When we return, Tiney is back from town, and her brother begins cooking the meal. He cooks in a kitchen that is separate from the house, a tradition that prevents the house from getting hotter. While Tiney's brother is cooking, Iaa states that we need to give her brother money to help cover his expenses. The ensuing conversation highlights a drastic misunderstanding about the money. The day before, when talking about this trip, Iaa had made it sound as if he were doing a favor for friends, helping us to learn more about Jamaican culture so that I could write about it more accurately. He had stated that he was only expecting to get around $500 Jamaican to cover gas and so on (around $15 American). As it turns out, he is highly insulted by that amount—or at least he acts as if he is—and narrates four or five stories, each one illustrating how much money he has made for comparable trips. The compensations range from $75 to $150 American.

We feel a terrible sense of guilt. And at the same time anger and disillusionment. Was Iaa a friend? Or were we simply being hustled? And if, as is usually the case, the truth lay somewhere in the middle, exactly where? And how could we locate it? Why would they invite us to eat dinner, which we could have easily done without, and then charge us for it? Iaa smooths things over, in part, as the tension of the conversation rises, by suggesting that perhaps we could give him more money the next day. He walks back to the roadside stand, sits and smokes, while LuAnne and I talk.

The meal is an assortment of different starches. Okra, boiled bananas, pumpkin (squash), dumpling, dasheen, and several roots: all boiled without spices that we could detect. After eating we say goodbye to Tiney and start back, Gregory Isaacs turned up so loudly we can barely hear each other speak. In fact, there is little speaking, as the tension of the previous conversation is still quite palpable. Iaa stops at his house, still not conversing. We get out and follow him, feeling a bit fearful and insecure. He goes upstairs and, after a while, returns, suggesting once again that we should stay there rather than go back to Negril. I answer that we really need to get back, to which he responds, "You sure? You sure you want to go? You could stay here. Wake up. Bathe in the mineral water. Relax." It is evident that he does not want to make the drive back. One reason for his reluctance is probably his car, which had started having trouble going into gear. To compensate, he drives extra fast, picking up momentum to get up hills and around curves, recklessly swerving in and out of other cars and pedestrians, scaring us as we barely miss accident after accident. Needless to say, the ride back is a nightmare, as we ponder how much of the silence and recklessness is directed toward us. Once back at our hotel, however, Iaa becomes a little more social, and we make plans for him to come by the next day.

When he arrives the next day, we sit and talk for a while. He asks once more about us staying at his house. I explain that, in fact, it would not save us money, as he assumes. We are paying for the hotel with a credit card, because we have no cash. If we stayed at his house, we would have to buy groceries and give him "a little something." We could not use the credit card for those things, and so, we'd just have to return to the United States sooner than we had planned. At last he seems to understand our economic situation, and with the realization that we really are broke, his enthusiasm to have us as guests quickly dissipates. He responds with a proverb: "**Well, I guess we'll just have to call it a day.** Just call it a day. Yeah, Just like that." Minutes of silence pass between us, sitting there on the porch.

The day before, he had opened his trunk, saying "I just want to give you a gift, something to remember me by. So that you won't forget Iaa." He had an assortment of hand-carved wooden pipes, which I had mentioned that I collect. "Which one of these you like?" he asked, and I picked one with a ganja leaf carved on the front. "OK, OK, so you won't forget Iaa." Today, after those minutes of silence, he asks, "So, how much do you feel to give me for the chalice?" I almost laugh. By now, this comes as no surprise. Nor do I begrudge him his request. He has given me such richness. I only wish that we had met him at the beginning of our trip, when money was not such an issue, rather than at the end, when we were broke. We agree on a price, based on the little money that I could spend and still have enough for the last few taxicab rides and the departure tax. As he is about to leave, to indicate that everything is OK between us, he says, "**No cup no mash, no coffee no throw away.** Yeah, Just like that. Just like that."

A number of general comments can be made about Iaa's proverb use. Many of the proverb applications are concerned with economic hardships and strategies for coping and transcending the harsh reality of poverty. This seems almost too obvious to note, since this is perhaps the overriding influence on the tenor of his, and most, Jamaican lives. Almost all of the proverbs assist in maintaining a precarious balance between hopefulness and realism. One cannot afford to be overly optimistic, for this would set one up for unnecessary disappointment and leave one vulnerable to despair. But neither can one allow oneself to be overcome with hopelessness. The key to staying alive lies in life's ever-present potential for transformation and transcendence. No matter how bad things might be at any moment, they can get better. Hence, the proverbs convey an attitude that whatever one has is precious, not to be taken for granted or easily discarded. This applies to human relationships as well as to material circumstances.

Another aspect of proverb use is clear, not only in Iaa's case, but with others whom I observed. The speakers' use of proverbs reflects primarily their own issues and efforts to resolve them; our presence has a relatively minor impact on their repertoires or frequency of usage. For example, Chin's chief concern was relationship, and he used proverbs that reflected this. The driver who was stopped on our trip from Ocho Rios to Kingston has a "bone to pick" with police, as evidenced by his tirades and sermons about them. His use of the proverb reflected his cynicism and anger about the unfairness of police behaviors. As I mentioned above, Iaa's proverbs are concerned with economic struggles and the impact of poverty on the human spirit. They also reflect another of his major concerns: the accurate representation of Jamaican culture. This latter issue is especially important to him because of the obvious disregard for African Jamaican culture reflected in neocolonial governmental policies, as well as in attitudes displayed by many tourists, who ironically keep the economy in this part of the country afloat. The ambiguity produced by this situation characterized his relationship with us and complicated the *situational* meanings of several proverbs.

For instance, **Dog more than bone** was simultaneously a simple expression of how hard his life was, a plea for support, an advertisement for his business, and a veiled criticism of us as American tourists whom he assumed knew nothing of hard times. This was also evident with the proverbs **You never too old to learn, Seein is believing, Rain a fall but the dutty tough, Seven times rise and seven times fall**, and **When in Rome, do as the Romans do**, and contributed to our constant feeling of unsureness about the relationship. On one hand, he took seriously the charge of providing us with accurate information about Jamaican culture. At one point he said, "If I you find me worthy in my humble way to be your teacher," rhetorically deferring to my wishes. However, this posture carried an element of resentment and served as a banner for his business. Hence, at any given moment, the use of a proverb might, in fact, assert his dominance and power. This happened on several occasions, most notably with **You never too old to learn**. On one hand the proverb spoke to our earnest desire to learn and his willingness to inform us. At the same time, though, it rhetorically established that the teacher was in charge and could chastise the pupils as he saw fit. A similar dynamic occurred again with **When in Rome . . .** , which may, on the surface, have sounded like an innocent invitation for us to relax and learn about Jamaican culture. The assertion was tinged, however, with an insistence that reminded us we were at *his* house, in *his* country, effectively stranded many miles away from our lodging and our home. As we will see in succeeding chapters, the issue of power and dominance is central to the uses of proverbs in reggae discourse.

NEW BROOMS SWEEP CLEAN

Proverbs and the Rhetorical Strategies of Address in Reggae Discourse

In the previous chapters, I contextualized reggae proverbs culturally, historically, and rhetorically. I established that Rastafari ideology is a prevailing influence on the philosophical orientation of roots artists, profoundly impacting the lyrical and musical content of songs, performance styles, and narrative personas, hence affecting the use of proverbs. Beyond these general contextual elements, however, a variety of more specific factors affect proverb meanings in reggae performances. These include (1) the specific artist; (2) the particular rhetorical and aesthetic characteristics they tend to rely upon; (3) how the audience perceives that artist; (4) sociolinguistic components of a given performance (on record or live), such as inflections, intonations, gestures, and so on; (5) to whom the song is rhetorically addressed; (6) the ritual dissonance of the song; and (7) the proverb's intended function. In this chapter, I will focus on the latter three of these elements, exploring their impact on proverbs in reggae. Factors that have to do with particular artists will be examined in subsequent chapters.

Practically all the compositions of roots artists can be placed in four major content-oriented and rhetorical categories: (1) sermons, (2) prayer, (3) praise, and (4) love songs. The sermon song is by far the most prevalent: the remaining three categories of romantic, prayer, and praise songs are much less common among these artists. Moreover, resonances of sermonic traditions are often found in the other song types. I use the term "sermon" loosely to refer to songs that serve instructional, expository, and/or didactic functions. In many cases these songs contain the structural elements of sermons—for instance, chanting, repetitive formulaic lines, and a gradual buildup to heightened intensity. It is common that artists begin sermon songs with a thesis or idea that is explicated, illuminated, and expounded upon. Parables or other narratives making ethical or moralistic points are woven into such songs, just as they customarily are in more recognizable sermonic traditions. To some extent the genre of reggae crafted by artists such as Bob Marley, Bunny Wailer, the Wailing Souls, Culture, and the Itals becomes primarily a platform for musical and lyrical sermonizing.

Within these four larger categories, we can further delineate songs based on who is being addressed. My research indicates that songs are addressed to (1) Babylon, (2) Jah, (3) a lover, (4) the Rastafari community, (5) the African Diasporic community, (6) a nonspecific listener or general audience, (7) the speaker, or (8) some combination of these. It is critical to note that while the larger four categories mentioned above influence and limit, they do not always determine the addressee. Only in the case of prayer songs can we automatically assume who will primarily be addressed. This is somewhat true for love songs, which are in most instances directed to the speaker's lover, but not necessarily. Many romantic laments are rhetorically addressed to a general audience. Praise songs are usually addressed to the Rastafari or Diasporic community, a general audience, in some cases Babylon, and in other instances a combination of these. Thus, in praise songs the speaker talks to someone else *about* Jah rather than addressing the deity directly. Similarly, there is a variety of possible addressees for sermon songs.

The addressee in roots reggae is one of the most important elements bearing on proverb meaning. I refer here to Seitel's theory of proverb speech (1969), in which he distinguishes between a first-, second-, and third-person correlation, and argues that this distinction can significantly alter a proverb's message. In a first-person correlation, the speaker applies the proverb to himself. With second-person correlation, the proverb is applied to the person to whom one is speaking. For example, person A says to person B, **New brooms sweep clean**, as a way of criticizing person B for spending all of his time with newly made friends. With a third-person correlation, the speaker applies the proverb to a third party, although that person may not be present. For instance, person A says the above proverb to person B *about* person C. As we shall see, an exploration of who is addressed in reggae can illuminate not only proverb meaning but other facets of reggae discourse as well.

Negotiating Power and the Rhetoric of Address

We established in our examination of Rastafari that an inherent aspect of the ideology is a concern with deconstructing the power base and philosophical underpinning of colonial and neocolonial societies. This consideration insists on nothing short of a construction of a new world order, based on the spiritual, aesthetic, and ideological tenets of Rastafari. That new world order would value the spiritual over the material, and the quality of human relationships over all other standards by which one might measure "progress" or civilization. One of the fundamental tasks of warrior/priests is to assist in the deconstruction of the Babylonian reality. At the same time, they facilitate the construction of a new system of thought, being, and action that can potentially transform the nature of human relationships and bring an end to the suffering caused by the greed, avarice, and ego-centered perspectives characterizing Western society up to this point. This mission informs the composition of songs, lyrically and musically, and is prominently reflected in the use of proverbs. As I have noted in my discussion of the Itals, for instance, a proverb may simultaneously critique and deconstruct the Babylonian system, while constructing an ideological foundation for the new and imminent, Rasta-influenced reality (Prahlad 1995).

As such, the negotiation of power is one of the most significant functions of proverbs in roots reggae. The warrior/priests find themselves in similar roles as the leaders of Obeah, Myalist, Convince, Revivalists, Kumina, or other African-influenced religious groups in Jamaica and throughout the Diaspora. They assume the role of visionaries and healers, often on the front line between the haves, the representatives of Western power, and the have-nots. While this role is to some extent symbolic, it has often been very socially and politically real. Those in power in Jamaica, for instance, recognized that Bob Marley's voice was at one point more influential than the voices of Jamaican political figures. The American CIA also recognized Marley's local and international influence, as evidenced by the detailed files they kept on him.

It is not coincidental that the rise of this genre of song corresponded with political changes in Jamaican society (Jones 1988, 22; Chang and Chen 1998, 53). Following Jamaican independence in 1962 came a period of social unrest, triggered by a widening gap between the ruling class and the poverty-stricken masses, and a strengthening of the color caste system privileging whites and lighter-skinned peoples. By the mid 1960s, when the first general election occurred, Kingston was embroiled in unprecedented political violence and tension. Among the other possible currents in the music developing at that time was a concern with basic social and psychological issues confronting those who, after four hundred years of slavery, were faced with a future offering no signs of significant improvements in their condition. Roots reggae addresses this social and political dilemma, giving expression through the symbols and aesthetics of Rastafari to the range of emotions and ideas that this period of time evoked. Some of the ritualized dissonance of reggae, for example, can be viewed at least in part as a response to the social crises of this period.

The escalation of proverb use can also be seen in this context. As Jones writes: "To add spiritual and philosophical weight to a particular song, the reggae lyricist is also able to draw on the rich source of rhymes, riddles, folk-stories and proverbs in Jamaican oral culture. . . . In this way, reggae lyricists attempt not only to articulate the collective consciousness of their audience, but also to organise and politicise it, by working on the practical ideologies and elements of 'good sense' that already exist in the popular culture of the Jamaican working class" (27). The negotiation of power in these songs concerns relationships between any number of polarities, as well as among members of the Diasporic or other oppressed groups. Jones lists, for example, such oppositional elements as the haves/have-nots; natty dread/baldhead; us/dem (them); and righteous/wicked (1988, 27). The connections between negotiation of power and proverb meaning will become evident as we consider the forms of address in reggae. This aspect helps to explain, for instance, why proverbs are found more frequently in sermon songs and in songs addressed to Babylon, Rasta, and the Diasporic community than in prayer songs or songs addressed to a lover.

Prayer Songs: Addressing the Deity

Songs in which most or all of the text directly addresses the deity are by far the rarest, and their presence among the repertoire of the most well-known roots reggae performers is minuscule. In most cases, Jah is addressed in introductory invocations, asides, occasional lines or stanzas during songs, or he is spoken *about*, not spoken *to*. For example, in the chanted introduction to the Itals' "Titanic," the deity is spoken about: "He that dwelt in the secret place of the most high, shall abide under the shadow of the almighty. Jah Rastafari" (*Modern Age*). Prayer songs are those directed primarily to the deity, asking for strength and guidance, or simply confessing love and devotion. The structure of prayer songs can be rendered as:

stanza—to Jah
chorus—to Jah
stanza—to Jah
chorus—to Jah

One of the most enchanting examples of a prayer song is Michael Prophet's "Hear I Prayer," from his LP *Serious Reasoning*:

Help me Father
while I put my trust in you
'cause I just want to do
that which is right
Have mercy on me
and help I prayer
so brighten up my days
and let me be nearer.

Another example is Don Carlos's "Jah Jah Hear My Plea," from *Raving Tonight*:

Jah Jah please hear my plea oooohh
Jah Jah please answer me
for so long I have been in Babylon
No one to give me a helping hand.

And a final illustration comes from an artist called Danny Dread I:

Oh Jah Jah Jah
I really love you so
I want the world to know
I really love you so
I want the heathen to know

("Oh Jah Jah," *Hit Me with Music*)

Thus far, I have found no proverbs in this genre, which validates some of the noted functions that proverbs serve in reggae discourse. There is no power relationship being challenged or negotiated in prayer songs, nor is there any advice or criticism being offered. The imbalance of power between the speaker and Jah is accepted and embraced. Hence, most of the functional reasons for proverbs in reggae do not apply to this rhetorical form.

Songs of Romance

Songs addressed to lovers give us further insights into how proverbs traditionally function in reggae. This is a common genre and even the most religiously oriented artists, at one time or another, pen love songs. For roots reggae artists, however, such songs make up a small percentage of their repertoires. This is understandable, given the primary mission of the warrior/priests and the subordinate role that romantic relationships seem to have in Rastafari ideology. While proverbs are found in this genre, they comprise a minute percentage of the expressions found in reggae. For singers such as Gregory Isaacs and Dennis Brown, who are known for romantic and sermonic songs, we are more likely to find proverbs in their sermonic compositions. In most cases, proverbs in love songs function as friendly forms of negotiation and as parts of persuasive arguments being made by the speakers to their lovers. The kind of power struggle that is so prominent in sermon songs is absent. The structure of this genre is roughly:

stanza—to lover
chorus—to lover
stanza—to lover
chorus—to lover.

Several proverbs are found in an early love song by the Itals. The speaker is telling the loved one not to be bothered by malicious rumors spread about them. The song begins, "Hearing is not seeing my love / **Seeing is believing my love**," and continues with a testimony to how much the relationship means to the speaker. Much later in the song, another proverbial expression is used: **Sticks and stones may break my bone / but my darling words will never hurt.** Both proverbs are used persuasively as a way of affirming the speaker's love and dispelling any doubts that his partner may have about the relationship. There is no power struggle being negotiated or critical comment being made to the addressee.

"Give Me What I Want" from *Brutal* is another classic tune by the same group. It tells the story of the speaker's burning love and desire for the beloved. He has stood "in the pouring rain," and "in the burning sun," waiting "patiently for you to come." He needs "just one more dance with you" and begs for his beloved to give him another chance. The apex of emotions in the song occurs with the use of the proverb halfway through. The vibrant soulfulness of the singing and the perfect insertion of traditional wisdom at this moment in the song is enough to evoke goosebumps for the close listener. Just after the proverb is sung, the backup singers harmonize on a sweet "Oooh yeahhh," that is like the "Amen" of a congregation during a sermon. By calling upon traditional wisdom, the speaker adds another dimension of authority to his plea, making it that much more compelling:

Absence makes the heart grow fonder. (Oooh yeahhh)
I think it's time we should be together
Give me one more chance to prove
my true romance,
Gee whee, let me dance, let me dance.

As in the previous example, the proverb here is used persuasively, as part of a "rap," or "sweet talk."

This song also provides an excellent illustration of how elements of the sermonic tradition can be present even when the subject matter is romantic love. The performance of the proverb reverberates with the aesthetics and intensity of the heightened portion of a preacher's sermon, the vocal harmonies echoing with tinges of Revivalist singing. There is a double level of meaning inherent in the proverb and throughout the stanzas of the song. A comparable example would be Aretha Franklin's "Respect," in which her voice and piano playing signify on the black Baptist church's singing and sermonic traditions. But "Respect" also exemplifies how lyrics of a "love" song can signify the historicity of African American life, giving each line a double meaning. At the same time that Aretha is demanding respect from a lover, the lines resonate with listeners for whom respect has been an issue in the historical context of slavery and neocolonial America. When the Itals sing, **Absence makes the heart grow fonder** and "Give me what I want," the same duality of meaning occurs.

Bob Marley's romantic songs are few in comparison to his sermon songs; however, he ensured the immortality of the proverb **Don't rock my boat** in reggae parlance with his hit, "Satisfy My Soul." The proverb is used in the first stanza.

Oh please, **don't you rock my boat,**
cause I don't want my boat to be rocking
Don't rock my boat (backup singers).

The speaker's message is that he likes things just as they are: "I like it, like this." **Rock my boat** would then mean "upset my OKness with the way things are," or "disturb the space I'm in." Inasmuch as the proverb is concerned with establishing a state of balance within the relationship or with setting boundaries and establishing who is in control, it is being used to negotiate power. The second proverb supports this interpretation.

You satisfy my soul, satisfy my soul
Every little action, there's a reaction.
Oh can't you see, what you have done for me.
I'm happy inside, all, all of the time.

With this reading, the "action" would be the partner's attempt to get more from the speaker than he is willing to give. The "reaction" would be his possible withdrawal from the relationship.

As with many of Marley's songs, however, the message can be read on multiple levels; in fact, this is an instance in which the audience's knowledge of the singer might influence their interpretation of the proverb. Marley was known for his social, spiritual, and politically conscious lyrics. The album from which this song comes, *Kaya,* was somewhat controversial because of its romantic, seemingly nonmilitant appeal. Released after an assassination attempt on his life, there was speculation and criticism that Marley had gone "soft." Some listeners, however, assumed that there were militant messages on the album; they were simply more disguised. So, assuming the romantic lyrics were masking political commentary, the proverbs would have social/political applications. Both **Don't rock my boat,** and **For every little action** . . . , for instance, would be directed toward those who attempted to assassinate Marley.

Perhaps the most proverbially rich love song in roots reggae is an oracular composition by the Itals, "Easy to Catch." It illustrates how the warrior/priest persona colors discourse even in matters of romance. This persona comes across strongly in the use of the proverbs here, which resound like the rhetoric of an African oracle, clearly defining the speaker as more than just a man communicating with his lover. While he may be addressing a lover, he is speaking so that we, the audience, will be sure to overhear. The song begins with phrases that sound proverbial, "What happen in a year / happen in a day no I-ya," before moving on to the chorus, which contains the central proverb.

Old firestick
So easy to catch.
[repeat]
Won't you sata let me tell you this
Cause it's a natural fact.

The proverb is a familiar one to most Jamaicans. Its social meaning is that just as a fire can be rekindled easily from cinders that are still aglow, an old relationship can be easily reignited. This leads us to conclude that the speaker is talking to someone with whom he has been in a relationship previously, or he is giving advice to someone else who is in this situation. The next verse begins, **New broom sweep clean and / old broom know the corners**, and ends, "**The older the moon, the brighter it shines** / I'm a want to tell you this from a very long time." The meanings of these two proverbs converge in the theme of "old things are better than the new." This theme, specifically applied to the relationship, is echoed by the proverb in the next stanza, **You've got to come from some place / before you can go back.** The proverb suggests that separating for a period of time was a necessary condition for the relationship finally to work. A stanza later, another proverb is used: **Them say what drop off the head / always drop on the shoulder.** The social meaning I have obtained from Jamaican informants for this one is that unfinished business does not just disappear; one has to deal with it at some point. Hence, there is no escape from eventually confronting and resolving the relationship.

Songs to Babylon

Compositions in which all or most of the text directly addresses the system are far less frequent than songs in which there are simply occasional lines and phrases with such direct address. However, proverbs occur more frequently in this type of song than in either of the previously discussed categories, probably because songs to Babylon are usually sermon songs. The structure of this genre is comparable to the previous types, with the substitution of "Babylon" for "Jah" or a loved one:

Stanza—to Babylon
Chorus—to Babylon
Stanza—to Babylon
Chorus—to Babylon

Culture's "Frying Pan" is a sermon with a mocking attack on the Babylon system and its insatiable greed, immorality, and violence. Rather than facing up to their crimes, Babylonians keep running away, further losing themselves in distractions. Underlying the sermon here is the Rastafari emphasis on a spiritually based, socially just vision of human society. Babylon signals the Western materialistic empires, which include politicians and all others whose reality revolves around the capitalist ethic. The song begins with a spoken warning, "Babylon, your days are numbered," with the chorus as a repetition of the proverb:

Babylon, **you jump outta frying pan**
Jump ina fire.
You jump outta frying pan
Jump ina fire.

Later in the song, the chorus is changed:

Babylon, **you jump outta frying pan,**
Jump ina fire.
You cannot be satisfied,
All the time you want more.

Rhetorically, the speaker is urging Babylon to own up to its transgressions and repent. Power is being negotiated, as the speaker lifts himself morally above the addressee, both through taking the ethical higher ground and by using a proverb. As much as anything else, the song functions to portray the Babylonian in an almost pitiable light.

Another such composition is "Stop Red Eye," by the Wailing Souls. The dominant referential frame in this one is the middle passage and the days of the slave trade. The song is at the same time mocking, sarcastic, and bitter. Much of the sarcasm is communicated through the ritualized dissonance of ironically playful musical phrases that occur throughout, which is unfortunately lost on readers of the text alone. Counterpoised against the seriousness of the lyrical message, these phrases become chillingly critical. The sarcasm is also conveyed by the mocking phrases of the chorus: "Eh eh eh eh eh, Lord / Eh eh eh eh eh, Jah," which are sung almost like a children's taunting game but are followed by the lines: "Ol Pirates make you raid I so / (Jump overboard and drown!)."

This composition is similar to Culture's in that it reiterates the theme of Western greed and the crimes resulting from a materialistic mindset: "Every little thing you want / every little thing you see you run down pon." The proverb, **Finger mash no cry** comes in the third stanza and conveys the idea that the oppressors will ultimately fall; and when they do, they should not cry about it. The social meaning of the proverb is that a person doing something that can lead to injury or harm should not complain when the harm comes.

Dem coming like a hungry shark
Up from the bottom for another bite, yeah
finger mash no cry, oh no
Watch the saints no watch the crowds.

The proverb is lifted from "Emmanuel Road," a popular Jamaican game song. Bilby gives this description of the game and provides lyrics: "The players rapidly pass stones in rhythm as they sing, attempting to avoid an accidental collision between the circulating objects and their hands" (1985, 143):

Go dung [down] Emmanuel Road, gyal an' bwai [girl and boy]
fe go bruk [break] rock-stone, gyal an' bwai
bruk dem one by one, gyal an' bwai
bruk dem two by two, gyal an' bwai
bruk dem three by three, gyal an' bwai
bruk dem four by four, gyal an' bwai
finger mash, no cry, gyal an' bwai
memba, da play we da play [remember, we're only playing]

(143; see also Dance 1985, 189–90)

In "sampling" the proverb from the children's game and applying it to the historical dynamic between European enslavers and "downpressed" Africans, the Wailing Souls have created complex layers of meaning. What stands out is the same aesthetic dissonance generated by juxtaposing a playful melody with serious lyrics. One can read the proverb as placing the relationship between Africans and Babylon in the context of a game, insinuating a winner and a loser. One can interpret the proverb to mean that Babylon's way of operating is tantamount to playing Russian roulette: sooner or later the gun will go off. In either case, the proverb "signifies" on Babylon, carrying with it the same taunting tone as the lyrical phrases, "eh eh eh eh eh."

A final example of a song in which Babylon is addressed directly is the Itals' "To the Bone," which is one of the most militant statements made in reggae music. The basic message of the song is that Babylon should not disturb King Rastafari or his children. The price for doing so will be Babylon's absolute annihilation, read as the destruction of the Babylonian mindset and the power system that produces this mentality. The song is not only a sermon but contains, as many roots reggae songs do, the flavor of a Rastafari gathering, complete with the sounds of the kete and simulated sounds of funde and bass drums, and chanting. The effect of a campground meeting is heightened by the call-and-response structure of the chorus and the entire last part of the song. In this last part, Keith Porter is "preaching," counterpoint to the lines of the chorus sung by the other two Itals.

Two proverbs—both occurring in the first stanza—are central to the song. However, this stanza gains meaning in the context of the chorus, "To the bone / to the bone / oooh yeah / eat you to the edge of the bone," and the militant message that saturates the song.

Still waters run deep.
don't you wake the Lion
when he's asleep.
For cause when he's sleeping
he's like a lamb to the slaughter.
So don't you try to wake him
He will devour you
To the bone . . .

Porter has said of the proverb, **Still waters run deep**:

Definitely. That's why a lot of people. God created people and caused all these things to happen. You know what I mean? Cause I've been through that several times you know. But you know he said, you know I mean, he's watching. There's nothing he don't see and you know I mean. What one takes unto himself is one destruction and until that day you know, I mean. So the silent river is the Almighty himself who watches over all of us. And, I mean, yeah. And he will stay there and say, "Okay, I'm going to watch over you cause you said you would do the work, you said you would do the wills, so I'm going to sit here and see how much positive you are." (See Appendix 3)

So the proverb refers explicitly to His Majesty, Jah Rastafari, and the idea that He is silently watching the thoughts and actions of each individual. Connected to this idea is a sense of mythical time: it references the timeless foundations of creation. The proverb amplifies the threat imminent in the rest of the song, implicating the temporal nature of Babylon and all those who pay it homage.

The second proverb, **Don't wake the Lion**, which further bolsters this meaning, also refers to the deity and warns that He is best left alone. The lion is an important Rastafari symbol, derived from a combination of biblical passages, Selassie's actual "pet" lions, and the lion's strength, nobility, and ferocity as symbols of dreadlocked Rastas. The power resting in the nonviolent deity and His followers is crystallized in the terrifying image chanted repeatedly in the refrain: "The Lion will eat you, the Lion will eat you / He will conquer you." Certainly, negotiation of power is one of the proverb's functions here. The boasting, defiant tone of the lyrics are as overt a challenge to Babylon's sovereignty as one will find in reggae. The first proverb suggests the consummate power of Rastafari that overshadows all other powers, thus relegating the "system" to a subordinate position. The second proverb intensifies this message by further depicting the ferocious nature of Jah and Rastas.

Addressing Rastas and the Diasporic Community

Songs that primarily address either the Rastafari or the African Diasporic communities are usually sermon songs and contain the majority of proverbs that are used. A range of recurring topics are treated in these. The songs chastise members of the larger community for behaviors that are counterproductive to the ultimate goals of unity and liberation for African-derived peoples. Along with the critical comments, we also find words of encouragement and inspiration. Proverbs within these songs are a part of the wisdom and guidance being offered by the warrior/priests. Structurally, this genre simply substitutes members of the community for Babylon, lovers, or Jah:

Stanza—to brother, sister, community member
Chorus—to brother, sister, community member
Stanza—to brother, sister, community member
Chorus—to brother, sister, community member

"Who Lives It" (*Firehouse Rock*) by the Wailing Souls exemplifies songs in which the warrior/priest chides the addressee. As with most songs, it is impossible to know if an actual person is being addressed; nevertheless, the general meaning of the song and proverbs can be extrapolated. Two recurring stanzas and a chorus essentially make up the lyrical composition. The chorus is comprised exclusively of one proverb: **Who lives it, really knows it**, a variation of the popular **Who feels it knows it**, one of the most common proverbs in reggae. The social meaning of the proverb is that an understanding of the harshness of life and of what it means to be oppressed comes only through experience. The two stanzas of the song are as follows:

Your momma say you was to stay at home,
But that's what happens when you choose to roam,
Crab walk too much, yes him lose him claw, now,
It sick, no care, then the doctor worse.
You had to go and find out for yourself,
Nobody couldn't keep you on the shelf,
Rain a fall but the dutty tough,
Time like lightning strikes without warning.

The two stanzas contain four proverbs. In each case, the first two lines are narratives to the addressee, noting his or her rebellion against parental and communal advice. The second two lines, containing the proverbs, comment on the behavior mentioned in the first two. The proverb **Crab walk too much, him lose him claw** is said about people who have a difficult time choosing a "sensible" direction for their lives and working toward achieving specific goals. It is a negative critique, reinforcing the idea that one should not wander, be idle or fickle, or spend too much time exploring different interests. To do so is a character flaw and can lead to any number of problems such as chemical addiction, criminal activity, or physical harm. **It sick, no care, then the doctor worse** suggests an apathy toward one's own illness, and a resulting indifference from the physician. In other words, why should the doctor care about patients who are unconcerned about their own health? The doctor can be metaphorically anyone able to lend assistance, be it a parent, an elder, or even the government. As such, the proverb criticizes the addressee for not being more proactive and energetic in improving his circumstances.

Rain a fall but the dutty tough is a popular traditional Jamaican proverb, meaning literally that the rain cannot penetrate the ground because the earth (dutty) is too dry and hard. Metaphorically and socially, its meaning is that good things may come but conditions are so overpowering that these things do not make much of a difference. Centuries of economic and social oppression are likened to an earth parched by drought. **Time like lightning strikes without warning** suggests the impending nature of calamity that can come at any unforseen moment. Together the two proverbs convey the psychological attitude resulting from an oppressed condition: that one cannot afford frivolities, that survival depends on finding a livelihood and direction in life that ensures stability and maintenance of whatever material necessities one can accrue.

The proverbs can also be read within the context of Rastafari ideology. In this case the behavior being criticized would be a lack of spiritual focus. Whichever interpretation one gives the song, the lyrics are a kind of parable in which the proverbs suggest consequences for willfully disregarding traditional advice. The issue of power centers on the negotiation between the individual and the community, and on the suggestion that, if for no other reason than survival, the individual should accommodate social expectations. It should be noted that cultural and community survival and health depend on the well-being of the individuals within it.

Another composition by the Wailing Souls further exemplifies songs of reprimand and intracommunity conflict. This one addresses a person who is so infatuated with new friends that he turns his back on old friends and community. The speaker tells his friend that he is making a mistake, that old alliances should never be so easily cast aside:

You run gone left your old friends
Say you found some new friends.

Where you ago come when your new friends gone?
New broom only sweep clean I say
Old broom know the corners
Oh what a la la la la, what a la la la la la la la
De same stone that the builders refuse
always be the headstone
oh what a la la la la la

Here, as in many of the Wailing Souls' songs, we find a dissonance between the seriousness of the lyrics and playful lyrical and musical sounds reminiscent of children's games. Such dissonance affects the proverb's meaning. The proverbs themselves are sung to a gamelike melody and cadence, adding an ironic, sarcastic dimension to their meanings. The proverb **De same stone . . .** is another very common one in reggae lyrics, but in most other cases it has a seriousness that is diffused here. The "stone" usually refers to the Rastafari or African who has been overlooked by Babylon. But here it refers more specifically to an old friend. The popular social meaning, which carries religious overtones, bleeds into the stanza adding extra layers of meaning. The ideas of being neglected and eventually redeemed are amplified. A later stanza further insinuates this wider meaning:

Never turn your back on the ghetto walls.
Never burn your bridges behind you mon.

The speaker is concerned with more than simply abandoning old friends; "bridges" has a much broader correlation here. At the heart of the message is a focus on cultural and personal identity, and the pitfall of thinking that one can casually walk away from one's historical, cultural, and social self. The cultural theme is strengthened by the use of the previous proverb, **De stone that the builders refuse**, which is saturated with Rastafari resonances. This illustrates an identical rhetorical strategy to one found in African American blues. For example, the proverb **You reap what you sow** is often used in traditional blues stanzas addressing a lover. However, the social meaning of the proverb entails its application to slaveowners and white America, as a way of wishing them misfortune because of their inhumane treatment of African Americans. This social meaning cannot be divorced from the proverb within the context of the culture. Thus when a singer uses the proverb to a lover, this other relationship is also evoked (Prahlad 1996, 96–97). Likewise, in this case, it is not simply the particular friendship that is highlighted but the experience of being overlooked, rooted in ancient and colonial history, and the certainty that in the end those who have been neglected will ultimately occupy the most significant roles. For Rastas this reflects the belief that Africans will eventually rule and Europeans will be relegated to subordinate positions. This belief has been modified over time to include other oppressed and righteous people among the "stones that the builders refused."

Culture's "Iron Sharpeneth Iron" also fits into the genre of songs that chastise and advise. It begins with the playful sounds "La la la la la la la la lay la la la la la," although both vocal and musical tones are more serious than those in the previous song. This composition criticizes those people who fall prey to gossip and negative thinking about their brothers and sisters, warning them that any efforts they make to sabotage another person will also undermine themselves. It encourages instead a philosophy of unity. There are essentially three stanzas in the song, two of which are entirely proverbial. The first proverbial stanza is:

So, **when you're gonna dig a pit**, I tell you my brother [lead singer]
Don't dig one always dig two. [backup singers]
[repeat]

The other stanza contains two proverbs.

The countenance of one man brighteneth another, [lead singer]
Iron sharpeneth iron. [backup singers]
[repeat]

The proverb **Iron sharpeneth iron** is a favored Rastafari expression, capturing the philosophies of reasoning, unity, and cooperative effort that are so integral to this movement. It takes iron (a committed brethren or sistren with strong will and clarity of vision) to sharpen (spiritually elevate) iron, which happens through reasoning, love, and sharing. In fact, "iron" is an important symbol among Rastas, suggesting force of will, resolve, and pride.[1] It is often coupled with the rhyming symbols *lion* and *Zion*, as in Bob Marley's "Iron, Lion, Zion," forming a trinity of power. Consequently, the use of the proverb here carries with it the power of Rastafari theology and philosophy, whether or not the persons being addressed are actually Rastas. The message is to live up to Rastafari teachings, and to develop mutually supportive, positive intragroup relationships.

In some songs the speaker does not chastise but simply consoles, advises, or gives encouragement; Culture's "Don't Cry Sufferer" is an example. The song is dedicated to all those who are suffering the pangs of oppression, hunger, imprisonment, and injustice. It urges them not to weep but to "Keep the good faith," for "Jah provide for the poor mothers and fathers," and someday "Things will be sweet, sweet, sweet." In the third stanza, one of the most common proverbs in reggae is used:

The harder the battle be,
a go sweeter the victory.

The proverb can be taken literally, its meaning layered by its connection to the colonial and neocolonial history to which it refers. Another layer of meaning is added by the Rastafari perspective that views present-day Africans throughout the Diaspora as descendants of biblical tribes who, even in ancient times, were engaged in the same struggle.

Perhaps no other lyricist has penned so many songs in this vein as Bob Marley. The popular "Get Up, Stand Up," cowritten with Peter Tosh and Bunny Wailer is a classic example. The composition is a persuasive argument for those struggling beneath the weight of oppression to stand up for themselves, to rebel. Its central focus is a rebellion against traditional Christian teachings that prevent black people from seeking their freedom in the here and now. According to the song, preachers who insist on heaven "in the sky" are in collusion with politicians and neocolonial powers to subvert black people's liberation by keeping them focused on otherworldly things. The speaker extols Rastafari ideology as the basis for revolutionary thought and action: God is "a living man." Three proverbs are used in the song, two in the first stanza:

Preacher man don't tell me
Heaven is above the earth.
I know you don't know
What life is really worth.
It's not all that glitters is gold.
Half the story has never been told.

The first proverb suggests that the idea of heaven preached by Christian ministers is a deceptive lie. The fantasy sounds alluring (glitters), but there is no substance (gold) to it. The second proverb refers not only to history but to theology. The story is historical but also cultural and theological. The African's voice in history has been silenced by colonial influences, but so has an entire philosophical and theological perspective. The third proverb occurs in the final stanza and intimates that many people are "wise" to the trickery of Christian propaganda:

We know and understand
Almighty God is a living man
You can fool some people sometimes
But you cannot fool all the people all the time.

All of these proverbs, favorites among Rastas, are used in the negotiation of power. The speaker addresses the imbalance of power between the ruling class and the oppressed and points specifically to the use of Christian texts and teachings to ensure the status quo. Knowledge and control of educational and other media are major themes. The proverbs emphasize that even in the face of neocolonial propaganda, each individual can take control of his or her own acquisition of knowledge.

A second song penned by the trio of the Wailers is similar in the simplicity of its structure. In "One Foundation," the speakers encourage listeners to put aside whatever categories separate them and to work together to build a peaceful world. People should put aside "segregation," "denomination," and "organization," or risk destroying any opportunity for love to flower on the planet. The second stanza includes an allusion to the proverb **Birds of a feather flock together**, an image that fits with the idyllic vision of paradise on earth that the song depicts. The irony of the proverb is that it has often been used to point to differences among people, inasmuch as certain characteristics distinguish one group from another. Here it is being used to suggest that *all* humans belong to one family.

Got to come together
'cause we're birds of a feather.

Nonspecific Addressee, the Speaker as Addressee, and Multiple Addressees

Three other categories of address include songs in which (1) a general audience empathetic to the Rastafari perspective is addressed; (2) the speaker is talking almost to himself; and (3) there are multiple addressees. As mentioned earlier, the form of address is a rhetorical device, and Rastas, Babylon, or others may be indirectly addressed in the lyrics. Thus far I have been considering what is referred to by proverb scholars as second-person forms of address; that is, the speaker is directly addressing the person to whom the proverb is applied. I have not discussed instances in which the speaker might be addressing the proverb to himself, or saying it to one person while intending its message for someone else.

Such songs have rhetorical intensity much greater than those using direct forms of address. A number of songs by the Wailing Souls and Culture fit into this category. One could say that these singers are fond of signifying on Babylon in the most militant ways. The 1981 hit by the Wailing Souls, "Run Dem Down," exemplifies these characteristics. The speaker is in one way talking to himself, as he reflects on the history and relationships between the dominant and subordinate groups in society: "When I think of all the nice times we've missed / And I think of all we been suffering." The speaker could then be directing the proverb stanza either to himself or to those who share his experiences. While listeners who are neither Rastas nor of African descent could quite possible identify with the general sentiment of the proverb, it is impossible to divorce it from the Rastafari worldview with which it is associated.

The battle is not yet won
The battle is neither for the swift
Neither for the strong.

The "swift" and "strong" in this case both refer to Babylon, and so the proverb comments on a third party, one not present in the speech event between the speaker and the listener. In essence, it says that "they" cannot win, that the qualities required to win this particular battle are ones that "they" do not possess. Babylon is more directly alluded to in the chorus:

Say we gonna run dem down
Say we gonna run dem down
Say we gonna run dem from
The corners of the world.

The meaning here is quite apparent. Eventually, those who have been oppressed will metaphorically chase the heathen to the ends of the earth.

A similar structure is found in another hit from the same period, "A Fool Will Fall." This song is from the same album as the previous one, and the rich horn sounds by Dean Frazier and Nambo resonate with urgent prophecy and militancy. The bittersweet melody is smooth and meditative, as the bass drives forward like a tidal wave and the drum recalls the sounds of whips cracking on black backs, spitting back, into the face of the oppressors, the sounds of oppression. Once again, Babylon is spoken about, in the repetitive chorus: "A fool will fall / oh yeah / a fool will fall, oh yeah." Once again the reflective priest uses a biblical proverb: **A lying tongue just for a moment / But righteousness is everlasting foundation.** The "lying tongue" captures the essence of "dem," Babylon, whose reality is a false construction. This is an excellent illustration of proverbial negotiation between opposing sides of the war, between those who are in power now and those who will ultimately claim the glory.

Culture's proverbially dense "Hand A'Bowl" (*Good Things*) is another of those songs that resound with the voice of the oracle. It is almost entirely composed of proverbs and is one of the most poignantly critical songs in roots reggae. A number of characteristics are delineated in the critique of "them." "They" are loveless, scheming people who pretend to be friends while secretly plotting "our" demise. The title proverb, located in the recurring chorus, captures the essence of the song:

They all are:
Hand a bowl, knife a throat,
No love in their hearts.

The proverb refers to people who are "wolves in sheep's clothing." On the one hand, they offer food (sustenance, material goods, opportunity) while on the other, they are poised to cut one's throat (sabotage, murder, and so on). The first stanza consists of another proverb, repeated twice. This one encapsulates the idea that, although their lives *seem* to be positive and good, living among "them" one sees that, in fact, their character is repugnant and reprehensible.

See them, go live with them,
It's a different thing.

The next stanza contains a third proverb, centered on the same theme: "they" pretend to be helpful, while actually undermining one's efforts for success. This one, like the two above, are common Jamaican proverbs that may be unfamiliar to the foreign listener. Its image is powerful and biting, carrying with it the resonances of everyday life for African Jamaicans in slavery and neo(post)-colonial history. The effect of such images as "bowls" and "baskets" is to ground the song in historical and contemporary African Jamaican traditional culture, a presence that exudes from the stanzas. Rhetorically, this practice of proverb use intensifies the sense that the speaker is talking to fellow Jamaicans (oppressed peoples). His comments about "them" are likewise intensified, in part by the emotional thread connecting him to the addressed audience. This makes the feelings being expressed more "raw" than they might be if "they" were being directly addressed:

They love to give you
basket to carry water.
When deep within their hearts,
Feel what they are after.

Two final proverbs appear a few stanzas later.

Sometimes you try to do good to others,
And they tell you that
The more you look
The less you see.
The quickness of your eyes, they say,
It does deceive your body, but—

A common *social* application of the first proverb **The more you look . . .** is
to criticize someone who is nosey or intrusive. It might be said critically, for
instance, to someone who is staring or showing too much interest in one's
affairs. Although this meaning fits into the context of the song, exactly to
whom and how it is being applied remains ambiguous. We can hypothesize
that those same people who handed the speaker a "bowl" are being addressed
by the proverb. On the other hand, the speaker may mean that continuing to
look (trying to figure out or to understand or rationalize) at them and their
behavior simply obscures what is more obvious at only a glance. They are an
enigma, which becomes only more puzzling as one continues to scrutinize
them. It could also mean that one gradually sees through the enticements of
their reality. At first glance, there seemed to be so much there, but upon further inspection, there is hardly anything of value there at all. The meaning of
the second expression is similar to **See them . . .** implying that one can be
fooled by the seductiveness of "their" world.

A favored rhetorical strategy found in songs by Bob Marley is the critique
of Babylon while speaking to the Diasporic community. "The Heathen" is an
excellent illustration. First, simply the title—which depicts the contemporary
Babylonian as a historical extension of the uncivilized, barbaric tribes of ancient times—is a form of signification. The chorus consists of one line, repeated four times: "Heathen back there pon the wall." The two stanzas
contain four proverbs and are essentially words of encouragement to the Diasporic community. The first proverb suggests there is no shame in having
made compromises in the context of slavery and postcolonialism: black people did what they had to do to survive. But now the time has come to rally

the forces of African peoples, to battle against the influences of colonialism, and once again become a proud, independent world power:

Rise O fallen fighters,
Rise and take your stance again.
'Cause he who fight and run away
Live to fight another day.

The other stanza is an oracular proverb cluster, consisting entirely of proverbs.

As a man sow, shall he reap.
And I know that talk is cheap.
But the hotter the battle
Is as sweet as the victory.

The first proverb may be interpreted as another signification on Babylon, meaning that the corrupt and violent system is going to reap ruin, violence, and destruction. It could also be directed to members of the Diaspora, as an encouragement to "sow" the necessary "seeds" to ensure a new era of strength and political solvency. The next proverb can also be taken on two levels, applied either to the Diaspora or to Babylon. In one case, it would support the idea that black people need to commit to actions and behaviors that will bring about the goals they seek, not just give lip service to those ideals. In the other case, it would imply that the Babylonian system may talk about helping black people but in fact is just as hostile as ever (a recurring motif in Marley's songs). The final proverb, which is familiar to any reggae listener, is clearly directed toward the Diasporic audience. It is a way of gathering consolation and even inspiration from the very pain that oppression inflicts. It extends the central metaphor of the song—war—and reminds the fighters that the most profound sorrows of battle are to be embraced, for the depth of that suffering will be the measure of gratification when the struggle is finally won. As in numerous other Marley songs, this one is like a sermon to the fighters, the warriors, and draws upon analogies from the Old Testament as well as from the Rastafari ideological connection to warriors from African societies.

Marley's "So Much Things to Say" (*Exodus*) is another composition in this mold. It mocks and signifies on the character of Babylonians, criticizing their penchant for endless, empty rhetoric and babble. It also connects contemporary oppressors to ancient forces of wickedness that have historically fought against and tried to murder every righteous person who has ever lived, such as Jesus, Marcus Garvey, Moses, and Job. The chorus, a repetition of the line "They got so much things to say," is preached by Marley throughout the song, his contempt for "them" completely unveiled. Toward the end of the song he adds the kind of mocking imitative sounds that one would find in Diasporic "marking," or "mocking" speech acts,[2] poking fun at Babylonian babble: "Na na na na na na na na na / Every morning time / Na na na na na na na na na." The proverb comes in a musical bridge about two-thirds of the way through the song:

Oh when the rain fall
It won't fall on one man's house.
Remember.
[repeat]

The proverb can be interpreted in several ways, depending on whom one assumes is being addressed. If applied to the Babylonian, it would be a reminder that people are judged equally by higher laws, an implicit condemnation of the unjust political, social, and judicial systems that characterizes Western powers around the world. If directed toward the Diaspora, the same meaning would resound with comfort and encouragement. No matter how biased and corrupt the political system might be, the divine powers are indiscriminate; and sufferers should therefore stay rooted in the knowledge that "So while they fight we down / Stand firm and give Jah thanks and praises." These differing interpretations depend on our reading of the images "rain" and "house." On one hand, "rain" could be a positive, natural phenomenon; on the other hand, it could indicate calamity.

In all the above instances in which proverbs are used, the negotiation of power is a prominent concern. One can almost take for granted that an adversarial message will underlie songs signifying on Babylon and that the historical struggle between "them" and the righteous will be referenced. Within this context, the proverb quite naturally becomes a tool in rhetorically resolving the crises. In some cases, the speaker accomplishes this by using proverbs that insinuate the speaker's moral superiority. I have noted that simply using a proverb can effectively achieve this end. According to Abrahams (1968a), conflicts are resolved in the rhetorical world of the proverb, symbolically resolving them in the real. This function is evident in the songs under discussion. In almost all instances, song lyrics challenge the dominant ideology, which includes the way in which power is conceptualized. In the dominant society, power rests on material and economic privilege; in Rastafari philosophy, however, the locus of power lies in knowledge, spirituality, and connection to divine and nature forces. Hence, the proverbs assist in shifting the concept of the real in a way that automatically transforms the site of power. Through word/sound/power, the mythological/real war is won.

Proverbial images facilitate this metamorphosis. Proverbs are chosen carefully so that the images accomplish several goals. First, they become part of a symbolically coded language, easily understood by those well versed in reggae sermons. Second, they are used parabolically, as signs of a story with a moral at the end. As such, they not only describe recurrent social problems (Abrahams 1968a, 1968b) but reinforce the group's attitudes and responses to those problems. Again, those immersed in this discourse are able to discern the stories and the moral. For example, the proverb **Rain a fall but the dutty tough** evokes not simply an image of rain falling but an image of *people* looking out at the rain, their hopes once again shattered as the earth remains hard, of people who have been oppressed, who have suffered for hundreds of years, having to take a deep breath, gather their resolve, and keep struggling. The implicit "moral" of the story is that one cannot count on occasional "rains" of good fortune to transform a life of struggle into one of comfort and ease; one has to keep pushing ahead, trodding the hard road.

The poetry of reggae exploits the *social* level of proverb meaning, which is especially powerful for a group as closely knit as Jamaicans but also for serious reggae fans and disciples internationally. The *social* level is that level of meaning commonly shared by members of the group, which includes the weight of connotative associations. This is distinguished from the *symbolic* level of meaning, which refers to the associations and shades of meaning a particular individual might bring to a proverb; and from the *situational* meaning, which refers to nuances that apply to a specific instance in which the proverb is used (Prahlad 1996). I return to the proverb above by way of illustration. Let us say that a listener first heard the proverb in a Bob Marley song that was playing as she or he was breaking up with a partner. For that listener the *symbolic* level of meaning might involve sadness related to a relationship, and this level would exist in conjunction with the *social* level; however, it would not replace it.

My main point here is to qualify the common assumption that listeners construct their own meanings of reggae lyrics. Of course, this is true to an extent. Cooper notes that, "Indeed, the lyrics become open to a wide range of interpretations" (1993, 118), and quotes Marley on the subject: "You have to play it and get your own inspiration. For every song have a different meaning to a man. Sometimes I sing a song and when people explain it to me I am astonished by their interpretations" (118). She further argues that the meanings of lyrics can never be limited to the artist's intention, and that, "The audience, as much as the performer, engages in the making/spreading of the text and its meanings" (118). Although I am in agreement with Cooper that each instance of interpretation becomes another performance, characterized by reciprocity between artist and listener, I contend that reggae discourse, like other traditional narrative performances, *directs* the listener's interpretation. The discursive frame of reggae lyrics is encoded with certain values that are bound to influence the meanings attached to them by their audience. As such, lyrical and proverbial interpretations are not completely open-ended.

Jones's study of young white British fans supports this contention. His study indicates that many of these listeners studied reggae lyrics, sensitizing themselves to their nuances, and became socialized to Jamaican culture by attending dances and having Jamaican friends. Thus their interpretations were based to an extent on the Jamaican social meanings for particular expressions and their understanding of Jamaican and Rastafari ideology and worldview. Even when they lifted elements of this philosophy out of the Rastafari context and used them in their own lives, they applied them in a manner that reflected the dominant threads of Rasta ideology. For example, a woman might apply the paradigm of the oppressor versus the oppressed to her personal struggle with gender issues and discrimination. This adaptation, however, still recognizes that a power struggle is at the root of much reggae discourse. Hence the *situational* or *symbolic* meanings given to proverbs are influenced by the proverbs' *social* meanings.

In reggae, and particularly with proverbs that tend to recur within this discourse, proverb images tell stories and become symbolic markers for strategies of negotiation. When one hears **The stone that the builders refuse**, for instance, one envisions the story and its parabolic application. The warrior/priest and disciples are thus able to communicate large quantities of information through short metaphorical and symbolic statements. Imagine for a moment two people conversing only in proverbial language. This is essentially what warrior/priests often do and is exemplified most dramatically in oracular songs containing proverb clusters, such as Culture's "Weeping and Wailing," *More Culture:*

Every tub must sit on its own bottom.
And what your hand commit
your body must bear.
So sow good seed today
and you will reap good crop tomorrow.

The use of this symbolic language, among other things, facilitates the shift in power from Babylon to Rasta. The use of oracular narratives in this facilitation will be explored further in the next chapter.

STILL WATER RUN DEEP

Proverbs of the Itals

I first encountered the Itals in 1980 in a club in the Bay Area of California. Reggae clubs then were always packed. We entered one by one, two by two, coming in from the chilled San Francisco air thick with eucalyptus, sea water, and the aromas of night jasmine, into the temple where musk and sandlewood incense burned. Someone would always be burning frankincense and myrrh crystals on a small bed of charcoal in an iron pan, the thick smoke cascading up into the rafters and wafting through the music hall, mixing with the scents of sweat and patchouli; of sensimilla, acapulco gold, vanilla, coconut butter, ylang a ylang, and other essential oils; of Red Stripes and Heinekin, gin and cigarettes, mints and hormonal secretions. There'd be vendors at tables as you entered, selling Rasta crafts such as tams, bracelets, earrings and other jewelry, belts, incense burners and incense—and photographs, tapes, posters, and buttons of reggae stars like Bob Marley, clothes, books, and pamphlets.

Sometimes there'd be food. Curry chicken, rice and peas. Fried plantains, brown-nut stew. Vegetable patties. Cold juices of tamarind, coconut, mango, or banana. There'd be small groups of older dreads, their thick locks draped down to waist level or buried under tall tams. There'd be multitudes of younger dreads. Whites and blacks. Sometimes whole families with their children running around. There'd be the deadhead types in Indian dresses and tie-dyes, and the punker types, with shaved or spiked hair, tatoos and pierced lips, tongues, ears, and eyebrows. Wall to wall there were bodies. And as soon as you entered the temple, the holy yard, the booming bass would assault your body. Get inside your body. Start lifting you up into a meditation. If the deejay was good, he stuck to the roots. Something deep and persistent. U-Roy, Culture, Burning Spear, Johnny Osborne, the Gladiators, Augustus Pablo, or any of those hundreds of uncompromisingly rootsy singles by artists who never made it big on the international scene. If the deejay played the right selections, by the time the first band came on we were fully prepared to be taken to the next level. To dance praises, surrender our spirit/bodies to the power of the warrior/priests. All boundaries broken. Identities temporarily merged into one.

The thing that struck me most about the Itals was the absolute foreignness of their sound. There was nothing of the American aesthetic in it. It demanded you expand, reach, let go of the known, the familiar. The three singers seemed strangely angelic, rooted more firmly in some invisible earth power than any persons I had ever witnessed up to that point. They exuded that permanence, that disconcerting unshaken anciency you feel emanating from redwoods that have been around for thousands of years. But their sound. First there was the raw power of their vocal harmonies that blended like the voices you might hear lying on a cot in the mountains of Jamaica at night, all mingling together wafting along: Pocomania, Revivalist, Rastafari and/or Holy Ghost singing, drumming, and shouting; gospels on the radio, preachers from nighttime churches across the hills; deejays from somebody's boombox in the gully below; barking dogs; children playing; nightbirds. The Itals sing in the rich tradition of the three-part harmony groups such as the Mighty Diamonds, the Abyssinians, the Gladiators, and the Heptones. And the music. The music destroyed all notions of beginning, middle, and end, as the rhythmic patterns surged and resurged, circular but never quite arriving any place it had been before. Like Anancy, mischievous. Deceptively complex. A country in itself, sweeping us along like a river. An ancient spirit emerging from the earth. A certain space created by the purity of the instrumental tones, capturing electricity, stroking it, melting it into an oral substance as pleasant as sanded wood. A certain silence sculpted by the sound, which you could enter, like a river, and renew your bones.

The three songs I remembered most from that first concert were "Herbs Pirate," "Brutal," and "Rastafari Chariot." I remembered segments of them as one might phrases of the preacher's sermon from last Sunday, turning them over and over in my mind, contemplating their meanings. I recalled the sound of those songs that rocked my being full force, blasting from the stage, those soulful harmonies and delightful guitar and kete drum voices. And I recalled how I felt, dancing that night in the club, as the word/sound/power washed over us and the Itals never wavered from their rootedness but swayed or danced occasionally as the spirit moved them. "**Rolling stone don't gather no moss** / no more slavemaster, no more boss / just roll Rastafari chariot along, I say roll," echoed in my mind; as did **Man cannot live by only bread**, and **Never bite the hand that feed you**. From that time forward, as I continued to buy the Itals records and to attend their concerts whenever they performed in a place where I lived, their proverbs have lived with me.

Like many listeners, I have made meaning out of the Itals' lyrics that apply to my own life's situations. In all likelihood, many of my fellow concertgoers were not attuned to the proverbial expressions, unless they were used repeatedly, as in some refrains. My background has many parallels to poor Jamaicans moving from rural to urban areas and operating within the confines of a neocolonial system designed to ensure that its philosophical vision remains the norm. More specifically, I am an African American, first-generation college student, born on a plantation to parents for whom slavery was no more than a generation past. Thus I held my experiences, frustrations, fears, nightmares, determinations, and interactions with the white world and academe within this neocolonial context. I remember walking across campus at UCLA, for instance, singing to myself: "Whoi whoi whoi, man it brutal out deh," overwhelmed by the breadth of the university, the cold and impersonal nature of not only the school but the city itself, and the absolute absence of any familiar cultural markers or of others who shared my background.

One of the aspects of the Itals' music that drew me to them was their frequent use of proverbs. In fact, Keith Porter is the greatest living proverb master among reggae artists. Only Bob Marley's use of proverbs is comparable. To acclaim Porter the greatest roots reggae proverb master, alongside Marley, is not only to acknowledge that his collective works include by far the largest number of proverbial expressions of any artist but also to recognize that the proverbs he draws upon come from the widest ranges of sources, biblical, English, American, and Jamaican. Furthermore, his use of proverbs entails the most consistently complex rhetorical strategies of any artist. In my survey of six albums, I have identified no fewer than eighty-five proverbs, which averages between fourteen and fifteen proverbs per album.

A number of stylistic features stand out in songs containing proverbs. One is a recurring structure in which a desired goal and obstacle are presented. In these songs the proverbs help in rhetorically resolving the conflicts and ensuring the success of the goal. Another feature is what I have referred to as the oracular use of proverb clusters. A third is an innovative use of traditional proverbs and the invention of new proverbs based on traditional ones. In this chapter, I focus on these elements of the Itals' proverb use, placing them within the contexts of the warrior/priest persona, forms of address, and negotiative strategies; and I examine potential meanings of proverbial items.

Rhetorical Structure of Songs: Desired Goal/Obstacle

Several elements of the Itals' proverb use are striking and connect to aspects of my previous discussions. The persona of the warrior/priest is certainly prominent. A close examination of this group's lyrics reveals more particulars of this persona and its relationship to proverb use. I noted in the previous chapter that proverbs often play roles in the rhetorical negotiation of power between two opposing forces. In the Itals' compositions, the most common strategy of songs is to identify an obstacle and the accompanying frustration or pain one encounters in confronting it. Alongside the obstacle, a desirable goal is also presented. Some of the emotional tension of the songs arises from this structure, which mirrors the dominant experience of Africans in the New World, as well as of other colonized, marginalized, or oppressed peoples. This structure reflects the epic and heroic journey and the mythical battle between good and evil that is so central to Rastafari ideology.

In some songs the conflict is between the speaker (the righteous) and external forces. For example, in "Herbs Pirate," the desired goal is for the speaker to have the freedom to plant, cultivate, and harvest his crop, make a good living, and live a peaceful life. The impediment to this goal are the "pirates" who steal the crop. In "Roll Rastafari Chariot," the confrontation is between the righteous and the "weak head," or those who would be "stumbling blocks" to the fulfilling of Rastafari prophecy. Just as often the struggle involves internal forces. The desirable goal in "Jah Calling" is spiritual surrender, and the obstacle, earthly temptations. Similarly, "Temptation" is a sermon concerned with the war between internal urges; on the one hand, to become involved in "fussing and fighting" and, on the other, to stay on the righteous path of word/sound/power. As such, the songs are focused on practical problems that are faced particularly by oppressed people; hunger, poverty, crime, self-respect, and negotiations with those in power.

Proverbs in Itals' songs play a decisive role in the proposed resolutions of problems, as they typically do in social discourse (Abrahams 1968a, 1968b; Seitel 1969; Briggs 1985). In some cases proverbs help to critique the problem or obstacle, and in other instances they negotiate the conflict, proposing—or more accurately, becoming—symbolic solutions. In the tradition of word/ sound/power, the proverb encapsulates the new reality. To put it another way, proverbs deconstruct not only the Babylonian system (Prahlad 1995), but many specific social situations that grow out of that system's influence. In keeping with Rastafari ideology, social circumstances or events are viewed in the larger context of a hostile and oppressive philosophy, not as isolated phenomenon. Thus, the solution always involves creating a new and radical reality based on spiritual principles. These elements will become clearer as our discussion continues.

"Truth Must Reveal" is a beautifully crafted, somber composition whose instrumental introduction creates a meditative mood upon which build the lyrics of the song. Musically, the song is introduced by a serene singular organ note that becomes the central thread, changing as chords change but remaining a sustained, singular sound. Beneath this sound is a bubbling, grumbling bass that exudes simultaneously agitation and reflection, evoking an image of an African priest in a posture similar to that of Rodin's *The Thinker*. In this case, however, the figure's brow is furrowed, as he reflects on the indecency of colonialization and the pain it has inflicted on millions. And, in this portrait, he is standing, staff in his hands. The dominant drum sound is an insistent, defiant splash on the three beat; and the kete punctuates periodically. The kete is especially narrative in response to the proverbs and during the last stanza, in which the power of Jah is lyrically summoned. The vocal emphasis is on the one and three beats; thus, the bass drum doubly accents the second emphasis of the measure. For example, in the phrase "Got to Reveal," "got" is on the one, and "veal" on the three. So the heavy drum splash is coming at the same time that the voices sing "veal," making it more accurately "veal!" The overall mood of the song is not only reflective but wise, even joyful. The joyfulness arises from the persona's source of meditation, Jah, and from contemplation of the deity and His power.

The rhetorical goal in the song is a just world, and the obstacle, the colonial system and those with wealth and power who perpetuate that system. The song is rooted in the experience of hardship and historical oppression endured by African Jamaicans and colonized people worldwide. A component of this experience is an acute awareness of the gap between the haves and have-nots. Some of these sentiments are captured in the first verse, which contains two proverb allusions, and in the chorus, in which two proverbs are used:

I and I who live
out here in the ghetto
We a feel it, Jah know-ow!
So we **bound to reveal it.**
[chorus, sung by backup singers] Got to reveal,
[sung by Porter in antiphony] **Who can't hear will feel.**
[sung by backup singers] Got to reveal,
[sung by Porter in antiphony] Then you know what I mean.
[sung by backup singers] Got to reveal,
[sung by Porter in antiphony] **Truth that is hidden must reveal, reveal.**

The first allusion is to the proverb **Who feels it knows it**, and the second to **The truth that is hidden must reveal**. The use of these allusions reveals Porter's ability to borrow from the language of proverb in composing and to play with the syntax, sense, and images to create new shades of meaning and poetic tropes. Here the two allusions foreshadow the proverbs that follow, suggesting the closeness of Jah to his people and the imminent revelation of truth.

Who can't hear will feel is a common reggae proverb, meaning generally that those (the oppressors) who seem incapable of hearing and heeding pleas for justice, humaneness, moral and spiritual principles, and who seem oblivious to warnings and prophecies will ultimately suffer and be damned. The proverb examines the same human capacity as the allusions above—feeling. In the first case, feeling precipitates insight and truthtelling. In the latter, feeling is a negative consequence of being unable to hear and respond to external or internal voices. In the first, feeling is the validation of cultural pain; in the second, it signifies punishment eventually reaped by oppressors.

In the second stanza, several lines are drawn from the proverb **Money is**

the root of all evil. The same creative license that characterizes the allusions above are reflected, as the proverb is transformed into an active picture.

when the rich man do wrong
them walk with them money
the root of all evil and violence.
And when the poor man, yes
when the poor man do wrong
Them got to stand the penalty,
and Jah know this should never be.

The proverb here functions to characterize the oppressors, pointing to a particular moral deficiency: their obsession with material wealth that leads to cruelty, corruption, and violence. The critique is strengthened through the use of a biblical proverb.

"Herbs Pirate" is another song that illustrates this structure, which can be compared to Dundes's "lack/lack liquidated" motifeme for Native American folktales (Dundes 1965, 206–5). Innovating upon Propp's folktale morphology, Dundes delineates a number of structural types of Native American tales, each type having a different set of "motifemic" elements. The simplest type, regardless of how elaborate the details and descriptions may be, can be reduced to two motifemes: lack and lack liquidated. In these tales, the narrative is set in motion by the absence of a particular object or state of being; and that "thing" is acquired by the tale's protagonist. For example, in one tale a monster is holding all of the water in the world (lack, for the people); and a hero slays the monster, releasing the water (lack liquidated). This mirrors the structure of the songs involving a goal and an obstacle. The songs go a step further, however, adding an analysis of the social factors that produced the lack. The most recurrent lack in Itals' songs is freedom, in every sense of the word, and lack is usually liquidated through the power of Jah.

"Herbs Pirate" is the story of a farmer whose crop is stolen by pirates (those who sit around doing nothing, preying on the harvest of others). Like most Itals songs, this one is grounded in social/historical critique. The speaker "was born and growed in the ghetto." His parents could not afford to send him to school, so he "turned to do some cultivation." The critique characterizes the pirates: "Them rob from them mother, even them brother too / Don't know what to say, thief a man won't do." They are people without ethics, who will do anything to get what they want. While the pirates are the obvious obstacle to the speaker's freedom and peace of mind, they are foregrounded in the larger context of the system, which limited the speaker's options in the first place; thus, the system itself is implicated as the most significant obstacle. In fact, the symbols "pirate" and "cultivation" cannot be divorced from the historical referents of colonizers and African civilizations. Echoes of these larger markers are responsible for much of the song's poetic and emotional depth. The proverb used to liberate the speaker is one of those we encountered in the previous song. Its placement in the last stanza gives it the quality of a moral at the end of a parable:

Seven days a week, I've got to work the field.
And they know it's the only way I can get my meal.
Who can't hear, dem bound to feel,
It was written in the book, thief a man,
thou shalt not steal.

Who can't hear . . . invokes the prophecy of *Revelation* and the inevitable punishment of the wicked. Its occurrence twice on *Brutal* reflects the strong "fire and brimstone" sermonic tone of the album, on which sermon songs carrying the message "repent or be damned" represent a significant subgenre. Within this subgenre, the threat of divine retribution is used as a vehicle to intensify the nationalistic impulse for radical social change.

Another example of the lack/lack liquidated structure negotiated by a proverb is "Rastafari Chariot," whose title and central metaphor demonstrate the poetic brilliance of Porter's songwriting. Drawing upon biblical images, Porter creates a memorable metaphor—Rastafari Chariot—evoking the dramatic and relentless power of Jah, while also signifying on the chariot of traditional spirituals ("Swing low sweet chariot / comin' for to carry me home"). There is an element of humor in the song, owing to the dissonance between the semantic meaning of the lyrics and the playfulness of the melody line. This melody line is established initially and carried throughout by the horns. Thus the lines of the chorus, "Roll Rastafari chariot along, I say roll," is sung to a playful melody. This playfulness infuses the stanzas, even when semantic meanings are serious, affecting the way in which we hear the proverbs.

The first proverb in stanza 1 presents a militant solution to the obstacle, or problem, of nonspiritual people:

If a weak heart get in the way,
I and I will roll it over him

Stumbling block must be removed,
once and for all let's get in the mood
and roll Rastafari chariot along . . .

The next proverb comes in stanza 2, which illustrates the historical contextualization of Rastafari experience, the divine mode through which lack is liquidated, and the role of proverb in this structure. Rastafari is depicted in the
context of biblical history, and the speaker's ultimate consolation is in the
knowledge that Jah is in control. All roads and all chains of events are leading
to oneness with the deity, and the momentary period of slavery and neocolonialism is transcended as the system falls:

Jah so loved the world,
so he sent I and I his son
On earth to be prepared
to meet Him when Him come
[backup singers] It a go red
Rolling stone don't gather no moss,
[next two lines sung in harmony by entire group]
No more slave master
No more boss.

The proverb is also chosen in part—and quite ingeniously—to link with the
central song motif of "rolling." Because of the prominence of this motif, one
naturally connects the stone to the chariot. The further contextualization of
the proverb in the stanza makes it easy to read "rolling stone" as "New World
African" or "righteous." The proverb defines the resolution to an ancient
conflict, captures the joy of liberation, and insinuates the spiritual demeanor
reflected in the expression "In the world, but not of the world."

Oracular Proverbs

Another prominent feature of the Itals' songs is the grouping together of several proverbs. I refer to these groups as proverb clusters. Individual proverbs
and clusters become symbolic signifiers, carrying associative meanings, evoking images of recurring social interactions, and establishing through the principle of word/sound/power the manifestation of a desired goal. I have also
mentioned that these clusters are oracular and would like to explore this aspect in more detail.

Although there is no research data suggesting a direct link between Rastas and traditions of West African divination, I wish to draw theoretical parallels here. Ifá divination, which is derived from the Yoruba of West Africa, is widespread among New World African communities in the Caribbean and South America. Within this system, clients typically come to the diviner (or *babalao*) for counsel and guidance. Similar to roots reggae, divinations offer strategies for coping with everyday problems. According to Matibag, divinations "must be understood as mediating between the client's misfortunes and the social structure" (1997, 152). The diviner's method for obtaining insights may vary, from casting palm nuts or cowry shells, for example, but the configurations of how these objects land are generally called *odu*. For each possible *odu* a corresponding set of verses, proverbs, and sacrifices is narrated to the client, who "listens quietly through irrelevant verses until the diviner recites one that deals with his particular problem; this he accepts as the answer to his question" (Bascom 1981, 15). The idea that the interpretation and the application of texts rest with the client is critically important and contradicts stereotypical notions suggesting that the diviner imposes remedies. The client is an active participant in the identification of and prescriptive medicine for his problem.

The themes of this system are divided into five kinds of good and five kinds of evil. The good include "long life or 'not death,' money, marriage or wives, children, and victory . . . over one's enemies." The evil include "death, sickness, fighting, the want of money, and loss" (Matibag 1997, 153; see also Bascom 1969). One is struck immediately by the similarities between the system of Ifá and the discursive structure of roots reggae. With the exception of familial concerns, the conflicts focused upon by warrior/priests are similar to those found in Ifá divination. Long life (as in eternal life), victory (over Babylon), fighting (the spiritual and political war), loss (the removal from the African homeland and loss of cultural elements), sickness (brought about by oppression and cultural brainwashing), the desire for a more comfortable material existence (money), and death are certainly recurring motifs in roots reggae.

Obviously, reggae artists are not working within as elaborate a system as Ifá; nor are they in most cases speaking only to a specific individual. Nevertheless, they are offering spiritual/practical guidance, and individual listeners often respond as if the songs were written to them about their particular situations. Of note is the tendency in Ifá divination and in reggae to use symbolic and metaphorical language in offering solutions to social problems. One effect of this strategy is to leave the interpretation somewhat open-ended. Another result is to ground the proposed solution in a specific cultural and spiritual worldview that, in effect, defines the parameters of the problem and the appropriate attitudes toward it. Reggae discourse is filled with examples of oracular songs. An extreme illustration is Justin Hinds's beautiful "In This Time," which consists almost entirely of proverb clusters, without the benefit of other lyrics that might identify a specific problem.

The higher the monkey climbs
the more he expose.
Grief comes to those
who love the crowd the most.
Plant corn, can't reap peas
Whatever you sow, you shall reap.
[Chorus]
In this time in this time
It's only the strong will survive
[repeat]

When you go to Rome
Do as the Romans do.
If you . . .
That you must also do.
No cup no break, no coffee won't throw away
No cup no break, no coffee won't throw away.

Come here to drink milk
Don't come here to count cows.
When you go to Rome
Do as the Romans do.
You play with fire, fire will burn you.
Spit in the sky, will fall in your eye.

[Chorus]

By contrast, proverb clusters within the Itals songs are always found in the context of nonproverbial language. More time is taken to analyze, critique, and diagnose the malady for which the proverbial balm is prescribed than in the above example. In fact, time is a prominent concern, for the proverb is sung within the context of sacred time, which is carefully sculpted by the players of instruments to fit the thematic issue being addressed. One effect of the reggae rhythm is to open up a cultural sphere of time and space, where the essence of Rastafari sensibility, or vibe, can be experienced. This experience is a substantial part of the "medicine."

There is evidence that reggae proverb users draw upon the same *social* meanings of certain proverbs in composing their lyrics. Similar goal/obstacles are identified and associative images evoked by the same proverb in different songs. There are a number of proverbs that recur in reggae discourse and, in fact, even clusters that have become traditional. Common expressions include **The hotter the battle, the sweeter the victory; Teeth and tongue have fe meet some day; A hungry man is an angry man; What you sow, you reap; Iron sharpeneth iron; They give you basket to carry water; The half has never been told; Who feels it knows it; The stone that the builder refuse shall be the head cornerstone; Rain a fall but the dutty tough; Every tub must sit on its own bottom; and Habee habee no wantee wantee, and wantee wantee can't gettee gettee.**

A listener closely attuned to reggae discourse will recognize immediately the goal addressed in a particular song, as well as the range of possible obstacles, simply by hearing one of these proverbs. They will know, for instance, that a song containing the proverb **Iron sharpeneth iron** is in some way going to engage the goal of cultural unity and an obstacle to that goal. When we compare Culture's "**Iron sharpeneth iron**" and the Itals' "Temptation," we find that this is the case. As a second example, a well-versed listener will recognize that a song using the proverb **Every tub must sit on its own bottom** will in some way reference the days of Armageddon, include the goal of ultimate spiritual salvation, and critique possible impediments to achieving this goal. Again, when we listen to Culture's, "Weeping and Wailing," and The Itals' "Hallelujah," this argument is confirmed.

Proverbs and proverb clusters have a traditionality within reggae that substantiates the view of these songs as primarily diagnostic and healing. That this rhetorical strategy would become a key marker in roots reggae (and the recurrence of particular proverbs) is not surprising, when we consider that the pioneers of this genre were drawing upon the same spiritual and cultural sources and sharing freely among themselves as they developed as songwriters and musicians. Even a casual survey of song titles reveals a substantial number of proverbs or allusions to proverbial expressions. Consider Bob Marley's "Time Will Tell," "Small Axe," "Who the Cap Fit," Them Belly Bull," and "Rat Race"; the Wailing Souls' "Lay it on the Line" (from the album of the same title), "Old Broom," "Things and Time," "Who No Waan Come,"

"Who Lives it"; and the Itals' "Jah Helps Those," "Easy to Catch," "Time Will Tell," "Seeing Is Believing," "Don't Wake the Lion," "Action," "Truth Must Reveal," "Never Say Never," "Blood (Thicker Than Water)," "Wanti Wanti," "Time (Take No Share)," and "Happen Before the Time."

From an American perspective, we might view these titles as trite or catchy, but when considered within Rastafari reggae philosophical discourse, their significance as components of ritualistic healing becomes apparent. Such titles validate the songs' claim as medicinal balm offered by wise and divinely inspired warrior/priests. The effect of this rhetoric is intensified in the overall context of an album, and even more so if a listener is familiar with several of the artist's albums. We might glance first at the list of song titles on a given album, which in themselves reflect the warrior/priest persona and their role relative to their audience. Consider, for example, the Itals' *Brutal*, which contains "Run Baldhead," "Action," "Rastafari Chariot," "Truth Must Reveal," "Give Me What I Want," "Time Will Tell," and "Smile Knotty Dread."

Additional prescriptive or oracular allusions can be read in album cover art and in musical and lyrical texts, which are based on Rastafari ideology and ritual. While the productions of most artists are rooted in the same philosophical elements, different artists draw upon different ritualized practices for their rhetoric and prescriptions. In general, however, the most influential ritualized Rastafari practice in reggae discourse is "reasoning," which is one element that separates this kind of reggae from others. The absence of songs explicitly suggesting the liberating qualities of dance, for instance, is striking when comparing roots reggae with ska and dancehall. The absence of romantic compositions is just as prominent. While music and dance have implicit medicinal potential, roots reggae privileges the power of the word. Chang and Chen credit Bob Marley with this influential shift in the focus of Jamaican music: "For the first time reggae had found a singer whose lyrics were so striking that sometimes you stopped dancing and actually listened to the words. Rhythm and melody were slowly pushed into the background until lyrics and harmony came to almost completely dominate" (1998, 58). These authors fail to note that this shift has ideological foundations. Singers in this tradition view their song performances as invitations to reasoning sessions with their audiences. *Reasoning becomes the dominant ritualistic frame of reference for the rhetorizing of warrior/priests; and prescriptions are offered within this contextual frame.*

Oracular songs by the Itals promote reasoning and intensify the rhetorical portrait of the artists as healers. Such songs, which can be found on every album beginning with the earliest compositions and following through to the most recent, are so numerous that I can only touch on some of them here. One of the earliest oracular songs is "Time Is Getting Harder." This composition critiques the increasing difficulty of life for poor Jamaicans, in part by echoing commonly heard phrases: "time is getting harder," "rich are getting richer / poor are getting poorer." The speaker goes to a friend to borrow money, but his friend is trying to borrow money for himself. The song also criticizes poor people for fighting among themselves, and the proverb cluster follows this criticism:

All of these things were written in the book a long time:
Fittest of the fittest shall survive in a while.
Simple trash can blind eyes.
But blind a lead blind in a this yer time.

The cluster serves the same function as the singular proverb in the goal/ obstacle/resolution structure, except that the resolution is more complex. One effect of the cluster is to intensify and strengthen the representative power that is ultimately responsible for dissolving the obstacle. That power is referenced less directly here than in later Itals compositions, alluded to only in the line "All of these things were written in the book." The first proverb takes on tremendous import in this context. It suggests that the righteous are the fittest and, by implication, argues for a conversion to Rastafari. The next proverb encompasses two meanings. First, "trash" can be equated to the madness of life in a neocolonial society and "blind eyes" to losing sight of the ultimate reality—Jah. It is, thus, a reminder to stay focused on a spiritual reality. The last proverb of the cluster suggests that the ungodly are leading the ungodly. The cluster identifies neocolonial social madness as the obstacle and a focus on Jah as the solution.

One of the strongest oracular songs is "Brutal," which has a proverb cluster in each of the two stanzas. "Brutal" focuses on the recurrent themes of (1) hardship and (2) spirituality as a vehicle for social change, which appear in so many other songs. The chorus affirms the brutality of "out deh" while cautioning the Rasta brethren and sistren to face the harshness with continued dignity, patience, and aplomb: "Whoi whoi whoi, man me say it brutal out deh / But if fe cool Jah man, cool Jah man." The first stanza is comprised almost entirely of proverbs.

If I should feed one child and starve the other.
I'd rather be down with my brothers and sisters.
'Cause a hungry man is an angry man.
And a drowning man will catch at straws.

While the material meanings of the proverbs within the context of an economically struggling society like Jamaica are apparent, they are not, in fact, the meanings that Porter intended most to emphasize. With an understanding of the intended meanings, the reference to spiritual power as the determining factor in "liquidating" lack becomes clear. Porter's encoding of all of the proverbs is based on a spiritual ideology; thus the images of food refer to spiritual nourishment, and drowning alludes to being without a spiritual center. The food motif is continued in the next stanza:

Man cannot live by only bread,
But every mouth must be fed.
Never bite the hand that feed you,
'Cause the good you do will live with you.
Man got to practice what them preach, now and then
Else he'll never reach the land where there's no night,
there's only day.

Four of the seven proverbs contain food-related motifs, creating a complex of reflective meditations on the relationship between human beings and the deity, and driving home the idea that spirituality is at the heart of solutions to social crises. Specifically, **Feed one child** . . . and **A hungry man** . . . refer to the presence or absence of not only material but also spiritual sustenance. **Only bread** . . . is a playful twist of expected meaning, as the food motif is reversed and applied to material reality. **Never bite the hand** . . . is a warning against forgetting that the gifts of life and abundance come from Jah. Thus, against the background of economic poverty and desperation, the critique that envisions spirituality as a primary solution is foregrounded. As such, the obstacle/lack is redefined. It is not simply the brutality of the system that is addressed, but the ungodliness of its perpetrators and many of its victims. The last two proverbs speak specifically to this latter issue, asserting the importance of living a spiritually centered life, in practice as well as in theory, as a condition for reaching "the land where's there no night, only day."

Several other songs illustrate the same relationship between proverb clusters and spiritual resolutions to lack—for example, "Jah Calling," "Kill

Crime," and "Make Merry," all from *Give Me Power*. "Jah Calling" is a sermon declaring "This could be the very last train to Zion" and urging listeners to take heed. Proverb clusters occur in both the first and second stanzas, addressing the obstacle of earthly temptations:

Some would say that **the chip don't fly
too far from the block.**
But in this time, I and I got to
Hold on to what we've got.
So long ago I keep a tellin' dem a say, tellin' dem a say,
Should **never the foolish one try to fool you**, no way.
Teeth and tongue they got to meet some sweet day
I wanna be among the number to share the sweet I say
Won't you hear when Jah call.

Porter's correlations for the images in the first proverb are chip = people and block = Jah. The suggestion is that people should not stray too far from their spiritual nature. The second proverb asserts the speaker's determination to remain close to Jah. Proverb 3 is a warning against being led astray. The final proverb signifies the ultimate meeting between Jah (teeth) and Satan (tongue), good and evil. As such, it effectively conveys the proposed resolution to the conflicts addressed in the song: Jah will be the victor, ushering in a new age characterized by truth and purity.

"Kill Crime" conveys a similar message, except its rhetorical mask is the prevalence of crime and the urgency to rid it from society. As with other songs, the obstacle is rooted in the system, as the final lines declare: "This kind of system keepin' my people driftin' / This kind of system . . . / I can't stand the system!" The proverb cluster in stanza 1 offers social critique as well as defining the "answer" to the problem:

**Too much rat never dig good hole.
Some ha fe come, some ha fe go.
If your heart is willing and your flesh is weak**
now is the time, Jah Jah you've got to seek.
**If you want to get to heaven
You got to build ahead on earth.**

Too much rat . . . is a traditional Jamaican proverb, which means that too many people working on a project will ensure its failure. The second proverb means that people are coming and going (birthing and dying) all the time. Together, the two proverbs convey a reflective and mystical view of life: the natural cycle of birth and death is a good thing, for it ensures space and opportunity for each person to work on his or her salvation. The next item is a biblical proverb, used here as any Christian minister might use it. One should enlist God as support in one's efforts to live a righteous life; otherwise, earthly temptations may lead one off the path. The final proverb echoes the meaning of the previous one. The cluster advises each individual to realize his or her place in the natural and cosmological cycles and actively pursue spiritual salvation. The cluster is offered as a solution to ills within the system; more specifically, it is a "prescription" to "Kill Crime, shame and disgrace / overcome hunger and poverty."

Similar sentiments are conveyed by a proverb cluster in "Make Merry." On the surface, the song seems simply to celebrate the capacity of Jamaicans to have fun, in spite of hardships. But a deeper analysis reveals a subtext containing the recurrent motifs from clusters discussed above. In the first stanza the speaker observes people "dancing in the street," although "Some don't have a bite to eat." But the cluster that follows casts these lines in a different light:

Some try to put the best outside.
Some try to find a place to hide.
What you sow, it's that you reap.
Silent river runs deep, yeah, oh yeah.

Porter's intended meaning for the first proverb is that some people wear a false face, pretending to be morally good when, in fact, their smiles are attempts to cover up the immoral things they have been doing. The "place to hide" in this case is "making merry." The second proverb takes on a specific, *situational* meaning in the context of the cluster, as it refers to those people who have been committing crimes but who are now feigning innocence. The final proverb, which refers to Jah's omnipresence, anchors the cluster in divine intervention as a source of resolution. It is important to note that the cluster does not refer to everyone dancing in the street nor does it negate the positive claim being made for the unconquerable, lively spirit of Jamaicans. Its application extends beyond those making merry and becomes a signifier for wrongdoers wherever they may be.

Creativity and Innovation

Among the challenges faced by the Itals over the years has been one that confronts every other reggae artist: how to continue making marketable records as the trends and tastes of consumers change. For roots artists equally committed to a Rastafari message and music that remains anchored in Nyabinghi aesthetics, this has been a particularly difficult task, and only a few individuals and groups have been able to achieve it—Burning Spear, Culture, Bunny Wailer, and the Itals, for example. One obstacle has been the decline of interest among Jamaicans in this type of music, as dancehall became the favored popular form. As Chang and Chen note, "Reggae magazines lavish ecstatic reviews on 'cultural' groups like Israel Vibration, The Congos and The Itals, but ghetto massives mostly couldn't care a hoot about such music" (1998, 61). This has meant a reliance on foreign markets, a situation with inherent complications. Another struggle has been to find record companies to produce and market the music. Artistically integrating contemporary trends and Nyabinghi has proved another formidable challenge, as has continuing to produce songs with fresh and innovative lyrics that convey the cornerstone messages of roots music.

In the effort to meet these challenges, the music of the Itals has to an extent become less "rootsy" as it has integrated more and more elements of contemporary jazz, rock, and rhythm and blues. There are fewer echoes of Revivalist singing and Nyabinghi chanting and drumming. The narrative voice of the kete is heard less often. As the tempo has increased, there is less time and space in the music. Once inside the interior of songs on *Brutal*, for instance, one can wander for days; however, the space and time in songs on the most recent CDs is less expansive, more fast-paced and American. There has also been a lyrical movement toward more romantic songs and compositions that address a general audience, which means a decrease in sermonic songs and those that specifically address members of the Diasporic community. The remarkable thing, however, is the extent to which the Itals' music remains rooted in Nyabinghi aesthetics.

One of the lyrical features that has persisted through all of the different periods and helped root Itals songs in the Rastafari reggae tradition is the continued use of proverbs and proverb clusters. In some cases, proverbs have been worded and applied in much the same way they were in songs from the earliest recordings; but in many instances there are innovations in form and application. "Sing Hallelujah" from *Easy* is a good illustration of the group's efforts to keep up with the times while continuing to retain elements of roots reggae tradition. Musically, the tune is sparse and more up-tempo than songs from the three previous albums. Instead of the heavy splashing sound on the drum, there is a cleaner, less emotionally charged sound. The bass and keyboard are more akin to the sounds of digitally produced (as in drum and keyboard machines) music, rather than the rich, resonant tones of earlier reggae that told such elaborate and moving stories. The beat is an updated ska rhythm, but there are no horns. The focus of the song lyrically, in terms of addressee and subject, is more ambiguous than in previous compositions, and the lines, much shorter and choppier. The song is more "pop." However, we can still find resonances of recurrent Itals themes; and the song is filled with proverbs. There is an innovation on the tradition of proverb clusters here as, rather than occurring next to one another, proverbs come at the end of short stanzas and at the end of the chorus:

[Chorus]
Sing Hallelujah
Sing Hallelujah
Every heart a get them desire.
Sing Hallelujah
Sing Hallelujah
Never seen smoke without fire.

The world is out there
Gwan go get your share
**Jah will never give a one
more than he can bear.**
In this kind of evolution
**Every tub a sit
upon its own bottom.**

The I will be the conquering
Sit upon the throne
with king of kings.

Say mi heart, mi soul
To Jah Jah the control
That's when I know
The half has never been told.

The world is out there
Gwan go get your share
Even if you climb on a broken chair.

There are a number of themes alluded to here, but none convincingly explored. Nor is the structure of goal/obstacle as discernible as it is in songs from the previous albums. As a result of these elements and the ambiguity of whom the song is addressed to, there is a greater vagueness about the proverb meanings. The central issue (goal) is getting one's heart's desire. However, one cannot tell if the desire is godliness or social/material progress. The first two lines of stanza 1 would suggest the latter. The proverb's most likely meaning in this context is that Jah will allow only so much suffering before granting more material comforts. The second stanza poses similar difficulties. Does "evolution" refer to the unfolding of prophecy or to social progress? In the larger context of the Itals' works, we would suppose the former; and the proverb in reggae discourse has usually connoted armageddon. Stanza 3 supports this reading, as does stanza 4, which contains another common reggae proverb, **The half has never** . . . , which usually refers to the colonial/Babylonian denial of the African/righteous experience and contribution to civilization.

The composition would seem then to follow the structure and theme of most Itals songs. The resolution is the coming revelation, at which time the righteous will sit by Jah's side. There is, however, no clearly articulated obstacle to this goal. This effectively removes the element of social critique that is usually prominent in songs by this group, thereby eliminating most of the tension that usually adds to the songs' impact. Because the lyrical context surrounding the proverbs is so sparse, and the musical context so devoid of traditional Rastafari signifiers, it is more difficult to extrapolate much depth of meaning from the proverbs. A listener unfamiliar with either the Itals or the traditional *social* meanings of the proverbs in reggae will certainly be at a disadvantage. Or perhaps the song is composed to allow listeners a chance to interpret the proverbs in whatever ways they wish.

Other songs on *Easy* are more successful in conveying proverbial depth, even without the benefit of rootsy musical contexts. "Time (Take No Share)," for instance, contains several proverb clusters and several singular proverbs, all of which resonate with profound poetic and philosophical beauty. Musically, the song has a similar sparseness as most tunes on *Easy*, placing more burden on the lyrical content. The rhetorical structure is classically goal/obstacle, with an extended critique of "them" and their absurd and misguided philosophy.

The first proverb is used in stanza 1, which contains a critical analysis of "them." We have already encountered this proverb from a Culture song,

"Hand a Bowl," and discussed its *social* reference to the pretense of support from those who would keep the righteous oppressed. Its meaning here echoes that *social* usage:

Them nuh want us to share the sweet
Them want I carry them heavy load
They want **to give I basket to carry water.**
See them a try and them just can't conquer.

The second line of this excerpt signifies on a song by Larry Marshall, "Heavy Heavy Load." The line evokes memories of slavery, spoken of in that song, and Marshall's rootsy musical and singing styles. Lines of Marshall's song are as follows:

It's a heavy heavy load Jah Jah children a carry.
Through this rocky rocky mountain.
Through this bushy bushy valley.
Big big men them walking behind us
If we ever make a slip now
we feel it by them whip.
If we ever make a slide now
them stick us with their sword.
Great tribulation along this journey.
Victimization along with sufferation.
["Heavy heavy load Jah Jah children a carry" is sung by backup singers after each line]

Hence, the well-versed listener will hear, in the Itals' song, echoes of Marshall's hit, "Heavy Heavy Load." The listener, furthermore, may be reminded of two of this artist's other hits, "Nanny Goat" and "Throw Me Corn," two of the earliest examples of reggae proverb songs. "Throw Me Corn," along with tunes by Justin Hinds, pioneered the tradition of using proverbs in reggae to address social/political/ethical problems:

Me throw me corn a door me no call no fowl
Suppose you want to pick it up is your business.
O Yeah. Yeah Yeah Yeah.
Whether you are black, or you are white.
It is you, It is you.
Why won't you stop your fussing and your fighting.
Why won't you stop your and killing,
It is you, I'm talking to.
[Spoken] **If the cap fits you mon,
then wear it!**

The tune "Nanny Goat," like "Heavy Heavy Load," is a seminal recording in the history and evolution of roots reggae, sharing this distinction with songs like "O Carolina" by the Folkes Brothers, "Carry Go Bring Come" by Justin Hinds and the Dominoes, "Simmer Down" by Bob Marley and the Wailers, "The Israelites" by Desmond Dekker, and other recordings that mark periods, styles, and musical/lyrical genius. A stanza of "Nanny Goat" reads:

You said that you don't need my love anymore
Because you found someone new.
But I'm not gonna let you go.
Because I know you are the only one for me.
Old time people used to say,
Sweet nanny goat have to run him belly.
O no, oh no, I'm not gonna let you go.

The main point here is that, with one phrase, the Itals evoke a deep vein of reggae heritage that helps to compensate for the absence of lyrical and musical depth in their song. A second proverb and cluster in stanza 2 also connect to the song's title and theme of time:

You see time
Ain't no substitute for time.
Time is a master
and **time waits on no one.**
See length of days
How Jah got it in his hand.

Here the proverbs are used to elaborate on Rastafari mythology, specifically articulating the relationships between Jah, human beings, and time. Time is viewed as a tool of the deity, a device for ordering creation, and a gift offered to human beings. The paradox of the gift, though, is that it casts a foreboding shadow over human lives, and people are forever at its mercy. Taken together, the three expressions convey quite emphatically the power of external forces over human lives and, implicitly, the deity and His power as a resolution for the crises spoken of in the song.

The social critique is furthered in subsequent stanzas, becoming crystallized in the last stanza, which contains a proverb cluster. The stanza uses proverbs in much the same fashion as the proverbial painting by Breughel, to portray the "world upside down." A compelling tension is created between the serious message being conveyed and the humor of images depicting "them" in all their absurdity. This depiction is an innovation on clusters in previous songs that used a much more religiously oriented rhetoric in drawing critical comparisons between Babylon and the righteous:

I see them **trying to force water
over a hill**.
Saying them a try to get the
Time to stand still.
I even see them **putting the cart
before the horse**.
That's when I know
they put **the first thing before the last**,
I don't give a damn or blast.

In essence, the stanza is a list of absurdities, characterizing people who are out of touch with reality and suggesting this as their defining characteristic. The lines capture a common sentiment of African-derived people about Western society and those in power: they are fools.

"Wanti Wanti" is more akin to "Hallelujah" in its absence of a clearly articulated addressee or obstacle. It seems to be directed toward a lover but is even more open to interpretation than "Hallelujah." The main innovation here lies in the title's allusion to the proverb, **Habee habee no wanti wanti, and wanti wanti no habee** and in the personification of the proverb in the song: "A me name wanti wanti [My name is wanti wanti] / Me wanti / And if me get it me will tek it." As with the phrase "heavy load" in "Time," the proverb here signifies on several previous instances of its use in reggae discourse. Most notably, it is used by Max Romeo in "Smile Out of Style" from another seminal album, *War Ina Babylon*. Romeo's song critiques economic hardship in Jamaica. Selected lines from two stanzas and the chorus are as follows:

Cost of living is rising high while
poverty flowing
Rain is falling but
no seeds is growing.

[Chorus]
Smile out a style, love on the walls
screwface is back in town.

**Wanti wanti
can't gettee**.

**Gettee gettee
them no wanti.
Habee habee no wanti while
wanti wanti can't gettee.**

Thus the *social* meaning of the proverb from both Jamaican vernacular and reggae discourse resonate in the Itals' song. The proverb criticizes the disparity of resources and power between the haves and the have-nots. This meaning is muted in the song, however, because of what seem to be sexual innuendos and allusions to romance in stanza 2 and the recurring lines: "Won't you give it to me / Give it up, give it up." The musical context adds to these innuendos, as it echoes dancehall and American disco or "rave" as much as roots reggae.

I've got something here in store
And if you get it once
You've got to come on down for more
Keep a walking through the same door
Like you did just once before
How I wanna check you out . . .

The combination of these factors makes the proverb cluster all the more difficult to translate.

Small mercy thankful received
I wonder what is really **up the sleeve.**
Eat little me say eat long.
That's how the weak can get strong strong.
Licki licki til you bite it.
Get on up, **hold tight**
if you are in doubt . . .

The first line of the stanza contains the only words in the song that might evoke religiousness. This is followed by a proverbial expression that sounds more American than Jamaican. The third line of the stanza is a common expression in Jamaica, suggesting a strategy for survival in harsh circumstances. It also recommends a philosophical approach to achieving longevity and convalescence, possibly keying the idea of cultural struggle. The next proverb reiterates the meaning of the previous, also communicating on another level a sexual innuendo. This duality of meaning is latent in the final expression. We can note in this cluster an experimental approach to creating and stretching the meanings of proverbs. Many such elements that pertain to proverbs in "Time," "Hallelujah," and "Wanti Wanti" also apply to other songs on *Easy*, including "Never Say Never," "Blood (Thicker Than Water)," and the title song, which we have previously discussed, "Easy to Catch." In comparison to earlier (and even later) works, these are not as rootsy and do not contain as compelling a use of proverbial materials.

While the Itals' more recent CD, *Modern Age*, continues the trend toward more romantic songs, it is at the same time a refreshing return to more rootsy sounds and lyrics. The warrior/priest persona dominates and is expanded to allow room for romance that is deep and spiritual. The songs on the LP are framed by a roots version of one of their earliest hits, "In a Dis Ya Time," at the beginning of the CD, and a ska version of the same song at the end. The second song, "Titanic," is a sermon, invoking the names of biblical figures such as Daniel, David, Jonah, Elijah, Moses, Joshua, Peter, Paul, Barabas, and John the Baptist. It offers a Rastafari commentary on the popular American interest in the SS *Titanic* by comparing the moment when the ship was sinking to the moment of Jah's second coming. "Render Love" is a beautifully poetic praise song, containing moments of prayer: "Wonderful counselor, my redeemer / Jesus Christ, Iyesus Christus / Tica-Amia, Alla praise Jah." The title song, "Modern Age," invents a proverb and applies it to contemporary people: **Modern age, primitive people**. The three proverb songs, "Together Forever," "Happen Before the Time," and "Almighty" all come toward the end of the CD.

"Together Forever" is a prayerful sermon that rings with joy and celebration. Its primary addressee is a general audience. The song is distinct from many earlier sermon songs in that its message is gentle rather than fiery and condemning. The chorus conveys the sense that a milestone has already been passed, implying that the unity spoken about in the rest of the song has already happened. This makes a significant rhetorical difference, especially in the context of a song with the goal/obstacle structure. In previous examples, the lack is liquidated through the invocation of the deity, sometimes involving the use of proverbs. The deity is not invoked here, though. The onus for resolution is placed entirely on the shoulders of fellow human beings. As such, an appeal to reasoning is made and many expressions connoting unity and mutual support are used. Speaking from a place of joy becomes a rhetorical strategy that helps to compensate for the absence of a direct invocation of Jah, capturing the pleasure that one might feel in His presence and conjuring the goal into existence.

Hurrah!! Hurrah!! Hurrah!!
Together forever.
Hurrah!! Hurrah!! Hurrah!!
Together forever.

The succeeding stanzas are rich with invented and traditional proverbs and clusters:

Be slow to anger, you better decline.
The more we stick together,
that's the way we survive.

That's why them trying so hard **to divide and conquer,**
but I and I know **seh no weak heart can enter.**
Because of *words, sound, power,*
I got to throw down my anger.

One to one is so unjust,
in this time you got to be conscious.
No victimization, no segregation,
Iron sharpen iron.

Remember, **One hand can't shake,**
a two it really take,
One hand wash the other.
It must be now or never,
Everyone is his brother's keeper.

The overriding concern of the proverbs is unity. This theme is expressed through images that convey intimacy and others that comment on separation and boundaries. The first proverb, for instance, depicts anger as a barrier to the unification spoken of in the second proverb. Both proverbial expressions in stanza 2 are concerned with separation. The first articulates one obstacle to unity—"their" age-old strategy of dividing those they seek to conquer. The next expression declares that they (the weak heart or ungodly) cannot enter Zion (the home of the righteous). Thus, both proverbs assist in painting a picture of "them," although one depicts separation negatively while the other portrays division in a positive light. The last two lines of the stanza allude again to the obstacle of anger, viewing it within Rastafari thought. To give in to anger could lead to negative word/sounds and material manifestations, ultimately undermining efforts for peace and unification.

The third stanza uses several proverblike expressions to promote fairness, justice, and humane interactions among human beings and societies. The underlying spiritual nature of the argument is apparent in the last line, a Rasta proverb we have already discussed. In fact, it would have been surprising had the proverb **Iron sharpeneth iron** not been used in this song, as it signifies—as much as any expression in reggae—the idea of unity and mutual support.

In the final cluster, we see the linking of proverbs by central image that is so characteristic of Itals compositions. "Hands" become a central image, symbolizing the work involved in creating a new society and suggesting touch as a symbol for brotherly love and cooperation. The references to simple everyday actions contained in the first two proverbs concretize the abstract theme of unity, giving the listener pleasant, sensory images on which to focus. **One hand can't shake** effectively conveys the loneliness of being apart from others, and **One hand** . . . captures the comfort of physical closeness and cooperation. The third proverb asserts the urgency for unity, and the fourth is a final appeal, grounding the sermon in biblical authority. Cumulatively, the cluster is one of the most effective and moving in the Itals' repertoire.

"Happen Before the Time" addresses those who are impatient for social change or material progress. Much of the song is in a didactic vein, offering advice. The goal is not only ultimate change but a patient and relaxed state of mind while working toward change. The obstacles are the addressee's impatience and the system that created the problem in the first place. The title and refrain are used proverbially, **Nothing ever happen before its time**; and several other invented and traditional proverbs are used in conjunction with this one, posing strategies for achieving the goal:

Nothing never happen before the time,
I mean it, can't you feel it?
Anything you wanna find,
it's there in the mind.
The things you want is not what you always get.
Use what you got till you get what you want.

This sermon song also represents a departure from many earlier ones. The song begins: "Be gentle, meek, and mild, we are of a kind," a tone that carries throughout and contrasts with the more aggressive tones of many songs on previous albums. Striking in this and other songs on the CD are the signs of a significantly different historical point in time from that one finds on albums such as *Brutal*. As the CD title suggests, these are songs for a modern age. There is a recognition that although the war may remain the same, the particularities of the battles have changed, owing to a number of factors. These include a rise in the economic and social status of some throughout the Diaspora; the internationalization of Rastafari; and the changing nature of Babylon itself, from the age of industrialization to the age of communication. Thus, the advice offered by the warrior/priests is often applicable to those whose major concerns are no longer survival or repatriation. They are speaking as well to survivors who now have before them the difficult task of operating within the system.

The proverbs in "Happen Before the Time" fit this general mode. They prescribe a mental attitude of patience, thoughtfulness and shrewdness, as well as promoting the notion that whatever becomes manifest begins with mental imaging. Again, the individual rather than the deity is given primary responsibility for providing solutions. Individuals and groups should apply their full creative powers to utilizing whatever means are available eventually to gain the things they most desire. However, one should not be downhearted if one's desires are not immediately fulfilled. Human power is limited, and the unfolding of events is ultimately "in the hands of time."

One final example of a proverb song from *Modern Age* is "Almighty," a creative synthesis of the prayer, praise, and sermonic genres. The chorus, for instance, incorporates elements of both prayer and praise songs and includes several proverbial statements. The second of these expressions parallels the structure of the first, leading to the playful use of "jolly" as an adjective formed from "Jah."

Almighty, you're my king, you're my Jah
You're my emperor.
Praise him as king, you get a kingly reward.
Praise him as Jah, you get a jolly reward.

The first stanza contains a proverb cluster and one of Porter's most interesting innovations:

Everyone got paid according to their work.
A them kind of things happening through the earth.

Some might think that it's **mind over matter,**
but the victory must be won though,
the battle is getting hotter.

The last proverb of this cluster is disguised by virtue of syntax. A traditional expression has been broken apart and reassembled in a different form to create this new one. For this reason, it may be unrecognizable as a proverb to listeners new to reggae. Customarily the proverb is **The hotter the battle, the sweeter the victory.** Here it has been transformed into an active mode, an imperative instead of an observation.

More than anything else, this composition is a praise song. Most of the text consists of testimonies to Jah's power and beauty, the speaker's love for him, and the speaker's encouragment to others to also praise Jah. It is this context that gives the proverbs such concentrated meanings. For instance, the proverbs in the stanza above speak to the relationship between a human being and the deity. The "victory" that must be won is individual and planetary spiritual salvation. The proverb in the next stanza can be read within this context as well:

He's the shepherd and I am the sheep
in his hands my whole life to keep.
Give me strength when I'm weak,
What you sow is what you shall reap.

Again, the importance of establishing a personal relationship with the deity is stressed, as this will lead to inner fulfillment and the robe of immortality granted the righteous.

A Proverb Performance

The Blue Note is a club in Columbia, Missouri. During my first four years in Columbia, from 1991 to 1995, the club regularly booked major reggae artists, often bringing in at least one a month. Thus Columbians were treated to annual appearances by bands such as Eek-a-Mouse, Culture, Burning Spear, and the Itals, and occasional concerts by other performers such as Jimmy Cliff, the Wailers, Lloyd Parks and We the People Band, Ziggy Marley, and the Skatalites. In addition to major acts, a number of local reggae bands (from Kansas

City, St. Louis, or other Midwestern cities) played each month at the Blue Note.

Although the Blue Note offered little of the ceremonial paraphernalia of clubs in which I had attended reggae concerts in West or East Coast cities (the smell of incense, foods, visible numbers of Rastas, and so on), the crowd was usually large and the dance floor packed with enthusiastic spirits and bodies. The night of the Itals' performance was no different. Their band laid down a "murderous" roots rhythm that held the near capacity crowd in a smoothly swaying, hypnotic groove from the first bar of the first song until they filed off the stage at the end. The hot, sweaty, excited mass of bodies remained, yelling and stomping, as the colored stage lights glinted magically off the metal rims of drums, the glossy finish of guitars, and the phallic chrome of mic stands. The crowd yelled and kept yelling until the band came back on stage for the encore. Smiling serenely, Porter, Ronnie Davis, and David Isaacs launched into "Blood Thicker Than Water."

Riding the crest of intensity that pulsed through the crowd, Porter motioned for the musicians to lower the volume, which they did, as the three singers sang the refrain more softly: "**Blood, thicker than water,**" holding the mic out to the audience for them to sing back. Porter "preached," between the lines of the refrain. He moved back and forth at the edge of the stage, reaching out occasionally to touch the hands of people in the audience, as the stage was transformed into a pulpit, and those of us on the dance floor, in the balconies, at the bar, seated at tables, the congregation. Some pushed forward to the stage and reached out, as if grasping for the holy water of sweat. Some kept on dancing. Some stood on the side, eyes closed in silent ecstasy, swaying in trance. Some jerked and smiled, filled with the reggae spirit. Some jumped up and down. "**Blood thicker than water** / And every man and man a brother / And every sistren a me sister," the singers harmonized, again and again, driving home the idea we were all of one blood, as our spirits melted momentarily into oneness. Scented by cigarette and ganja smoke that clung to our skin and clothes, the pungent odor of beer sticky beneath our feet, a hundred failed perfumes and deodorants laid at the altar of sweat and hormones like joyful sacrifices.

We watched them say farewell, this time not to return. The house lights came on, and we milled around for some minutes longer, wanting the high to last. "Blood thicker than water," I hummed, "**Blood thicker than water,**" and I could see others still humming to the beat that buzzed in the lingering vibrations of damaged eardrums. We glanced around, began to see each other. "Blood thicker than water." Walking out, past stale scents of beer and tobacco, along with the crowd that spilled ever so slowly onto the sidewalk, I looked around. "Blood thicker than water." I wondered. And I'm sure I was not the only one.

FIRE, CORN AND POTS

Proverbs of Bob
(Robert Nesta) Marley, O.M.

Children get your culture,
and don't stand there and gesture.
Or the battle will be hotter
and you won't get no supper.

Bob Marley, "Natty Dread"

My brother Bob Marley
paved a clean way for Rasta
and for every decent one in
every society.

Culture, "A Double Tribute to the O.M."

Of the reggae emissaries, Bob Marley, the "King of Reggae Music," is
without question the most widely known and is given credit for being
the one who did the most to internationalize reggae and Rastafari. Throughout the world, Marley is a symbol of resistance to colonial mentality, of spiritual and social revolution, and of freedom of expression. A story told to me

The statue of Bob Marley in front of the Marley Museum (Marley's former residence on Hope Road), Kingston. Pictured at the bottom of the statue are Haile Selassie, The I-Threes (his backup singers Rita Marley, Judy Mowatt, and Marcia Griffiths), and Marcus Garvey. At his feet is a soccer ball, representing the game he loved so passionately. (Courtesy of the author)

by a friend who recently returned from the Ukraine illustrates the place this visionary holds in the minds of many, even in remote areas of the world. My friend encountered a young Ukrainian man who practically worshiped Marley. He said to her that, when he died, he hoped he would go to heaven and that heaven was a place where one could wake up every day listening and dancing to Bob Marley. Another friend who had been traveling in Southeast Asia reported similar testimonies from groups of people in Thailand and Cambodia and even told me about a reggae café she frequented in Thailand. It would not be an overstatement to say that Marley is perhaps the most widely known and influential performer/philosopher in the modern Third World. Excerpts of a letter written by a young man from the Ivory Coast on the occasion of Marley's passing capture the adulation paid him internationally:

In Ivory Coast, West Africa, all the ghetto of Abidjan [capital of Ivory Coast] was in a kind of meditation, a kind of Nyabinghi [Rasta Bredren Reunion]. People were awake in the streets, day and night, forgetting for about two weeks the existence of the sun and moon. In Williams Ville, North Abidjan, a young Rasta association organized a special Bob Marley night during which they listened to all the records of the Wailers, by candlelight. Meanwhile in the streets of the town, some local musicians holding torches were moving from one section to another, creating a massive human energy flow simply by means of unity.

In the air, Bob's voice coming from either radio sets or record players, vibrated the cars. "Zion train is coming our way" was the favorite sentence that people repeated strongly with hands up, like a magical recital. So was the atmosphere till the daylight came, and Abidjan was sparkling with the "uprising sun" now like it had never been before. Spreading over the town was a kind of "natural mystic" in the air that brings people to accept the reality of nature.

The walls of many inhabitants had been scratched with drawings and scripts about Bob and the Rasta philosophy: "Bob is not Jamaican, he is African," "the Rasta will win," "tribute to his Imperial Majesty Haile Selassi," "this district quarter is named Zion City," "Here is Jah people city," "Jah no dead," "Rastafari."

How could I say it was a funeral, because funerals reflect death, but in this case it was like a feast. As the young Abdoul . . . told me, "They used our physical energy, they sold many parts of our culture, they left us in poverty, but never will they take from us the reason of our existence: the promised land, Zion." Rest in peace, Bob, we understood the message.

Kone Baru Omar—Ivory Coast (cited in Whitney and Hussey 1984, 135)

Known as the "King of Reggae" music on the basis of his lyrical and musical achievements, his international influence, and his personal charisma, Marley would easily maintain his title on the basis of his use of proverbs. Only songs by the Itals are comparable in number and variety of proverbs, and in the lyrical and poetic skill with which they are applied. Like Porter, Marley drew equally from Jamaican, Rastafari, English, American, and biblical sources; however, there are some stylistic differences between the uses of proverbs by these two artists. Although the goal/obstacle structure discussed in the previous chapter applies to the majority of Marley's songs, we do not find the complexity of proverb clusters characteristic of many Itals compositions. A few songs that do have clusters include "Heathen," "Real Situation," "Stiff Necked Fools," and "Jah Live." The cluster from "Heathen" contains common reggae proverbs:

As a man sow, shall he reap.
And I know that **talk is cheap.**
But the hotter the battle
Is the sweeter the victory.

The cluster from "Real Situation" innovates upon one proverb to make two, and adds a third and fourth:

Give them an inch, they take a yard.
Give them a yard, they take a mile.
Once a man and twice a child.
And everything is just for a while.

A cluster comprised of biblical expressions is found in "Stiff Necked Fools":

The lips of the righteous, teaches many.
But fools die for want of wisdom.
The rich man's wealth is in his city,
The righteous wealth is in his holy place.

"Jah Live," which was written in response to Selassie's passing, contains another cluster:

The truth is an offense,
but not a sin.
Is he who laugh last, children,
Is he who win.
It's a foolish dog
bark at a flying bird.

Marley is particularly fond of using two proverbs together. Most often, proverbs are used at the end of stanzas or following argumentative statements as parabolic morals, rhetorical support, and to lend the voice of authority to what has just been stated. Frequently the statements used in conjunction with traditional proverbs also have a proverbial sound and structure. The care with which Marley constructs his stanzas, using proverbs to embellish and support his critique of particularized situations, gives the listener a firmer ground to stand on in interpreting the proverbs than one has, for instance, in many of the Itals' songs. In general, the greater the number of proverbs there are in a cluster, the greater the difficulty in interpreting their meanings, as the cluster becomes almost a unit of meaning, with its own internal dynamics, separate from the rest of the lyrics.

We can note several examples of Marley's characteristic use of proverbs in "Coming In from the Cold," "So Much Trouble in the World," "Who the Cap Fit," "Ride Natty Ride," and "I Shot the Sheriff." In "Ride Natty Ride," the proverb is used as a summary response to the description of how Babylon fights down the Rastaman:

All and all you see a gwan
Is to fight against the Rastaman.
So they build the world in great confusion
To force on us the devil's illusion.
But the stone that the builder refuse
shall be the head cornerstone.

In "So Much Trouble," an allusion to the same proverb is used within an identical structure:

So you think you have found the solution
But it's just another illusion.
So before you check out your tide,
Don't leave another cornerstone
standing there behind.

"Coming In from the Cold" contains another excellent illustration of this strategy:

Well you, it's you, it's you
It's you I'm talking to now.
Why do you look so sad and forsaken?

When one door is closed
Don't you know another is opened.

Several examples are found in "Who the Cap Fit," which also demonstrates how proverblike lines are sometimes paired with traditional proverbs:

Some will hate you
pretend they love you, now.
Then behind they try to eliminate you.
But who Jah bless, no one curse.
Thank God, we're past the worse.

Hypocrites and parasites
will come and take a bite.
And if your night should turn to day
A lot of people would run away.
And who the sock fit,
let them wear it.
Who the cap fit, let them wear it.

Perhaps the quintessential example of the proverb as explanatory statement for the story that precedes it is in "I Shot the Sheriff." This stanza also illustrates Marley's penchant for using proverb pairs in his lyrics:

I shot the sheriff
but I didn't shoot no deputy.
Reflexes got the better of me,
and **what is to be must be.**
Every day the bucket a go a well,
one day the bottom a go drop out.

These and other aspects of Marley's proverb use will be covered in the following discussion, which critiques proverbs in the context of the albums in which they appear.

Proverbs by Album

Proverbs appear in some of Bob Marley and the Wailers' earliest compositions. For example, there are several proverbs in the Wailers' first hit, a ska tune called "Simmer Down," released in 1963 in Jamaica. It is impossible to tell where the inspiration came from to use these proverbs in the song, although, around the same time, other rootsy groups were emerging who also used proverbs in their compositions—Justin Hinds and the Dominoes, for example, and the Ethiopians. The proverbs from "Simmer Down" would probably be quite puzzling to a foreign listener. The song was written in part to dispel anxieties Marley's mother had about his association with rudeboys, and it speaks directly to rudeboy subculture. The song employs a rhetorical voice and strategies that foretell of the warrior/priest that would emerge some years later, embroidering social, spiritual, and political commentary so intricately into his lyrics:

[backup singers] Simmer down . . .
Long time people dem used to say
What sweet nanny goat ago running belly
so, [backup singers] simmer down
[Marley] or the battle will be hotter
[backup singers] simmer down
[Marley] or you won't get no supper.

[Marley] **Chicken merry, hawk must be near**
a when a dem near, you must beware.
so [backup singers] simmer down . . .

This single began a steady string of ska and American soul-influenced singles and albums by the Wailers, on the Clement Dodd and Leslie Kong labels. Most of these tunes were love songs; however, a number of them take on social themes and several contain proverbs. During the period between 1964 and 1970, the Wailers identified themselves with rudeboy culture and even called themselves the Wailing Rude Boys for a time. A number of songs written during this period contain proverbs and became a part of the Wailers' later repertoire—"Who Feels It," for example, and "Small Axe."

The Wailers entered another period in 1969 when they began recording for producer Lee "Scratch" Perry. With Perry as producer, the group released another long string of hits. Whitney and Hussey write, "The Upsetter label was where they laid their tracks, producing wondrous waxworks that have become Jamaican music classics seemingly glued to the Jamaican Hit Parade" (1984, 65). Countless singles and six albums were released by Perry, and many of these songs also became permanent parts of the Wailers' repertoire in later years, although, only a few of these contain proverbs (such as "Don't Rock My Boat"). By this time their lyrics had begun to take on more political consciousness; still missing was the reliance on proverbs and influences of Rastafari that developed later.

Songs with Rastafari influences and in which proverbs begin to play more central roles do not really come until the period after Marley started his own recording studio, Tuff Gong International, in 1970. Among the Rasta-inspired tunes released by Tuff Gong were "Selassi Is the Chapel," "Knotty Dread," "Lion," "Chant," "Jah Live," "War," "Exodus," "Rastaman Live Up," and "Blackman Redemption." The focus on songs with a revolutionary flavor and a persona reflecting Rastafari teachings began in earnest with the Wailers' association with producer Chris Blackwell and Island Records. Blackwell was interested in promoting the Wailers and their music. Understandably, a part of his concern was to develop an image that would sell to American and European markets. It was the record company's decision, for instance, to change the group's name from the Wailers to Bob Marley and the Wailers; to capitalize on Rastafari symbols; and to promote elements of the group that would appeal to rock-oriented audiences and young consumers of popular culture.

In spite of their prolific career prior to signing with Island Records in 1973, Marley and the Wailers' recordings on the Island label comprise the bulk of the work for which they are known to international audiences. These twelve albums, along with the many forms of promotional materials and press coverage, were the channels through which audiences worldwide came to know of Bob Marley. Although many of the songs from these albums were recorded previously—released as singles in Jamaica or Great Britain, or even on albums—most listeners abroad know them from the context of the Island LPs. Thus, these are the recordings that I will focus on in my discussion.

Of the twelve albums, *Babylon by Bus, Live . . .* , and *Legend* are essentially anthologies of songs found on the other LPs. They do not have, as the other nine albums do, a conceptual and thematic thread that ties the songs together. Of the remaining nine LPs, *Catch a Fire* and *Confrontation* contain no proverbs. The remaining seven albums contain roughly seventy songs, about twenty of which have fifty proverbs among them. There are no convenient markers indicating which albums might have the largest or smallest number of proverbs. For example, factors such as how commercial or rootsy the recordings are, how early or late in Marley's career they come, or their thematic concerns are not determining factors of proverbs. *Natty Dread*, one of the earliest and most rootsy LPs, has only three proverbs; *Exodus*, a later, very militant work has only five; and *Kaya, Rastaman Vibration, Survival, Burnin'*, and *Uprising*, which represent a range of periods and styles, contain an average of nine or ten proverbs apiece.

Nor can one draw conclusions about the importance of proverbs to an album based on the number of expressions the work contains. In fact, one cannot argue from an emic perspective about the significance of particular proverbs at all. We must consider the varied ways in which an album can be perceived, and the diverse categories of audiences. Many listeners are only familiar with Marley's hit songs, those that have received the most radio airplay and that appear on compilations: "I Shot the Sheriff," "Get Up, Stand Up," "Is This Love," "Buffalo Soldier," and so on. More serious Marley fans may own numerous or all of his major LPs. Also, some audiences may be attracted primarily to the music, while others delve deeply into the lyrics in search of meaning. Certainly, those at both extremes—and listeners who fall somewhere in between—will have different responses to elements of the lyrics, such as proverbs. So my consideration of how important proverbs are to Marley's recordings represents a critical point of view that, in all likelihood, many listeners will not have thought much about. Like Cooper, I claim no "authority for my own readings" (1993, 118) except a legitimacy accorded any other listener who has lived with this music or who, because of a literary or oralic sensibility, can feel his or her way to possible meanings.

1973

I have chosen to treat 1973 as a single period for one reason: it represents the very short time frame in which the Wailers, complete with the trinity of Bob Marley, Peter Tosh, and Bunny Wailer, achieved international success. Up to and during this year, The Wailers' songs were penned by all of these artists; however, after this year, Marley was the sole composer. Bunny Wailer, one of the founding members of the group, decided to withdraw. Peter Tosh set out on his own separate recording career. In 1973, the Wailers released two albums on Island records, *Catch a Fire* and *Burnin'*. As White indicates in his discussion of the Wailers' discography, it is difficult to pin down the dates on which songs were either written, recorded, or released. In many cases:

A Jamaican producer might play an acetate dub plate or a pre-release pressing of a "hit" record at Sound System dances for as much as a year before issuing the record commercially. The single might then enjoy "hit" status on the Jamaican radio charts for another year before being picked up for British release. As a result, by the time

"Simmer Down," for example, was deemed a "hit" in the London roots community (1965), it had been popular in Jamaica for almost two years. Yet if you ask the producer or the artists when they recorded the song, they'll tell you it was the winter of 1963—the period during which they were in the studio cutting it. (1998, 394)

Hence, a number of the songs from the two albums in question enjoyed airplay, underwent numerous different versions, and were popular among Jamaican audiences prior to their release by Island Records. These include "Stop That Train," "Small Axe," "Baby We've Got a Date," "Midnight Ravers," "Stir It Up," "Duppy Conqueror," "400 Years," and "Put It On," a number of which contain proverbs. *Catch a Fire* was in certain ways a repackaging of Marley and the Wailers, with an international audience in mind. It reflects the Wailers prior to their conversion to Rastafari and gives us a glimpse of Marley as the songwriter and visionary he would soon become.

That development begins to flower on *Burnin'*, which continues the trend of reversioning older materials but is clearly weighted toward newly penned compositions. Those songs that are reversioned fit perfectly with the other spiritually based and socially conscious songs and with the general vision that emanates from this album. The album title clearly suggests this vision, continuing the theme of fire begun with *Catch a Fire*. This theme both reflects the Rastafari insistence that Jah is coming this time with fire to burn down Babylon, and captures the symbolism of the favored ritual, lighting the chalice or the spliff. The Rastafari priest emerges for the first time here, using all of the rhetorical strategies discussed in the previous chapters. Proverbs are used in five of the ten songs: "Small Axe," "Get Up, Stand Up," "One Foundation," "I Shot the Sheriff," and "Pass It On."

The general tone of the compositions on *Burnin'* is soft and reverent, heavily influenced by the meditative spirit of Peter Tosh and by the vocal harmonies of Tosh, Wailer, and Marley. There is a sense of containment and particularized references to Jamaican culture, which are amplified by the cover art. On the inside cover, which opens like a book, the lyrics of each song are printed in alternating colors of red, gold, and green. Dispersed throughout the lyrics are photographs of Marley and other Jamaican urban and rural scenes. The overall effect is to convey the sense of community and the beauty of Jamaican people, as well as to cast certain cultural activities and contexts in a symbolic light. For instance, we see people in the marketplace, on the street corner, in the doorways of shops; children playing or at work; a Rastafari man in a rural setting, with a small child in one scene and with a goat in the other.

One of the gems on this album is "Small Axe," which had been released in Jamaica and the UK as early as 1971. The song's title is taken from a traditional Jamaican proverb, **Cotton tree never so big, but lilly axe cut him.** The social meaning of the proverb parallels the metaphor of David and Goliath, from biblical lore. No person or situation is so immense that a much smaller and seemingly weaker person cannot destroy it. Of course, everything depends on the smaller person having a quality comparable to the hardness and sharpness of an axe, and the determination to wield it. Marley expands the proverb into an allegory, applying the metaphor of the tree to the "evil men" and the axe to himself, Rastas, the righteous, the oppressed.

Beginning the song with "Why boasteth thyself, oh evil men," Marley adopts the role of the righteously indignant, the epic hero, a sort of David poised against Goliath.[1] Here we have an example of the direct address to Babylon, who is "capped" on in the first stanza: "Playing smart and not being clever," and "working iniquity to achieve vanity." In an ironic twist, the narrative engages in boasting, as if entering a verbal duel in which the warrior/priest declares himself ready for battle. It is in the context of this assumed struggle that the allusion to the proverb occurs, as the chorus goes: "**If you are the big tree / we are the small axe** / Sharpened to cut you down / ready to cut you down." It is no accident that Marley chooses an implement made of iron and one that can symbolize the strength and ruggedness of rural Jamaicans. We have already noted the importance of iron to Rastafari thought, and the experience of sharpening and cutting with iron blades, be they axes or machetes, is a familiar one to Jamaican people.

Just as the allusion to the first proverb functions as a warning, so does the second proverb, **Whosoever diggeth a pit, shall fall in it.** The warning is amplified by the repetition of the proverb, by the change of "fall in it" to "bury in it" the second time, and by the antiphonal, "fall in it" and "bury in it," by the backup singers, following the lead singer's original lines. The thematic message of the first stanza is reiterated here: Babylon's business is to subvert and undermine any efforts by the oppressed to better their lives, and to keep the underprivileged weak and disempowered. This agenda on the part of the system (digging a pit) will ultimately prove their undoing (falling in it).

Whereas these two proverbs rely solely on the weight of the traditional voice for their impact, a third expression references Jah as a source of authority. This authoritative voice colors the narrative throughout the rest of the song: "These are the words of my Master / telling me that **no weak heart shall prosper** / oh no they can't." The term "weak heart" is a Rastafari expression denoting a non-Rasta, someone without the strength that comes from a knowledge of oneself. This proverb, like the previous two, are rhetorical put-downs in the context of the verbal duel; and we should bear in mind that the verbal reality, as in word/sound/power, is no less substantial than the material. Thus the battle *is* being fought, as the word/sound/power of the song is activated by the musical, vocal, and corporeal performance.

Having examined the song and its proverbs in this vein, it is interesting to note legends about its origin. Stephen Davis writes: "When the Wailers originally merged with Lee Perry, Upsetter Records was facing competition from the 'big three' studios in Kingston—Federal, Studio One and Dynamic. One day Bob and Peter and Scratch were playing with lyrics at the Upsetter shop and Scratch was complaining about the 'big t'ree'. Brash and boasty as usual, Tosh spoke up: 'If dem is the big t'ree, we am [sic] the small axe!' And one of the canniest double-entendres in reggae music was born" (from Cooper 1993, 119). According to this legend, the song was written about larger, competing record studios. Another such account claims a very different origin: "Psalm 52 was used by Bob Marley to create 'Small Axe'. The Psalm opened with: 'Why boasteth thyself, O mighty man? The goodness of God endureth continually.' Marley changed or scrambled the words around to say, 'Why boasteth thy self, O evil man? The goodness of Jah endureth for Iver.' The song was also strengthened by the inclusion of bits of Ecclesiastes 10: 'He that diggeth a pit shall fall into it.' Marley's slightly changed lyrics say, 'And whosoever diggeth a pit shall fall in it' " (120).

These accounts are significant for a number of reasons. The first one suggests particular *situational* meanings and applications for the proverbs in Marley's songs. Certainly such information would, when proven accurate, deepen our appreciation of individual songs and the proverbs that occur in them. The two stories, however, alert us to the difficulty of ever confirming stories of origin, especially when so many legends circulate about such a phenomenal and ofttimes mysterious figure as Bob Marley. Finally, the accounts bring an important aspect of our endeavor into sharper focus. The possibility that Marley had a specific *situational* meaning in mind does not limit the poetic breadth of either the song or the proverbs used in it. Nor does our ignorance of that *situational* meaning in any way discredit possible interpretations we might make on the basis of the song's performance and our interpretive role as audience in each performance. This highlights the fact that there are no absolute or correct "hearings" of the songs and proverbs: there are only hearings that are closer to or further afield from what the artists were intending to communicate.

"Small Axe," as well as the next several songs I will discuss, are classic examples of proverb songs. As one can readily observe, the central message of the song is conveyed in proverbs. In this case (although not always), the main portion of the composition is proverbial language. The same is true of "Pass It On," in which every stanza is composed of proverbs or proverblike statements having the sound of ancient wisdom and prescribing moral courses of behavior. The speaker here addresses the Rastafari/Diasporic community, offering spiritual guidance, using invented and traditional expressions. The first stanza begins with **What your hands do / it's your own eyes that've seen**, and the second stanza with, **It's your own conscience / that is going to remind you.** Lines of the chorus go: "Be not selfish in your doings," "Help your brothers in their needs / Pass it On," **Live for others / you will live again**, and "In the kingdom of Jah / man shall reign." The traditional proverb **What's in the darkness, must be revealed to light**, comes in the third verse and extends the central theme of the song—a re-creation of a subtle, traditional religious ethos. The listener is advised that the evaluation of one's life comes from within, and that man is God, a central element of Rasta worldview. This theme, which is expressed through symbols of light and dark in the song, is beautifully picked up in the final stanza.

On a hot sunny day
follow the shadows for rescue
but as the day grows old
I know the sun is gonna find you.

"One Foundation" is similar to "Pass It On" in its didactic strategy. It directly addresses the Diasporic and other international communities, and its stanzas are repetitions of a few social/spiritual principles. These include "Got to build our love on one foundation" and "Got to put aside them segregation." An allusion to the proverb **Birds of a feather, stick together** comes in the chorus: **Got to come together / 'cause we're birds of a feather.** Whereas a common social meaning of the proverb would support the idea of separation and boundaries, the proverb here reflects a vision of unity and the realization of "oneness" as a condition for a peaceful and loving world.

The composition "I Shot the Sheriff" is similar in narrative voice to "Small Axe." Instead of the reverent musical tone, however, its timbre is harsher and more aggressive, just as its message is more overtly militant. Instead of building upon a proverbial metaphor, the story becomes metaphorically allegorical of the relationship between white authorities—the system—and the African Jamaican male, culminating with a proverb at the very end that sums up the message of the narrative. As the story goes, the sheriff has devoted his life to the harassment and oppression of the speaker and his people—as the colonial system has been committed to the "downpression" and genocide of black people.

Sheriff John Brown always hated me
for what I don't know.
Every time I plant a seed
he said kill it [them] before it [they] grow.

Eventually, the speaker fights back, shooting the sheriff: "I shot the sheriff / but I swear it was in self-defense." The reference to rudeboy subculture is inescapable, as are parallels to Ivan in the film *The Harder They Come*, and the novel by the same name (Thelwell 1980). The concluding stanza contains two proverbs, intensifying the song's message by explaining and justifying the speaker's actions:

Reflexes got the better of me
and **what is to be must be.**
Everyday the bucket a go a well
One day the bottom a go drop out.

In other words, people can only allow themselves to be the victim of genocidal policies for so long before something within them inevitably strikes out at their killers. In such a case, there can be no regrets, only a recognition of how the act will be viewed by the white authorities: "All around in my home town / they're trying to track me down." As in "Small Axe," an everyday object comes to symbolize an important aspect of African Jamaican culture. In this case, the bucket speaks metaphorically of people's self-control, and even their brainwashed submission to colonial rule. **What is to be must be** indicates the inevitability of rebellion. The seed is another agricultural image that takes on symbolic significance in this and other Marley songs. Imagistically, the two images of the seed and the bucket dominate the landscape of the song.

This composition also gives a glimpse into Marley's sense of humor. First, the decision to tell a Jamaican story using symbols of "the Old West" is amusing. And the claim that he shot the sheriff "but I didn't shoot no deputy" is hilariously mocking of the neocolonial system of justice, "law and order." What difference can it possibly make to the authorities that the speaker *only* shot the sheriff? And yet this is the kind of legal distinction that the authorities would make an issue of, as if it would in any way alter the verdict of the court. By mocking the law enforcement officers, he condemns and ridicules the entire system.

The final song from *Burnin'* that contains proverbs, "Get Up, Stand Up," is coauthored by Tosh, Marley, and Wailer. Just as in some of the preceding examples, proverbial wisdom here is connected to the overall advice being given to the Diasporic community. The tone is more overtly fiery and militant than the more subtle reference to rebellion in "I Shot the Sheriff." But as much as the song encourages rebellion, it is in essence a critique of Christianity that has enslaved the minds of black people, deluding them and making them docile. The critique is purely Rastafari, in that it argues that God, spirit, and divinity do not exist independently of the material world. The belief that it does is a major obstacle to revolution. Thus the song is about spiritual awakening, which leads to cultural and self-knowledge, and ultimately to a militant commitment to the restoration of black people's dignity and political sovereignty. All four of the proverbial expressions embellish these ideas: **It's not all that glitters is gold, Half the story has never been told, Now you've seen the light, You can fool some people sometimes / but you can't fool all the people all the time.**

1974–1976

The next period, from 1974 to 1976, is the one in which Marley's identity as a reggae priest crystallizes. During this period, the band jells into basically the group it will be for the duration of Marley's career. Marley comes into his own as songwriter and performer during this period. He is not just admired by Jamaicans but tours and becomes famous abroad. Three albums are released during this period, two of which are of concern here, *Natty Dread* and *Rastaman Vibration.*

In some ways, one can view *Natty Dread* as Marley's debut album, although he had been recording for over twelve years. The album is full of militant Rastafari ideology, soulful conviction, and exquisitely clear and resonant instrumental work. In it we can see the expansion of reggae as a musical form, as the tones, timing, and chord progressions extend the basic reggae formula. With the combination of Carlton Barrett's eclectic drumming, Aston Barrett's melodic bass, a horn section resonating with sounds from the varied ethnic mixes of the entire Caribbean and the United States, and Marley's vision of music, reggae moves next door to jazz in its conceptual approach, keeping one foot, however, firmly grounded in the Jamaican soil. Chang and Chen write of *Natty Dread:* " 'Natty Dread,' Bob's first 'solo' album, was an unqualified masterpiece and perhaps his finest album. Its cohesiveness of vision and execution more than made up for the loss of Peter's and Bunny's artistic contributions. It was received with tumultuous praise in Jamaica, and never before or since has any album been so unanimously admired here" (1998, 51).

But only one song on the album contains proverbs, "Them Belly Full." This song occurs in the context of militant compositions such as "Rebel Music," "So Jah Seh," "Revolution," and "Natty Dread," which continue to expound on Rasta philosophy and critique the social plight of black people relative to the white power system, offering encouragement, wisdom, and inspiration; giving praises to Jah; and chanting down fire on Babylon. "Them Belly Full" contrasts the social condition of the haves and the have-nots. But more than that, the song offers a prescription for coping with the realities of poverty and oppression, and transcending psychological or physical ailments resulting from these social conditions: "We're gonna dance to Jah music, dance / Forget your troubles [sickness, weakness], and dance."

The song begins with the repetitive dissonance of a phrase recalling a children's play rhyme: "Na na na na na na na na." This common rhetorical element in reggae simultaneously celebrates the wider range of traditional Jamaican oral art and mocks the powers that be. Both proverbs come in the first stanza following "na na na":

Dem belly full but we hungry
A hungry mob is an angry mob
A rain a fall, but de doti [ground] **tuff** [tough].
A yot [pot] a yook [cook], but de yood [food] no nuff [is not enough]

The first proverb is a common one in reggae lyrics, sometimes having "man" instead of "mob." It is a literal proverb that needs little explanation. The second expression is a traditional Jamaican proverb that poet Louise Bennett "set to verse over forty years ago" (Bilby 1985, 145). The last line is a marker of Rastafari Dread talk, in which the "y" replaces the first consonant in the word. Although this is not a traditional Jamaican proverb, it has become proverbial in Jamaican speech, perhaps because of the popularity of the song (see chapter 3). Together, the lines of this stanza capture the dilemma confronting the multitudes of African Jamaicans and, perhaps, Third World people globally. There never seems to be enough. There never seems to be an end to the suffering. In fact, the pressure and tribulation seem to be escalating as the world moves forward into the technological age. Once again Marley has used an image from the everyday lives of Jamaicans to represent a far-reaching issue.

This song provides an excellent example of how the proverb lives beyond the simple oral text. The melody line played by the bass throughout is the proverb and, along with the accompanying instrumentals, forms a musical unit of meaning. Thus the proverb echoes extend much further than the oral performance. If one were to listen to the dub version of the song, for example, one would hear, in the instrumental interplay, the proverb being played. And when audiences dance to the song, they are dancing to the proverb. This helps to explain why when Iaa mentioned the proverb (chapter 3), he sang it, his body moving subtly to the remembered beat of the song.

Rastaman Vibration is more personal and less overtly political in tone than many other albums. There is less of a tendency to preach large philosophical truths; in fact, rhetorically speaking, the priest comes down from the mountain and has more face-to-face conversations. Yet many of the same themes pertain: encouragement for unity and spiritual growth, reggae as a prescription for suffering, the cruelty of the system, and the necessity to rebel. These are conveyed less overtly, however. I sometimes refer to this as "the corn album," because corn is one of the dominant images. In "Crazy Baldhead," as in other examples, this agricultural image takes on significant symbolic value, representing the civilization and labors of black people that have been consistently exploited by colonial powers:

I and I plant the corn.
Didn't my people before me
slave for this country
now you look me with a scorn
then you eat up all my corn.

The image appears again in "Who the Cap Fit," a deeply personal song about a friend's betrayal. This composition exemplifies the kind of song in which the speaker is not directly addressing anyone else, in which we seem to be overhearing his contemplation about a particular issue. This strategy is deceptive, however, for he is "signifying" on a particular person, someone who was once a friend. Just as with "Small Axe," the title is taken from a proverb. One of the most plaintive and delicately crafted of Marley's songs, this speaks of the pain of being betrayed by a close friend and the sad actuality that many friends are only loyal as long as it is convenient or profitable for them. It assumes an observational tone from the beginning and establishes the narrative voice as teacher. However, the song remains grounded in the personal experience of the narrator:

Some will eat and drink with you
then behind them su-su pon you,
only your friend know your secret
so only he could reveal it.
Who the cap fit, let them wear it. [Repeat]

The repetitive refrain **Who the cap fit, let them wear it** is coupled here with another phrase that sounds equally proverbial. The proverb is applied to the situation described by this phrase, and in the previous narrative. It comes almost as a voice of resignation, a signal that the narrator has accepted the untrustworthy nature of human relationships. With the use of the proverb, the impersonal voice of wisdom provides a solution to the incredulous narrative voice.

With the next stanza we see another example of Marley's humor and artistry. Using a proverb made famous by Larry Marshall, Marley draws upon the images within the expression as a source for mocking and derisive sounds, characterizing those to whom he speaks.

I say I throw me corn
me no call no fowl.
I saying cok, cok, cok;
cluk, cluk, cluk, yeah!

One writer describes the proverb's meaning in this way: "The phrase refers to the conversational technique of throwing out a provocative statement (throw corn) in an indirect manner, thus forestalling any accusations of personal insult" (Turner 1996, 30). In other words, the proverb is itself a comment on practices such as "signifying," "capping," or "mocking." The speaker, who has signified on another person, feigns innocence. "Yes I did 'throw corn,'" the speaker says, "but I didn't tell you to pick it up." Contained in the expression is the idea that a chicken could not possibly walk by without eating corn thrown in the yard, regardless of whose yard it may be. Hence, there is an implicit suggestion of "being in someone's else's business"; otherwise, the listener may not have even heard the comments in question. One can see the perfect match between this proverb and the central expression of the song, **Who the cap fit. . . .**

Succeeding stanzas build upon proverblike statements, just as stanza 1 does, each statement containing thoughtful, wise expressions. In the next stanza another proverb is used, addressing the central idea of betrayal by invoking the power and ultimate justice of the deity:

Some will hate you
pretend they love you, now.
Then behind they try to eliminate you.
But who Jah bless, no one curse.

In the next stanza, which follows this same structure, the central proverb is used again. We might note that the proverb is sung as an accompaniment to the musical "bridge" of the song, that is, the climactic segment at which the musical progression turns around and begins to repeat. The rhetorical sense of a concluding remark is further reinforced by the deliberate deepening of the singer's voice, moving to a lower octave while singing the proverb segment of the stanza. "Who the Cap Fits" is illustrative of the artful layering of meaning that is characteristic of Marley's songs. On one hand, the composition tells, though indirectly, of an event in the singer's life and his emotional responses to that event. At the same time it communicates on a cultural level, using nouns that are cultural markers, and placing the story of the song within the context of Jamaican values and ways of perceiving the particular event in question.

The title of a second composition, "Rat Race," alludes to the song's central proverb, **When the cat's away, the mice will play.** The use of sarcastic wit is taken a step further and rivals political cartooning in its sensibility, as the song criticizes the viciousness of politics and the social climate generated by political corruption. Written during the political campaigns for the 1976 elections in Jamaica, the song was probably a comment on those involved in the rioting and other violent outbreaks that occurred, and the political parties responsible for these events. Jamaican officials certainly interpreted the song in this context, for along with several others ("War," "Crazy Baldheads," "Who the Cap Fit") it was banned from the radio (Whitney and Hussey 1984, 79).

**When the cats away
the mice will play.**
Political violence fill your city
Yeah!
Don't involve Rasta in your say say.
Rasta don't work for no C.I.A.
Rat race, rat race, rat race.
When you think it's peace and safety
A sudden destruction
Collective security for surety,
Yeah!

The cat here would seem to be the authorities and the mice the people who would give in to looting and shooting. The proverb succeeds in criticizing both parties through the demeaning quality of its animal referents. This one, like **Throw me corn . . .** , illustrates the derisive use of proverbs with animal images, a characteristic found in African and African American proverbial speech (Prahlad 1996, 65–66). A second proverb is used in the next stanza, which first pleads for a grounding in cultural knowledge and then offers a proverbial critique of those caught up in the ugliness of the political process. The proverb carries the Rastafari perspectives that spirituality and self-knowledge are solutions to social crises, that these qualities are abundant within, and that people tend to search instead for material answers:

Don't forget your history
know your destiny.
**In the abundance of water
the fool is thirsty.**

1977–1981

The last period of Marley's career, from 1977 to 1981, is characterized by his coming into full flowering as a prophetic and priestly voice. The sound of his music is fuller, harder, and more insistent. *Exodus* followed *Rastaman Vibration* and was reportedly Marley's best seller. Dermott Hussey writes:

An attempt was made on Marley's life and the singer went into exile for over a year, his ego wounded. The first side of the album is a complete statement in response to that event. He interprets much of that experience through the wisdom and teachings of the Bible, but at the same time his criticisms are trenchant. The five part chapter concludes with a triumphant soul-stirring "Exodus." The second side is celebratory, delving into love songs, a previously unheard of preoccupation, at least on a sustained basis in militant reggae. (Whitney and Hussey 1984, 140)

Despite its strident militancy, however, the album contains only seven proverbs, all of them in four songs: "So Much Things to Say," "Guiltiness," "Jamming," and "Heathen." The first song is a one-dropped composition firmly grounded in a Nyabinghi heartbeat rhythm. The narrative prophet/priest is at the height of his power. He defines his mission, allied with Garvey, Jesus, Moses, and Job, and derides and mimics the enemy who hides behind a clever and sophisticated rhetoric while attempting to crucify the innocent. Marley is preaching, sermonizing, full of conviction. "They got so much things to say" is repeated four times, comprising the chorus, and at one point Marley sings mockingly: "Na na na na na na na na na na na / na na na na na na / every morning time!" The proverb occurs in the bridge of the song, following a stanza commenting on "their" persecution of him and other righteous people:

I and I don't expect to be justified
By the laws of men.
Oh jury find me guilty
But through Jah prove my innocence.

Oh when the rain fall
it don't fall on one man's house,
remember that.

The proverb reinforces the message that spiritual and natural forces are no respecters of humanly constructed social or political divisions.

The second proverb song on *Exodus* is "The Heathen," which contains similar sentiments to those in "So Much Things to Say," similar, in fact, to those in most of the songs on this side of the album. "Heathen" is straightforward and condemning. The warrior/priest encourages the Diasporic community to take heart, depicting Babylon as losing ground in the war. A proverb is used in the first stanza (discussed in chapter 2), and a cluster of three proverbs comes in the second and final stanza (mentioned earlier in this chapter):

Rise o fallen fighters
Rise and take your stance again.
Cause he who fight and run away
live to fight another day.

"Guiltiness" is a sermon song in the same structural and thematic vein. The song contains one proverb, whose history has been explored in an excellent essay by Wolfgang Mieder. Mieder traces the proverb from its origin in antiquity among the Chinese, Sumerians, Turkish, and Africans, through the Indo-European languages and up to contemporary society. He cites examples of the proverb from settings as diverse as a poem by Greek writer Hesiod in the eighth century B.C.; the Sanskrit epic *Mahabharata* (600 B.C.–200 A.D.); Habakkuk of the Old Testament in seventh century B.C.; Shakespeare's *Coriolanus, All's Well that Ends Well,* and *Pericles*; a passage from St. Augustine; Bosch's paintings *The Hay Wain* and *The Temptations of Saint Anthony*; Pieter Breughel's paintings *The Netherlandic Proverbs* (1559) and *The Triumph of Death*; a popular song by Gary Geld, "Big Fish, Little Fish" (1969); Bertolt Brecht's 1930 essay "If the Sharks Were Humans"; and countless other texts and modern advertisements (1987, 178–228).

The original social meaning of the proverb was that people needed authority and government to keep their baser impulses in check; without such visible restraints, human beings would devour each other. Over time the meaning changed to reflect the idea that the rich and powerful follow the laws of the animal kingdom: they feed off the less powerful. Whereas the proverb reflected the attitude "this is just the way it is" in earlier periods of history, its wisdom has been questioned in contemporary times. The expression is sometimes used nowadays to criticize the rich and to protest policies that threaten the natural environment or reinforce classism, sexism, or racism. In the Marley song, it is used as a central metaphor in a sermon denouncing those in power. Musically, the bass line weaves itself around the singing of the proverb, and a characteristically eclectic one drop on the drum punctuating the expression. Within the goal/obstacle structure, the proverb assists in the critique of the problem, whose resolution is suggested in the chorus:

Guiltiness.
Rest on their conscience,
o yeah.
And they live a lie

of false pretense
everyday,
each and every day.
These are the big fish
who always try to eat down
the small fish.
Tell you what,
They would do anything
to materialize their every wish.

[Chorus]
Woe to the downpressors,
They'll eat bread of sorrow.
Woe to the downpressors,
They eat the bread of sad tomorrows.

The next album released by Bob Marley and the Wailers, *Kaya*, was controversial for a number of reasons. It was also put together in the period of self-imposed exile following the assassination attempt, and was a departure from the militancy and radical tone of the other albums. While many were critical, others recognized the more adventurous, carefree, and playful nature of *Kaya* as a positive period of Marley's development. Certainly *Kaya* is one of the LPs that is richest in proverbs. Proverbs are found in five of the ten songs: "Satisfy My Soul," "She's Gone," "Crisis," "Running Away," and "Time Will Tell." Of these, the first two are songs whose focus is the relationship between lovers. Cooper has written that such songs "illustrate one of the remarkable accomplishments of Marley's lyrics—the seriousness with which he treats sexual love, a subject that is often trivialised in Jamaican popular music" (127). The two love songs between them contain five proverbs, and the other compositions ten.

We have already discussed the two proverbs from "Satisfy My Soul" in chapter 4: **Don't rock my boat** and **For every little action, there's a reaction.** "She's Gone" is a reflective lament for a departed lover, which uses three proverbs in the first stanza:

She felt like a prisoner, who needs to be free.
Fools have tried, wisemen have failed.
Oh listen to me honey, life could never be another jail.
Still we know, **we'll never see smoke without fire.**
And **everyone you see has a heart desire.**

The first and last expressions are not found in proverb collections but are used as proverbs in the context of the song. The first stanza of "Crisis" contains several expressions that are introduced with formulaic phrases but that are also absent from collections.

They say **the sun, shines for us all.**
but in some peoples world, it never shines at all.
They say **love is a stream, that will
find its course, and every river runs to sea.**
Some people still think life is a dream
so **they making matters worse.**

"Running Away" is an introspective composition in which Marley reflects on going into exile after the attempt on his life. It is as self-scrutinizing a song as one will find in reggae, employing a haunting, repetitious refrain to capture one of the apparent internal voices with which he had to contend: "You running and you running and you running away." The first proverbial line comes in conjunction with this refrain and is also repeated numerous times:

You running and you running
but **you can't run away from yourself.**

Two more proverbs comprise the next stanza. They are expressions we find commonly in reggae, but they have a distinct *situational* meaning in this context. The first can be taken as an accusatory comment spoken by one voice, the second as a defense uttered by another persona.

Every man thinketh his burden is the heaviest (repeated)
But who feels it knows it Lord. (repeated three times)

The scrutiny continues in a later stanza, and, in the last segment of the song, it becomes a dramatization of someone desperately struggling with himself, his psyche deeply troubled to the point of near madness:

You must have done, something, something, something
something, something, you don't want nobody to know about.
You must have done, Lord, something wrong.

Why you can't find a place where you belong?

Well, well, well, you running away . . .
[the next lines spoken, dramatically, voice distorted for emphasis]
no, no, no I'm not running away, don't say that

I've got to protect my life
and I don't want to live with no strife.
It is better to live on the housetop
than to live in a house full of confusion.
So I made my decision, and I left you
now you coming to tell me that I'm running away
but it's not true, I am not running away.

One of the strengths of the song is that those unfamiliar with the events of Marley's life can interpret the song as another sermonic composition, addressing "them." The proverbs applied in this context would work as well if we applied them to the crisis of conscience resulting from Marley's exile and the accusations of others that he had abandoned his fellow warriors. Heard from this alternative perspective, some of the proverbs and other lines of the song would be ironic, used to caricature "them."

"Time Will Tell" is in the sermonic tradition, addressed both to the righteous and to "them," and calling upon Jah's power for ultimate resolve. The first proverb functions as a resolution and the second as a critique of the situation. The song is sung to the musical accompaniment of Nyabinghi heartbeat drumming and a beautifully melodic, twelve-string, acoustic guitar:

Jah would never give the power to a baldhead [non-Rasta]
run come crucify the dread.
Time alone, time will tell.
Think you're in heaven but you're living in hell.

In 1979 Marley released what was perhaps his most powerfully integrated, most musically and lyrically developed album, *Survival,* considered by some to be his crowning achievement. On *Survival,* every rhetorical element of his repertoire and every instinct of his musical genius comes to a full flowering. The personal voice, tinged with innocence and striving for the truth; the priest, filled with zeal and conviction; the prophet, aflame with visions of past, present, and future and how the three converge at a given moment in history; and the warrior, armed for battle—all merge in one of the most insightful critiques of the African's plight in Western societies ever recorded. These narratives are firmly rooted in the Rastafari vision and grounded in Jamaican culture and the harsh realities of political and social conditions, particularly for Africans, but also for oppressed people throughout the world.

The tone and focus of the album is announced by its cover art. The front cover is a collage of the many flags of African nations. Across the upper part of the collage is a band depicting an aerial view of the inside of a slaveship, with the bodies of Africans packed closely together like sardines. Across this band, in large letters, is the word, "Survival." The musical flavor of the LP is slow and rootsy, several songs recalling the tempos found on *Natty Dread*. "Babylon System," for instance, employs a burro beat (Whitney and Hussey 1984, 141). There is even a song titled "One Drop," which may be the first in reggae to explore lyrically the potential of this musical element (the one drop) for healing and transformation, and its symbolic significance as a weapon in the struggle against Babylon.

The first song, "So Much Trouble," contains several proverbs. Like all the songs on the album, it is permeated with a strong sense of crisis. This urgency results from an acute awareness of the destructive forces of technology. In fact, the Rastafari theme that Babylon's "wrong" thinking has culminated in technological madness is a prominent feature of the album. Technology (space exploration and nuclear weapons, for example) more effectively perpetuates the oppression of black people but also threatens to destroy the environment and even the planet. The "trouble in the world" alluded to in the song results in one way or another from Babylon's misguided philosophy and unethical behavior:

You see men sailing on their ego trips
Blast off on their spaceship
Million miles from reality
No care for you, no care for me

The first proverb allusion is almost a plea that those in power recognize and embrace as equals the oppressed: "So before you check out your tide / **Don't leave another cornerstone / standing there behind.**" Two additional proverbs are linked to an uncharacteristic hint of resignation in this song, arising perhaps from prospective events that Rastafari ideology does not account for, such as the destruction of the world by nuclear bombs:

Now they're sitting on a time bomb
Now I know the time has come.
What goes on up is coming on down.
What goes around it comes around.

In keeping with Rastafari philosophy, the first proverb probably means that Babylon and its technological world is beginning to crumble. The second suggests that Babylon will inherit the suffering it has inflicted upon millions of oppressed people. Hence, the stanza would seem to be a positive and celebratory one. The tone of the song, however, is not at all joyful. Perhaps at the same time that Marley uses the proverbs from a Rastafari perspective, he is equally cognizant that—regardless of changes in political world order—there are, because of Babylonian practices, inevitable and devastating consequences to be reaped by everyone.

The image of the "cornerstone" appears a second time on the album, in "Ride Natty Ride," coupled with a rhetorical portrait of the epic hero. The composition depicts an apocalyptic scenario, including a vision in which fire is "burning down everything," destroying all Babylonian institutions: "Destroying and melting their gold / Destroying and wasting their souls." Meanwhile, Natty Dread is safe, as Marley invokes the Wild West motif again, "Natty Dread Rides Again." Like the previous song, this one centers around the struggle between good (Natty Dread) and evil (Babylon):

So they build their world
In great confusion
To force on us the Devil's illusion
But the stone that the builders refuse
Shall be the head cornerstone.

The proverb captures the sentiment that Natty Dread—Rastafari, or the righteous—shall ultimately be the leaders of the earth. Several other proverbial expressions give testimony to the urgency of the present moment for the unsaved, and to the struggles of Natty Dread. Similar to **Every tub has to sit on its bottom**, in a Culture song discussed earlier, **Pull your own weight** functions in this song to suggest that each person is responsible for his or her own redemption. No declarations from institutions or leaders can save the individual: "Fire is burning / **Man pull your own weight.**" The certainty that Natty Dread will survive the apocalypse is perhaps the most important message of the song and is restated in many ways throughout the composition. In the very last lines, it is reiterated with a proverbial expression, "We riding **thru the thick** / We riding **thru the thin.**"

"Wake Up and Live" is a motivational sermon in which the priest gives advice and encouragement, preaching with a seasoned fire and wisdom. The messages are the same ones we hear repeatedly in Rastafari and reggae discourse. Live life fully—which can only be done with the acquisition of knowledge. Stay on the spiritual path. Work toward unity in your everyday actions, not just in philosophy. Heed the word/sound/power of reggae, and surrender to its healing and liberating puissance. The first stanza begins, "**Life is one big road with lots of signs /** So when you're riding thru the ruts / Don't you complicate your mind." The expression in the song is suggesting an alert but non-anxious attitude toward life. It advises listeners how to "be" and how to survive and transcend this complicated, oppressive period of history. "Wake up and live now!" Marley sings, repeatedly, "Riiiiise, from your sleepless slumber!" There are obvious parallels between this call and those of eastern mystics. Not only is the idea of living in the here and now similar to elements of Buddhism, Zen, and so on, but so is the notion that one must "awaken" to some essence found within.

A second proverb continues Marley's penchant for raising agricultural images to the plateau of cultural and spiritual symbol:

You see **one, one cocoa full a basket**
Whey you use you live big today
Tomorrow you bury ina casket.

This traditional Jamaican proverb contains layers of social meaning (as noted in chapter 3). First, it encapsulates the idea that little by little someone who goes to market or the garden can get enough food. One gets a few yams, a few bananas, and so on, until the basket is full. Underlying this observation about how the basket is filled is a very strong communal philosophy. One should (if shopping at the market), buy from as many vendors as possible, thus giving financial support and affirming social ties to the maximum number of people. To buy everything from one person would be an antisocial act. On the metaphorical level, the proverb suggests that wisdom and understanding should also be attained little by little, from a variety of sources. Implicitly, physical hunger and nourishment are correlated to spiritual hunger and fulfillment. The proverb can be read, then, as a plea to take advantage of the wisdom being offered by any number of sources in the community—and to do so now, while one still has breath. Forsake the "vanity" of life, as Ecclesiastes warns, the drive for material wealth and social status, and turn your attention to the spiritual.

Several additional proverbial expressions are used in "Survival," a composition that mirrors the ideas in those discussed above. Again we have the extreme urgency of appeal to the Diasporic community, integrated with testimonies to its anciency and ability to survive the most severe persecutions. In the following lines is an expression that fits perfectly with the song's theme: "We better hurry, oh hurry woe now / Cause we **got no time to lose.**" Three other expressions are used in a stanza stating emphatically that black people need to "seize the moment." "So my brethren, my sistren / the preaching and talking is done / we gotta **live up** woe now." **Live up** is a traditional Rastafari expression meaning to live in a dignified, spiritual manner, according to the precepts of knowledge. The stanza continues: **Some people put the best outside / Some people keep the best inside.** This is another popular Rastafari proverb, referring to how people relate to their inner essence. The social expectation is in keeping with Jesus' admonition that one should not hide one's light under a bushel basket. One should share one's inner wealth, and through such sharing the entire community will be stronger and more able to accomplish its goals.

The final proverb, used near the end of the song, is a rhetorical gem, combining humor and dual levels of personal and community meaning. The stanza begins with the by-now familiar rhetorical use of children's taunts: "Na-na-na-na-na / We're the survivors; the black survivors." It moves from there to a biting depiction of the contemporary "lion's den" into which the ancient tribe has been thrown:

In this age of technological inhumanity
[backup singers] We're the survivors
Scientific atrocity. (We're the survivors)
Atomic mis-philosophy. (We're the survivors)
It's a world that forces life-long insecurity
All together now, we're the survivors

[Spoken] **A good man is never honored in his own country.**

On one level, the proverb seems out of place, as it makes a personal statement near the end of a sermon about the survival of a community. Certainly Marley was targeted not only by Jamaican authorities but (as CIA files attest) by foreign governments as well. His unwavering radicalism, his attacks on the system, his Rastafari identity, his international influence, all made him a threat to the established powers-that-be. Perhaps, though, the proverb goes beyond Marley's concern with his personal situation and refers to the plight of Rastas or, even more generally, of New World Africans in countries throughout the world.

Many of the same concerns and the same sense of urgency carry over into Marley's next album, *Uprising*. The cover art of this one returns to the depiction of Marley on the front. The red, green, and gold are still basic elements of the cover painting. In the background is a large yellow circle of sun rays, emanating from a red center. In front of this are green mountains, and in the front of this the upper body of a brown, muscular Marley, with arms outstretched and fists clenched, and a mountain of thick, black dreadlocks falling around him. In the very foreground is the title, *Uprising*, in large red letters. The painting gives the impression of a dreadlocked figure militantly rising from the earth.

The themes on *Uprising* are familiar ones, although the musical style of the songs on the surface are a little more pop than on the previous LP. The genius of Marley, however, is his ability to mold music that, on the surface, satisfies the pop flavor that many Western audiences craved while at the depths it remains true to the aesthetic vision of roots reggae. There are as many sustained hours of sublime, mystical ecstasy on *Uprising* as on any of his other LPs. The Barrett brothers (drummer and bassist) are "mashing it up" as hard as they ever did. There, on that deeper level, each tune rocks steady on into tomorrow, whipping, stomping, and marching on yesterday; and one-dropping on today. One stills hears the echoes of whips and gunshots. Fists against bone smashing. Kete and cowbells. Africans dancing secret dances under the full moon. The determined and persistent "uprising" of the enslaved.

Another relevant dimension of *Uprising* is its tempo. In spite of the rock musical touches on top of the songs, their tempo is that loping, laid-back Jamaican—and, more specifically, Rastafari—sense of time. It is a sense without anxiety, without hurry, a wide patience in which everything is moving slowly and things happen organically in their own time. The proverbs are spoken within the space of this sacred time, and once spoken, they, like other word-sounds, have agency, force, tangible consequences and effects. They come blasting from the speakers, having gathered momentum as they rushed along the currents of copper wires, like salmon carried along by raging river waters, accelerating the speed of their own wills, finally pouring into the sea. They come through the crackling of worn vinyl scratched by worn diamond; or above the stutter of laser light reading the etchings on a dust-covered or tea-stained disk. The proverbs come, like pebbles thrown in a lake, distorting the image of the sky, carried by Marley's voice, smooth, yearning, full of ecstatic conviction. They come to the accompaniment of Nyabinghi undercurrents and the pop veneer of songs like "Pimper's Paradise"; a trendy veneer that fades, becomes cloudy, like the echoes of the almost disco beat, evaporating, leaving one dancing, instead, ancient steps.

The first song on the LP, "Coming In from the Cold," is a sermon celebrating the redemption of the righteous. It is rhetorically similar to traditional spirituals with lines such as "The winter, chillun, the winter soon be over," or "I looked over Jordan / and what did I see / a chariot coming after me / coming for to carry me home." Marley declares, "In this sweet life / We're coming in from the cold." The song has the characteristic Marley synthesis of encouragement and social critique, punctuated with the wisdom of proverbs. As in many compositions, his form of address to the righteous and oppressed is very direct:

It's you, it's you, it's you I'm talking to

Why do you look so sad and forsaken?
When one door is closed
Don't you know another is open.

Marley's singing of the proverb is punctuated, interwoven, with the voice of the bass—both voices call and respond to each other—sometimes calling, sometimes singing back. The proverb is one that I have heard used often by African Americans as a form of encouragement to keep striving and not become depressed in the face of racism. In the Rastafari context, however, the ultimate goal is freedom from the system rather than freedom to become a part of it. Hence, the metaphorical doors must be interpreted on this basis. Marley is speaking about the struggle not just for job opportunities but for cultural liberation. Closed doors, then, might refer to economic disadvantages—but taken within this larger context.

A second proverb comes in the chorus, which begins with a series of questions to Rastafari and other brothers and sisters: "Would you let the system / make you kill your brotherman? / No Dread, No." Would you succumb to the tempting entreaties of the system and, in doing so, throw away your values in favor of theirs?

Would you make the system
Get on top of your head again?

[Marley and backup voices]
No Dread No. [Crashing symbols, melodic, rhythmic turn around]
[Marley simultaneously] No No No No No Dread No

[Marley's voice] **Well the biggest biggest biggest**
man you ever ever ever did see was a once a once a once a baby.

The proverb is dramatically preached here. A listener who has seen Marley perform might envision his intense stage enactments upon hearing the stanza. The proverb meaning is wide open to interpretation. Perhaps it is as a conciliatory encouragement for those who might be embarrassed by their stage of consciousness. In other words, never mind about where you happen to be. If it is further back than you would like, don't worry about it. We, as a group, should not beat ourselves up or be embarrassed by our condition. Just take a look around, reflect on the things that have to be done, and set about doing them. Everybody starts from somewhere. Or the proverb could be a way of demystifying those in power. Rich or poor, "a man puts his pants on one leg at a time."

The second song, "Real Situation," contains one of Marley's most beautiful proverb clusters. The composition sounds a disturbing note about the inevitability of nuclear war. Its refrain, "Ain't no use, no one can stop them now," is a haunting shift from the images that appear in other songs. One is forced to ponder Rastafari ideology more deeply to understand how such a prophecy as certain nuclear war—a vision that states, "Seem like total destruction / the only solution"—is reconciled with the certainty of "a new world." Of note in this regard are the lines from the last song on the LP, Marley's acoustical version of "Redemption Song." He sings, "Have no fear for atomic energy / cause none a them can stop the time." The proverb cluster comes in the second stanza:

Give them an inch, they take a yard.
Give them yard, they take a mile.
Once a man and twice a child.
And everything is just for a while.
It seems like total destruction . . .

The first two proverbs—or, rather, variations of the same proverb—speak to the character of the madmen who rule the planet. But more profoundly, these expressions go to the heart of human nature. The oppressors are greedy opportunists; but everyone carries the potential for greed within himself. The next proverb, **Once a man and twice a child**, suggests the decline of those in power. The most common *social* meaning is that a person eventually reverts back to the vulnerability of infancy. This reading is consistent with the next proverb, which calls attention to the temporality of all things. Its scope, however, encompasses all that has been constructed by human hands, specifically Western empires.

"Zion Train" is the next proverb song. Between it, "Coming In from the Cold," "Redemption Song," and lines from other compositions on the album, there are hints of a man who is coming to the end of his work on earth. This aspect of the album becomes eery in retrospect, now that we know this was Marley's last offering before his untimely death from cancer, at age thirty-six. In this hard-hitting tune, Marley returns to the theme of imminent salvation and rescue, relying on a traditional image from New World African religion— the train. The image conveys simultaneously the inevitability of freedom and repatriation to Africa (mentally, spiritually, and corporeally), and liberation from the physical body. The song skanks along, suspended between melodic, snakelike bass lines that resonate with the tones of an electric keyboard or an orchestral string instrument, clean, pure, determined; explosive one drops that splatter, hammer, and whip; and bells and symbol sounds of iron and tightened skin that sink into the far reaches of a displaced, colonized soul, tearing scabs off memory, and almost bringing the listener to tears. Marley's voice, filled with revelation, wedges itself tightly between pulses of the rhythm, while dancing with beats and offbeats, like an eagle on wind, a boat on water, a spirit dancer on earth. In trance, he sings, trying to share the rapture of his vision with those gathered around the sacred fire: "Zion train is coming our way / Oh Children."

The gems of proverbial wisdom begin in the first stanza, flowing like cool waters or mana, and continue in the "bridge" stanza:

Which man can save his brother soul
Oh man it's just self-control
Don't gain the world and lose your soul
Wisdom is better than silver and gold
To the bridge—

Marley is cautioning listeners, in the words of Jesus and other biblical visionaries. Read in the context of Rastafari ideology, the warning is to stay focused on the knowledge and not to be tempted by Babylonian reality. "Gaining the world" is not equivalent to becoming economically solvent, for one can have money and reject a Babylonian mentality. But to become accepted in Babylonian society suggests "making a deal with the devil," for it is felt that the corrupt will only accept those who agree to live by their codes or to become like them. The second proverb reflects the Rasta perspective that knowledge is indeed the ultimate possession, that the inner world is more precious than the outer.

The stanza that accompanies the musical bridge of the song is comprised of one proverb, repeated several times. Coming in the bridge, the proverb is highlighted. The bridge is similar in function to the soliloquy in a drama. By this I do not mean to emphasize the element of speaking to oneself but that of the metaphorical lights dimming on the main drama, as it recedes into the background. For a brief, reflective moment, a single idea takes center stage. One is always aware that the basic progression of the song is gathering momentum and will, like an ocean wave, come roaring back. In fact, the bridge is a musical strategy for allowing the melody to circle back on itself. Thus the word/sounds of the bridge claim a special place in our memories: **Oh where there's a will / There's always a way.** The proverb comes on the edge of the bass, with accents/responses from a crashing drumbeat. Its meaning is obvious: Keep the faith. Don't be discouraged. As long as we have the determination to become free, to "catch the Zion train," it can happen.

Three other proverbs are used in "Could You Be Loved," another composition that warns against "selling out." **What's in the darkness must come out in light** comes at the end of the first stanza. This stanza states emphatically that "our" way of thinking is "right," and theirs is wrong. The proverb suggests that eventually this realization will **come out to light.** The second proverb appears in stanza 3:

Don't let them change you
or even rearrange you, oh no!
We've got a life to live
They say only, only
only the fittest of the fittest shall survive.
Stay alive.

The meaning of the proverb is also somewhat obvious, although shades of meaning derived from Rastafari worldview bear mention. For example, the fittest are not simply those who are more physically healthy. The term extends to a consideration of one's spiritual consciousness; thus wisdom, self-reflection, humility, and knowledge of Selassie-I define the state of fitness as much as physical characteristics. "Stay alive" speaks as much to nurturing these qualities as it does to keeping the physical body alive.

Proverb number 3 begins the next stanza:

You ain't gonna miss your water
until your well runs dry.
No matter how you treat him
The man will never be satisfied.

This is one of the instances in which it is difficult to penetrate Marley's intended meaning. To begin with, the stanza is sung by the I Threes, the backup singers, not by Marley. Another aspect of difficulty arises from the ambiguity of who is being addressed.

The final proverbs on the album are found in "Forever Loving Jah," a sermon song testifying to unwavering devotion to Jah in the face of outside criticism and rebuke. The repetitive line of the chorus, "We'll be forever loving Jah," is directed toward those who "say we're going wrong." Three biblical proverbs are used in conjunction to reflect the perspectives of the righteous, as Marley allows the authority and poetry of established text to critique the skeptics and to contextualize Rastafari worldview.

Cause only a fool lean upon, lean upon
his own misunderstanding.
And what has been hidden from the wise and
the prudent
been revealed to the babe and the suckling.

We'll be forever loving Jah [repeat three times]
Cause just like a tree planted planted by the river of water, that bringeth forth
fruits in dry season
Everything in life got its purpose
Find its reason in every season.

The combination of the proverbs, musical tone, and tempo creates a meditative effect, leading one to reflect more generally on the whole sound than on the meanings of individual expressions. This is often the case when biblical proverbs are used, as the rhetorical authority and poetry of the expressions seem to be more important than particular meanings. Or, to put it another way, a large part of the meaning is the effect of hearing quotes from the Bible so lyrically strung together to the background sound of reggae rhythms.

In an earlier work (Prahlad 1996), I coin the phrase "proverb masters" to refer to speakers who have an extensive repertoire of proverbs at their command and demonstrate a marked sophistication in their ability to apply them. I note further that proverb masters are known for being wise and reflective, and for having deep insight as well as the skill to utilize metaphor in commenting on personal and societal concerns. Finally, my research illustrates that proverb masters are acutely aware of their role in keeping alive the spirits, memories, and cultural and personal associations embodied in the proverbs they use. Undoubtedly, Marley is a consummate proverb master, and this aspect of his lyrics, performances, and persona played a significant part in his popularity and in the high regard with which he is held by fans, fellow artists, and all those associated with reggae music in some capacity. More than any other artist, he epitomized the warrior/priest, and a major component of his appeal derives from the auras he so effectively projected of the mystic, visionary, freedom fighter, and spiritual guide. An integral feature of these auras was the use of proverbs, which contributed perhaps more than any other single rhetorical component. Hence, Marley's stature exemplifies, along with other things, the prevailing power of the proverb in modern societies and, particularly, in the Third World and among societies in the African Diaspora.

Partial Discography

This discography is not intended as a complete guide to the recordings of the artists noted here but as a list of those recordings that I primarily drew upon for this study. Not included are the thousands of singles and CDs by other artists or tapes from reggae radio programs that complete my reggae collection, most of which did not have proverbs or whose inclusion would have made this project too lengthy. The focus here is on albums. For a more complete discography of artists affiliated with the Wailers, see Timothy White's *Catch a Fire*. Those interested in pursuing a more complete listing of recordings by other artists might check the *Reggae and African Beat* magazine, which often has back issues available with interviews and discographies of specific reggae singers. Another possible source is Steve Barrow and Peter Dalton's *Reggae: The Rough Guide.*

Discs

Abyssinians, the
1993   [1970s] *Satta Massagana,* Heartbeat, CD HB 120.
1998   *Reunion,* Artist Only Records.

Ann, Lady
1983   *Informer,* Joe Gibbs Music, JGML-60074.

Broggs, Peter
1982   *Rastafari Liveth,* RAS.

Byles, Junior
  1997   *Curly Locks: The Best of Junior Byles and the Upsetters, 1970–1976*,
              Heartbeat, CD 208.

Carlos, Don, and Gold
  1983   *Raving Tonight*, RAS, 3005.

Carol, Sister
  1991   *Mother Culture*, RAS, 3003.

Cliff, Jimmy
  1973   *Unlimited*, Reprise, MS 2218.
  1973   *The Harder They Come*, Mango, MLPS-9202.
  1974   *Music Maker*, Reprise, MS 2188.
  1975   *Follow My Mind*, Reprise, MS 2218.
  1982   *Special*, Columbia, CXBL-38099.
  1983   *The Power and the Glory*, A L 38986.

Congos, the
  1979   *Congo*, Congo Ashanti, 002.
  1996   [1977] *Heart of the Congos*, Blood and Fire, BAFCD 009.
  1997   *Natty Dread Rise Again*, RAS, CD 3238.

Culture
  [1976]   *Two Sevens Clash*, Joe Gibbs Music, JGML 3201.
  1978   *Africa Stand Alone*, April Records, ADI-735 x 32.
  1979   *International Herb*, Virgin Music.
  1979   *Cumbolo*, 200–388.
  [1978–79?] *Culture in Dub*, SKY-LP-16.
  1981   *More Culture*, Joe Gibbs Music, JGML-6038.
  1982   *Lion Rock*, Heartbeat, HB-12, 1982.
  1986   *Culture at Work*, Blue Mountain, BMLP-014.
  1989   *Nuff Crises*, Shanachie, 43064.
  1989   *Good Things*, RA 3048-A.
  1991   [1986] *Culture in Culture*, CD HB 67.
  1991   *Three Sides to my Story*, Shanachie, 43088.
  1992   *Wings of a Dove*, Shanachie, 43097.
  1993   *Trod On*, Heartbeat, C HB 137.
  1993   [1980] *Baldhead Bridge*, Shanachie, 44017.
  1994   *Culture in Dub*, Heartbeat, CD HB 173.
  1996   *One Stone*, RAS, CD 3188.
  1997   *Stoned*, RAS, CD 3177.
  1997   *Trust Me*, RAS, CD 3240.
  1997   *Ras Portraits*, RAS, CD 3321.
  1998   *Cultural Livity*, RAS, CD 3241.
  1999   *Payday*, RAS CD 3252.

Diamonds, the Mighty
  1970s   *When the Right Time Come,* Channel One, Jamaica.
  1994   *Speak the Truth,* RAS, 3152.

Dillon, Leonard, and the Ethiopians
  1991   *On the Road Again,* Heartbeat, HB108.
  1992   [1978] *Slave Call,* Heartbeat, CD HB 56.
  1980   *Everything Crash,* Studio One, Jamaica.
  1980s   *Owner Fe De Yard,* Heartbeat.

Donovan
  1989   *Banzani-!,* Mango, MLPS 9838.

Dread, Danny
  [1970s] *Hit Me with Music,* Jet Star Records, LPARC005.

Dread, Mikey
  1991   *Best Sellers,* RYKOdisc, RDC 20178.

Dube, Lucky
  1992   *House of Exile,* Shanachie, 43094.

Ellis, Alton
  1995   *Sunday Morning,* Heartbeat, CD 3511. [Studio One masters from the
           1960s and 1970s]

Far I, Prince
  1970s   *Under Heavy Manners,* Joe Gibbs, Kingston, Jamaica.

Griffiths, Albert, and the Gladiators
  1987   *In Store For You,* Heartbeat, HB-41.
  1970s   *Presenting the Gladiators,* Studio One, Jamaica.
  1998   *The Gladiators at Studio One: Bongo Red,* Heartbeat, CD11661–7662–2.
           [Reissues of Studio One recordings from the 1970s]

Heptones, the
  1976   *Nightfood,* Island Records, ILPS-9393.
  1978   *In Love with You,* United Artist, UA-LA805-H.
  1996   *Rainbow Valley,* St. Clair Entertainment Group, CD REG26122

Hinds, Justin, and the Dominoes
  1976   *Jezebel,* Island Records, ILPS-9416.
  1985   *Travel With Love,* Nighthawk, 44159.
  1992   *Know Jah Better,* Nighthawk, NHC-313.

I-Roy
  [1970s] *African Herbsman,* Joe Gibbs Music, JBML-6045.

Isaacs, Gregory
  1980   *The Lonely Lover,* PRE.
  1982   *Mr. Isaacs,* Shanachie, 430006.
  1982   *The Sensational Gregory Isaacs,* Vista Sounds, VSLP 4001.

1982	*Night Nurse,* Island Records, CD 162–539 721–2.
1990	*Consequence,* Rohit Records, RRTG 7777–4.
1992	*Pardon Me,* RAS, CS 3100.
1993	*Unattended,* Pow Wow Records, PDW 7436.
1997	*Ras Portraits,* RAS CD 3309.

Itals, the

1981	*Brutal Out Deh,* Nighthawk, NH 303.
1983	*Give Me Power,* Nighthawk, 307.
1987	*Early Recordings 1971–1979,* Nighthawk, 45715.
1988	*Cool and Dread,* Nighthawk, NH 311.
1991	*Easy to Catch,* Rhythm Safari, 4xl 57159.
1998	*Modern Age,* RAS CD 3180.

Jackson, Vivian (Yabby You)

| 1972 | *Conquering Lion,* Kingston, Jamaica. [reissued by Shanachie] |
| 1985 | *A Musical Prophet,* Shanachie, 43026. |

Jerry, Brigadier

| 1990 | *On the Road,* RAS, 3071. |

Marley, Bob, and the Wailers

1973	*Catch a Fire,* Island, ILPS 9241.
1973	*Burnin',* Island, ILPS 9256.
1974	*Natty Dread,* Island, ILPS 9281.
1975	*Live! Bob Marley and the Wailers,* Island, ILPS 9376.
1976	*Rastaman Vibration,* Island, ILPS 9383.
1977	*Exodus,* Island, ILPS 9498.
1978	*Kaya,* Island, ILPS 9517.
1978	*Babylon by Bus,* Island, ISLD 11 1298.
1979	*Survival,* Island, ILPS 9542.
1980	*Uprising,* Island, ILPS 9596.
1983	*Confrontation,* Island, ILPS 7 90085–1.
1984	*Legend,* 7 90169–1.
[?]	*Interviews,* Tuff Gong.

Marshall, Larry

| 1992 | *I Admire You,* Heartbeat, CD HB 57. |
| 1992 | *Come Let Us Reason,* King's Music Records, KMR-2. |

Meditations, the

1983	*No More Friend,* Greensleeves, GREL 52.
1984	*Greatest Hits,* Shanachie, 43015.
1992	*Return of the Meditations,* Heartbeat, HB CHB 130.

Melodians, the

| 1983 | *Irie Feeling,* RAS, 3003. |

Miller, Jacob, and Inner Circle

| 1993 | *The Best of Inner Circle: The Capital Years, 1976–1977,* Capital, T4 27170. |

Mowatt, Judy
  1983   [1979] *Black Woman,* Shanachie, 43011.

Mundell, Hugh
  1980   *Time and Place,* Muni Music, MMLP-001.
  1983   *Africa Must Be Free by 1983,* Corona Records, 99–18.

Osbourne, Johnny
  1981   *Warrior,* Starlight Records, DHLP 2001.

Pablo, Augustus
  1978   *Earth Rightful Ruler,* Pablo Music, RP 011.
  1990   *Blowing with the Wind,* Shanachie, 43076.
  1999   *Valley of Jehosaphat,* RAS CD 3184.

Prophet, Michael
  1980   *Serious Reasoning,* Island, ILPS 9606.

Romeo, Max, and the Upsetters
  1976   *War Ina Babylon,* Island, ILPS-9392.

Souls, the Wailing
  1992   [1981] *Fire House Rock,* Shanachie, CGR 21.
  1983   [1982] *Inchpinchers,* Shanachie, GREL 47.
  1986   *Lay It on the Line,* RAS, LL-024-2.
  1990   *The Very Best,* Shanachie, 48018.
  1995   *Wild Suspense,* Island, 162–539–952-2.
  1996   *All Over the World,* Columbia, 48653.
  1999   *Reggae Legends Vol. 1,* Artists Only Records, Canada. CD AOR24.
             [Recordings from the 1960s and 1970s]

Spear, Burning
  1975   *Marcus Garvey,* Island, ILPS-9317.
  1976   *Man in the Hills,* Mango, MLPS-9412.
  1976   *Garvey's Ghost,* Mango MLPS-9382.
  1977   *Live,* Mango, MLPS-9513.
  1977   *Dry and Heavy,* Mango, MLPS-9431.
  1980   *Hail H.I.M.,* Rondor Music, RDC 2003.
  1987   [1983] *The Fittest of the Fittest,* Heartbeat, CD HB-22.
  1991   *Jah Kingdom,* Mango, 162–539915.
  1993   *The World Should Know,* Heartbeat, C HB 119.
  1995   *Rasta Business,* Heartbeat, CD HB 179.
  1997   *Appointment with His Majesty,* Heartbeat, CD HB 211.
  1999   *Calling Rastafari,* Heartbeat, CD 11661–7744.

Tosh, Andrew
  1994   *Original Man,* Heartbeat, CDHB 140.

Tosh, Peter
  1976   *Legalize It,* Columbia, BL 34253.

1977	*Equal Rights*, Columbia, PC34670.
1978	*Bush Doctor*, Columbia, COC 39109.
1979	*Mystic Man*, Columbia, COC 39111.
1981	*Wanted: Dread and Alive*, EMI-America, SO 17055.
1983	*Mama Africa*, EMI-America, RDC 2005.
1984	*Captured Live*, EMI, EG 2401671.
1987	*No Nuclear War*, EMI-America, ELT 46700.
1988	*The Toughest (The Selection, 1978–1987)*, Capital CI 90201

U-Roy

| 1991 | *True Born African*, Ras Records, ARICS 071. |

Wailer, Bunny

1976	*BlackHeart Man*, Solomonic.
1977	*Protest*, Mango, MLPS 9512.
1980	*Bunny Wailer Sings the Wailers*, Mango, MLPS 9629.
1980	*Time Will Tell: A Tribute to Bob Marley*, Shanachie, 43072.
1981	*Rock 'n Groove*, Solomonic.
1983	*Roots Radics Rockers Reggae*, Shanachie, 43013.
1985	*Marketplace*, Shanachie, SM LP 010.
1988	*Liberation*, Shanachie, 43059.
1994	*Crucial*, Shanachie, 45014.

Wailers, the Original

| 1993 | *Never Ending Wailers*, RAS 3501. |

Youth, Big

| 1995 | [1970s] *Jamming in the House of Dread*, Roir, DRCD A- 198. |

Compilations and Field Recordings

1990	*Rastafari Elders*, RAS, 3068.
1991	*Dancehall Reggaespañol*, Columbia, CT 48526.
1994	*Word Sound 'Ave Power: Dub Poets and Dub*, Heartbeat, CD HB15.
1997	*By the Rivers of Babylon: Timeless Hymns of the Rastafari*, Shanachie, 45031.
1998	*The Roots All Stars: Gathering of the Spirits*, Shanachie, 45040.

Films

The Harder They Come
Red X—Stepping Razor
The Land of Look Behind
Reggae Sunsplash
Bob Marley, Time Will Tell
Bob Marley and the Wailers: Live at the Rainbow
Heartland Reggae

Legend: The Best of Bob Marley and the Wailers
Rockers
Countryman
Babylon
Reggae
Rasta in A-Babylon

Appendix 2

List of Major Proverb Users

JIMMY CLIFF: Cliff was born in 1944, in the village of Somerton, the Parish of St. James, Jamaica. Although the beginning of his recording career predated roots reggae and he has remained outside the mainstream, he is highly respected in Jamaica and internationally and is generally considered a living legend. One may argue, in fact, that Cliff introduced the world to reggae before the coming of Bob Marley, although his music was much more pop and less infused with the spirit of rebellion or religious zeal. He was rocketed to international fame with the release of the film *The Harder They Come*, in which he plays Rhygin, the main character. The film achieved cult status in many countries, including the United States, and was the inspiration for Michael Thelwell's novel by the same name. Cliff, who is still actively recording and touring, is one of the unsung proverb users in reggae.

CULTURE: The group Culture is composed of three singers: Albert Walker, Roy "Kenneth" Dayes, and lead singer Joseph Hill. Joseph Hill, who was born in the parish of St. Catherine, Jamaica, is the founder, leader, producer, and songwriter of the group. He put himself through the Jamaica School of Arts, Science, and Technology, and says that his youth was "not spent in idle dalliance, but in thinking about life, about serious things" (Paladino 1990, 34). The group was founded in 1976 and was called at first the African Disciples. One might call them an instant success, as their first recording session was so stunning that, legend has it, "all other activity in the area came to a halt" (34). Initially, they recorded nine songs for producer Joe Gibbs, some of which would later appear on their first and seminal album, *Two Sevens Clash*. From the beginning, they gained a reputation as one of Jamaica's most militant and spiritually centered harmony groups, a status that has only grown over time.

JUSTIN HINDS AND THE DOMINOES: Justin Hinds was born in 1942 in Steertown, St. Anns Parish, Jamaica. Although this group is known as a vocal trio, I have been unable to find the names of the Dominoes. The group's career began in 1963 on the Duke Reid label, and most of their hits were during the ska and rock steady periods. One of Bob Marley's favorite groups, they were known for Hinds's beautiful tenor voice, songs that reflect Rastafari perspectives (before this trend became popular), and mastery of proverbs and biblical parables.

IAA (delta weit): Iaa is a forty-year-old Jamaican Rastafari who lives in the mountains east of Negril, where he was born (in 1957) and raised. He currently divides his time between Negril, where he comes occasionally to make money by using his car as a taxi and selling wood-carved souvenirs, and his home in the mountains, where he farms and lives with his family.

NEVILLE O'REILEY LIVINGSTON (bunny wailer): Wailer was born in April 1947, in Kingston, Jamaica. A childhood friend of Bob Marley's, he helped to form the Wailers, but became unhappy with the trappings of tours and media and retired from the group to spend several years living in a Rastafari community in Bull Bay. He continued to record, keeping a low profile and preferring to serve his role of social critic and spiritual advisor via records rather than through live performances. He reemerged into the international limelight in 1988 and has continued to produce roots music, earning the acclamation of artists around the world as well as two American Grammies.

BOB MARLEY AND THE WAILERS: Robert Nesta Marley was born around 6 April 1945, in the Parish of St. Ann, in the village of Nine Mile, Jamaica. He was raised in the country by his mother, Cedella Marley Booker, his grandfather and grandmother, Omeriah and Yaya Katherine Malcolm, and other elders. Marley was known since childhood for having a mystical aura around him and a mind of his own. He cut his first record, "Judge Not" in 1959 with producer Leslie Kong. Around the same time, he formed a group with his two friends, Peter Tosh and Bunny Wailer, who were coached by Rastafari singer/songwriter, "the godfather," Joe Higgs. By 1962 the group was recording regularly on a number of Jamaican labels. Marley devoted the rest of his life to his music, becoming increasingly popular in Jamaica. He converted to Rastafari in 1968, and by 1973 had gained international fame. He went on to become a spokesman for the underprivileged and colonized; he comes as close as one can come, in fact, to being a patron saint in the non-Catholic country of Jamaica. More than any other artist, Marley defined the genre of roots reggae and spread the message of Rastafari internationally. He passed away, tragically, from cancer on 11 May 1981.

LARRY MARSHALL: Larry Marshall was born in 1945 in Lawrence Park, St. Ann's Parish, Jamaica. His stature in reggae derives not only from his early recordings but also from his work as a producer, arranger, and advisor to many aspiring reggae stars. His sound—which incorporated American soul and R & B, Jamaican popular and folk music, ska, and Jamaican religious music (he maintained a career as a gospel singer) and country-style singing—helped to move Jamaican music from ska into the rock steady and reggae eras. His lyrics incorporated folk wisdom, proverbs, social commentary, and Rastafari philosophy.

KEITH PORTER AND THE ITALS: Members of the Itals began their recording careers with other groups around 1971. In 1976, Keith Porter, Ronnie Davis, and Lloyd Ricketts formed the Itals. Their first song, "In A Dis Ya Time" was a hit in Jamaica, followed by "Brutal" and other remarkable singles that never reached the top of the charts. Ironically, the three-part harmony tradition that is one of the strengths of the group lost popularity in Jamaica, and the Itals began recording for the American Nighthawk label and building a following primarily in the United States. Thus, the proverb mastery that distinguishes the group has never been widely appreciated in Jamaica. After their first LP, *Brutal,* Lloyd Ricketts left the group and was replaced by David Isaacs. In 1997, Ronnie Davis left the Itals and formed his own group, Ronnie Davis and Idren. Keith Porter's wife, Kada Porter, replaced Davis. Lloyd Ricketts also joins with David Isaacs doing backup vocal harmonies.

PETER TOSH: Tosh was born in Church Lincoln, in the parish of Westmoreland, Jamaica, in 1944. An only child, he was raised by an aunt in Savanna-la-Mar and later in the Denham Town section of Kingston. He moved in with an uncle in Trench Town after his aunt died and turned to music in part to ward off loneliness and as a means to a better standard of living than he found around him. He left the Wailers in 1973, embarking on a solo career. The personas of Bush Doctor and Mystic Man—as well as the militant, angry ones employed in many interviews—surrounded Tosh in his personal life, gaining him the reputation of being difficult or embittered. He was a steadfast, evangelical crusader for Rastafari and social justice, and his conversational rhetoric was filled with proverb, parable, and allegory. Although his musical stature was overshadowed by Marley's, he was popular abroad, enjoying a successful recording and touring career until his brutal assassination by thugs on September 11, 1987, at his home in Kingston.

THE WAILING SOULS: The Wailing Souls are one of the finest vocal harmony groups in Jamaican roots reggae. They began recording as a quartet in 1970 and had a number of singles reach number one on the Jamaican charts. The group was initially Winston "Pipe" Matthews and Lloyd "Bread" McDonald, with harmony singers Oswald Downer and Norman Davis. After the first two LPs, Downer and Davis left, and from 1976 to 1985, harmony singers George "Buddy" Haye and Rudolph "Garth" Dennis sang with the group. In 1986, Winston "Ziggy" Thomas joined the group for at least one album. Matthews and McDonald have remained the core of the Wailing Souls, with Matthews doing most of the songwriting. The two primary singers grew up together in Trench Town, Jamaica. Matthews was among the young teenagers tutored by Joe Higgs, along with Bob Marley, Peter Tosh, and Bunny Wailer. They remain a popular band, primarily in the United States.

Interview with Keith Porter

The following is a transcript of an interview I conducted with Keith Porter, in Columbia, Missouri, in 1991. Upon hearing that the Itals were coming to Columbia, I contacted their managers, Jeff Colvin and Mary Perkins, and informed them of my project. They were excited to hear about my proposed book and granted me permission to do the interview. By ethnographic standards, the interview was poorly conducted, owing to a number of factors. I had begun collecting proverbs from reggae songs but had only the vaguest idea of how the book would eventually unfold. This made it difficult to know what questions would ultimately be the most important. The interview environment was also a factor. I met with Porter (and subsequently with the other Itals, Ronnie Davis and David Isaacs) in their rooms at the Ramada Inn, hours before the show. Time was relatively short, as they were scheduled for an interview on a local radio station and needed to get dinner and get prepared for the concert. The telephone rang several times during the interview. At least one of those times the radio station was calling to say that the Itals were late for their engagement there.

To add to all of this, I was so completely starstruck that I lost my focus and composure. There I was, sitting down face-to-face with Keith Porter, whose music I had listened to and loved for more than twenty years. The Itals were one of my favorite groups and the admiration I feel for them is very deep. I never dreamed I would actually get an opportunity to sit and reason with them, much less in such a private setting. Porter was so composed, meditative, and serene it made my nervousness even greater. My first question, for instance, was actually three or four questions put together, which made it difficult for him to answer. Although I settled down as the interview progressed, the combination of nonideal factors led to a number of poorly worded questions. In other cases, I failed to pursue issues that cried out for further reasoning, largely because I knew that at any moment the interview would be terminated. With this in mind, I tended to go for breadth rather than depth, asking about as many proverbs as possible, rather than spending very much time on any particular item or idea.

There were, in spite of everything, parts of the interview that took on the tenor of reasoning. Unfortunately, some of this does not translate onto tape. For instance, in some cases when Porter says, "Yeah, definitely," a paralinguistic connection occurs that communicates important information and feeling. However, this is difficult to represent in a written transcription. Also considerable essence of the interview is lost on those who are not familiar enough with Jamaican patois to fill in for themselves how the transcribed lines might be intoned and spoken. Finally, as most of the questions pertain to proverbs used in specific songs, readers unfamiliar with those songs will be at a disadvantage. The Itals have recorded seven albums with which I am familiar (see discography); however, the interview questions pertained primarily to *Brutal Out Deh* and *Give Me Power*. Although from time to time Ronnie Davis or another of the Itals have penned songs, 98 percent of the compositions are written by Keith Porter.

P: I'd like to ask you about some of them [proverbs] that I notice you use, and you can tell me, like, what kind of meaning you have behind them. On the album *Brutal*, on the song "Brutal" there's a lot. You say, "**If I should feed one child and starve the other,** I'd rather be down with my brothers and sisters," and then **Cause a hungry man is an angry man,** and **A drowning man will catch at straws.** They all sort of come together. When you hear one or think of one does that trigger your memory of the others? Is that why they come together?

KP: Yeah, definitely. Because, you know, I write every, each verse and you who living and I like to know every, each time people can find food for themselves. You know, if it's not natural food, but even physical and spiritual food, you know, in that sense. You know, I don't **Feed one child and really starve the other.** You know, I want you to know that they both must be fed.

P: And you're not just talking about physical food . . .

KP: No, I'm not talking about physical food, I talk about, you know, I talk about physical and spiritual, you know, natural.

P: A drowning man will catch at straws. What do you mean by that?

KP: Well, most likely if one is desolated or are, you, have nothing else to turn to and I mean what is out of His [Jah] sight or comes close to his reach or however, you know what I mean, even cross his thinking, he's going to try to get at it. It's like seeing a drowning man drowning. And it don't matter what is there, he's going to try to grab at it.

P: So when later you say, **Man cannot live by only bread . . .**

KP: See that kind of explains the whole thing. I'm not talking about only the physical but you know, the spiritual.

P: And what about **Never try to bite the hand that feeds you.**

KP: Well, definitely, because, you know, who gives life? Where does this life come from? Because, you know, that's the hand that feeds you every time.

P: OK, OK, that's beautiful. In "Herbs Pirate" you say, **Who can't hear, them bound to feel.**

KP: Yeah, well. It's like our farm. I do a lot of cultivating. I cultivate my own food stuff for eating and other different kind of herbs, you know. And it's, like, I get so deep into the stuff. I do my own farming, planting food, etc. You know, it happens that other times I felt that when it's time to reap, you know, I mean it's all gone. You know, people just sit there, the pirates, just sit aside, and wait until everything is close to maturity. You know, I mean that's the time you go and take it. Up until that time it's been so much so hard. I mean you've done it with your hands, down to earth. You know, it's a fine food, you know, and to know that the pirate is right there for the taking. All the time I going to prepare for a later day.

P: And so the pirate is not just the government then . . . ?

KP: The pirate is not just government. The pirate is like anyone who try to destroy your livelihood, your sensibility.

P: OK, I got that . . . In "Truth Must Reveal . . . "

KP: Yes, you get right down to it because the truth must reveal every time, and, I mean, it makes no sense that one tries to hide behind the things, you know, that one do because you know sooner or later you gonna have to get down to the thing and say, you know, "well I've done this." If you hide behind sheet, you know, or underneath the sheet, or between the 8 or 10 inches concrete or whatever with steel, the guilt is still there. It's always there. So the truth must reveal at some point.

P: So that's like **The truth will come to light?**

KP: The truth must come to light.

P: Here's one I was wondering about. In "Temptation" there's a line when you say, "It's full time, you should know that," are you saying **Iron sharpeneth iron?**

KP: Yeah, because if you look on materially, you know, iron like a file to sharpen a knife or a machete. I mean it's like brother or sister, like I know something you know and I want to get you enlightened so you can use the thing I know.

P: So it's a song Culture has, **Iron Sharpen Iron.** I don't know if you know that song, but Joseph Hill has a song, **Iron Sharpen Iron.** So **Iron sharpen Iron** is like you are your brother's keeper in a way.

KP: Yeah, naturally.

P: Okay, **The countenance of one man brightenth another . . .**

KP: Definitely. [We share a laugh, reflecting on the truth of the proverb.]

P: Is **Iron sharpen iron** one you learned from someone or did you learn that from the Bible?

KP: I learned that you know, through everyday living. I mean, because in island community, you know, there's a lot of intelligent people who live in my circle, you know, and we like sit down and when there's not much things to do and focus on lot of different stuff. You focus on, like, present, past, future, and even things that we haven't seen. You know, you just try to think about these things.

P: Is it, are there certain people that say these a lot or does everybody use them?

KP: I wouldn't say everybody, you know. People who really know that the word is what it is. It's like whoever take hold of the words as active you know.

P: Because where I grew, I grew up, I grew up in the country and my great grandmother who always used these kinds of things, but to other people didn't use them much so I learned a lot of them actually from her.

KP: Yeah, I learned a lot from my mother, my father and some of my grandparents and I learned from other folks around.

P: When you use them in the songs do you use them the same way that people used when you were growing up, or do you try to give them new meaning?

KP: Most likely, growing up like partly religious people, because, you know, my ah mother's into, like, religious stuff. I go to church, like stuff like that, so I learn a lot, you know. And by seeing things, and I read different Bible, different version. I come across a lot of different, ah, what say ah, paragraph, so you know, I develop way of seeing different things I sing together different dictions from what I learned. Learning, is like learning from, you know, from the Bible. You know, learning from day to day stuff and things that I've seen and things that I've thought about.

P: In "Rastafari Chariot" you say, **A rolling stone gather no moss** . . .

KP: Yeah, naturally.

P: But I didn't understand how you were using it in that one. Is that a good thing that it doesn't gather moss or . . . ?

KP: Well, you know, if it could keep moving, I mean. It's, like, normally you would be going down a street, just for instance, right? And you just make a quick stop, like, here. Like check in on a friend. You could use it this way, okay? And right away something happen, you know, and you get caught in the act. Then if you're moving, you wouldn't be there. So it's like to be in the wrong place at the wrong time, you know, it's like you're gathering moss. You get caught in the act.

P: So keep moving?

KP: Yeah.

P: Keep the momentum going.

KP: Yeah, every time.

P: Okay, and then negative things won't catch you?

KP: Won't catch you at all. Because if you keep your mind focusing on positive things, you know, then you have no time for negative. It's, like, you know, people have to look into themselves to understand or overstand the diction that is being used in a lot of different songs.

P: Do you think that listeners here in North America understand what you sing as well as people, say, in Jamaica or the Caribbean?

KP: Lot of people, because right now the culture or the language or the way Jamaicans speak is catching on all over the world, you know. I'm in no doubt because I've been to, like, lot of shows, lot of concerts, and, like, the previous tour, and even this mini tour that we are on right now.

P: So they get it?

KP: Yeah.

P: Do you feel like in the songs you're teaching people . . . ?

KP: Well definitely. You know, definitely, that's one of the intentions, to teach people so people can learn and understand. You know, just for instance, people say understand what you know. Growing up on . . . I even start figuring a different sense of knowledge by saying *overstand* because if you *under* you just *under* you know, because if you *over* you *over,* you know.

P: It seems like on each album you have maybe one sort of love song, I guess on *Brutal* it was "Give Me What I Want."

KP: Well, love songs, you know, I love. It's always there, because love is the universe and, I mean, you know. When you talk about give me what I want, it could be anything as long as it's positive.

P: And **Absence makes the heart grow fonder?**

KP: Yeah, definitely.

P: Are you thinking about a person you're missing, or do you mean that in a general way?

KP: Well, you could say, you know, both. Both.

P: I like that one, **Absence makes the heart grow fonder.** Let's see. Oh yeah, here's one that I've been trying to understand and it's in the song "Jah Calling." It says, **Teeth and tongue, teeth and tongue will meet.** What do you mean by "teeth and tongue got to meet some sweet day"?

KP: Well, it's, like, normally we are learned about Lucifer. Some people say Jesus, Allah, some say God, some say Yahweh, or whatever, right? It's normally, thousands of different names. And remember he was one that created Lucifer. You know, who was the bright sun of the morning. And then, when they got into, like, exchanging words and stuff like that, you know, even to a point Lucifer said, "I wrestle till the break of day. I will not let you go." You know, one is saying that he want to do this, and the next one is saying "No, you should do this."

P: So it becomes like opposites?

KP: Yeah.

P: Conflict.

KP: Conflict.

P: I got it, because I was thinking of, like, when your teeth and your tongue meet.

KP: Yeah, if you look at it that close. Your teeth and tongue meet every time. You know, so it's, like, the diction that is being used. Everyone will have a different feel for it and it will mean something to the person who is thinking about the song.

P: Yeah, right, I see. Another one that I've been trying to understand is, "Some would say that **The chip don't fall too far from the block.**"

KP: Well, naturally. Because in His own likeness, in His own image. You know, like the father, like so the son. You know, if you got a son or a daughter, chances are one of them are going to do in life the stuff that you know have been doing. Now you can look at it that way.

P: In "Kill Crime," you say **Too much rat never dig good hole.**

KP: Definitely.

P: Can you help me with that one?

KP: Well, you see. Too much stability can never create anything that's positive.

P: If too many people are trying to do it you mean?

KP: Yeah. I mean, too many people like too much rat, you know, learned, like, ah that's a saying that goes around Jamaica. I mean, that it's, like, one person but not a whole bunch. So if you got too much gathering, you know, I mean, we all should gather, right? But there comes a time when it's too much gathering and too much things are being said and, I mean, it cause like friction, you know.

P: Okay, I see.

KP: And it, even, you know, it goes beyond that. Because, if you talk about "Kill Crime," because people could just kill crime. I mean, because crime is a thing where people can kill. You don't have to use a knife, or a gun, or machete to kill. You just use you. You know? Just think about it. Think about the hurt, you know, of the next person. How the next person is gonna get hurt, or how you could be hurt, you know, and result into things that are not necessary.

P: When you say, **Some ha fe come, some ha fe go.** How does that connect with the idea?

KP: Well, He said I'll give men for thee and people for their life. From beginning until this time, you know, man fall on this earth and man leave. And, I mean, some must come and some must go. Because if everybody that was born from that time was still here today, while you or I don't know that would be. It's, like, you grow from a kid into grown a man into an old man, you know, it's like **Once a man, twice a child.**

P: So coming and going in that way. And then later you say, "I can't stand the rat race." Are you making any kind of connection between those two or did it just happen to be in there?

KP: Well, you see, the rat race is like the race out there, a lot of people out there, just come out and shout out, "Oh Jah!" and just try to get ahead of the crowd. And really, check it out. I mean, it's like a race to see who first can shout out, you know. I mean, but you are learned to be civil. It's not a low tone of the voice, it's the inner.

P: I only have a few more, I don't know if you're getting tired. In "Make Merry," there's a verse where you say, **Some try to put the best outside,** some try to find a place to hide, **What you sow, it's what you reap** . . .

KP: You see there are so much thing in the world that everyone can partake of and still [the telephone rings]. A lot of people, just trying to put the best outside and some trying to find a place to hide because there's so many things in the world can spread out and everyone, I mean, have something so they can be comfortable. You have these so-called big guys who claim that they are leaders and rulers and whatever, and, I mean, so far, the people and I know it's unbelievable. So right now when they find out that people are getting conscious or aware of what's really going on, I mean, they trying to hide behind their big speeches. You know and stuff like that, but there will be no place for them to hide.

P: So putting the best outside is like putting a false face to the people?

KP: Yes. Putting a false face to the people, and still deep behind that they are killing them. You know?

P: So then when you say, **What you sow it's that you reap,** you're saying that about those people?

KP: Yeah, that's right. That goes for everyone. You know, whatever you want. If you want corn, plant corn and reap peas. You can't expect that to be living and doing all these wrong things like pushing your brother down, you know, stepping in your sister's face, and you know . . .

P: And then, **Silent rivers run deep** . . .

KP: Definitely, that's why a lot of people, God created people, and caused all these things to happen. You know what I mean? Cause I've been through that several times. But, you know, He said, He's watching. There's nothing he don't see. What one takes unto himself is one's destruction and until that day, you know. So the silent river is the Almighty Himself who watches over all of us. And I mean, yeah. And he will stay there and say, "Okay, I'm going to watch over you cause you said you would do the work, you said you would do the wills, so I'm going to sit here and see how much positive you are."

P: That's a really deep one. What about **This race is not for the swift, neither is the battle for the strong?**

KP: Definitely. There's only One who can do it, you know, from the beginning till the end. So, you know, good, your mind done too, but keep marching because you have a whole bunch of money and you have, you know, your facilities, you have a whole lot of access. I mean, you figure, "Oh, I'm strong. I can do this and that." But, you know, it can all get gone too. You check it out, it's like, no one believes that it's "because I have big powers, I have big garment, I have big car, the whole big mansion" that they live in and all those people have to be running around and doing stuff and like that, and I'll just sit. I just can't help you.

P: In "In Deh," you say **If knife would only speak it would attack. When lamp out, finger walk.**

KP: Yeah, if *night* could only speak.

P: Night. Okay, cause I got it wrong, it's not knife. Okay.

KP: Yeah. Okay, it's really "night." Yeah, because a lot of people tends to use the darkness, which is night, to do so much fanatic stuff. You know what I mean. So you're more or less, "Oh well, this is night nobody see me, you know, so I can get away with it." It's like I said before, He's watching over us. To see what we are doing. So if night could turn to daylight a lot of people even try to run away from themselves. Which they can't.

P: So when you say, **When lamp out, finger walk**, you mean when the lights go out, people start doing bad things?

KP: Yeah, crazy things. You know what I mean? Because they figure, "Oh it's dark nobody is going to see me." But you know the guilt is there. Whatever you do is still there.

P: And later I hear you say, **Hawk dem near—chicken merry**.

KP: That's another Jamaican term. Like **Chicken merry you know, hawk is near**. You know what I mean? We all sit at, like, when I was a child, or a little child you know, I see the chicken that follows the mother hen and keep playing and a lot of times. When they, they see they going and making merry like that, soon after there comes a hawk, you know. Come down, and, like, "I really want to get one, I will get one and go again." And they are silent for a time. And just like with people, right now. A lot of people all just making merry because they are so guilty you know. They are so guilty themselves so all they try to do is make merry to cover up that. But deep inside, deep inside, they not making merry, you know, so it's, like, why make merry?

P: There was one I've been listening to a lot and I want to make sure I understand what you mean. When you say, **A friend in need is a friend in deed**. And then you sorta talk about your friends turning out not to be friends.

KP: Yeah, because sometimes I don't know who to trust. You have a close one to you, say he's a friend and we sit and talk and, you know, and see him as a person who want to get to you all of his life. So **A friend in need is a friend in deed** because I don't know who to trust or who to believe. I mean, you to first trust in yourself and believe in yourself, because I said again that **The arms of flesh will not give you a choice of war**. So, you know, we right down to it, sometimes you can't even trust your own. Because, I don't know sometimes the things that I will do. Yeah, definitely. Because I'm not going to sit there and be killed. You know, I'm not just gonna, you know. I going to do something to emancipate myself and whatever it is.

P: There's one more I wanted to ask you about, and I think this is from the last album, and you say, **Blood is thicker than water**. I like to get what you meant when you said that. [Another telephone interruption.] Some people when they say that mean people that are kin to each other stick together, but I don't think you mean that.

KP: Let's check it out. **Blood is thicker than water**, okay. This is your bond for life. You have one mother. You are not going to stand here and see them get hurt. You're going to want him to be a partaker of some of what you got. You know whatever you got to use. I mean, when you check it out, not because you might be born from a different mother, you might live in a different country, and you might be of a different color from me. I mean, it's one blood. You know, it's one eternity. It's like cut your skin and run the blood out there and cut mine and run the blood there. Cut a white man and run the blood there, or a Chinese man, or whatever, you know, it's the same blood that goes through everyone vein.

P: So you're taking it deeper than just . . .

KP: So many times it's much deeper than some people thought, you know. Every man and man that lives is brother and sister, every, each one. It's the same blood that goes through everyone veins.

P: For me, the proverbs are the parts of the song that really stand out. Do you think it's like that for other people, or do you think it might be just my thing?

KP: I think it reach out to lot of people, lots and lot of people. Because I've seen people come to Ital show, you know, and lot of people walk away saying, "Oh, I'm blessed." You know, I can even remember, like I've been to shows, like here in America, where people go down on their knees and ask me to, like, just touch them. And by doing that, they said, "Oh, I'm blessed, I'm healed, I feel so good inside, I've never felt this way before." I ask some people, you know, don't do that to me. You know, because thou should not bow down my self to them and I serve them because who I am? Give and live, follow who created you. One should give thanks to Him, and not to me.

P: I know you need to get going. I have just two more questions. One is, out of all these proverbs, do you have a favorite one that you think about more than others?

KP: I know of a favorite one that I think most definitely. You know, all of our proverbs, you know, I mean love. Cause I fight against tribal, I fight whatever fight against a brother or sister, I mean, that's not love. You know? Love means one thing. Love. Love mean two things. We know not love as a universe. It's like **Love thy neighbor as they self**. Love one another. Love your brother, love your sister. You know, love your enemy. One final thing I would to say is that captivity, it's anything that goes beyond your will. Young people don't get any jobs, and getin' the blues because of fights. Anything that does that, restrict your mind and retards your personal self. That's captivity.

P: Thank you so much for taking the time to sit and talk with me.

KP: Yes, Yes. Irie. Jah love.

List of Proverbs by the Itals and Bob Marley, by Album and Song

The following proverbs and proverbial expressions are taken from albums by Bob Marley and the Wailers and by the Itals. Most of them can be easily annotated using standard collections, whereas a few cannot. Those not found in standard collections have been included either because Jamaican informants considered them to be proverbial or because they are used proverbially in songs. Key words, designating the location of the proverbs in the appendix, have been italicized.

Proverbs of the Itals

I. *Easy to Catch* (Rhythm Safari, 4XL-57159, 1991)

"Take No Share"
1. Trying to force *water* over the hill.
2. Give I *basket* to carry water.
3. Putting the *cart* before the horse.
4. Put the *first* thing last.
5. *Time* waits on no one.
6. Ain't no substitute for *time*.

"Easy to Catch"
7. Old *fire* stick so easy to catch.
8. New *broom* sweep clean, but old broom knows the corner.

9. The older the *moon,* the brighter it shine.
10. What never happen in a *year,* happen in a day here.
11. You've got to *come* from somewhere before you can go back.
12. What drop off the *head,* always drop on the shoulder.
13. Give it your best *shot.*

"Blood"

14. *See* and blind, hear and deaf.
15. *Blood* is thicker than water.
16. *Anything* you do to me you do to yourself.

"Wanti Wanti"

17. *Habee* habee, no wantee wantee, wantee wantee no habee habee.
18. Eat *little,* eat long.
19. *Lickie* lickie til you bite it.
20. *Hold* on tight.
21. What you got up the *sleeve.*

"Never Say Never"

22. *Never* say never.
23. Sometimes you *win,* sometimes you lose.
24. Nothing beats a *failure* but a try.

"Hallelujah"

25. Never see *smoke* without fire.
26. Every *tub* must sit on its own bottom.
27. The *half* has never been told.
28. *Jah* never give you more than you can bear.
29. Every *knee* shall bow and every tongue confess.
30. Even if you *climb* on a broken chair.

"Rescue Me"

31. One *love,* one aim, one destiny.

"Stage"

32. The whole *world* is a stage.

II. *Brutal Out Deh* (Nighthawk, NH-303, 1981)

"Brutal"

33. Never try to bite the *hand* that feed you.
34. A drowning *man* will catch at straws.
35. A hungry *man* is an angry man.
36. To *practice* what you preach.
37. *Man* cannot live by only bread.
38. Who can't *hear* must feel.
39. Thou shalt not *steal.*
40. If I should feed one *child* and starve the other.

"Temptation"

41. The life of all *flesh* is the blood thereof.
42. You take up the *sword,* you'll perish by it.
43. *Iron* sharpeneth iron.
44. Give unto *Caesar* what is Caesar.
45. To be your *brother's* keeper.

"Action"

46. *Action* speak louder than words.

"Truth Must Reveal"

47. *Money* is the root of all evil.
48. *Truth* that hidden got to reveal.

"Give Me What I Want"

49. *Absence* makes the heart grow fonder.

"Rastafari Chariot"

50. A rolling *stone* gathers no moss.

"Time Will Tell"

51. Don't let *time* catch up on you.
52. *Time* will tell.

III. *Give Me Power* (Nighthawk Records, 307, 1983)

"In Deh"

53. The hotter [harder] the *battle,* the sweeter the victory.
54. Hawk near, *chicken* merry.
55. If *night* would only speak, it would attack.
56. When *lamp* out, finger walk.

"Kill Crime"

57. The *heart* is willing but the flesh is weak.
58. Too much *rat* never dig good hole.
59. We all got to *start* from the bottom.
60. Some ha fe *come,* some ha fe go.
61. If you want to get to *heaven* you've got to build ahead on earth.

"Make Merry"

62. Silent *river* runs deep.
63. What you *sow,* it's that you reap.
64. The *race* is not for the swift, nor the battle for the strong.
65. He [*Jah*] never gives a man more than he can bear.

"Jah Calling"

66. *Teeth* and tongue will meet.
67. The *chip* don't fall too far from the block.
68. *Hold* on to what you've got.

"Love Affair"

    69. Every *heart* feels its own vibration.

IV. *Cool and Dread* (Nighthawk Records, 311, 1988)

"Jah Helps Those"

    70. *Jah* helps those who help themselves.

    71. A *friend* in need is a friend indeed.

    72. When you're *up,* you're up.

"Sing Farewell"

    73. What's to *be* is gotta be.

"Easy Now"

    74. *Business* before pleasure.

    75. A *bird* in the hand is better than a thousand in the bushes.

    76. *Something* for something, nothing for nothing.

V. *Early Recordings, 1971–1979* (Nighthawk Records, 310, 1987)

"Seeing Is believing"

    77. *Seeing* Is Believing.

"Don't Wake the Lion"

    78. Don't wake the *lion* when he's asleep.

    79. Still *waters* runs deep.

"Time Is Getting Harder"

    80. The *fittest* of the fittest shall survive.

    81. *Blind* man lead blind.

    82. Simple *trash* blind eyes.

"In A Dis Ya Time"

    83. Anyone can tell a lie, but the *truth* reveal itself.

    84. *Birds* stand up by him feet, man understandeth by him tongue.

VI. *Modern Age* (Ras Records, CD 3180, 1998)

"Modern Age"

    85. *Modern* age, primitive people.

"Together Forever"

    86. Slow to *anger,* better decline.

    87. The more we stick *together,* that's the way we stay alive.

    88. *Divide* and conquer.

    89. No weak *heart* shall enter.

    90. *Iron* sharpeneth iron.

    91. It must be *now* or never.

    92. Everyone is his *brother's* keeper.

    93. One *hand* can't shake, two it really take.

94. One *hand* wash the other.

95. *One* to one it's so unjust.

"Happen Before the Time"

96. *Nothing* ever happen before the time.

97. It's not always the thing you *want* you get.

98. Use what you *got* to get what you want.

"Almighty"

99. Get paid according to their *works*.

100. *Mind* over matter.

101. What you *sow* you reap.

102. The *battle* getting hotter.

"Give This Love a Try"

103. Put you on the *spot*.

104. Leaves me *high* and dry.

Proverbs of Bob Marley

I. *Catch a Fire*

No proverbs.

II. *Burnin'* (Island, ILPS 9241, 1973)

"Small Axe"

1. If you are the big tree, we are the small *axe*.

2. No weak *heart* shall prosper.

3. Whosoever diggeth a *pit* shall fall in it.

"Put It On"

4. Got to come together cause we're *birds* of a feather.

"I Shot the Sheriff"

5. Every day the *bucket* goes to the well, one day the bottom drop out.

"Get Up, Stand Up"

6. All that glitters is not *gold*.

7. *Half* the story has never been told.

8. *See* the light.

9. You can *fool* some people sometimes, but not all the people all the time.

"Pass It On"

10. What's in the *dark,* must come to light.

III. *Natty Dread* (Island, ILPS 9281, 1974)

"Dem Belly Full"

11. A hungry *man* is an angry man.

12. *Rain* a fall but de dutty tough.

13. The *weak* must get strong.

IV. *Rastaman Vibration* (Island, ILPS 9383, 1976)

"Who the Cap Fit"

14. Who the *cap* fits, let them wear it.
15. Throw me *corn,* me no call no fowl.
16. Your worst *enemy* could be your best friend.
17. Only your *friend* knows your secret.
18. Who Jah *bless,* no one curse.

"Johnny Was"

19. The wages of *sin* is death, gift of Jah is eternal life.

"Rat Race"

20. When the *cats* away, the mice will play.
21. In the abundance of *water,* the fool is thirsty.

V. *Exodus* (Island, ILPS 9498, 1977)

"Heathen"

22. As a man *sow,* shall he reap.
23. *Talk* is cheap.
24. The hotter the *battle,* the sweeter the victory.
25. He who *fights* and runs away, live to fight another day.

"So Much Things to Say"

26. The *rain* don't fall on one man housetop.

"Guiltiness"

27. These are the big *fish,* always try to eat down the small fish.

"Jamming"

28. *Life* is worth more than gold.

VI. *Kaya* (Island, ILPS 9517, 1978)

"Satisfy My Soul"

29. Don't rock my *boat.*
30. For every *action,* there's a reaction.

"She's Gone"

31. You never see *smoke* without fire.
32. Every *man* you see has his heart desire.

"Time Will Tell"

33. *Time* alone, time will tell.
34. Think you're in *heaven* but you're living in hell.

"Misty Morning"

35. Don't jump in the *water* if you can't swim.

"Crises"

36. Love is a *stream* that will find its course.

37. The *sun* shines for all.

38. So much been *said* but so little been done.

39. Every *river* runs to sea.

40. Making *matters* worse.

"Running Away"

41. It's better to live on the *housetop* than to live in a house full of confusion.

42. You can't *run* away from yourself.

43. Every man thinks his *burden* is the heaviest.

44. Who *feels* it knows it Lord.

VII. *Survival* (Island, ILPS 9592, 1979)

"Wake Up and Live"

45. One one *cocoa* full a basket.

46. *Life* is one big road with lots of signs.

"So Much Trouble"

47. What goes *around* it comes around.

48. What goes on *up* is coming on down.

49. Don't leave another *cornerstone* standing there behind.

"Ride Natty Ride"

50. Through *thick* and thin.

51. The *stone* that the builders refused, shall be the head cornerstone.

"Survival"

52. Some people put the *best* outside, some keep the best inside.

53. A good *man* is never honored in his own country.

VIII. *Uprising* (Island, ILPS 9596, 1980)

"Real Situation"

54. Give them an *inch* they take a yard.

55. Give them a *yard* they take a mile.

56. Once a *man* and twice a child.

57. *Everything* is just for a while.

"Coming In from the Cold"

58. When one *door* is closed, another is open.

59. The biggest *man* you ever did see was once a baby.

"Zion Train"

60. Where's there's a *will*, there's always a way.

61. Don't gain the *world* and lose your soul.

62. *Wisdom* is better than silver and gold.

"Forever Loving Jah"

63. Cause only a *fool* lean upon his own misunderstanding.

64. What has been *hidden* from the wise and prudent revealed to the babe and suckling.

65. *Everything* in life got its purpose.

IX. *Confrontation* (Island, ILPS 7 90085–1, 1983)

"Stiff Necked Fools"

66. The lips of the *righteous* teaches many, but fools die for want of wisdom.

67. The rich man's *wealth* is in his city, the righteous wealth is in his holy place.

68. *Destruction* of the poor is in their poverty,

69. *Destruction* of the soul is vanity.

X. Singles

"Simmer Down"

70. *Chicken* merry, hawk near.

71. Sweet nanny *goat* run him belly.

"Jah Live"

72. The *truth* is an offense, but not a sin.

73. Is he who *laugh* last, children, is he who win.

74. It's a foolish *dog,* bark at a flying bird.

Proverb Index

Proverbs in this index are given alphabetically according to the key word in the expression. At times the key word corresponds to that found in other collections, but in some cases it is based more on factors such as the Jamaican version of the proverb or words that might link proverbs by subject. For example, **Putting the *first* thing last** would precede **Big *fish* eat little fish.** The name of the person from whom the proverb comes (performer), along with the song and the album, is given first. In some instances, the song is a single or 45rpm and thus no album is mentioned. The performer (Prfrmr) is followed by the performance (Prfrmnc), which includes the version of the proverb used by that particular performer. In some cases a stanza is provided to contextualize the proverb, especially if a different version of it is used. The absence of a performance category indicates there is no difference between the version given initially for the proverb and the one used by the performer. Following the performance category are annotations of the proverb, that is, examples of its occurrence in collections. The annotations consist of (1) the abbreviation of the collection in which the proverb is found; (2) the page number on which the proverb can be found, sometimes followed by a number or letter given to it in that particular collection; (3) versions of the proverb found in that collection, sometimes with the author's explanation of the proverb; and (4) an occasional comment further explaining the proverb, preceded by an asterisk. A typical annotation might read, for example: [MB 21:10, "A bird in hand is worth twenty in the bush (One should keep what one has rather than being jealous of other people)." *This is often applied to relationships.] The entry tells us that the proverb is number 10 on page 21 of Marion-Brown's *Jamaica Handbook of Proverbs*. It also gives the version and an explanation of the proverb found in MB, as well as my note on the proverb's application. The annotations have been separated into British or American and Caribbean or African with the symbols "//." British and American sources precede the "//" and Caribbean and African sources follow it.

The index can be used in a number of ways. First, it documents particular proverbs and how commonly they are found in reggae. One can note with only a glance, for instance, that **You reap what you sow** is popular in reggae, just as it is in African Amerian blues. The index can also at times indicate the likely origin of proverbs, and certainly the regions in which they are most often found. For instance, annotations show that a favored Rasta proverb, **Iron sharpeneth iron**, can be traced back to Biblical origin and was used in fourteenth-century Europe. However, the proverb is more commonly used today in Jamaica than in the United States.

I readily acknowledge that a number of the proverbs may not be traditional; however, I have included them because of their obvious proverbiality in reggae lyrics. I further note that this is not an exhaustive list of proverbs either from reggae or even from the artists discussed in the book. It is, nonetheless, more than merely representative: it reflects the overwhelming majority of proverbs used by the artists under consideration and the core of expressions found in reggae in general.

Abbreviations (For more complete bibliographic information, see Bibliography)

AB	Roger D. Abrahams, "Proverbs from Nevis"
ABR	Roger D. Abrahams, "West Indian Proverbs and Proverb Collections"
AC	Izett Anderson and Frank Cundall, *Jamaican Negro Proverbs and Sayings*
AP	G. L. Apperson, *English Proverbs and Proverbial Phrases*
BA	Francis Barbour, *Proverbs and Proverbial Phrases of Illinois*
BH	Alene L. Barnes-Harden, "African American Verbal Arts: Their Nature and Communicative Interpretation"
BN	Louise Bennett, *Jamaican Labrish*
BR	Francis W. Bradley, "South Carolina Proverbs"
BRU	Harold Brunvand, *A Dictionary of English Proverbs and Proverbial Phrases from Books Published by Indiana Authors before 1890*
BT	William Bates, *Creole Folklore from Jamaica: I. Proverbs"*
BW	Martha Warren Beckwith, *Jamaica Proverbs*
CL	Al Cleary, *Jamaica Proverbs*
CU	Frank Cundall, "West Indian Negro Proverbs"
DA	Jack L. Daniel, *The Wisdom of Sixth Mount Zion from Members of Sixth Mount Zion and Those Who Begot Them*
DC	Daryl C. Dance, *Honey Hush*
DSDJ	Jack L. Daniel, Geneva Smitherman-Donaldson, and Milford A. Jeremiah,

"Making a Way Outa No Way: The Proverb Tradition in the Black Experience."

FA	Arthur H. Fauset, *Folklore from Nova Scotia*
FR	Harry A. Franck, "Jamaica Proverbs."
HA	Margaret Hardie, "Proverbs and Proverbial Expressions Current in the United States East of the Missouri and North of the Ohio Rivers"
HD	Walter Hoard, *Anthology: Quotations and Sayings of People of Color*
HY	Albert M. Hyamson, *A Dictionary of English Phrases*
MB	Vivien Morris-Brown, *The Jamaican Handbook of Proverbs: With Standard English Translations and Explanations*
MKH	Wolfgang Mieder, Stewart A. Kingsbury, and Kelsie B. Harder, *A Dictionary of American Proverbs*
NC	B. J. Whiting, "Proverbs and Proverbial Sayings," in *The Frank C. Brown Collection of North Carolina Folklore*, v. 1
OX	F. P. Wilson, *The Oxford Dictionary of English Proverbs*
PA	Elsie C. Parsons, "Riddles and Proverbs from the Bahama Islands"
PAR	Elsie C. Parsons, *Folklore of the Antilles, French and English*
PR	Sw. Anand Prahlad, *African American Proverbs in Context*
RT	Robert Southerland Rattray, *Ashanti Proverbs*
SM	John A. Simpson, *The Concise Oxford Dictionary of Proverbs*
SN	Emma L. Snapp, "Proverbial Lore in Nebraska"
ST	Burton E. Stevenson, *The Macmillan Book of Proverbs, Maxims and Familiar Phrases*
T	Morris P. Tilley, *A Dictionary of the Proverbs in England in the Sixteenth and Seventeenth Centuries*
TA	Archer Taylor, *The Proverb and an Index to the Proverb*
TU	Michael Turner, "Old Time People Used to Say"
TW	Archer Taylor and B. J. Whiting, *A Dictionary of American Proverbs and Proverbial Phrases, 1820–1880*
WH	B. J. Whiting, *Modern Proverbs and Proverbial Sayings*
WS	Llewellyn G. Watson, *Jamaican Sayings: With Notes on Folklore, Aesthetics, and Social Control*
WT	B. J. Whiting, *Early American Proverbs and Proverbial Phrases*

Absence makes the heart grow fonder.
Prfrmr: The Itals, "Give Me What I Want," *Brutal Out Deh*
Annot: MKH 3; OX 1; WH 2; TW 2.

Action speak louder than words.
Prfrmr: The Itals, "Action," *Brutal Out Deh*
Prfrmnc: I want to see your action—it speak louder than words.
Annot: OX 3; ST 2616:11; BH 68; DA 2, 11; WT 3; SM 1; TW 3; BR 59; NC 360; WH 4:A24; PR 204.

Every little *action*, there is a reaction.
Prfrmr: Bob Marley, "Satisfy My Soul," *Kaya*
Prfrmnc: Every little action, there is a reaction.
Prfrmr: Mighty Diamonds, "Looking for Trouble"
Prfrmnc: In every action, there is a reaction.
Annot: MKH 6; TW 3.

What goes *around* it comes around.
Prfrmr: Bob Marley, "So Much Trouble," *Survival*
Prfrmnc: See "What goes on up is coming on down."
Prfrmr: Wailing Souls, "Them a Fret," *Lay It on the Line*
Annot: PR 205; BH 61; DA 12:55; DSDJ 504:1.

Lilly *axe* can cut down big tree.
Prfrmr: Bob Marley, "Small Axe," *Burnin'*
Prfrmnc: If you are the big tree
          I am the small axe
          sharpened to cut you down.
Annot: // AC 15:13; BW 27: 122 "Cotton tree neber so big, but lilly axe cut him"; FR
          99:75, "Cotton tree ever so big but little axe cut him"; WS 159:16, "is used to
          indicate that great feats can be accomplished by the lowly and humble if they
          persevere, and that they are capable of surpassing or overthrowing the
          great"; MB 88:196, "Small hax fall big chree."

What come *bad* in the morning can't come good in the evening.
Prfrmr: The Ethiopians, "Everything Crash," *Everything Crash*
Annot: // TU 31; "Wha' gone bad a maanin, cawn come good a evening." Refers to
          children who are spoiled by their parents. Used as a reminder to people to
          socialize their children in an acceptable manner while they are young; MB
          23:21, "It is unwise to spend valuable time worrying about those problems
          we cannot solve. Also it makes no sense to take precautions after we have
          carelessly allowed a situation to get out of hand."

They love to give you *basket* to carry water.
Prfrmr: Culture, "Han' a Bowl," *Good Things*
Prfrmr: Chin. A Jamaican taxicab driver, approximately 25 years old. Kingston,
          Jamaica, August 1999.
Prfrmr: The Itals, "Take No Share," *Easy to Catch*
Annot: // AC 16:24 "If neyger hate you, him gi' you basket fe carry water; but if you
          cleber, you put plaintain-leaf a bottom." In Trinidad and Hayti—"Hate
          people, but don't give them baskets to fetch water in"; BW 63:427 "People
          hate you, dem gi' you basket fe carry water; but if you ha' sense you wi' tek
          clay-clay." "If anyone hate you, him gib you basket fe carry water; but if you
          cleber you put plaintain-leaf in him." "They give you basket to carry water
          in and fork fe drink soup." (Applied to the efforts made to drive an
          unpopular person out of a disrict. Plastering a basket with clay in order to

hold water is a common device in folk poetry); FR 103:239 "Man hate you him gi' you basket fe fetch water"; HD 117, "Give the basket to carry water"; WS 112:15; MB 96:218, "When nayga hate yu, im gi yu baskit fe kya wata. When someone hates you, he will deliberately try to embarrass you or put you in trouble."

The harder the *battle* be, ago sweeter the victory.

Prfrmr: Culture, "Don't Cry Sufferer," *Nuff Crises*
Prfrmnc: The harder the battle be
      a go sweeter the victory.
Prfrmr: Jimmy Cliff, "You Can Get It If You Really Want It," *The Harder They Come*
Prfrmnc: Rome was not built in a day
      Opposition will come your way.
      But the harder the battle you see,
      It's the sweeter the victory.
Prfrmr: Bob Marley, "The Heathen," *Exodus*
Prfrmnc: As a man sow, shall he reap.
      And I know that talk is cheap.
      But the heat of the battle
      Is as sweet as the victory.
Prfrmr: The Itals, "In Deh," *Give Me Power*
Prfrmnc: When you tell them of the Almighty
      Some of them would want to try stay one side and fight me.
      But the hotter get the battle, it's the sweeter Jah victory.
Prfrmr: Bunny Wailer, "Blackheart Man," *Blackheart Man*
Prfrmnc: No cross, no crown,
      No sorrow, no laughter,
      Trial and crosses in I and I.
      But the hotter the battle
      Is the sweeter Jah Jah victory.
Prfrmr: The Wailing Souls, "Them a Fret," *Lay It on the Line*
Prfrmnc: The longer it takes, the sweeter the victory.
Annot: MKH 39, "The harder the battle the sweeter the victory."

What is to *be* is got to be.

Prfrmr: The Itals, "Sing Farewell," *Cool and Dread*
Prfrmr: Gregory Isaacs, "Number One," *Tougher than Tough*
Annot: MKH 39; WH 684, "What will be will be."

***Beggars* can't be choosers.**

Prfrmr: Mikey Dread, "Knock Knock," *Best Sellers*
Prfrmnc: They say a beggar have no choice
      But I won't be a beggar all my life.
Annot: MKH 44; OX 42; ST 149:2; TW 24; WH 41.

Dem *belly* full, but we hungry.

Prfrmr: Bob Marley, "Dem Belly Full," *Natty Dread*

Annot: // AC 17:43, "When belly full, jaw mus' stop."

It ain't no *big* thing.
Prfrmr: The Wailing Souls, "No Big Thing," *Lay It on the Line*
Prfrmnc: It ain't no big thing / that's how the people sing.

***Birds* tangle by them feet, man tangle by them tongue.**
Prfrmr: The Itals, "In a Dis Ya Time," *Early Recordings,* and *Modern Age*
Annot: MKH 51, "A bird is known by his note, and a man by his talk"; OX 59; ST
         177:8; WH 48.

**You can't stop the *bird* from flying over your head, but you can stop them from
building a nest.**
Prfrmr: Chin. A Jamaican taxicab driver, approximately 25 years old. Kingston,
         Jamaica, August 1999.
Annot: MKH 53; // AC 19:65; BW 124:951, "You can't keep crow from flyin but you
         wan' keep him from pitchin 'pon you' head"; WS 53:104, 36:24, "Yu cawn
         stap crow fram flying, but yu can stap 'im fram flying 'pon yu head. In other
         words, while we cannot prevent others from doing whatever they will, we
         can certainly prevent them from influencing us."

A *bird* in the hand is worth a thousand in the bushes.
Prfrmr: The Itals, "Easy Now," *Cool and Dread*
Annot: MKH 51, ". . . two in the bush"; OX 59; ST 182:6; AP 48; DA 3:50; DSDJ 499;
         SN 70:270; TW 27–28; BR 62; TA 13,22; T B363; NC 370; WH 47:B229; HA
         461; BA 16; BRU 10: WT 31; PR 211; DC 323; // BW 92:674, "One bud a han'
         wort' two a bush."

***Birds* of a feather flock together.**
Prfrmr: Bob Marley, "One Foundation," *Burnin'*
Prfrmnc: Got to come together
         'cause we're birds of a feather.
         Or there will never be
         no love at all.
Prfrmr: U-Roy, "Birds of a Feather," *True Born African*
Annot: MKH 52; ST 1403:3; OX 60; AP 48; BR 62; HA 462; HY 46; NC 370; TB 393;
         PR 210; TW 28; WH 49; DSDJ 502; // BW 20:64.

You *bite* off more than you can chew.
Prfrmr: Culture, "Walk with Jah," *Trust Me*
Prfrmnc: How you a go walk with Jah
         When your greedy belly too full
         You bite off too much more than you chew
         now you gonna choke on it.
Annot: DA 7:2, 7:30.

The *blacker* the berry, the sweeter the juice.
Prfrmr: I-Roy, "Welding" *Tougher Than Tough*

Prfrmnc: The higher the mountain the greener the grass,
    The blacker the girl the sweeter her —————.
Annot: MKH 48; PR 209; BH 64:2,3, ("the blacker the berry/meat . . ."); DSDJ 503:4,
    505; DC 132.

Who Jah *bless,* let no one curse.
Prfrmr: Bob Marley, "Who the Cap Fit," *Rastaman Vibration*
Prfrmnc: Who Jah bless let no one curse
    Thank God we're past the worse
Annot: MB 124:296, "Who God bless, no man cuss (Despite the tribulations of life,
    one should trust God to keep his promise to bless those who keep His
    commandments)."

Blind man lead blind.
Prfrmr: The Itals, "Time Getting Harder," *Early Recordings*
Annot: MKH 56; OX 50, 67; ST 199; AP 56; DA 5:4, "The blind can't lead the blind";
    DSDJ 503:2; NC 372, "If the blind lead the blind both shall fall into the
    ditch"; TW 32–33; HY 51; T:B452; WH 55:B283; BA 18; SM 21; WT 35; PR 209;
    Luke 6:39, "And he spake a parable unto them, Can the blind lead the blind?
    Shall they not both fall into the ditch?"

Blood is thicker than water.
Prfrmr: The Itals, "Blood (Thicker than Water)," *Easy to Catch*
Annot: MKH 57; OX 68; ST 202:7; AP 56; BH 65:2; NC 372; TW 33; BR 62; WH
    56:B291; SN 107; BA 18; BRU 13; WT 36; SM 22; // WS 185:42; PR 213; BW
    21:74; MB 65:133, "Blud ticka dan wata."

If you can't take *blows,* don't throw blows.
Prfrmr: Peter Tosh, "Glass House," *Mama Africa*

Don't rock the *boat.*
Prfrmr: Bob Marley, "Satisfy My Soul," *Kaya*
Prfrmnc: Oh please don't you rock my boat.
Annot: WH 60:B320, "To rock the boat."

Don't judge a *book* by its cover.
Prfrmr: Gregory Isaacs, "Don't Call Me Baldhead," *Unattended*
Prfrmr: The Wailing Souls, "Mix Up," *Reggae Legends, Vol. 1*
Prfrmnc: Can't check the book by its cover.
Annot: MKH 62; ST 83:3; BH 61:2, "You can't judge . . ."; DSDJ 503:6; WH 65:B351,
    "Never judge . . ."; HA 465, ". . . by its binding"; SN 84; BA 20; SM 23; PR
    214; DA 7:11.

We all got to start from the *bottom.*
Prfrmr: The Itals, "Kill Crime," *Give Me Power*
Prfrmnc: A lot o' dem a try to reach to the top
    But we all got to start from the bottom.

Don't burn your *bridges* behind you.
Prfrmr: Mikey Dread, "Roots and Culture," *Best Sellers*

Prfrmr: The Wailing Souls, "Old Broom," *The Very Best*
Annot: MKH 71; ST 245; BH 62:5, ". . . that carried you across"; DSDJ 503, ". . . you have to cross"; PR 215; DA 7:2; WH 75:B428, "To burn one's bridges"; TA 198; BA 23; HY 55; // WS 181:16; FR 99:79, "Don't broke down de bridge you jus' cross'; AC 21:105 "Don't bruh dem bridge you jus' cross."

New *brooms* sweep clean.
Prfrmr: The Itals, "Easy to Catch," *Easy to Catch*
Prfrmr: The Wailing Souls, "Old Broom," *The Very Best*
Prfrmnc: New broom only sweep clean
but the old broom know the corners.
Prfrmr: Horace Andy, "New Broom"
Prfrmr: Tony, a Jamaican man approximately 35 years old. Collected at Maya Lodge in the Blue Mountains outside Kingston in August 1992.
Prfrmnc: New brooms sweep clean but old broom knows the corners.
Annot: MKH 72; OX 450; ST 246–47; AP 443; NC 376, ". . . but an old brush knows the corners / fine de corner / corners of the house"; SN 93:3; TW 44; BR 64; HY 250; TA 51; T B682; WH 75:B432; BA 24; BRU 16; WT 47; SM 161; PR 215–16; // WS 185:41; AC 21:105; TU 31; MB 27:31; FR 108:458.

Everyone is his *brother's* keeper.
Prfrmr: The Itals, "Temptation," *Brutal Out Deh*
Prfrmnc: It's full time that you should know
Everyone is his brother's keeper, yeah.
Prfrmr: The Itals, "Together Forever," *Modern Age*
Prfrmnc: Everyone is each other keeper.
Annot: Genesis 4:9, "Am I my brother's keeper?"

Every day the *bucket* a go a well one day the bottom a go drop out.
Prfrmr: Bob Marley, "I Shot the Sheriff," *Burnin'*
Prfrmnc: Reflexes had got the better of me
and what is to be must be
Every day the bucket a go a well,
one day the bottom a go drop out.
Prfrmr: The Ethiopians, "Everything Crash," *Everything Crash*
Annot: // AC 22:107; BT 39:15, "Eberyday bucket go da well, one day bottom drop out"; BW 45:265, "Eberyday bucket go a well, one day bottom mus' drop out"; CW 22:107, "Ebery day bucket go a well, one day him battam drop out." (. . . one day rope will break.) Spanish Don Quixote, Irish, 13th century French; FR 100:120, "Ebery day bucket go a well, one day him bottom wi lef da"; HD 119, "Everyday bucket goes to well one day the bottom is going to drop out"; WS 187:46; AB 22; TU 31; MB 118:278, "No matter how long it takes, we reap the results of our actions."

Every man thinks his *burden* is the heaviest.
Prfrmr: Bob Marley, "Running Away," *Kaya*

Prfrmnc: Every man thinks his burden is the heaviest.
But who feels it knows it Lord.
Who feels it knows it Lord.
Prfrmr: Bunny Wailer, "Who Feels It," *Protest*
Prfrmnc: Every man thinks his burdens the heaviest,
But it common they know because they feel.
And who feels it know it
Who feels it knows it.
Annot: MKH 74; ST 256:7.

Business before pleasure.
Prfrmr: The Itals, "Easy Now," *Cool and Dread*
Annot: MKH 75; OX 93; ST 263:1; TW 48; WH 82; DA 3:67, (Business comes . . .).

Let by-gones be by-gones.
Prfrmr: Buju Banton, "A Close One," *Inna Heights*
Prfrmnc: If he has done you no harm
Let by-gones be by-gones.
Prfrmr: Frankie Paul, "Bygones."
Annot: MKH 78; OX 96; ST 270:5; TW 51; WH 86.

What is for Caesar, give it unto Caesar.
Prfrmr: The Itals, "Temptation," *Brutal Out Deh*
Prfrmnc: What is for Caesar, give it unto Caesar
what is for Jah Jah, come on, let's chant it over.
Annot: MKH 79; OX 671; WH 88; ST 272:6; Matthew 22:21, "Render therefore to
Caesar the things that are Caesar's."

Many are called, but few are chosen.
Prfrmr: Judy Mowatt, "Many Are Called," *Black Woman*
Prfrmnc: Many are called, but few are chosen
You got to beware of the wolf in sheep's clothing.
Prfrmr: Wailing Wailers, "Together Again," *Wailing Again*
Annot: MKH 80; TW 237; ST 348:4; Matthew 22:14.

If the cap fits, wear it.
Prfrmr: Bob Marley, "Who the Cap Fit," *Rastaman Vibration*
Prfrmnc: Only your friend know your secret,
so only he could reveal it.
Who da cap fit, let them wear it.
Prfrmr: Larry Marshall, "Throw me Corn," *Come Let us Reason*
Prfrmr: The Meditations, "Babylon Trap Them."
Annot: MKH 82; OX 77–78; AP 81; BR 91; HY 73; NC 379; TA 18; PR 247, (shoe); DA
11, (shoe); WH 91:C32, "If the cap fits wear it"; DC 88, 456; // AC 27:181, "Cap
no fit you, you no tek i' up"; BW 24:97, "Cap not fit you, you no tek i' up";
WS 188:53, 188:54; HD 119, "If the cap fits you, why don't you wear it?"; MB
68:144, "Who de cap fit, weari."

Carry go bring come.
Prfrmr: The Wailing Souls, "Old Broom," *The Very Best*
Prfrmr: The Wailing Souls, "Informer," *Lay It on the Line*
Prfrmr: Justin Hinds, "Carry Go Bring Come," *Jezebel*
Annot: // WS 188:55; TU 30; MB 77:164.

Putting the *cart* before the horse.
Prfrmr: The Itals, "Take No Share," *Easy to Catch*
Annot: MKH 85; OX 104; WH 93; ST 290:9; TW 56; DC 85, "Don't put the cart before the horse."

When the *cat's* away, the mice will play.
Prfrmr: Bob Marley, "Rat Race," *Rastaman Vibration*
Annot: MKH 87; OX 109; ST 301:2; WH 102:C115; DA 4, 5; // WS 98:316, "Puss a sleep, ratta teck charge," "Puss gone, ratta tek 'ouse"; MB 114:265, "Puss gawn, ratta tek chaaj (When the cat is gone, the rat takes charge)"; RT 89:263, "Agyinamoa wu a, nkura yam (When the cat dies, the mice rejoice)."

Chicken merry, 'awk deh near.
Prfrmr: The Itals, "Make Merry," *Give Me Power*
Prfrmr: Bob Marley, "Simmer Down," *Tougher Than Tough*
Annot: // WS 40:44, "Children engaged in rough, noisy play are usually warned. . . . This also applies to the adult who mirthfully engages in negative behavior but eventually pays the price, such as one who steals a radio and, while dancing to its music, is apprehended by the police"; FR 101:145, "Fowl merry hawk a go pick him chicken"; AC 56:564, "When fowl merry, hawk ketch him chicken," "Hen da cackle and da 'joyment himself, him no know say hawk da watch him"; HD 119, "Chicken merry hawk is near"; BW 118:889; MB 19:9, "Danger can lurk in some of the most unexpected places. We should temper, therefore, our most light-hearted moments with a litte sobriety"; RT 80:211, " Akokonini bow nsā na ne were afi akorōmā (When the cock is drunk he forgets about the hawk)."

The *chip* don't fall too far from the block.
Prfrmr: The Itals, "Jah Calling," *Give Me Power*
Prfrmnc: Some would say that the chip don't fly too far from the block.
Annot: MKH 23, "An apple never falls far from the tree"; OX 93; AP 97; BEY 16.1, 383.2; HY 84; NC 384; DC 87, "He's a chip off the old block, and the chip don't fall too far from the block / the leaves don't fall too far from the tree"; // AC 29:196, "De chip nebber fall to furr from de block"; BW 25:104, "Chip nebber fly far from de block"; MB 172:438, "Chip noh fly fur fram de blak."

Cock mouth kill cock.
Prfrmr: Justin Hinds, "Cock Mouth Kill Cock."
Annot: //TU 30; HD120; BW 25: 110, ". . . implying that a person tells more than he

should to his own harm"; AC 59:598, "Applied to the evil effects of jealousy and gossip. I.e. Through too much talking one is apt to get oneself into trouble"; WS 53:103, 21:13.

One one *cocoa* full a basket
Prfrmr: Bob Marley, "Wake Up and Live," *Survival*
Prfrmr: Gregory Isaacs, "One One Cocoa."
Prfrmr: Iaa (Delton Waite). A Jamaican Rastafari man, 42 years old, Negril, Jamaica, August 1999.
Prfrmr: Culture, "The Boss," *Payday*
Annot: //HD 117, "One coco at a time fills a basket"; WS 161:27, "It serves to remind us that wealth can accumulated by fervently saving a little at a time"; MB 109:255, "Do not expect to achieve success overnight."

***Some ha fe come,* some ha fe go.**
Prfrmr: The Itals, "Kill Crime," *Give Me Power*
Prfrmnc: Too much rat never dig good hole,
          some ha fe come, some ha ge go.

You've got to *come* from somewhere, before you can go back.
Prfrmr: The Itals, "Easy to Catch," *Easy to Catch*

The harder they *come,* the harder they fall.
Infmant: Jimmy Cliff, "The Harder they Come," *The Harder they Come*
Prfrmnc: The harder the come,
          the harder they fall, one and all.
Annot: MKH 51, 610, "The bigger the tree, the harder she falls"; OX 373, 18; ST 748:13, 749:2; PR 218, (bigger); WH 45.

Me throw me *corn,* me no call no fowl.
Prfrmr: Bob Marley, "Who the Cap Fit," *Rastaman Vibration*
Prfrmnc: I say I throw me corn
          me no call no fowl.
          I saying cok, cok, cok;
          cluk, cluk, cluk, yeah!
Prfrmr: Larry Marshall, "Throw Me Corn," *Come Let Us Reason*
Prfrmr: Culture, "Have E Have E," *Payday*
Prfrmnc: Me a go throw me corn, and me no call no fowl
          And you see who want pick up a macka corn and swallow it.
Annot: // BW 84:598, "Me t'row corn, me no call neighbor fowl." Retort to one who, although no names have been used, thinks himself the abused one"; FR 103:253; WS 192:74, "Me trow me kaan a doh, but me no call not fowl"; AC 32:233: MB 43:72.

The *countenance* of one man, brighten another.
Prfrmr: Culture, "Iron Sharpen Iron," *More Culture,* and *Africa Stand Alone*
Prfrmnc: The countenance of one man, brighteneth another, Iron sharpeneth iron.

Annot: Proverbs 27:17, "Iron sharpeneth iron; so a man sharpeneth the countenance of his friend."

Crab walk to much, him lose him claw.

Prfrmr: The Wailing Souls, "Who Lives It," *Fire House Rock*
Prfrmnc: Crab walk to much, yes him lose his claw, now.
          It sick, no cure, then the doctor worse, now.
Annot: // AC 33:246, "When crab walk too much him los' him claw." 34:247,
          (. . . him go a cutacoo)/basket. *Identical structure but different images:
          42:365, "Darg walk too much, los him share"; BT 38:3, 40:34, (. . . him get in
          kutakoo); BW 29:137, also 35:181, "Darg walk too much los him share"; FR
          99:48; DN 99; HD 133, "Crab walks to much loses his claw; he does not walk
          he does not get fat"; WS 52:95; 52:97.

Creep before you walk.

Prfrmr: The Gaylads, "Creep Before You Walk."
Prfrmr: The Heptones, "Backstabbers," *Rainbow Valley*
Prfrmnc: You have to mumble before you talk.
          You have to creep before you walk.
Annot: MKH 126, "You must creep before you can crawl"; OX 120; ST 722; BH 63;
          DA 12:72, (You must creep before you can crawl); BA 42; AP 214, "First
          creep, then go"; SM 240; WT 70; PR 221, (crawl); WH 138; DC 84, "You got
          to crawl before you can walk"; // T:C820; WS 256:167; BT 42:74, "Pickney
          mus'creep before him walk"; AC 93:1048; WS 114:23; TU 31; MB 108:253.

No cup no break, no coffee no throw away.

Prfrmr: Justin Hinds, "In This Time," *Know Jah Better*
Prfrmr: Iaa (Delton Waite). A Jamaican Rastafari man, 42 years old, Negril, Jamaica,
          August 1999.
Prfrmnc: No cup no mash no coffee no throw away.
Prfrmr: The African Brothers, "No cup no Bruk."
Annot: // TU 31; AC 89:999, "Mug no broke, coffee no t'row away (Keep clear of
          trouble and you won't come to grief)"; WS 209:161, "No mug nob bruk, no
          kaafi no trow weh. (Quite frequently a person finds him/herself encumbered
          by acquaintances or relatives whom that person would gladly be rid of.
          When those persons decide to sever the relationship, they are in fact doing
          the person a favor, rather than harming him.)"; MB 17:1, "Even in the most
          difficult of times, if total devastation has not occurred, one should count his/
          her blessings. Do not blow simple matters out of proportion."

Cuss cuss no bore hole ah me kin will never hurt me.

Prfrmr: A plaque on a hotel wall in Kingston, Jamaica, August 1999.
Annot: // AC 35:270,271; BT 41:60; BW 31:150; WS 193:79, "Cuss cuss no bruk no
          bone," 115:27, (". . . no bore 'ole ina man 'kin.")

What's in the darkness must be revealed to light.

Prfrmr: Bob Marley, "Pass It On," *Burnin'*

Prfrmnc: What's in the darkness
　　　　　must be revealed to light.
Prfrmr:　Jimmy Cliff, "You Can't Be Wrong and Get Right," *Music Maker*
Prfrmnc: You can't be wrong and get right,
　　　　　no matter how you my try, try, try.
　　　　　Everything that's done in darkness
　　　　　must come out in light.
　　　　　For you can't be wrong and get right.
Prfrmr:　Justin Hinds, "Book of History," *Travel with Love*
Prfrmnc: Take what was in the darkness
　　　　　bring it into the light.
Prfrmr:　The Heptones, "Backstabber," *Rainbow Valley*
Prfrmnc: What you do in the dark must come to light.
Annot:　MKH 134, "What goes on in the dark must come out in the light"; ST 537:9;
　　　　　BH 65:5, "What you do in the dark will come to the light"; DA 12:51; DSDJ
　　　　　504:3; PR 221–22.

Man no *dead* no call him duppy [ghost].
Prfrmr:　Iaa (Delton Waite). A Jamaican Rastafari man, 42 years old, Negril, Jamaica,
　　　　　August 1999.
Prfrmr:　Gregory Isaacs, "Where There Is Life There Is Hope."
Prfrmnc: While there is life there is hope
　　　　　Man no dead, no call him ghost.
Annot:　// AC 48:455; BW 82:581; MB 173:443, "Wha noh ded, noh dashi wey."

***Destruction* of the poor is their poverty.**
Prfrmr:　Peter Tosh, "Fools Die," *Wanted*
Prfrmr:　Bob Marley. "Stiff Necked Fools," *Confrontation*
Prfrmr:　Buju Banton, "Destiny," *Inna Heights*

***Dog* no nyam dog** (Dog don't eat dog).
Prfrmr:　Culture, "Dog a Go Nyam Dog," *Africa Stand Alone*
Prfrmnc: Dog, a go nyam dog in the city.
Annot:　MKH 159, "Dog will not eat dog"; OX 194; ST 611:9; WH 174:D215, "Dog
　　　　　does not eat dog"; TW 106; // AC 39:322, "Darg no nyam dog"; BW 34:171
　　　　　"Darg nabber nyam daag"; "Daag don't nyam daag"; "Dog no eat dog,"
　　　　　"You nebber see de day dog nyam dog"; FR 99:80, "Dog nebber nyam dog";
　　　　　HD 122, "Dogs don't eat dogs"; MB 159:400, "Daag nyam daag (People
　　　　　destroy each other to gratify their own selfish desires)."

***Dog* more than bone.**
Prfrmr:　Iaa (Delton Waite). A Jamaican Rastafari man, 42 years old, Negril, Jamaica,
　　　　　August 1999.

Every *dog* has got his day.
Prfrmr:　Jimmy Cliff, "Money Won't Save You," *Music Maker*
Prfrmnc: Every dog has got his day

Annot: MKH 159; OX 195: ST 609:8: TW 106; WH 175:D222, "Every dog has his day"; DC 513, "Every dog has his day"; // AC 40:333, "Ebery darg hab him day, but every puss hab Sunday"; MB 17:3.

Same *dog* bite you a morning, bite you again at evening.
Prfrmr: Andrew Tosh, "Magga Dog," *Original Man*
Prfrmr: Peter Tosh, "Magga Dog."
Prfrmr: Mr. Weir. A Jamaican man, approximately 65 years old, Kingston, Jamaica, August 1999.

It's a foolish *dog* barks at a flying bird
Prfrmr: Bob Marley, "Jah Live," *Countryman*
Prfrmnc: The truth is an offense,
　　　　but not a sin
　　　　Is he who laugh last, children,
　　　　is he who win.
　　　　It's a foolish dog,
　　　　barks at a flying bird.
Annot: // WS 62:152, "Fool-fool dawg bark at flying bud"; MB 81:175.

Magga *dog* turn around and bite you every time.
Prfrmr: Andrew Tosh, "Magga Dog," *Original Man*
Prfrmnc: Sorry for magga (starving) dog
　　　　turn around and bite you every time.
　　　　Jump from the frying pan I say
　　　　Into the fire hot.
Prfrmr: Peter Tosh, "Magga Dog," *Mama Africa*
Annot: // TU 31; WS 63:154, "Sorry fe mawga dawg, mawga dawg tun 'round bite yu. (There are many people who will 'bend over backwards' to assist someone who is in need, in this case, 'a meager dog.' But only too often, once success has been achieved, the assisted person turns his back on the one who assisted him/her in the first place, or repays that kindness with ingratitude.)"; MB 43:73, 171:435.

When one *door* is closed, another is opened.
Prfrmr: Bob Marley, "Coming in from the Cold," *Confrontation*
Prfrmnc: Why do you look so sad, and forsaken?
　　　　When one door is closed
　　　　Don't you know, another is opened.
Annot: MKH 165, "When one door closes, another opens"; OX 596; TW 109; ST 618:8; // HD 121, "When one door is shut another is opened"; WS 195:91, "When wan door shut, nudda one open."

You'll be playing with *dynamite.*
Prfrmr: Jimmy Cliff, "Treat the Youths Right," *Special*
Annot: WH 191:D343, "To play with dynamite."

Your worst *enemy* could be your best friend.
Prfrmr: Bob Marley, "Who the Cap Fit," *Rastaman Vibration*
Prfrmnc: Your worst enemy
          Could be your best friend,
          and your best friend
          your worst enemy.
Annot: // WS 245:33, "Yu wuss enemy live ina yo' 'ouse wid yu"; 264:46, "Yu bes;
          fren a yu wuss enemy"; BW 126:970; AC 49:469.

***Enough* is enough.**
Prfrmr: Iaa, (Delton Waite). A Jamaican Rastafari man, 42 years old, Negril, Jamaica,
          August 1999.
Prfrmr: Gregory Isaacs, "Enough Is Enough," *Ras Portraits*
Annot: MKH 181; OX 224; TW 121; ST 699:8; WH 204.

***Everything* is everything.**
Prfrmr: The Wailing Souls, "No Big Thing," *Lay It on the Line*

***Everything* is just for a while.**
Prfrmr: Bob Marley, "Real Situation," *Uprising*

The quickness of your *eyes* deceives the body.
Prfrmr: Culture, "Hand-a-Bowl," *Good Things*
Prfrmnc: Sometimes you try to do good to others,
          And they tell you that
          the more you look, the less you see.
          The quickness of your eyes, they say,
          it does deceive your body, but . . .

Nothing beats a *failure* but a try.
Prfrmr: The Itals, "Never Say Never," *Easy to Catch*
Annot: MKH 195.

Follow *fashion* monkey never drink good soup.
Prfrmr: Bunny Wailer, "Follow Fashion Monkey," *Protest*
Annot: // AC 53:533, "Follow fashion Juba nebber boil good soup." 86:962, "Follow
          fashion bruk monkey neck"; BT 42:65, "Follow fashion broke monkey
          neck"; BW 49:302, + six versions; FR 101:137, (. . . mek monkey cut him
          tail.); WS 267:82, same as AC ("Juba = woman"), 93:299, 93:300; MB
          100:231.

Who *feels* it knows it.
Prfrmr: Bunny Wailer, "Who Feels It," *Protest*
Prfrmr: Bob Marley, "Running Away," *Kaya*
Prfrmr: Jimmy Cliff, "Who Feels It Knows It," *Follow My Mind*
Prfrmnc: Did you ever have to laugh,
          to keep from crying?
          Who feels it kno-ows it.

Prfrmr: The Wailing Souls, "Who Lives It," *Inchpinchers*
Prfrmnc: Who lives it really knows it.

He who *fights* and runs away will live to fight another day
Prfrmr: Bob Marley, "The Heathen," *Exodus*
Prfrmnc: Rise o fallen fighters,
      rise and take your stand again.
      Cause he who fight and run away
      live to fight another day.
Annot: MKH 207; OX 200–201, 256; AP 74; BR 74; NC 407; WH 222:F100, "He who
      fights and runs away may live to fight another day"; TW 132.

Ole *fire* stick easy to catch.
Prfrmr: The Itals, "Easy to Catch," *Easy to Catch*
Prfrmr: Chin. A Jamaican taxicab driver, approximately 25 years old. Kingston,
      Jamaica, August 1999.
Annot: MKH 209, "A smothered fire may rekindle"; DC 134, "Old kindlin' easy to
      catch fire"; // BA 37:18; FR 104:288; HD 123, "Old fire stick easy to catch";
      WS 199:110, "Ole fiah 'tick eezy fe ketch"; CU 52:511, "Ole fire 'tick no hard
      fe ketch"; BW 92:671; AC 52:511; AB 23; MB 12:6; see Barrett 1976, 37, "Ole
      fire stick no hard fe ketch."

If you play with *fire* you must get burned.
Prfrmr: Jimmy Cliff, "You Can't Be Wrong and Get Right"
Prfrmnc: If you play with fire then you must get burned.
      There's a little thing you had better learn.
Prfrmr: Justin Hinds, "In This Time," *Know Jah Better*
Prfrmnc: Play with fire, fire will burn you.
Annot: MKH 209; OX 632; WH 226:F127, "To play with fire. . . ."

Putting the *first* things last.
Prfrmr: The Itals, "Take No Share," *Easy*
Annot: MKH 211; OX 82; WH 618.

Big *fish* eat little fish.
Prfrmr: Bob Marley, "Guiltiness," *Exodus*
Prfrmnc: These are the big fish,
      always try to eat down the small fish.
Annot: MKH 213; OX 333; ST 817:2.

**Even if a *fish* would keep his mouth shut, he wouldn't end up as food down
somebody's throat.**
Prfrmr: The Wailing Souls, "Spread Propaganda," *Reggae Legends, Vol. 1*
Annot: MKH 211, 613, "Even a fish would not get in trouble if he kept his mouth
      shut"; DC 84, "You ever see a fish what kept his mouth shut caught on
      anybody's hook?"; // TU 31.

The *fittest* of the fittest shall survive.
Prfrmr: The Itals, "Time Getting Harder," *Early Recordings*

Prfrmr: Burning Spear, "Fittest of the Fittest," *Fittest*
Prfrmnc: The fittest of the fittest of the fittest of the fittest of the fittest . . .

Walk with a *fool*, you shall be fooler.
Prfrmr: Justin Hinds, "Weeping Eyes," *Travel with Love*
Prfrmnc: Walk with the fool, you shall be fooler
          Walk with the wise, you shall be wiser.
Annot: // AC 54, "You follow fool, you fool you' self.

***Fools* die for want of wisdom**
Prfrmr: Peter Tosh, "Fools Die," *Wanted*
Annot: MKH 222.

Cause only a *fool* lean upon, lean upon his own misunderstanding.
Prfrmr: Bob Marley, "Forever Loving Jah," *Confrontation*

Never let the *foolish* one try to fool you no way.
Prfrmr: The Itals, "Jah Calling," *Give Me Power*

You can *fool* some people sometimes but you can't fool all the people all the time.
Prfrmr: Bob Marley, "Get Up, Stand Up," *Burnin'*
Prfrmnc: You can fool some people sometimes,
          but you can't fool all the people all the time,
          and now we've seen the light,
          we gonna stand up for our rights.
Prfrmr: Peter Tosh, "Get Up, Stand Up," *Equal Rights*
Prfrmr: Bunny Wailer, "Get Up, Stand Up," *Protest*
Prfrmr: U-Roy, "Prophecy," *True Born African*
Prfrmnc: You can fool some idiots some of the time, but you can't fool Natty Dread
          none of the time.
Annot: MKH 460; ST 534:1.

Only your *friend* know your secret.
Prfrmr: Bob Marley, "Who the Cap Fit," *Rastaman Vibration*
Prfrmnc: Only your friend know your secret
          So only he could reveal it.

A *friend* in need is a friend indeed.
Prfrmr: The Itals, "Jah Helps Those," *Cool and Dread*
Annot: MKH 233; OX 289; ST 902:2; TW 146; WH 242.

Sweet nanny *goat* a go run him belly.
Prfrmr: Bob Marley, "Simmer Down," *Tougher Than Tough*
Prfrmnc: Old time people used to say
          What sweet nanny goat a go run him belly.
Prfrmr: Larry Marshall, "Nanny Goat," *Come Let Us Reason*
Annot: // FR 107:394, "What sweet billy goat a't da go run him belly"; AC 62:634,
          635, "Dat something wha sweet nanny goat run him belly," "If nanny goat
          know how him belly 'tan,' him no swallow jackfruit seed"; WS 82:249, "The

above registers a warning against idle pastimes which, though pleasurable, might have detrimental consequences"; 77:166, "Wha sweet Nanny goat ah go run im belly (What appears to be the most delightful or precious possession a person may have, may produce a bitter end)." *Literally refers to the goat's habit of eating indiscriminately, which often leads to diarrhea (run im belly).

All that glitters is not *gold*.
Prfrmr: Bob Marley, "Get Up, Stand Up," *Burnin'*
Prfrmnc: It's not all that glitters is gold
          half the story has never been told.
Prfrmr: Bunny Wailer, "Get Up, Stand Up," *Protest*
Prfrmr: Peter Tosh, "Get Up, Stand Up," *Equal Rights*
Prfrmr: Peter Tosh, "Brand New Second Hand," *Legalize It*
Prfrmnc: It's not everything glitter is gold.
Annot: MKH 256; OX 316; BH 66; DA 11:18, "All that glitters ain't gold"; DSDJ 504; AP 6; BR 77; HA 461; TA 36; T A146; NC 416; BA 77; TW 154; WT 181; NC 416, "All is not gold that glitters"; SM 92; PR 228; DC 381; // BW 88:637, "No eberyt'ing wha' glitter a gold," "Eberyt'ing shine like gold no gold," "No eberty'ing shine a gold"; PAR 484:592, pt. 3, "Not everything that glitters is gold," St. Thomas.

Got a *good* thing going.
Prfrmr: The Itals, "I Am What I Am," *Cool and Dread*

The *good* you do will live after you.
Prfrmr: Mikey Dread, "Roots and Culture," *Best Sellers*
Prfrmr: The Itals, "Brutal," *Brutal Out Deh*
Prfrmr: The Wailing Souls, "Informer," *Lay It on the Line*
Annot: MKH 258, "The good men do lives after them"; ST 1005:3; // AC 63:654, "Do good an' good wi follow you"; BW 42:241.

If you want *good* your nose must run.
Prfrmr: Bunny Wailer, "Blackheart Man," *Blackheart Man*
Prfrmnc: Ancient children used to say
          if you want good, your nose must run.
Annot: // AC 62:656, "You wuk good you nose mus' run'"; BW 74:509, "If you want good, you' nose mus' run"; HD 128, "If you want good your nostril has to run"; WS 120:52, ". . . yu nose 've fe run (Success does not come without maximum effort)"; MB 156:390, "If you want to succeed then you must be prepared to make many sacrifices and undergo much tribulation."

If we can't be *good,* we'll be careful.
Prfrmr: The Abyssinians, "Y Mas Gan," *Satta Massagana*
Prfrmnc: He will take us by the hand
          And lead us to that wonder land

If we can't be good we'll be careful
And do the best we can.

Annot: MKH 259, "Be good; and if you can't be good, be careful"; ST 995:8; WH 263.

Habee-habee no wantee-wantee, wantee-wantee no habee-habee.

Prfrmr: The Itals, "Wanti Wanti," *Easy to Catch*

Prfrmr: Culture, "Hav E Have E," *Payday*

Prfrmnc: Hey Mr. Hav E! Yuh Hav E already.

Prfrmr: Max Romeo, "Smile Out of Style," *War Ina Babylon*

Prfrmnc: Wanti wanti can't getti
Getti getti no wanti
habbi habbi no wanti
but wanti can't getti

Prfrmr: Johnny Clarke, "Wanti Wanti."

Annot: // BW 113:846, "Want i want i, no hab i'; hab'i,' no wanti," "habie habie, now want i'; no hab i, da dead fe he," "Want i,' no want i,' a dead for i' "; FR 100:103, "Habee-habee no wantee-wantee, wantee-wantee no habee-habee"; HD 125, "have nots can't get, and haves don't want"; WS 120:55; AC 66:686, "Habi Habi, no wanti; no habie, da dead fe he"; MB 26:30, 171:436, "Wanti wanti cyaan getti, an' getti getti noh wanti. (Be thankful for the blessings that come to you always realising that many of the things we take for granted are luxuries to others.)"

***Half* the story has never been told.**

Prfrmr: Justin Hinds, "Happy Go Lucky," *Know Jah Better*

Prfrmr: Bob Marley, "Get Up, Stand Up," *Burnin'*

Prfrmr: Peter Tosh, "Get Up, Stand Up," *Equal Rights*

Prfrmr: Bunny Wailer, "Get Up, Stand Up," *Protest*

Prfrmr: The Itals, "Hallelujah," *Easy to Catch*

Prfrmnc: The half has never been told.

***Hand* a bowl, knife a throat.**

Prfrmr: Culture, "Hand a Bowl," *Good Things*

Prfrmnc: Hand a bowl, knife a throat,
no love in their hearts.

Prfrmr: Culture, "Good Times," *Payday*

Annot: // AC 65:674, "Han' da a bowl, knife da a troat"; BW 56:368, "Han a bowl, knife a t'roat." "Han da bowl, knife da t'roat"; FR 108:465, "Han a bowl, knife a troat"; WS 248:62, Han' deh a bowl, knife deh a t'roat." *Pretending to do someone a favor while undermining their efforts.

When your *hands* do its your own eyes that have seen.

Prfrmr: Bob Marley, "Pass It On," *Burnin'*

Never bite the *hand* that feeds you.

Prfrmr: Mikey Dread, "Roots and Culture," *Best Sellers*

Prfrmr: The Itals, "Brutal," *Brutal Out Deh*
Prfrmr: Johnny Osbourne and Aswad, "Don't Bite the Hand"
Annot: MKH 54, 275; OX 62; ST 1242:9; DA 7:15; DSDJ 503; NC 419; HY 47; TA 37; WH 284:H51; BA 83; WT 195; PR 229.

What your *hands* commit your body must bear.
Prfrmr: Culture, "Weeping and Wailing," *More Culture*

One *hand* can't shake.
Prfrmr: The Itals, "Together Forever," *Modern Age*
Prfrmnc: One hand can't shake, two it really take.

One *hand* wash the other.
Prfrmr: The Itals, "Together Forever," *Modern Age*
Annot: MKH 276; OX 347; ST 1059:9; WH 283; DC 86, 617; // WS 121:58, "Wan han wash de other. (This is used throughout Jamaica to teach generosity [and communal and cooperative values in many areas of life, e.g., farming and finances].)"; MB 29:39.

Idle *hands* is devil's workshop.
Prfrmr: Donovan, "Devil's Workshop," *Banzani*
Prfrmnc: Can't stop, working at the devil's workshop.
Annot: MKH 411; OX 395; DA 4:83; WS 133:107, "Idle head"; SM 118; PR 236 (mind); // FR 102:192, "Idle man head . . ."; AC 72:766, "Idle man head . . . ,"; BW 61:412; WS 133:107.

Hard *head* pickney [child] dead ina sun hot.
Prfrmr: Iaa (Delton Waite). A Jamaican Rastafari man, 42 years old, Negril, Jamaica, August 1999.
Annot: PR 231, "Hard head makes a soft behind"; // MB 85:189, "Haad a hearin pikinny ded a sun hat (Children who will not listen to the instructions and advice of older folks will not succeed in life)."

What drop off the *head* fall on the shoulders.
Prfrmr: The Itals, "Easy to Catch," *Easy to Catch*
Prfrmr: Bunny Wailer, "Tagowar Game," *Crucial*
Annot: // BW 113:852 "What fall of a head mus' drop pon shoulder, i.e., what you do not give to a man you give to his children"; HD 125; FR 107:384; WS 147:173, "Wha drap off a head drap 'pon shoulder (In rural Jamaica, people practice a form of communal life by sharing labor, food, and other material things. An object that is sometimes useless in one household is the means of survival in another household)"; MB 155:388, "You really do not lose out if some of the benefits you expected to receive go to close friends or relatives instead of you. Sharing with others now could ensure your future gain . . ."

Who can't *hear* must feel.
Prfrmr: The Itals, "Herbs Pirate," *Brutal Out Deh*
Prfrmnc: Who can't hear,
        dem bound to feel.

Prfrmr: Culture, "Weeping and Wailing," *More Culture*
Prfrmnc: Who doesn't hear will feel it.
Prfrmr: The Maytones, "Who Can't Hear Will Feel."
Annot: MKH 290; // AC 66:694, "You no yearry a you aise (eyes), you wi' yearry a
         you 'kin.' " I.e., Those who persist in their evil ways and will not listen to
         advice will ultimately feel the effects. C.f. "He who will not hear must feel"
         (German); WS 266:62, "Yu no hear a ye aise, yu wi hear a yu skin."

No weak *heart* shall enter.
Prfrmr: The Itals, "Together Forever," *Modern Age*
Prfrmnc: No weak heart shall prosper.
Prfrmr: Bob Marley, "Small Axe," *Burnin'*
Prfrmnc: These are the words
         of my Master, telling me that
         "No weak heart shall prosper,
         oh, no they can't—"
Prfrmr: Burning Spear, "Door Peep," *Man in the Hills*
Prfrmnc: No weak heart shall enter this a hola [holy] land.

Every *heart* feels its own vibration.
Prfrmr: The Itals, "Love Affair," *Give Me Power*
Prfrmnc: Every heart feels its own vibration,
         every tongue, every nation has its own sensation.
Annot: MKH 293, "Two hearts never beat the same."

The *heart* is willing but the flesh is weak.
Prfrmr: The Itals, "Kill Crime," *Give Me Power*
Prfrmnc: If your heart is willing and your flesh is weak,
         now is the time, Jah time you've got to seek.
Annot: MKH 558, "The spirit is willing, but the flesh is weak"; OX 765; ST 2198:14.

If you want to get to *heaven* you got to build ahead on the earth.
Prfrmr: The Itals, "Kill Crime," *Give Me Power*

Think you're in *heaven*, but you living in hell.
Prfrmr: Bob Marley, "Time Will Tell," *Kaya*
Prfrmnc: Time alone, oh! Time will tell.
         Think you're in heaven, but you living in hell.

Jah *helps* those who help themselves.
Prfrmr: The Itals, "Jah Help Those," *Cool and Dread*
Annot: MKH 255, "God helps those . . ."; OX 310, "God (Heaven) helps them that
         helps themselves"; ST 979:4, 11; TW 154; WH 259; // MB 124:296.

For what was *hidden* from the wise and prudent now revealed to the babes and sucklings.
Prfrmr: Jimmy Cliff, "Treat the Youths Right," *Special*
Prfrmr: Bob Marley, "Forever Loving Jah," *Uprising*

Annot: Matthew 13:25, "Because thou hast hidden these things from the wise and prudent, and hast revealed them unto the babes."

For what was *hidden* in the first resurrection now revealed in the second resurrection.
Prfrmr: Jimmy Cliff, "Treat the Youths Right," *Special*

Every *hoe* ha fe stick a bush.
Prfrmr: The Gladiators, "Stick a Bush."
Annot: // AC 67:704, "Every hoe da shop, him 'stick da bush"; BW 46:274; HD 125, "Every hoe has its stick at bush"; WS 204:136, "Ev'ry hoe 've' 'im 'tick a bush (Applied to visibly unattractive people about finding a marriage partner. The gist is that there is someone out there for everyone.)"; MB 130:307. *Literally, for every hoe, there's a potential handle in the bush, or forest.

***Hold* on to what we've got**
Prfrmr: The Itals, "Jah Calling," *Give Me Power*
Prfrmnc: Some would say that the chip don't fly
          too far from the block.
          but in this time, I and I and I
          got to hold on to what we've got.
Annot: MKH 303, "Hold fast to that which is good."

If you live in a glass *house,* don't throw stones.
Prfrmr: Peter Tosh, "If You Live in a Glass House"
Prfrmnc: If you live in a glass house
          Don't throw stones.
          If you can't take blows brother don't throw blows.
Annot: MKH 252–53; BH 66; DA 11:37; BR 80; HA 464; SN 84; TW 194; TA 74, 84, 141; WT 225; WH 484:P108, "People who live in glass houses should not throw stones"; PR 234; SM 92; // BW 122:931, "Who in a glass house no fe t'row stone," "If you hab glass window, no fling rock-stone," "If you hab sash window, don't t'row stone," "If you hab sash window, neber t'row stone"; C716. FR 102:188, "If you hab sash window no trow stone"; WS 259:198, "If yu' 'av sash window, nebber trow 'tone."

It is better to live on the *housetop* than to live in a house full of confusion.
Prfrmr: Bob Marley, "Running Away," *Kaya*
Prfrmnc: And I don't want to live with no strife,
          it is better to live on the house top
          than to live in a house full of confusion.
Annot: Proverbs 24:9, 25:24, "It is better to dwell in a corner of the housetop, than with a brawling woman in a wide house."

Give them an *inch,* they take a yard.
Prfrmr: Bob Marley, "The Real Situation," *Uprising*
Prfrmnc: Give them an inch they take a yard,

give them a yard they take a mile.
Once a man and twice a child,
and everything is just for a while.

Annot: MKH 223, "Give a fool an inch. . . ."; OX 683, 238; AP 327; BR 69; HA 463;
           HY 197; NC 430; TA 42; WH 336:I26, "Given an inch one takes an ell," "Give
           them an inch, and they take an yard (mile)"; DA 9, "Give a child an inch,
           they'll take a mile"; DSDJ 503, (child); DC 87, "If you give an inch, they'll
           take a foot"; // BW 52:334, "Give you an inch, you tek an ell"; WS 267:75,
           "Gi' yu a inch yu tek a el; gi' yu a ole grey 'awse, yu ride 'im dung a hell."

Iron sharpeneth iron.

Prfrmr: The Itals, "Temptation," *Brutal Out Deh*
Prfrmnc: It's full time that you should know that
           iron sharpen iron,
           everyone is his brother's keeper, yeah.
Prfrmr: Culture, "Iron Sharpen Iron," *More Culture, Africa Stand Alone*
Prfrmnc: The countenance of one man, brightenth another,
           iron sharpen iron.
Annot: MKH 334; OX 406; ST 1255:5; NC 430; *Proverbs of Erasmus*, 1545; Proverbs
           27:17, "Iron sharpeneth iron; so a man sharpeneth the countenance of his
           friend"; // AC 72:772, "Iron cut iron, dutty water out fire."

No man is an *island*.

Prfrmr: Culture, "Be Honest," *Three Sides to My Story*
Prfrmnc: No man is an island
           No man stands alone.

Same *knife* cut the sheep throat, same knife cut the goat too.

Prfrmr: The Wailing Souls, "Old Broom," *The Very Best*
Annot: // FR 105:329, "Same knife stick sheep wi' stick goat"; AC 75:802, "De same
           knife dat cut goat troat can cut sheep troat"; WS 84:257, "De same knife weh
           'tick goat wi' 'tick sheep. (Applied to family discordances to warn against
           taking sides. The person who instigates disagreement with someone today,
           will attack someone else another day.)"; MB 50:85, "A butcher will use the
           same butchering knife, regardless of whichever animal he is butchering.
           Similarly, the bad things you do to others can easily be done to you."

Knock and it shall be opened, seek and ye shall find.

Prfrmr: Bunny Wailer, "Blackheart Man," *Blackheart Man*
Prfrmnc: And he said, "Knock and it shall be opened,
           seek and ye shall find,
           wisdom is found in the simplest places,
           in the nick of time."
Annot: MKH 29, "Ask, and it shall be given you; seek, and you shall find; knock,
           and it shall be opened unto you"; OX 20; ST 100:5.

What you don't *know* you don't know.

Prfrmr: Justin Hinds, "What You Don't Know," *Jezebel*

Prfrmr: Iaa, (Delton Waite). A Jamaican Rastafari man, 42 years old, Negril, Jamaica,
          August 1999.

Annot: // AC 75:808, "What you don't know older dan you"; BW 114:862.

Say when *lamp* out, finger walk.

Prfrmr: The Itals, "In Deh," *Give Me Power*

The man who *laughs* first is the last.

Prfrmr: The Pioneers, "Them a Laugh."

Prfrmnc: The man who laugh first, him are de last,
          Who laugh the last, him are the master,
          who laugh the last, him are the master; boss!

Prfrmr: Bob Marley, "Jah Live," *Country Man*

Prfrmnc: Is he who laugh last, children,
          is he who win.

Annot: MKH 361, "He who laughs last laughs best"; OX 445; ST 1356:1; WH 362:L54,
          "He that laughs last laughs best," varied; //AC 76:816, "Fus'laugh no laugh,
          as las laugh a de laugh," "He laughs best laughs last"; BW 50:327, "Fus' laugh
          a nod de ending." "Las' man laugh, laugh de sweetest"; CP 76:816 ("He
          laughs best who laughs last"); HD 127, "Who laughs last laughs best"; WS
          206:I41.

Lay it on the *Line*.

Prfrmr: The Wailing Souls, "Lay It on the Line," *Lay It on the Line*

Little and long.

Prfrmr: The Itals, "Wanti Wanti," *Easy*

Prfrmnc: Eat little me say eat long.
          That's how the weak can get strong.

Prfrmr: Iaa, (Delton Waite). A Jamaican Rastafari man, 42 years old, Negril, Jamaica,
          August 1999.

Prfrmnc: Lickle and long.

Life is one big road with lots of signs.

Prfrmr: Bob Marley, "Wake Up and Live," *Survival*

Prfrmnc: Life is one big road with lots of signs
          So when you're riding through the ruts
          don't you complicate your mind.

Prfrmr: Iaa, (Delton Waite). A Jamaican Rastafari man, 42 years old, Negril, Jamaica,
          August 1999.

The *life* of all flesh is the blood thereof.

Prfrmr: The Itals, "Temptation," *Brutal Out Deh*

Annot: Genesis 6:4, "Flesh with the life thereof."

Well if *life* is a thing money could buy, then you know the rich would live and the poor would die.
Prfrmr: Jimmy Cliff, "Love Is All," *Special*
Annot: A line from traditional African American spirituals.

For *linger* you must linger cry you must cry.
Prfrmr: Bunny Wailer, "Who Feels It," *Protest*
Prfrmnc: For linger you linger,
         cry you must cry.

Don't wake the *lion* when's he's asleep.
Prfrmr: The Itals, "Don't Wake the Lion," *Early Recordings*
Annot: MKH 378, "Don't wake a sleeping lion"; OX 863: ST 1437:9; // WS 92:293.

The *lips* of the righteous teaches many.
Prfrmr: Peter Tosh, "Fools Die," *Wanted*
Annot: MKH 378, ". . . feeds many"; ST 1440:6; Proverbs 10:21, "The lips of the righteous feed many."

The longest *liver* will see the most.
Prfrmr: Culture, "Why Worry," *Wings of a Dove*
Prfrmnc: Why worry about them, when you can pray them off?
         (Spoken) The longest liver will see the most.
Annot: // BW 38:205.

The more you *look,* the less you see.
Prfrmr: Culture, "Hand a Bowl," *Good Things*
Annot: // FR 100:91, "De more you look a de less you see"; AC 78:849, "De more you look, de less you see." BW 39:214, ". . . because one conceals things from an inquisitive person. A common reproof to one who is staring"; WS 128:87; MB 30:40.

***Man* cannot live by bread alone.**
Prfrmr: The Itals, "Temptation," *Brutal Out Deh*
Prfrmnc: Man cannot live by only bread,
         But every mouth must be fed.
         Never try to bite the hand that feed you,
         'cause the good things you do will live with you.
Annot: MKH 400; OX 144; ST 231:8; WH 396:M44, "Man does not live by bread alone"; Deuteronomy 8:3, ". . . that he might make thee know that man doth not live by bread only, but by every word that proceedeth out of the mouth of the Lord doth man live."

A hungry *man* is an angry man.
Prfrmr: The Itals, "Brutal," *Brutal Out Deh*
Prfrmnc: 'Cause a hungry man is an angry man,
         And a drowning man will catch at straws.
Prfrmr: Bob Marley, "Natty Dread," *Natty Dread*

Prfrmr: Big Youth, live concert, The Emporium, Kansas City, MO. January 1999.

Annot: MKH 318; OX 393; ST 1201:1; WH 396:M41, "A hungry man is an angry man."

Well the biggest *man* you ever did see was just a baby.

Prfrmr: Bob Marley, "Coming in from the Cold," *Uprising*

He (Jah) never gives a *man* more than he can bear.

Prfrmr: The Itals, "Make Merry," *Give Me Power*

Once a *man* and twice a child.

Prfrmr: Bob Marley, "Real Situation," *Uprising*

Prfrmnc: See "Give them inch, they take a mile."

Prfrmr: Justin Hinds, "Once a Man."

Prfrmr: Ronnie Davis and Idren, "Respect Your Elders," *Come Straight*

Annot: MKH 403; OX T M570; ST 26:1; TW 68; AP 464–65; BH 68:1; WT 70; AP 464–65:1631; NC 441; PR 236.

A drowning *man* will clutch at a straw.

Prfrmr: Jimmy Cliff, "House of Exile," *Music Maker*

Prfrmnc: A drowning man will
          clutch at a straw, now,
          Watching you now
          on your last mile.

Prfrmr: The Itals, "Brutal," *Brutal Out Deh*

Annot: MKH 169; OX 205; ST 643:5; TW 233; WH 394; // HD 122, "Drowning man will catch at a straw."

A good *man* is never honored in his own country.

Prfrmr: Bob Marley, "Survival," *Survival*

Annot: St. Mark 6:4, "But Jesus said unto them, a prophet is not without honour, but in his own country, and among his own kin, and in his own house."

Every *mickle* makes a muckle.

Prfrmr: Bunny Wailer, "Fig Tree," *Blackheart Man*

Prfrmnc: Now every man is a man and
          every mickle makes a muckle.
          Don't free some and put some
          in a shackle.

Prfrmr: Bunny Wailer, "Roots Man Skanking," *Rock 'N Groove*

Annot: MKH 410, "Many a mickle makes a muckle"; OX 508, "Many a little makes a mickle"; // TU 31, "Every mikkle makes a muckle refers to thriftiness, and is even more archaic than our 'a penny saved is a penny earned' "; WS 269:101; MB 42:70, "Ebry mikkle mek a mukkle. (Every little bit counts. By being content to save what little comes to you from time to time, eventually you will get all you need.)"

Come here to drink *milk*, didn't come here to count cows.

Prfrmr: Justin Hinds, "In This Time," *Know Jah Better*

Prfrmnc: Come here to drink milk,
didn't come here to count cows.
When in Rome, do as the Romans do.

Annot: // BW 125:957, "You come to drink milk an' no fe count cow, i.e., not to pry into my affairs"; TU 31, "Many people carry out their business in a straightforward manner, but others are merely a 'bag of mouth,' in such cases it may become necessary to remind them 'mi come here fi drink milk, mi noh come here fi count cow' "; WS 114:24, "Go backra cow pen fe count cow, no drink 'im milk; but w'en yu drink 'im milk, no count 'im cow (If you go to the Master's cow pen to count cows, don't drink his milk. But when you drink his milk, don't count cows." (Accept the good that comes from a situation but mind your own business.); MB 24:24, "Me come yah fe drink milk, me noh come yah fe count cow. (Mind your own business. Enjoy what you are entitled to.)"

Money is the root of all evil.

Prfrmr: The Itals, "Truth Must Reveal," *Brutal Out Deh*

Prfrmnc: When the rich man do wrong,
then walk with them money,
the root of all evil and violence.

Prfrmr: Jimmy Cliff, "Money Won't Save You," *Music Maker*

Annot: MKH 416; ST 1608:1; OX 150; BH 63 (love of money); BR 85; DA 2:29; HY 297; TA 49; NC 446; WH 387:L248; BRU 89; TW 230; WT 270; BEY 559.1; PA 705; I Timothy 6:10, "For the love of money is the root of all evil"; PR 238.

The higher the *monkey* climbs, the more he expose.

Prfrmr: Justin Hinds, "In This Time," *Know Jah Better*

Prfrmr: I-Roy, "Welding," *Tougher Than Tough*

Annot: DC 426, "The higher the monkey climb, the more you see his behind"; // AC 87:969, "The higher the monkey climb de plainer him tail show (in Italian, French, German)"; BW 38:202; WS 95:305.

The older the *moon*, the brighter it shine.

Prfrmr: The Itals, "Easy to Catch," *Easy to Catch*

Annot: DC 134; // MB 76:160, "Da olda de moon, de briyta it shine (Some people get better with age)."

Never say never.

Prfrmr: The Itals, "Never Say Never," *Easy to Catch*

Annot: MKH 428; OX 563.

Never too old to learn.

Prfrmr: Iaa (Delton Waite). A Jamaican Rastafari man, 42 years old, Negril, Jamaica, August 1999.

Annot: MKH 438; OX 563; ST 36:5; DA 3:59. (Never too old to learn new tricks.)

Nothing happen before it's time.

Prfrmr: The Itals, "Happen Before the Time," *Modern Age*

Annot: MKH 279, "Nothing don't happen till it takes place."

Now or never.
Prfrmr: The Itals, "Together Forever," *Modern Age*

You jump out of the frying pan ina fire.
Prfrmr: Culture, "Frying Pan," *Nuff Crises*
Prfrmnc: You jump outta frying pan
            jump ina fire.
            Babylon, you jump outta frying pan
            jump ina fire.
Prfrmr: Justin Hinds, "Jump Out of the Frying Pan."
Prfrmr: Peter Tosh, "Magga Dog," *Mama Africa*
Prfrmr: Andrew Tosh, "Magga Dog," *Original Man*
Prfrmnc: Jump from the fryin pan
            Into the fire hot.
Annot: MKH 448–49; OX 292; ST 814:1; AP 240; BH 69:23; NC 413; TW 147; TA 158,
            186; WH 244:F282, "Out of the frying pan into the fire"; BA 72; BR 75; HA
            470; SN 95; BRU 5405; WT 170; PR 241; DC 381, "Don't jump out the frying
            pan into the fire"; // BW 77:531, "Jump out a frying pan you jump ina fire,"
            "No jump from frying pan ina de fire"; MB 102:236.

When you think its *peace* and safety, sudden destruction sets in.
Prfrmr: Bob Marley, "Rat Race," *Rastaman Vibration*
Annot: // MB 48:82, "When you tink ah peace and safety, ah sudden dischukshan.
            (When you think all is well, you could be on the very brink of danger.
            Always be sensitive to warning signals.)"

Penny wise and pound foolish.
Prfrmr: The Wailing Souls, "War," *The Very Best*
Prfrmnc: Grandma said, penny wise and pound foolish
            See dem, . . .
            War in the east, war in the west . . .
Annot: MKH 458; ST 1771:15; OX 620; TW 280; WH 482.

Pie up in the sky.
Prfrmr: Jimmy Cliff, "The Harder They Come," *The Harder They Come*

Whosoever diggeth a *pit* shall fall in it.
Prfrmr: Bob Marley, "Small Axe," *Burnin'*
Prfrmr: Culture, "Iron Sharpen Iron," *More Culture,* and *Africa Stand Alone*
Prfrmnc: When you gonna dig a pit, my brother
            don't one always dig two.
Annot: MKH 465; OX 187; ST 1799:10; AC 69:723, "Dig hole, tak' ya fall in a i' "; DA
            12, (ditch); DSDJ 504, (ditch); WH 496:P225, "To fall into the pit one digs
            for others"; Ecclesiastes 10:8, "He that diggeth a pit shall fall in it, and whoso
            breaketh an hedge, a serpent shall bite him"; DC 87, "If you're gon' dig a

hole for someone, you better dig two"; // HD 121, "When you are digging a pit dig one for yourself"; WS 123:65; AB 22, (ditch).

Poverty is a crime.
Prfrmr: Andrew Tosh, "Poverty Is a Crime," *Original Man*
Annot: MKH 477, "Poverty is no crime"; OX 642; ST 1845:3.

Practice what you preach.
Prfrmr: The Itals, "Brutal," *Brutal Out Deh*
Prfrmnc: "Man got to practice what them preach"
Prfrmr: Mikey Dread, "Enjoy Yourself," *Best Sellers*
Prfrmnc: "Whatever I preach, I practice it."
Annot: MKH 479; OX 643; ST 1870:2; TW 295; WH 510:P319, "To practice what one preaches"; DA 7:26.

Preventing is better than curing.
Prfrmr: The Wailing Souls, "Mass Charlie Ground," *Inchpinchers*
Annot: MKH 482–83, "An ounce of prevention is worth a pound of cure"; OX 646; ST 1877:4; TW 272; WH 465; DSDJ 502; DA 3:44, (An ounce of prevention is worth a pound of cure).

Promise is a comfort to a fool.
Prfrmr: Mikey Dread, "Enjoy Yourself," *Best Sellers*
Prfrmr: Carolyn Tait, a 23-year-old woman at Maya Lodge in Blue Mountains above Kingston, Jamaica, August 1992.

Puss in a bag.
Prfrmr: Lee Perry, "Puss in a Bag."
Annot: MKH 463, "Don't buy a pig in a poke"; OX 95; ST 1791–92; T 31; PR 242, "Don't buy a pig in a bag"; AP 494; NC 458; TW 284; WH 489:P157; WT 335; T P304; BRU 109; // WS 97:313 (puss in a bag); AC 98:1109; MB 28:36.

The *race* is not for the swift, nor the battle for the strong.
Prfrmr: The Itals, "Make Merry," *Give Me Power*
Prfrmr: The Wailing Souls, "Run Dem Down," *Fire House Rock*
Prfrmnc: The battle is neither for the swift
           neither the race for the strong.
Annot: MKH 497, "The race is not always to the swift"; OX 661; ST 1903:2; TW 301; WH 521; DA 4; Eccliastes 9:11, "I returned, and saw under the sun, that the race is not to the swift, nor the battle to the strong, neither yet bread to the wise, nor yet riches to men of understanding, not yet favor to men of skill; but time and chance happeneth to them all"; // WS 215:189, "The race no fe who can run, but fe who run de end"; BW 39:215; AC 99:1124, "De race no fe who can run but fe who run a de end."

When the *rain* fall, it don't fall on one man house.
Prfrmr: Bob Marley, "So Much Things to Say," *Exodus*
Prfrmnc: Oh when the rain fall

It won't fall on one man's house,
remember that.

Annot: MKH 498, "Rain fall on the just and unjust"; ST 1284:9; // AC 100:1132 "Rain
nebber fall a' one man door. ('When it rains it rains on all.' Hindu) 'He
maketh his sun to rise on the evil and on the good, and sendeth rain on the
just and on the unjust.' Matthew: 5:45"; BW 100:738, "Rain neber fall a one
man door"; WS 257:174; RT 168:692, "Osu a *eto* Krobow no, ebit a*to* Siade
(Of the rain that falls on the Crobo hills some has fallen on the Shai
mountains)."

Rain a fall but de dutty tough.
Prfrmr: Bob Marley; "Dem Belly Full," *Natty Dread*
Prfrmr: The Wailing Souls, "Who Lives It," *Fire House Rock*
Prfrmnc: Rain a fall but the dutty tough.
Time like lightening strike without warning.
Prfrmr: Iaa, (Delton Waite), Negril Jamaica, August 1999.
Annot: // HD 130; "Rain is falling but the ground is tough"; BW 100:737, "Rain da
come but dutty stuff"; WS 214:187, "Rain a fall, but de dutty tough. Me belly
full but me hungry"; MB 143:346.

Too much *rat* never dig good hole.
Prfrmr: The Itals, "Kill Crime," *Give Me Power*
Prfrmnc: Too much rat never dig good hole.
some ha fe come, some ha fe go.
Annot: BA 36:14 (rat . . .); // AC 100:1134. "Too much ratta nebber dig good hole";
BW 110:826, "Too much ratta never dig good hole," "Too much rat can't dig
good hole"; FR 106:352, "Too much rat dig bad hole"; WS 99:325; MB 35:55;
RT 93:292, "Nkura dódow bɔre tú a, *ɛnno* (When a great number of mice
dig a hole, it does not become deep)."

Be careful of the white belly *rat*.
Prfrmr: Culture, "White Belly Rats," *More Culture*
Prfrmnc: Be careful I would say
Of whitebelly rats.
Annot: // AC 100:1140, "White belly ratta him bit and blow. The proverb is applied
to a hypocritical person who is friendly while trying to harm one"; WS
326:100.

Every *river* runs to the sea.
Prfrmr: Bob Marley, "Crisis," *Kaya*
Annot: MKH 512, "All rivers . . ."; OX 679; ST 1998:2; NC 467, "All the rivers run
into the sea, yet the sea is not fill"; AP 7, "All rivers do what they can for the
sea"; Ecclesiastes 1:7, "All the rivers run into the sea, yet the sea is not full;
unto the place from whence the rivers come, thither they return again"; //
WS 273:155.

The *road* to Rome is not I home.
Prfrmr: Culture, "Iron Sharpen Iron," *More Culture, Africa Stand Alone*
Annot: MKH 513, "All roads lead to Rome"; OX 679; ST 2003:5.

The *road* to Zion is not so easy.
Prfrmr: Culture, "Iron Sharpen Iron," *More Culture*

***Rome* was not built in a day.**
Prfrmr: Jimmy Cliff, "You Can Get It If You Really Want It," *The Harder They Come*
Annot: MKH 515; OX 683; WH 368; ST 2004:10; TW 310; AP 537; BR 90; GR 30; HY
         296; NC 486; TA 57; TR 163.

When in *Rome* do as the Romans do.
Prfrmr: Jimmy Cliff, "Originator," *Special*
Prfrmnc: Some talking bout a new economic order,
         a spiritual one I and I would rather.
         Cause we're in Rome, but we don't do,
         what those Romans do.
Prfrmr: Justin Hinds, "In This Time," *Know Jah Better*
Annot: MKH 515; ST 2005:1; OX 683; OX 547; T R165; AP 537; TA 40; BR 90; HA 465;
         SN 109; TW 310; WH 536; BA 154; SM 193; WT 368; HY 296; NC 468; TA 57;
         PR 245.

You can't *run* away from yourself.
Prfrmr: Bob Marley, "Running Away," *Kaya*

***See* them, come live with them, it's a different thing.**
Prfrmr: Culture, "Hand a Bowl," *Good Things*
Annot: // FR 99:63; HD 127, "See me is one, come live with me is the other"; WS
         139:135, "Come see me, an' come lib wid me an 2 different thing"; AC 31:228;
         BW 26:118; MB 68:143.

***Seeing* is believing.**
Prfrmr: The Itals, "Seein' Is Believing," *Early Recordings*
Prfrmr: Jimmy Riley, "Feeling Is Believing."
Annot: MKH 530; ST 2105:12; AP 556; BH 65; NC 471; TW 321–322; WH 551:S92; SM
         199; PR 245–246.

***See* and blind, hear and deaf.**
Prfrmr: The Itals, "Blood," *Easy*
Prfrmr: Johnny Osbourne and the Sensations, "See and Blind."
Prfrmr: Bunny Wailer, "See and Blind," *Gumption*
Annot: MKH 290, "Hear and say nothing"; ST 219:6; OX 362, "Hear and see and say
         nothing"; WH 206; DA 7:16, "Hear and don't hear, see and don't see"; T 31,
         "Discretion is highly valued when people live close together (sic). To avoid
         witnessing the improprieties of others and thus becoming entangled in their
         affairs one should 'See and blind, hear and dear.' "; DC 84, "See and be
         blind; hear and be deaf"; // AC 102:1166, "Used as a warning to servants not

to touch the things they see or repeat the things they hear in their master's house"; BW 101:752; WS 274:164; MB 91:207.

If you run down your *shadow,* you'll never catch it.
Prfrmr: The Meditations, "Woman Is Like a Shadow," *Greatest Hits*
Prfrmnc: If you run down your shadow, you'll never catch it.
          Woman is like a shadow, man is like an arrow.

Can't trust no *shadows* after dark.
Prfrmr: Bob Marley, "Revolution," *Natty Dread*
Prfrmnc: I don't want to live in the park
          Can't trust no shadows after dark.
Prfrmr: The Meditations, "Trust No Shadow."
Annot: // TU 31; BW 30:138, " 'Crab say him no trust shadow after dark'. . . for what
          he thinks is a shadow may be a man's hand"; WS 51:94, "Crab seh 'im no
          trus no shadder afta dark"; MB 67:140.

***Sick* no care, doctor worse.**
Prfrmr: The Wailing Souls, "Who Lives It," *Inchpinchers*
Prfrmnc: Crab walk too much him lose him claw, now
          It sick no care, the doctor worse.
          Who lives a knows it . . .
Annot: // BW 103:765, " 'Sick man no care, fe what doctor care.' If the sick man
          doesn't care, why should the doctor care?"

Three *sides* to my story.
Prfrmr: Culture, "Be Honest," *Three Sides to My Story*
Prfrmnc: Three sides to lyin (lion) story
          My side, your side, and then the truth.
          Please be honest with yourself.
Prfrmr: The Wailing Souls, "Mixup," *Reggae Legends, Vol. 1*
Prfrmnc: Every story there got to be two sides.
Annot: MKH 566, "There are three sides to every story, your side, my side, and the
          truth"; // BW 38:205.

The wage of *sin* is death.
Prfrmr: Bob Marley, "Johnny Was," *Rastaman Vibration*

Never see *smoke* without fire.
Prfrmr: Bob Marley, "My Woman Is Gone," *Kaya*
Prfrmnc: Still you never see
          smoke without fire.
          And every man you see,
          has a heart's desire.
Prfrmr: The Wailing Souls, "Fire Coal," *Reggae Legends, Vol. 1*
Prfrmnc: Never see smoke without fire
          What you sow you got to reap now.

Prfrmr: The Itals, "Hallelujah," *Easy to Catch*
Annot: MKH 549; OX 573; ST 812:1; TW 340; DA 12; WH 576:S282, "Where's there is smoke, there is fire"; DC 85, 87; // HD 123, "You never see smoke without fire"; WS 218:205, "Yu nebber se smoke widout fiah"; BW 126:965, "You never see smoke widout fire"; MB 33:50.

Snake in the grass.
Prfrmr: The Wailing Souls, "Informer," *Lay It on the Line*

Something for something, nothing for nothing.
Prfrmr: The Itals, "Easy Now," *Cool and Dread*
Annot: MKH, 433, 551, "Nothing for nothing," "Something for nothing, nothing for something"; ST 2161:7; TW 344; WH 582.

What you *sow*, shall you reap.
Prfrmr: The Itals, "Make Merry," *Give Me Power*
Prfrmnc: What you sow, shall he reap
            And I know that talk is cheap.
            But the hotter the battle,
            is as sweet as the victory.
Prfrmr: The Itals, "Almighty," *Modern Age*
Prfrmnc: What you sow is what you shall reap.
Prfrmr: The Wailing Souls, "Informer," *Lay It on the Line*
Prfrmr: The Wailing Souls, "Fire Coal," *Reggae Legends, Vol. 1*
Prfrmr: Culture, "Weeping and Wailing," *More Culture*
Prfrmnc: "Sow a good crop today, reap good crop tomorrow, I say."
Prfrmr: Jimmy Cliff, "House of Exile," *Music Maker*
Prfrmr: Justin Hinds, "In This Time," *Know Jah Better*
Prfrmnc: Sow corn, can't reap peas.
Annot: MKH 554–55; OX 757; OX 608; ST 2179:4; AP 591; BH 61; BR 92; DA 10; DSDJ 499; T S687; WH 585:S364; SN 61; BA 117; BRU 117; WT 408; SM 208; Galatians 6:7; "Be not deceived; God is not mocked: for whatsoever a man soweth, that shall he reap,"; 2 Corinthians, "But this I say, He which soweth sparingly shall reap sparingly; and he which soweth bountifully shall reap also bountifully"; NC 479; TS 687; PR 248–49; // MB 77:165, "Yu cyaan (cannot) sow caan (corn) an expek fe reap peas."

Spit in the sky, it'll fall in your eyes.
Prfrmr: Justin Hinds, "In This Time," *Know Jah Better*
Prfrmr: Delroy Wilson, "Spit in the Sky."
Prfrmr: The Heptones, "Backstabbers," *Rainbow Valley*
Annot: MKH 558, "Who spits against the wind spits in his own face"; OX 766; ST 2199:8; TW 405; WH 686; T 31; // BT 39:7; FR 107:431, "Spit in the sky it fall a you face"; MB 25:25, "Pit inna de sky, it fall inna yuh y'eye (What you do to, or wish for others, could eventually be the cause of your own downfall)"; AC 108:1226; BW 72:495, (face).

Sticks and stones may break my bones, but words will never hurt me.
Prfrmr: The Itals, "Seein' Is Believing," *Early Recordings*
Annot: MKH 563; OX 773; WH 594; ST 2609:6.

The *stone* the builders refused, shall be the head cornerstone.
Prfrmr: Bob Marley, "So Much Trouble," *Survival*
Prfrmnc: So before you check out your tide
          don't leave another cornerstone
          standing there behind.
Prfrmr: Bunny Wailer, "Blackheart Man," *Blackheart Man*
Prfrmnc: Them that drink of the old wine,
          have no place for the new.
          And the stones that the head of the corner
          are the some ones, that the builders refused.
Prfrmr: Bob Marley, "Ride Natty Ride," *Survival*
Prfrmnc: But the stone that the builders refuse
          shall be the head cornerstone.
          And no matter what game they play,
          we've got something they can never take away.
Prfrmr: Culture, "Where the Tree Falls," *Payday*
Prfrmnc: The same stone that the builder refused in the morning
          becomes the head cornerstone.
Annot: Matthew 21:42, "The stone that the builder rejected, the same is become the
          head of the corner. This is the Lord's doing."; Mark 12:10; Luke 20:17; Acts
          4:11; Peter 2:7–8; Psalms 118:22.

A rolling *stone* gathers no moss.
Prfrmr: The Itals, "Roll Rastafari Chariot," *Brutal Out Deh*
Prfrmnc: Rolling stone don't gather no moss.
Annot: MKH 565; OX 682, 547; ST 2218–19:6; AP 537; DA 3:48; TW 355; BA 173; BR
          93; HA 461; SN 73; TA 44; T S885; WH 597:S484; BRU 134; SM 193; WT 416;
          HY 296; NC 481; TA 61; PR 252; // PAR 462:121, pt. 3, Granada, "Rolling stone
          ketch no moss but him gader polish all de same"; BW 100:742.

Only the *strong* will survive.
Prfrmr: Justin Hinds, "In This Time," *Know Jah Better*

They say the *sun* shines for all.
Prfrmr: Bob Marley, "Crisis," *Kaya*
Annot: MKH 573, "The sun shines on all the world." ". . . on the evil as well as the
          good"; OX 787; ST 2233:1.

You take up the *sword,* you'll perish by it.
Prfrmr: The Itals, "Temptation," *Brutal Out Deh*
Prfrmr: The Wailing Souls, "Fire Coal," *Reggae Legends, Vol. 1*
Prfrmnc: Live by the gun, die by the gun.
Annot: MKH 577; ST 2265:3; TW 363; WH 608:S574, "He who lives by the sword

shall perish by the sword"; DC 85, "You live by the sword, you die by the sword."

Take it or leave it.
Prfrmr: Culture, "Natty Dread Taking Over," *Two Sevens Clash*
Annot: MKH 580; OX 799; WH 612.

Talk is cheap.
Prfrmr: Bob Marley, "The Heathen," *Exodus*
Annot: MKH 581; TW 365; WH 612; NC 484; WH 612:T22, "Talk is cheap"; PR 253; BH 68.

Teeth and tongue, they got to meet some sweet day.
Prfrmr: The Itals, "Jah Calling," *Give Me Power*
Prfrmr: The Wailing Souls, "Things and Time," *Inchpinchers*
Prfrmr: Stranger Cole, "Teeth and Tongue."
Prfrmr: The Wailing Souls, "Move On," *Reggae Legends, Vol. 1*
Annot: // WS 276:194, "Tongue an' teet' av' fe meet."

Thru the *thick*, thru the thin.
Prfrmr: Bob Marley, "Ride Natty Ride," *Survival*
Annot: WH 616:T50, "Through thick and thin."

As a man *thinketh*, so is he.
Prfrmr: Iaa, (Delton Waite), Negril, Jamaica, August 1998.
Annot: MKH 398; ST 2305:15.

You cut your own *throat*.
Prfrmr: Culture, "Walk with Jah," *Trust Me*
Prfrmnc: Something a go wrong tonight
          Those dirty ways not right.
          You use your own teeth
          to cut your own throat, tell me
          How you a go walk with Jah?
Annot: MKH 604, "Let not your tongue cut your own throat."

Time waits on no one.
Prfrmr: The Itals, "Take No Share," *Easy to Catch*
Annot: MKH 598, "Time and tide wait for no one"; OX 822; ST 2322:12; TW 373; WH 628.

There's a *time* and place for everything.
Prfrmr: Hugh Mundell, "Time and Place," *Time and Place*
Annot: MKH 185; OX 225; TW 374; ST 2329:1; WH 627; DA 12, (There's a place for everything and everything in its place.)

Time will tell.
Prfrmr: The Itals, "Time Will Tell," *Brutal Out Deh*
Prfrmr: Bob Marley, "Time Will Tell," *Kaya*
Prfrmr: Bunny Wailer, *Time Will Tell: A Tribute to Bob Marley*

Annot: MKH 599; OX 823; TW 375; WH 630.

Don't let *time* catch up on you.
Prfrmr: The Itals, "Time Will Tell," *Brutal Out Deh*
Prfrmnc: Don't let time catch up on you
           When you know you've got.
           The works of the father to do, yeah,

Time like lightning strikes without warning.
Prfrmr: The Wailing Souls, "Who Lives It," *Fire House Rock*

Time longer than rope.
Prfrmr: Prince Buster, "Time Longer Than Rope."
Annot: // AC 113:1286, "Time longer than rope" 72:774, "Jamaica longer dan rope";
          BT 41:52, "Day more long dan rope"; BW 36:185, (Day longer . . .), (world
          longer); FR 106:358; HD 132, "Time is longer than rope"; WS 223:225; MB
          158:396.

The more we stick *together*, that's the way we will survive.
Prfrmr: The Itals, "Together Forever," *Modern Age*
Prfrmr: Bunny Wailer, "The More We Stick Together"
Prfrmnc: The more we stick together / the happier we will be.

A lying *tongue* just for a moment.
Prfrmr: Wailing Souls, "A Fool Will Fall," *Fire House Rock*
Prfrmnc: A lying tongue is just for a moment.
           But righteousness is everlasting foundation.
Annot: Proverbs 12:19.

Simple *trash* blind eyes.
Prfrmr: The Itals, "Time Getting Harder," *Early Recordings*
Annot: MKH 608, ". . . blow in our eyes"; NC 489, "If you associate with trash,
          you'll flounder with trash"; DA 11:27, "If you play . . ."; PR 254, "If you fool
          with trash it'll get in your eyes.

Where the *tree* falls, there shall it lie.
Prfrmr: Culture, "Where the Tree Falls," *Payday*
Prfrmnc: Where the tree falls
           There shall it lie until judgment take its course.
Annot: MKH 610; OX 505; AP 644–45; NC 489, "As the tree falls, so shall it lie"; T
          T503; ST 2368:6; WH 452; WT 452; PR 254; // AC 114:1302, "Where de axe fall
          de tree, dere shall i' lay"; WS 261:1.

Trouble no set like rain.
Prfrmr: The Mighty Diamonds, "Looking for Trouble."
Prfrmr: Bunny Wailer, "Trouble Is on the Road," *Crucial*
Prfrmnc: Trouble is on the road again
           Dis ya trouble a go set like rain.
Annot: // AC 114:1306, "Trouble nebber set like rain"; BW 111:833, "Trouble never

set like rain," "Trouble no 'tan like when rain set a bush corner," "Sun set, but danger neber set." Explanation—"In Jamaica rain is usually seen long before it come. Trouble hardly ever gives warning"; FR106:348; WS 222:219, "Trouble no set laka rain."

If you're lookin' for *trouble* you get it on the double.
Prfrmr: The Mighty Diamonds, "Looking for Trouble."
Prfrmnc: If you lookin' for trouble
            you get it on the double.
            If you lookin' trouble with me,
            you cannot win.
Prfrmr: Tony Tuff, "Never Trouble Trouble."
Annot: MKH 612; ST 2377:7; AP 646; BR 73; DA 7:12; DSDJ 503, "Never trouble trouble"; NC 489; WH 645:T280, "Never trouble trouble 'til trouble trouble you"; SN 83; BA 187; SM 230; PR 254.//AC 115:1312, "Nebber trouble trouble till trouble trouble you"; HD 132; BW 73:500, "If you trouble trouble, trouble till trouble trouble you"; WS 222:220.

Pack up your *troubles*.
Prfrmr: The Itals, "Smile Knotty Dread Smile," *Brutal Out Deh*
Prfrmnc: Pack up your troubles,
            Dry your weeping eyes.
Annot: MKH 612.

The *truth* is an offense, but not a sin.
Prfrmr: Bob Marley, "Jah Live," *Country Man*

***Truth* that is hidden got to reveal.**
Prfrmr: The Itals, "Truth Must Reveal," *Brutal*
Prfrmr: The Itals, "In A Dis Ya Time," *Modern Age*
Prfrmnc: Anyone can tell a lie / but the truth reveal itself.

Every *tub* must sit on its own bottom.
Prfrmr: Culture, "Weeping and Wailing," *More Culture*
Prfrmnc: Every tub must sit on its own bottom.
            And what your hand commit
            your body must bear.
Prfrmr: The Itals, "Hallelujah," *Easy to Catch*
Annot: MKH 618; OX 845; ST 2397:4; AP 193; BH 67, "Every feet . . ."; NC 490; TW 384; WH 649:T306, (tub/barrel, stand); BR 96; GR 22; HA 463; TA 65; T T596; SN 93; BA 188; WT 456; SM 232; DC 86; // BW 46:282, "Every tub 'tan 'pon him own bottom"; FR 101:126, "Ebery tub sit down pon him bottom"; WS 222:224, "Ev'ry tub sidung 'pon 'im own bottom"; PR 254–55.

What goes on *up* is coming on down
Prfrmr: Bob Marley, "So Much Trouble," *Survival*
Prfrmnc: Now they are sitting on a time bomb,

Now I know the time has come.
What goes on up is coming on down,
What goes around is comes around.

Prfrmr: The Heptones, "Backstabbers," *Rainbow Valley*
Prfrmnc: What goes up must come down.
Annot: MKH 185, 626; OX 236; WH 257:G82, "What goes up must come down"; DA
          12; // RT 180:754, Biribi wo soro a, etwa se ebeba fam' (Whatever is above
          must come down to the earth)."

When you're *up*, you're up.
Prfrmr: The Itals, "Jah Help Those," *Cool and Dread*

Everyone should live under his own *vine* and fig tree.
Prfrmr: Bunny Wailer, "Fig Tree," *Blackheart Man*
Prfrmnc: Never never knew that the time would come
          When every fig must find its fig tree.
          Jump little figs into your fig tree
          and say your are free.
Annot: PR 255; Micah 4:4, "But they shall sit every man under his vine and under
          his fig tree; and none shall make them afraid: for the mouth of the Lord of
          hosts hath spoken it."

You can get it if you really *want*.
Prfrmr: Jimmy Cliff, "You Can Get it if You Really Want," *The Harder they Come*

The things you *want* is not what you always get.
Prfrmr: The Itals, "Happen Before the Time," *Modern Age*
Annot: MKH 639, "It ain't what you wants in dis world, it's what you gits"; ST
          2444:2.

Use what you got till you get what you *want*.
Prfrmr: The Itals, "Happen Before the Time," *Modern Age*
Annot: DC 87, "Take what you can get until you get what you want"; // MB 33:51,
          "Tek whey yuh get tell yu get whey yu want (Every opportunity, well used,
          can be a stepping stone to realization of your ultimate goals)."

In the abundance of *water* the fool is thirsty.
Prfrmr: Bob Marley, "Rat Race," *Rastaman Vibration*

Don't jump in the *water*, if you can't swim.
Prfrmr: Bob Marley, "Misty Morning," *Kaya*
Prfrmnc: One of my good friends said, in a reggae riddim,
          don't jump in the water, if you can't swim.
Annot: // AC 117:1345, "Try the water before . . ."

Trying to force *water* over the hill.
Prfrmr: The Itals, "Take No Share," *Easy*
Annot: MKH 642, "Don't try running water up a hill"; // BW 113:848, "Water never
          run up hill."

You don't miss the *water* until the well run dry.
Prfrmr: Peter Tosh, "Till Your Well Runs Dry," *Legalize It*
Prfrmr: Mikey Dread, "Roots and Culture," *Best Sellers*
Prfrmr: Bob Marley, "Could You be Loved," *Uprising*
Annot: MKH 642; OX 344; ST 2459:2; AP 670; BH 63; BR 97; HA 465; NC 493; WH
          666:W41; PR 257–58; SM 152; DC 86; // WS 131:98; AC 116:1342, "Man nebber
          know de use a water till de tank dry"; BW 125:960, "You neber know de use
          a water till de pon 'dry."

Still *waters* run deep.
Prfrmr: The Itals, "Make Merry," *Give Me Power*
Prfrmnc: Silent river runs deep.
Prfrmr: The Itals, "Don't wake the Lion," *Early Recordings*
Annot: MKH 642; ST 1894:3; AP 602–3; BH 70:33; BR 96; DA 11; HA 464; OX 775;
          TA 67; T W123; WH 666:W42, "Still waters run deep"; WT 471; SM 213; NC
          493; SN 74; TW 394; BA 193; DC 323; // AC 101:1145 ("Sof'ly riber run deep")
          cf. "Still waters run deep"; BT 42:67, "Sofely ribber run deep." FR 105:318;
          HD 120, "Softly rivers runs deep"; MB 18:4.

The rich man's *wealth* is in the city.
Prfrmr: Peter Tosh, "Fools Die"
Prfrmr: Bob Marley, "Stiff Necked Fools," *Confrontation*
Prfrmnc: "The rich man's wealth is in his city"
Annot: Proverbs 10:15, 28:11.

The poor man's *wealth* is in a holy place.
Prfrmr: Peter Tosh, "Fools Die"
Prfrmr: Bob Marley, "Stiff Necked Fools," *Confrontation*
Prfrmnc: The righteous wealth is in his holy place.
Annot: Proverbs 10:15.

Pull your own *weight*.
Prfrmr: Bob Marley, "Ride Natty Ride," *Survival*
Annot: MKH 399.

Where there's a *will*, there is a way.
Prfrmr: Bob Marley, "Zion Train," *Uprising*
Prfrmnc: Oh where there is a will,
          there always is a way.
Annot: MKH 655; OX 891; ST 2510:12; TW 402; SM 245; WH 683:W181; DA 4, 12; PR
          260.

Sometimes you *win*, sometimes you loose.
Prfrmr: The Itals, "Never Say Never," *Easy*
Prfrmr: Taxi driver in Ocho Rios, Jamaica, August 1998.

Them that drink up the old *wine* have no place for the new.
Prfrmr: Bunny Wailer, "Blackheart Man," *Blackheart Man*

Prfrmnc: Them that drink of the old wine
   have no place for the new.
   And the stones that the head of the corner
   are the same ones that builders refuse.
Annot: MKH 657, "Don't pour new wine in old bottles"; ST 2519:4; Mark 2:22, "No
   one puts new wine into old wineskins."

When the *wine* is in; the wit is out.
Prfrmr: The Heptones, "Mystery Babylon"
Prfrmnc: When the wine is in the wit
   Rasta don't drink wine,
   Mystery Babylon.
Annot: MKH 658; OX 895; ST 2523:7; TW 406; WH 688; // AC 101:1161; BW 117:883,
   "When the rum is in, de wit is out."

Wisdom is better than silver and gold.
Prfrmr: Bob Marley, "Zion Train," *Uprising*
Prfrmnc: Don't gain the world and lose your soul,
   wisdom is better silver and gold.
Prfrmr: Iaa, (Delton Waite), Negril, Jamaica, August 1998.
Prfrmnc: Perseverance is better than silver and gold.
Annot: MKH 660, "Wisdom is better than rubies (riches, wealth)"; ST 2537:10; TW
   695; NC 498; DA 3:62 (rubies).

Wisdom is found in the simplest place in the nick of time.
Prfrmr: Bunny Wailer, "Blackheart Man," *Blackheart Man*

Wolf in sheep's clothing.
Prfrmr: The Itals, "I Am What I Am," *Cool and Dread*
Prfrmr: Judy Mowatt, "Many Are Called," *Black Woman*
Prfrmnc: You got to beware of the wolf in sheep's clothing.
Annot: OX 907:1611, "Wolf in sheep's clothing (a lamb's skin)."

Don't gain the *world* and lose your soul.
Prfrmr: Bob Marley, "Zion Train," *Uprising*
Prfrmnc: Don't gain the world and lose your soul
   Wisdom is better than silver and gold,

You can't be *wrong* and get right.
Prfrmr: Jimmy Cliff, "You Can't Be Wrong and Get Right," *Music Maker*

A thousand *years* in Jah sight is just like a minute pass on.
Prfrmr: The Itals, "Time Will Tell," *Brutal Out Deh*

Notes

Introduction

1. Throughout this work, citations for song lyrics will include the song title in quotes, followed by the album from which the song comes.

Chapter I

1. White (1998, 113) describes the dungle [or dunghill] as "a piazza of flattened refuse ringed by cardboard huts behind which rose mounds of garbage. The Dungle did double duty as a municipal garbage dump and a derelict community erected on a platform of filth, human waste and the jetsam of the more discerning scavengers." The term, which originally referred to areas of Kingston on which the homeless erected makeshift shelters, sometimes refers to Rasta communities in the slums of the inner city.

2. See Rupert Lewis (1998) for more extensive discussion of Garvey's role in the development of Rastafari philosophy.

3. I cannot do justice to this central feature of African philosophy and worldview here. For fuller discussions see Janheinz Jahn, *Muntu: African Culture and the Western World*.

4. This deconstruction of the language should be quite familiar to contemporary literary critics, e.g., feminists who use a similar kind of linguistic critique in their own work.

5. The term "Nyabinghi" was first used to describe a liberation movement active in Uganda from 1850 to 1950. "It was centered around a woman healer, Huhumusa, who was possessed by the spirit of Nyabinghi, a legendary "Amazon Queen" (Turner 1991, 71). The term was later used by Emperor Haile Selassie in 1937 to refer to an Ethiopian organization, which included warriors. Rastas adopted the term, applying it to themselves. There is irony in the Rastafari choice of the term, given its original meaning, and considering the second-class status that women have held within the Rastafari movement.

6. Most of these rituals are performed in abbreviated versions in smaller, less elaborate gatherings. These consist of prayers, scriptures recitations, reasonings, and sometimes drumming and chanting, and are referred to as "groundings." The term "grounding" is sometimes used synonymously with "reasonings."

7. Vodou is a religion of African origin brought to the New World with African slaves. It involves an elaborate pantheon of loas (spirits), complex rituals, and an extensive cosmological system strikingly different from, for instance, that of Christianity. One of the most important aspects of Vodou is the synthesis of African and New World influences. Like most New World African religions, Vodou includes drumming, dancing, and spirit possession as pathways to communicate with supernatural forces. For more detailed discussions of Vodou, see Deren 1991, Brown 1991, Barnes 1997, Hurston 1990, and Cosentino 1995.

"Kromanti Play" or "Kromanti Dance" is a Maroon ceremony in which African-derived musical traditions have been preserved and passed down. "The name, 'Kromanti' is derived from the name of a historical slave port on the coast of what is today Ghana, from which a large number of slaves were transported to Jamaica" (Bilby 1985, 130). The rituals, which involve distinctive music and dance styles, are centered around possession by ancestral spirits. Among the surviving African elements is a musical style known as "Country," which uses a drum language to play songs and proverbs. At the center of Kromanti Play ceremonies is healing, achieved through music, dance, and possession. As with many other African-derived healing ceremonies, a possessed medium attends to patients, employing song, dance, sacrifice, and herbal remedies. A strong component is "a series of intricately choreographed ritual motions" (Bilby 1985, 132): in essence, drama and theater.

John Canoe festivals date back at least to the eighteenth century in Jamaica. The festival, which likely took its name from a notorious African, John Conny, incorporated elements of European mummers' plays, pre-Christian pagan survivals such as sword dances, and West African dance and masking traditions. In the 1700s it was linked to Christmas celebrations and characterized by a carnivalesque festival in which masked dancers paraded through the streets, dancing to the accompaniment of musicians playing African and European instruments. These dancers would stop periodically to perform speeches or parts of British folk plays, and even passages from Shakespeare. Later, "set dances" were added, as teams or "sets" competed in a similar fashion to groups in New Orleans's Mardi Grass, or Carnival Celebration in other Caribbean societies (See Bilby 1985, 138–40).

Chapter 2

1. Buffalo Soldiers were African American men who comprised the Ninth and Tenth Cavalries of the United States Army, during the nineteenth century. These men fought in the "Indian wars" and the Spanish-American War. Written out of history until recently, the Buffalo Soldiers had to fight against the racism of white America as well as the battles waged against others in the war for Westward expansion. The song, "Buffalo Soldiers" was written and recorded by King Sporty, who consulted with Bob Marley and gave him rights to do his own version (See "King Sporty," an interview by Roger Steffens, in *The Beat* 15:3 (1996), 50–51).

Chapter 3

1. Perhaps this illustrates the sound-based aesthetic of Jamaican culture in general, reflected in Rastafari *word/sound/power* and in deejaying traditions discussed earlier.

2. By this point, my son had returned to the United States and my wife and I were traveling alone.

3. Rent-a-dread is a male prostitution business supplying foreign white women tourists with dreadlocked escorts. The business is so popular that one can find parodies of it on postcards; and any man with dreadlocks seen with a white woman in Negril is suspected of being a rent-a-dread. Perhaps the most offensive aspect of the phenomenon to Jamaicans such as Iaa (aside from the idea that non-Rastas are cashing in on the "exotic" appeal of dreadlocks) is the rather shameless way in which these women flaunt their intentions.

Chapter 4

1. One is tempted to draw correlations between the symbol here and in other New World African groups in which iron is connected to the deity, Ogoun. While this is certainly a tentative link, it is especially conspicuous because a number of Ogoun's characteristics mirror those of Rastafari, e.g., he is associated with the hunter/warrior (See Barnes 1997).

2. A number of scholars have discussed "marking" or "mocking" among numerous other speech genres traditional within Diasporic cultures, and particularly associated with "signifying." "Marking" refers to derisive imitation, often unrecognized as such by the party being insulted. (See Mitchell-Kernan, 1972a, 1972b; Kochman 1970; and Abrahams 1972b.)

Chapter 6

1. As Owens notes, "men" is necessarily a negative concept. "Man" means an authentic, spiritual person, and "men" indicates a false, ungodly, evil person (people). To refer to someone as "men" is automatically an insult. (See Owens 1976, 67–68).

References

Abrahams, Roger D. 1963. *Deep Down in the Jungle.* Chicago: Aldine.

———. 1968a. "British West Indian Proverbs and Proverb Collections." *Proverbium* 10:239–43.

———. 1968b. "Introductory Remarks to a Rhetorical Theory of Folklore." *Journal of American Folklore* 81:143–58.

———. 1968c. "A Rhetoric of Everyday Life: Traditional Conversational Genres." *Southern Folklore Quarterly* 32:48–59.

———. 1972. "Proverbs and Proverbial Expressions." In *Folklore and Folklife: An Introduction,* ed. Richard M. Dorson, pp. 119–27. Chicago: University of Chicago Press.

———. 1983. *The Man-of-Words in the West Indies: Performance and Emergence of Creole Culture.* Baltimore: Johns Hopkins University Press.

———. 1994. "For Folklorists' Chanticleer: 'No Cry for Feathers, Cry for Long Life.' Proverbs from Nevis." *Proverbium* 11:15–26.

Abrahams, Roger D., ed. 1985. *Afro-American Folktales: Stories from Black Traditions in the New World.* New York: Pantheon.

Alleyne, Mervyn C. 1988. *Roots of Jamaican Culture.* London: Pluto Press.

Allie-I. 1998. "Reggae Moving Mountains: RAW Conference '97." *The Beat* 17, no. 1:14–15.

Anderson, Izett, and Frank Cundall. 1927 [1910]. *Jamaica Negro Proverbs and Sayings.* Kingston: Institute of Jamaica.

Apperson, G. L. 1929. *English Proverbs and Proverbial Phrases.* London: J. M. Dent and Sons.

Arora, Shirley L. 1994 [1984]. "The Perception of Proverbiality." *Proverbium: Yearbook of International Proverb Research* 1:1–38. Reprinted in *Wise Words: Essays on the Proverb,* ed. Wolfgang Mieder, pp. 3–29. New York: Garland, 1994.

Austin-Broos, Diane J. 1987. "Pentecostals and Rastafarians: Cultural, Political, and Gender Relations of Two Religious Movements." *Social and Economic Studies* 36, no. 4:1–39.

Baker, Christopher. 1996. *Jamaica: A Lonely Planet Travel Survival Kit.* Australia: Lonely Planet.

Bambury, T. 1894. *Jamaica Superstitions or The Obeah Book; A Complete Treatise of the Absurdities Believed in by the People of the Island, by the Rector (native) of St. Peter's Church, Hope Bay, Portland.* Jamaica.

Barbour, Francis. 1965. *Proverbs and Proverbial Phrases of Illinois.* Carbondale: Southern Illinois University Press.

Barnes, Sandra T., ed. 1997 [1989]. *Africa's Ogun.* Bloomington: Indiana University Press.

Barnes-Harden, Alene Leett. 1980. "African American Verbal Arts: Their Nature and Communicative Interpretation (A Thematic Analysis)." Ph.D. diss., State University of New York at Buffalo.

Barrett, Leonard E. 1976. *The Sun and the Drum.* Kingston: Sangster's Book Stores in Association with Heinemann.

———. 1988 [1977]. *The Rastafarians: Sounds of Cultural Dissonance.* Boston: Beacon.

Barrow, Steve. 1993. "The Story of Jamaican Music." Booklet for *Tougher Than Tough: The Story of Jamaican Music,* Island Records, pp. 6–65.

Barrow, Steve, and Peter Dalton. 1997. *Reggae: The Rough Guide.* New York: Penguin.

Bascom, William R. 1969. *Ifá Divination: Communication between Gods and Men in West Africa.* Bloomington: Indiana University Press.

———. 1977. "Oba's Ear: A Yoruba Myth in Cuba and Brazil." In *African Folklore in the New World,* ed. Daniel J. Crowley, pp. 3–19. Austin: University of Texas Press.

———. 1981. "The Sanctions of Ifá Divination." In William R. Bascom, *Contributions to Folkloristics.* Meerut, India: Folklore Institute.

Bates, William C. 1896. "Creole Folk-lore from Jamaica: 1. Proverbs. 2. Nancy Stories." *Journal of American Folk-lore,* 9, nos. 38–42:121–26.

Beckford, William. 1790. *A Descriptive Account of the Island of Jamaica.* London.

Beckwith, Martha W. 1922. *Folk Games in Jamaica.* Poughkeepsie, N.Y.: Publications of the Folk-lore Foundation, Vassar College.

———. 1923. *Christmas Mummings in Jamaica.* Poughkeepsie, N.Y.: Publications of the Folk-lore Foundation, Vassar College.

———. 1924. *Jamaican Anansi Stories.* New York: Memoirs of the American Folklore Society, vol. 17.

———. 1925. *Jamaica Proverbs.* Poughkeepsie, N.Y.: Publications of the Folk-lore Foundation, Vassar College.

———. 1928. *Jamaica Folklore.* New York: Memoirs of the American Folk-lore Society, vol. 21.

———. 1929. *Black Roadways.* Chapel Hill: University of North Carolina Press.

Bennett, Louise. 1975 [1966]. *Jamaica Labrish.* Kingston: Sangster's.

———. 1979. *Anancy and Miss Lou.* Kingston: Sangster's.

Bergman, Billy. 1985. *Goodtime Kings: Emerging African Pop.* New York: Quill.

Bilby, Kenneth. 1985. "Caribbean Crucible." In *Repercussions: A Celebration of African-American Music,* ed. Geoffrey Haydon and Dennis Marks, pp. 128–51. London: Century.

———. 1992. "Drums of Defiance: Maroon Music from the Earliest Free Black Communities of Jamaica." Booklet accompanying Smithsonian Folkways Recording, 40412. Washington, D.C.

———. 1995. "Chapter 7: Jamaica." In *Caribbean Currents: Caribbean Music from Rhumba to Reggae,* ed. Peter Manuel, with Kenneth Bilby and Michael Largey, pp. 143–82. Philadelphia: Temple University Press.

Bilby, Kenneth, and Illiott Leib, eds. 1983. *From Congo to Zion: Three Black Musical Traditions from Jamaica.* Cambridge, Mass.: Heartbeat Records, 1983.

Black, Clinton. 1966. *Tales of Old Jamaica.* London: Oxford University Press.

Bones, Jah. 1984. "Rastafari, a Cultural Awakening." In *The Rastafarians: The Minority Rights Group Report No. 64,* pp. 9–10. London.

Boot, Adrian, and Vivien Goldman. 1982. *Bob Marley: Soul Rebel and Natural Mystic.* New York: St. Martin's.

Boot, Adrian, and Chris Salewicz, eds., with executive editor, Rita Marley. 1995. *Bob Marley: Songs of Freedom.* New York: Penguin.

Bornstein, Valeria. 1991. "A Case Study and Analysis of Family Proverb Use." *Proverbium* 8:19–28.

Bradley, Francis. 1937. "South Carolina Proverbs." *Southern Folklore Quarterly* 38:167–86.

Briggs, Charles L. 1985. "The Pragmatics of Proverb Performances in New Mexican Spanish." *American Anthropologist* 87:793–810. Reprinted in *Wise Words: Essays on the Proverb,* ed. Wolfgang Mieder, pp. 317–49. New York: Garland, 1994.

Brown, Karen McCarthy. 1991. *Mama Lola: A Vodou Priestess in Brooklyn.* Berkeley and Los Angeles: University of California Press.

Brunvand, Harold. 1961. *A Dictionary of English Proverbs and Proverbial Phrases from Books Published by Indiana Authors before 1890.* Bloomington: Indiana University Press.

Burke, Eddie. 1975. *Water in the Gourd and Other Jamaican Folk Stories.* London: Oxford University Press.

Campbell, Horace. 1987. *Rasta and Resistance: From Marcus Garvey to Walter Rodney.* Trenton, N.J.: Africa World Press.

Cashmore, Ernest. 1979. *Rastaman: The Rastafarian Movement in England.* London, Boston: G. Allen and Unwin.

———. 1984. "The Rastafarians." *The Minority Rights Group Report No. 64,* pp. 3–11. London.

Chang, Kevin O'Brien, and Wayne Chen. 1998. *Reggae Routes: The Story of Jamaican Music.* Philadelphia: Temple University Press.

Chen, Ray. 1994. *The Jamaican Dictionary: A is fi aringe.* Ontario, Canada: Periwinkle.

Chevannes, Barry, ed. 1998 [1995]. *Rastafari and Other African-Caribbean Worldviews.* New Brunswick, N.J.: Rutgers University Press.

Chisholm, Clinton. 1998. "The Rasta-Selassie-Ethiopian Connections," In *Chanting Down Babylon: The Rastafari Reader*, ed. Nathaniel Samuel Murrell, William David Spencer, and Adrian Anthony McFarlane, pp. 166–77. Philadelphia: Temple University Press.

Christensen, James Boyd. 1958. "The Role of Proverbs in Fante Culture." *Africa* 28:232–43.

Cleary, Al. n.d. *Jamaican Proverbs.* Kingston.

Cooper, Carolyn. 1993. *Noises in the Blood: Orality, Gender, and the "Vulgar" Body of Jamaican Popular Culture.* Durham, N.C.: Duke University Press.

Cosentino, Donald J., ed. 1995. *The Sacred Arts of Haitian Vodou.* Los Angeles: University of California, Fowler Museum of Cultural History.

Courlander, Harold. 1976. *A Treasury of Afro-American Folklore.* New York: Crown.

Crepeau, Pierre. 1978. "The Invading Guest: Some Aspects of Oral Transmission." *Yearbook of Symbolic Anthropology* 1:11–29. Reprinted in *The Wisdom of Many: Essays on the Proverb*, ed. Wolfgang Mieder and Alan Dundes, pp. 86–110. New York: Garland, 1981.

Crowley, Daniel J., ed. 1977. *African Folklore in the New World.* Austin: University of Texas Press.

Cundall, Frank. 1910. *Jamaica Negro Proverbs and Sayings.* Kingston: Sangster's Books.

Cupmer, George E. 1979. *The Potential of Rastafarianism as a Modern National Religion.* Recorder Press.

Dalrymple, Henderson. 1976. *Bob Marley, Music, Myth and the Rastas.* Carib-Arawak Publishers.

Dance, Daryl C. 1979. *Shuckin' and Jivin': Folklore from Contemporary Black Americans.* Bloomington: Indiana University Press.

———. 1985. *Folklore from Contemporary Jamaicans.* Knoxville: University of Tennessee Press.

———, ed. 1998. *Honey, Hush!: An Anthology of African American Women's Humor.* New York: Norton.

Daniel, Jack. 1973. "Toward an Ethnography of Afro-American Proverbial Usage." *Black Lines* 4:3–12.

———. 1979. *The Wisdom of Sixth Mount Zion from Members of Sixth Mount Zion and Those Who Begot Them.* Pittsburgh: Self-published.

Daniel, Jack, Geneva Smitherman-Donaldson, and Milford A. Jeremiah. 1987. "Makin' a Way Outa No Way: The Proverb Tradition in the Black Experience." *Journal of Black Studies* 17: 482–508.

Davis, Stephen, and Peter Simon. 1977. *Reggae Bloodlines: In Search of the Music and Culture of Jamaica.* New York: Anchor/Doubleday.

Deren, Maya. 1991 [1953]. *Divine Horsemen: The Living Gods of Haiti.* New York: McPherson.

Dundes, Alan. 1965. "Structural Typology in North American Indian Folktales." In *The Study of Folklore,* ed. Alan Dundes, pp. 206–15. Englewood Cliffs, N.J.: Prentice Hall.

Dunham, Katherine. 1946. *Journey to Accompong.* New York: Henry Holt.

Edmonds, Ennis. B. 1998a. "Dread 'I' In-a-Babylon: Ideological Resistance and Cultural Revitalization." In *Chanting Down Babylon: The Rastafari Reader,* ed. Nathaniel Samuel Murrell, William David Spencer, and Adrian Anthony McFarlane, pp. 23–35. Philadelphia: Temple University Press.

———. 1998b. "The Structure and Ethos of Rastafari." In *Chanting Down Babylon: The Rastafari Reader,* pp. 349–60.

Evans-Pritchard, E. E. 1963a. "Meaning in Zande Proverbs." *Man* 4–7.

———. 1963b. "Sixty-One Zande Proverbs." *Man* 136–37.

———. 1964. "Zande Proverbs: Final Selection and Comments. *Man* 1–5.

Faristzaddi, Millard. 1982. *Itations of Jamaica and I Rastafari.* New York: Grove.

Fauset, Arthur H. 1931. *Folklore from Nova Scotia.* New York: Memoirs of the American Folk-lore Society, vol. 24.

Finnegan, Ruth. 1970. "Proverbs. The Significance and Concept of the Proverb. Form and Style. Content. Occasions and Functions. Specific Examples: Jabo; Zulu; Azande. Conclusion." In R. Finnegan, *Oral Literature in Africa,* pp. 389–425. Oxford: Clarendon. Also in *The Wisdom of Many: Essays on the Proverb,* ed. Wolfgang Mieder and Alan Dundes, pp. 10–42. New York: Garland, 1981.

Folsom, Steven. 1993a. "A Discography of American Country Music Hits Employing Proverbs: Covering the Years 1986–1992." In *Proceedings for the 1993 Annual Conference of the Southwest/Texas Popular Association,* ed. Sue Poor, pp. 31–42. Stillwater, Okla.: The Association.

———. 1993b. "Form and Function of Proverbs in Four Country Music Hits from 1992." In *Proceedings for the 1993 Annual Conference of the Southwest/Texas Popular Culture Association,* ed. Sue Poor, pp. 27–31. Stillwater, Okla.: The Association.

———. 1993c. "Proverbs in Recent American Country Music: Form and Function in the Hits of 1986–87." *Proverbium* 10:65–88.

Forsythe, Dennis. 1980. "West Indian Culture through the Prism of Rastafarianism." *Caribbean Quarterly* 26, no. 4:62–81.

Foster, Chuck. 1992. "Soul and Fire: The Wailing Souls." *The Beat* 11, no. 4:38–45.

Frank, Harry A. 1921. "Jamaica Proverbs." *Dialect Notes,* 5:98–108.

Franklin, C. L., Reverend, and Jeff Todd Titon. 1989. *Give Me This Mountain: Life History and Selected Sermons.* Urbana: University of Illinois Press.

Garrison, Len. 1979. *Black Youth, Rastafarianism, and the Identity Crisis in Britain.* London: Afro-Caribbean Educational Resources.

Gates, Henry Louis. 1988. *The Signifying Monkey: A Theory of Afro-American Literary Criticism.* New York: Oxford University Press.

Grant, Cyril F. 1917. "Negro Proverbs Collected in Jamaica, 1887." *Folk-lore* 28:315–17.

Griaule, Marcus. 1965. *Conversations with Ogotemmêli: An Introduction to Dogon Religious Ideas.* London: Oxford University Press.

Hardie, Margaret. 1925–29. "Proverbs and Proverbial Expressions Current in the United States East of the Missouri and North of the Ohio Rivers." *American Speech* 4:461–72.

Hawkeswood, William G. 1983. "I'N'I Ras Tafari: Identity and the Rasta Movement in Auckland." M.A. thesis, Department of Anthropology, University of Auckland, New Zealand.

Haydon, Geoffrey, and Dennis Marks, eds. 1985. *Repercussions: A Celebration of African-American Music.* London: Century.

Hebdige, Dick. 1979. *Subculture: The Meaning of Style.* London: Menthuen.

———. 1987. *Cut 'N' Mix: Culture, Identity and Caribbean Music.* New York: Methuen.

Hepner, Randal L. 1998. "Chanting Down Babylon in the Belly of the Beast: The Rastafarian Movement in the Metropolitan United States." In *Chanting Down Babylon: The Rastafari Reader,* ed. Nathaniel Samuel Murrell, William David Spencer, and Adrian Anthony McFarlane, pp. 199–216. Philadelphia: Temple University Press.

Hoard, Walter B. 1973. "Jamaican Proverbs," In *Anthology: Quotations and Sayings of People of Color,* pp. 117–34. San Francisco: Robert D. Reed.

Homiak, John P. 1998 [1995]. "Dub History: Soundings on Rastafari Livity and Language." In *Rastafari and Other African-Caribbean Worldviews,* ed. Barry Chevannes, pp. 127–81. New Brunswick, N.J.: Rutgers University Press.

Hopkins, John Barton. 1984. "Jamaican Children's Songs." *Ethnomusicology* 28, no. 1:1–17.

Hudson, Catherine. 1972. "Traditional Proverbs as Perceived by Children from an Urban Environment." *Journal of the Folklore Society of Greater Washington* 3:17–24.

Hughes, Langston, and Arna Bontemps, eds. 1972. *The Book of Negro Folklore.* New York: Dodd, Mead.

Hurston, Zora Neale. 1990 [1938]. *Tell My Horse: Voodoo and Life in Haiti and Jamaica.* Philadelphia: Lippincott.

Hutton, Clinton, and Nathaniel Samuel Murrell. 1998. "Rastas' Psychology of Blackness, Resistance, and Somebodiness," In *Chanting Down Babylon: The Rastafari Reader,* ed. Nathaniel Samuel Murrell, William David Spencer, and Adrian Anthony McFarlane, pp. 36–54. Philadelphia: Temple University Press.

Hyamson, Albert M. 1922. *A Dictionary of English Phrases.* London: Routledge.

Jahn, Janheinz. 1990 [1961]. *Muntu: African Culture and the Western World.* New York: Grove Weidenfeld.

Jekyll, Walter. 1966 [1907]. *Jamaican Song and Story.* New York: Dover.

Johnson, Linton Kwesi. 1976. "Jamaican Rebel Music." *Race and Class* 17, no. 4:397–411.

Jones, Simon. 1988. *Black Culture, White Youth: The Reggae Tradition from JA to UK.* London: Macmillan Education.

Jordan, Rosan A. 1982. "Five Proverbs in Context." *Midwest Journal of Language and Folklore* 8:109–15.

Kirshenblatt-Gimblett, Barbara. 1981 [1973]. "Toward a Theory of Proverb Meaning." *Proverbium* (Helsinki) 22:821–27. Reprinted in *The Wisdom of Many: Essays on the Proverb,* ed. Wolfgang Mieder and Alan Dundes, pp. 111–21. New York: Garland.

Kitzinger, Sheila. 1969. "Protest and Mysticism: The Rastafari Cult of Jamaica." *Journal for the Scientific Study of Religion* 8:24–262.

———. 1977. "The Rasta Brethren in Jamaica," In *Peoples and Cultures of the Caribbean*, ed. M. M. Horowitz. Garden City, N.Y.: Natural History Press.

Knappert, Jan. 1997. "Swahili Proverbs in Song." *Proverbium* 14:133–51.

Kochman, Thomas. 1970. "Toward an Ethnography of Black American Speech Behavior." In *Afro-American Anthropology*, ed. Norman E. Whitten Jr. and John F. Szwed, pp. 145–62. New York: Free Press.

Kuhel, Pat. 1991. "Lebanese-American Proverbs and Proverbial Lore." *Mid-American Folklore* 19:110–24.

Lake, Obiagele. 1994. "The Many Voices of Rastafarian Women: Sexual Subordination in the Midst of Liberation." *New West Indian Guide* 68, nos. 3, 4:235–57.

Leach, MacEdward. 1961. "Jamaica Duppy Lore." *Journal of American Folklore* 74:207–15.

Levine, Lawrence W. 1978 [1977]. *Black Culture, Black Consciousness: Afro-American Folk Thought from Slavery to Freedom*. Oxford: Oxford University Press.

Levy, Isaac Jack, and Rosemary Levy Zumwalt. 1990. "A Conversation in Proverbs: Judeo-Spanish Refranes in Context." *Proverbium* 7:117–32.

Lewin, Olive. 1974. *Brown Gal in de Ring*. London: Oxford University Press.

Lewis, Rupert. 1998. "Marcus Garvey and the Early Rastafarians: Continuity and Discontinuity," In *Chanting Down Babylon: The Rastafari Reader*, ed. Nathaniel Samuel Murrell, William David Spencer, and Adrian Anthony McFarlane, pp. 145–58. Philadelphia: Temple University Press.

Lewy, Gunther. 1974. *Religion and Revolution*. New York: Oxford University Press.

McFarlane, Adrian Anthony. 1998. "The Epistemological Significance of 'I-an-I' as a Response to Quashie and Anancyism in Jamaican Culture," In *Chanting Down Babylon: The Rastafari Reader*, ed. Nathaniel Samuel Murrell, William David Spencer, and Adrian Anthony McFarlane, pp. 107–21. Philadelphia: Temple University Press.

Manuel, Peter, with Kenneth Bilby and Michael Largey. 1995. *Caribbean Currents: Caribbean Music from Rumba to Reggae*. Philadelphia: Temple University Press.

Matibag, Eugenio. 1997. "Ifá and Interpretation: An Afro-Caribbean Literary Practice." In *Sacred Possessions: Vodou, Santería, Obeah, and the Caribbean*, ed. Margarite Fernández Olmos and Lizabeth Paravisini-Gebert, pp. 151–70. New Brunswick, N.J.: Rutgers University Press.

Mbiti, John S. 1970. *African Religions and Philosophy*. New York: Anchor.

Messenger, John. 1959. "The Role of Proverbs in a Nigerian Judicial System." *Southwestern Journal of Anthropology* 15:64–73.

Mieder, Wolfgang. 1987. *Tradition and Innovation in Folk Literature*. Hanover, N.H.: University Press of New England.

———. 1988. "Proverbs in American Popular Songs." *Proverbium* 5:85–101.

———. 1989. *American Proverbs: A Study of Texts and Contexts*. New York: Peter Lang.

Mieder, Wolfgang, and Alan Dundes. 1981. *The Wisdom of Many: Essays on the Proverb*. New York: Garland.

Mieder, Wolfgang, Stewart A. Kingsbury, and Kelsie B. Harder, eds. 1992. *A Dictionary of American Proverbs*. New York: Oxford University Press.

Miller, Marian A. L. 1993. "The Rastafarian in Jamaican Political Culture: The Marginalization of a Change Agent." *Western Journal of Black Studies* 17, no. 2:112–17.

Mitchell-Kernan, Claudia. 1972a. "Signifying, Loud Talking, and Marking." In *Rappin' and Stylin' Out*, ed. Thomas Kochman, pp. 315–35. Urbana: University of Illinois Press.

———. 1972b. "Signifying and Marking: Two Afro-American Speech Acts." In *Directions in Sociolinguistics: The Ethnography of Communication*, ed. John J. Gumperz and Dell Hymes, pp. 161–78. New York: Holt, Rinehart and Winston.

Morri, Sister. 1989. "U-Roy: Words of Wisdom." Interview in *The Beat* 8, no. 1:26–34.

Morris-Brown, Vivien. 1993. *The Jamaica Handbook of Proverbs*. Mandeville, Jamaica: Island Heart.

Morrish, Ivor. 1982. *Obeah, Christ, and Rastaman: Jamaica and Its Religion*. Cambridge, England: J. Clarke.

Murray, Thomas. 1951. *Folk Songs of Jamaica*. London: Oxford University Press.

Murray, Thomas, and John Gavall. 1960. *Twelve Folk Songs from Jamaica*. London: Oxford University Press.

Murrell, Nathaniel Samuel, and Lewin Williams. 1998. "The Black Biblical Hermeneutics," In *Chanting Down Babylon: The Rastafari Reader*, ed. Nathaniel Samuel Murrell, William David Spencer, and Adrian Anthony McFarlane, pp. 326–48. Philadelphia: Temple University Press.

Murrell, Nathaniel Samuel, William David Spencer, and Adrian Anthony McFarlane, ed. 1998. *Chanting Down Babylon: The Rastafari Reader*. Philadelphia: Temple University Press.

Nagashina, Yoshiko. S. 1984. *Rastafarian Music in Contemporary Jamaica: A Study of Socioreligious Music of the Rastafarian Movement in Jamaica*. Tokyo: Institute for the Studies of Languages and Cultures of Asia and Africa.

Noyce, John L. 1978. *The Rastafarians in Britain and Jamaica*. Brighton, England: University of Sussex Press.

Ogede, Ode S. 1993. "Proverb Usage in the Praise Songs of the Igede: *Adiyah* Poet Micah Ichegbeh." *Proverbium* 10:237–56.

O'Gorman, Pamela. 1972. "An Approach to the Study of Jamaican Popular Music." *Jamaica Journal* 6:50ff.

Oledzki, Jacek. 1979. "On Some Maxims on African Cars." *Africana Bulletin* 28:29–35.

Olmos, Margarite Fernández, and Lizabeth Paravisini-Gebert, eds. 1997. *Sacred Possessions: Vodou, Santería, Obeah, and the Caribbean*. New Brunswick, N.J.: Rutgers University Press.

Owens, Joseph. 1976. *Dread: The Rastafarians of Jamaica*. Kingston: Sangsters.

Owens, J. V. 1977/78. "Literature on the Ratafari: 1955–1974." *New Community* (Journal of the Commission of Racial Equality, London) 6:1, 2.

Paladino, Ed. 1990. "Culture: Visions and Prophecy." *The Beat* 9, no. 5:33–37.

Parsons, Elsie Clews. 1919. "Riddles and Proverbs from the Bahama Islands." *Journal of American Folklore* 32:439–41.

———. 1943. *Folk-Lore of the Antilles, French and English.* New York: Memoirs of the American Folk-Lore Society, vol. 26.

Pollard, Velma. 1980. "Dread Talk—The Speech of the Rastafarian in Jamaica." *Caribbean Quarterly* 26:32–42.

———. 1982a. "The Social History of Dread Talk." *Caribbean Quarterly* 28, no. 4:17–40.

———. 1982b. "Word Sounds: The Language of the Rastafari in Barbodos and St. Lucia." *Jamaica Journal* 17, no. 1:57–62.

Prahlad, Sw. Anand. [As Dennis Folly.] 1982. "Getting the Butter from the Duck: Proverbs and Proverbial Expressions in an Afro-American Family." In *A Celebration of American Family Folklore,* ed. Steven J. Zeitlin, Amy J. Kotlin, and Holly Cutting Baker, pp. 232–41. New York: Pantheon.

———. 1994. " 'No Guts, No Glory': Proverbs, Values, and Image Among Anglo-American University Students." *Southern Folklore* 51, no. 3:285–98.

———. 1995. "Persona and Proverb Meaning in Roots Reggae: Proverbs of the Itals Reggae Group." *Proverbium* 12:275–93.

———. 1996. *African American Proverbs in Context.* Jackson: University Press of Mississippi.

Priebe, Richard. 1971. "The Horses of Speech: A Structural Analysis of the Proverb." *Folklore Annual* 3:26–32.

Pulis, John W. 1993. " 'Up-Full Sounds': Language, Identity, and the World-View of Rastafari." *Ethnic Groups* 10:285–300.

Rampini, Charles l. G. 1873. *Letters From Jamaica.* Edinburgh.

Rattray, Robert Sutherland. 1916. *Ashanti Proverbs.* London: Oxford University Press.

Reckord, Verena. 1998. "From Burro Drums to Reggae Ridims: The Evolution of Rasta Music," In *Chanting Down Babylon: The Rastafari Reader,* ed. Nathaniel Samuel Murrell, William David Spencer, and Adrian Anthony McFarlane, pp. 231–52. Philadelphia: Temple University Press.

Regis, Humphrey A. 1994. "Changes in Reggae Music since the Mid-1970s and Cultural Domination by Re-exportation." *Western Journal of Black Studies* 18, no. 1:44–50.

Roberts, Helen H. 1925. "A Study of Folk Song Variants Based on Field Work in Jamaica," *Journal of American Folklore,* 38:149–216.

Robinson, Carey. 1969. *The Fighting Maroons of Jamaica.* Kingston: Collins and Sangster.

Rose, Tricia. 1994. *Black Noise: Rap Music and Black Culture in Contemporary America.* Hanover, N.H.: Wesleyan University Press.

Rowe, Maureen. 1980. "The Woman in Rastafari." *Caribbean Quarterly* 26, no. 4:13–21.

———. 1998. "Gender and Family Relations in Rastafari: A Personal Perspective," In *Chanting Down Babylon: The Rastafari Reader,* ed. Nathaniel Samuel Murrell, William David Spencer, and Adrian Anthony McFarlane, pp. 72–88. Philadelphia: Temple University Press.

Saakana, Amon Saba [Sebastian Clarke]. 1980. *Jah Music: The Evolution of the Popular Jamaican Song.* London: Heinemann Educational Books.

Savishinsky, Neil J. 1994. "Transnational Popular Culture and the Global Spread of the Jamaican Rastafarian Movement." *New West Indian Guide* 68, nos. 3, 4:259–81.

———. 1998. "African Dimensions of the Jamaican Rastafarian Movement," In *Chanting Down Babylon: The Rastafari Reader,* ed. Nathaniel Samuel Murrell, William David Spencer, and Adrian Anthony McFarlane, pp. 125–44. Philadelphia: Temple University Press.

Seaga, Edward, comp. and ed. 1956. *Folk Music of Jamaica.* Record album with explanatory notes. New York, Ethnic Folkways Library.

Seitel, Peter. 1969. "Proverbs: A Social Use of Metaphor." *Genre* 2:143–61. Reprinted in *The Wisdom of Many: Essays on the Proverb,* ed. Wolfgang Mieder and Alan Dundes, pp. 122–39. New York: Garland, 1981.

———. 1977. "Saying Haya Sayings: Two Categories of Proverb Use." In *The Social Use of Metaphor: Essays in the Anthropology of Rhetoric,* ed. David Sapir and J. Christopher, pp. 75–99. Philadelphia: University of Pennsylvania Press.

Sheffey, Ruthe T. 1989. "Behold the Dreamers: Katherine Dunham and Zora Neale Hurston among the Maroons." In *Trajectory: Fueling the Future and Preserving the African-American Past,* pp. 183–202. Baltimore: Morgan State University Press.

Sherlock, Phillip. 1966a. *Anansi the Spider Man.* London: Macmillan.

———. 1966b. *West Indian Folk-Tales.* London: Oxford University Press.

Simpson, G. E. 1956. "The Rastafarian Movement in Jamaica." *Social and Economic Studies.* Kingston, Jamaica.

Simpson, John A. 1992 [1982]. *The Concise English Dictionary of Proverbs.* Oxford: Oxford University Press.

Smith, Michael Garfield, Roy Augier, and Rex Nettleford. 1967a. "The Ras Tafari Movement in Kingston, Jamaica, Part I" *Caribbean Quarterly* 13, no. 3:3–39.

———. 1967b. "The Ras Tafari Movement in Kingston, Jamaica, Part II." *Caribbean Quarterly* 13, no. 4:3–14.

Snapp, Emma L. 1933. "Proverbial Lore in Nebraska." *University of Nebraska Studies in Language, Literature, and Criticism* 13:53–112.

Spencer, William David. 1998. "Chanting Change around the World through Rasta Ridim and Art." In *Chanting Down Babylon: The Rastafari Reader,* ed. Nathaniel Samuel Murrell, William David Spencer, and Adrian Anthony McFarlane, pp. 266–83. Philadelphia: Temple University Press.

Steffens, Roger. 1986a. "Jimmy Cliff: From Trenchtown to Paradise." Interview in *The Beat* 5, no. 4:16–19.

———. 1986b. "Peter Tosh: Rebel with a Cause." Interview in *The Beat* 5, no. 1:20–23, 49.

———. 1996. "King Sporty: 'Buffalo Soldier'—The National Anthem of Black People." Interview in *The Beat* 15, no. 3:50–51.

———. 1998. "Bob Marley: Rasta Warrior." In *Chanting Down Babylon: The Rastafari Reader,* ed. Nathaniel Samuel Murrell, William David Spencer, and Adrian Anthony McFarlane, pp. 253–65. Philadelphia: Temple University Press.

Steffens, Roger, and Bruce W. Talamon. 1994. *Bob Marley: Spirit Dancer.* New York: Norton.

Stevenson, Burton E. 1965. *The Macmillan Book of Proverbs, Maxims, and Familiar Phrases.* New York: Macmillan.

Taft, Michael. 1994. "Proverbs in the Blues: How Frequent Is Frequent?" *Proverbium* 11:227–58.

Taylor, Archer. 1950a. "Proverb." In *Standard Dictionary of Folklore, Mythology, and Legend,* ed. Maria Leach, pp. 902–05. New York: Funk and Wagnalls.

———. 1950b. "Proverbial Phrases." In *Standard Dictionary of Folklore, Mythology, and Legend,* ed. Maria Leach, pp. 906. New York: Funk and Wagnalls.

———. 1962. *The Proverb and an Index to the Proverb.* Hatboro, Pa.: Folklore Associates.

Taylor, Archer, and B. J. Whiting. 1958. *A Dictionary of American Proverbs and Proverbial Phrases, 1820–1880.* Cambridge, Mass.: Belknap.

Thelwell, Michael. 1980. *The Harder They Come.* London: Pluto.

Thomas, J. J. 1987 [1982]. *Chat Jamaican: The Authentic Jamaican Phrase Book.* Self-published.

Thomas, Polly, and Adam Vaitilingam. 1997. *Jamaica: The Rough Guide.* London: Rough Guides.

Tilley, Morris P. 1950. *A Dictionary of the Proverbs in England in the Sixteenth and Seventeenth Centuries.* Ann Arbor: University of Michigan Press.

Turner, Michael. 1996. "Old Time People Used to Say." *The Beat: Reggae, African, Caribbean, and World Music* 15, no. 2:30–31.

Turner, Terisa E. 1991. "Women, Rastafari, and the New Society: Caribbean and East African Roots of a Popular Movement against Structural Adjustment." *Labour, Capital, and Society* 24:1 (Apr.): 66–89.

Van Dijk, Frank Jan. 1998. "Chanting Down Outernational: The Rise of Rastafari in Europe, the Caribbean, and the Pacific," In *Chanting Down Babylon: The Rastafari Reader,* ed. Nathaniel Samuel Murrell, William David Spencer, and Adrian Anthony McFarlane, pp. 178–198. Philadelphia: Temple University Press.

Waters, Anita M. 1985. *Race, Class, and Political Symbols: Rastafari and Reggae in Jamaican Politics.* New Brunswick, N.J.: Transaction.

Watson, Llewellyn G. 1973. "Social Structure and Social Movements: The Black Muslims in the U.S.A. and the Ras-Tafarians in Jamaica." *British Journal of Sociology* 24:188–204.

———. 1991. *Jamaican Sayings: With Notes on Folklore, Aesthetics, and Social Control.* Tallahassee: Florida A & M University Press.

White, Timothy. 1998 [1983]. *Catch a Fire: The Life of Bob Marley.* New York: Henry Holt.

Whiting, B. J. 1952. "Proverbs and Proverbial Sayings." In *The Frank C. Brown Collection of North Carolina Folklore,* vol. 1, ed. Wayland Hand, pp. 329–501. Durham: Duke University Press.

———. 1989. *Modern Proverbs and Proverbial Sayings.* Cambridge, Mass.: Harvard University Press.

Whitney, Malika Lee, and Dermott Hussey. 1984. *Bob Marley, Reggae King of the World.* New York: E. P. Dutton.

Wilson, F. P. 1970. *The Oxford Dictionary of English Proverbs*. Oxford: Clarendon Press.

Yankah, Kwesi. 1986. "Proverb Speaking as a Creative Process: The Akan of Ghana." *Proverbium* 3:195–230.

———. 1989a. *The Proverb in the Context of Akan Rhetoric: A Theory of Proverb Praxis*. Bern: Peter Lang.

———. 1989b. "Proverbs: The Aesthetics of Traditional Communication." *Research in African Literature* 20, no. 3:325–46.

Yawney, Carol D. 1979. "Dread Wasteland: Rastafari Ritual in West Kingston, Jamaica." In *Ritual, Symbolism, and Ceremonialism in the Americas,* ed. R. Crumrine. Greeley: University of Northern Colorado Occasional Publications in Anthropology, Ethnology Series No. 33, Museum of Anthropology.

———. 1983a. "Rastafarian Sistren by the Rivers of Babylon." *Canadian Woman Studies* 5, no. 2:73–75.

———. 1983b. "To Grow a Daughter: Cultural Liberation and the Dynamics of Oppression in Jamaica." In *Feminism in Canada,* ed. A. Miller and G. Finn, pp. 119–44. Montreal: Black Rose.

———. 1987. "Moving with the Dawtas of Rastafari: From Myth to Reality." In *El Caribe y América Latina,* ed. Ulrich Fleischmann and Ineke Phaf, pp. 193–212. Berlin: Lateinamerika Institut.

Zindi, Fred. 1985. *Roots Rocking in Zimbabwe*. Harare: Mambo Press.

Index

Abednego, 11

Abel, 16

Abidjan, 172

Abrahams, Roger D., 34, 58, 135–36, 143

Abyssinians, The, 33, 140, 207

Accompong, 9

Adam, 16

Addis Kokeb, 82

Africa, 3, 14, 17, 35, 52, 59, 63–67, 73, 122, 127–29, 142, 148, 172, 194–95, 198–99, 208, 211–12; diviners (*see* Ifá Divination); Gold Coast, 172; Jamaican songs, influences on, 3, 7; languages of, 9; musical influences of, 51; nationalism, 14; proverbs from, 3, 123–37; Rasta ideology, importance to, 26, 28; Rastafari, influences on, 10, 17, 19, 23, 26, 27, 124, 161; Rastafari, spread of, 6, 66; repatriation to, 11–12, 15, 22, 202; slave trade, 8, 26, 53, 99, 121, 195; slave tribes from, 9,

33; warriors of, 42–43, 46; as Zion, 11, 27, 37, 39, 63, 96, 128, 154, 164, 172, 202–03

African Americans, 18, 39, 127, 200; Jamaican recordings, influence on, 1–4, 6–8, 34, 36, 45, 65, 118, 127, 141, 176, 189; music of (*see* Blues; Gospel; R & B; Soul); signifying, 34; toasts, 34

Akan, the, 3

Albums: covers as art, 36–38, 42–44, 108, 151, 155, 179, 194–95, 199, 224; warrior/priests persona, reflections of, 31–46, 58, 62, 64, 114, 117–19, 124–25, 137, 140–42, 148–51, 163, 166, 176, 180, 190, 205

Titles: *Appointment*, 49, 211; *Babylon by Bus*, 177; *Best Sellers*, 32, 209; *Blackheart Man*, 21, 37, 38; *Brutal*, 118, 146, 151, 152, 156, 166, 210, 216, 218, 221; *Burnin'*, 178–79, 184, 210; *Bush Doctor*, 57, 212, 216; *Catch a Fire*, 177–79, 207, 210; *Confron-*

pound foolish, 59, 83; Plant corn, can't reap peas, 149; Pot a cook but the food no nough, 98; Praise him as Jah, you get a jolly reward, 166; Praise him as king, you get a kingly reward, 166; Prevention is better than cure, 74; promise is a comfort to a fool, A, 78; Pull your own weight, 196; Putting the cart before the horse, 161; quickness of your eyes, they say, does deceive your body, The, 133; rain a fall, but de doti tuff, A, 185; Rain a fall but the dutty tough, 98, 111, 125, 136, 150; Rastafari Chariot, 146; rich man's wealth is in his city, the righteous wealth is in his holy place, The, 173; Rolling stone don't gather no moss, 141, 147; See them, go live with them, it's a different thing, 132; Seein' is believin', 88, 89, 92, 111, 117; Seven times rise and seven times fall, 87, 93, 111; Sow good seed today and you will reap good crop tomorrow, 138; Silent river runs deep, 3, 59, 123, 155; Simple trash can blind eyes, 152; So a man thinketh, so is he, 95; Some ha fe come, some ha fe go, 154, 222; Some people put the best outside, some people keep the best inside, 155, 198; Sometimes you win, sometimes you lose, 85; Spit in the sky, will fall in your eye, 149; Sticks and stones may break my bone, but my darling words will never hurt, 117; stone that the builder refuse shall be the head cornerstone, The, 150, 174, 196; Stumbling block must be removed, 147; Sweet nanny goat a go running belly, 76, 160, 176; Talk is cheap, 134, 173; Teeth and tongue have fe meet some day, 150, 154; These are the big fish who always try to eat down the small fish, 192; They give you basket to carry water, 84, 133, 150, 159; They say the sun, shines for us all, 193;

things you want is not what you always get, The, 165; Think you're in heaven but you're living in hell, 194; Time alone, time will tell, 194; Time is a master and waits on no one, 160; Time like lightning strikes without warning, 125, 126; Time longer than rope, and rope is running out, 75; Too much rat never dig good hole, 154, 222; truth is an offense, but not a sin, The, 173; truth that is hidden must reveal, The, 144; Trying to force water over a hill, 161; Use what you got till you get what you want, 165; We riding thru the thick, we riding thru the thin, 196; Well, I guess we'll just have to call it a day, 109; We've got no time to lose, 198; What drop off the head always drop on the shoulder, 120; What goes around it comes around, 195; What goes on up is coming on down, 195; What has been hidden from the wise and the prudent, been revealed to the babe and the suckling, 204; What is to be must be, 175, 183; What you don't know you just don't know, 90; What you sow is what you shall reap, 127, 149, 150, 155, 167; What your hand commit, your body must bear, 138; What your hands do, it's your own eyes that've seen, 182; Whatever one is doing, one should do it to be the best of one's ability, 75; What's in the darkness must come out in light, 182, 203; When in Rome, do as the Romans, 108, 111, 149; When one door is closed, don't you know another is open, 175, 200; When the cat's away, the mice will play, 188, 189; When the rain fall, it don't fall on one man's house, 135, 190; Where there's a will, there's always a way, 203; Who can't hear will feel, 144, 146; Who feels it knows it, 125, 144, 150; Who Jah bless, no one curse, 175, 188; Who the cap fit, let them wear it, 175, 187, 188; Who the sock fit, let them wear it, 175; Whosoever diggeth a pit, shall fall in it, 180; Wisdom is better than silver and gold, 96, 202; You ain't gonna miss your water, until your well runs dry, 204; You can fool some people sometimes but you cannot fool all the people all the time, 129, 184; You can't run away from yourself, 193; You can't stop bird from flying over your head, but you can stop him from building a nest, 83; You jump outta frying pan, jump ina fire, 121; You never too old to learn, 92, 111; You play with fire, fire will burn you, 149; Your heart is willing and your flesh is weak, 154; You're never too old to learn, 92; You've got to come from some place before you can go back, 120

Psalms, 99

Pulis, John W., 24

Quaco, 9

Ragga, 4, 53

Rasta Inn, 77

Rastafari, 2, 212, 215–16, 220; belief and world view, 6, 9, 10, 17, 19, 21, 22, 24, 37, 50, 58, 62, 65, 131, 137, 149, 182, 203, 204; and communities, 9, 29, 60, 62, 63, 64, 65, 66, 67, 74, 79, 104, 124, 148, 182, 213; militant ideology, 119, 123, 131, 146, 177, 183, 184, 185, 190, 215, 216; mythology, 5, 18, 38, 39, 40, 41, 160; in New Zealand, 66, 67; in the Pacific, 66; prophets, 14–18, 27, 31, 33, 38, 39, 45, 50, 190, 194; reggae, impact on, 6; rituals, 13, 23–25, 40, 65–66, 116, 128, 151, 163, 211, 218

Reasonings, 23–25, 40, 65–66; as frame for reggae, 151

Reggae Ambassadors Worldwide (RAW), 64

Reggae Instruments. *See* Drums; Guitar; Bass; Keyboards; Horns

Regis, Humphrey, 36, 68

Reid, Duke, 7, 215

Rent-A-Dread, 88

Repatriation. *See* Africa

Resistance, 7–11, 14, 17, 22, 72

Revivalist religion, 10, 17, 39, 51, 52, 118, 140, 156

Rhythm and Blues (R & B), 215

Ritual dissonance, 50, 52–55, 112, 115, 121–22, 126, 146, 185

Rock Steady, 4, 6, 54, 215–16

Rodin, 143

Romeo, Max, 161, 211

Rose, Tricia, 55

Roth, LuAnne, 92, 100, 104–09

Rowe, Maureen, 34

Russia, 65

Rudeboy, 8, 34–35, 57, 176

Rwanda, 66

Samoa, 66

Sampling, 55

Samson, 11

San Francisco, Calif., 139

Santeria, 29

Savishinsky, Neil, 15, 62, 63, 65, 66, 67

Scott, Dennis, 75

Sedaka, Neil, 6

Seitel, Peter, 113, 143

Selassie, King Haile, 8, 13–16, 22, 25, 37, 43–45, 65, 124, 171–73, 177

Senegal, 66, 67

Sermon songs, 112

Sermons, 34, 36, 53, 113–24, 134, 141–46, 154, 163–65, 191, 196–98, 200, 204

Seymour, A. J., 75

Shaddrack, 11

Sharpe, Sam, 10

Shashemane, 66

Shine Eye Girl, 51

Signifying, 55

Situational meaning, 136, 137, 181

Ska, 4, 6, 7, 151, 157, 163, 175–76, 215–16

Skatalites, The, 167

Slavery, 1, 9, 10, 15–16, 22, 25, 36, 75, 99, 107, 115, 118, 132–33, 141, 147, 159

Social meaning, 136–37

Solomon, King, 14, 41

Songs: "Action," 151; "Almighty," 39, 123, 129, 163, 166, 223; "Armagideon," 21; "Baby We've Got a Date," 179; "Black Starliner Must Come," 39; "Blood (Thicker Than Water)," 151, 163; "Blood Thicker Than Water," 168; "Brutal," 141; "Buffalo Soldier," 43, 178; "Carry Go Bring Come," 160; "Christopher Columbus," 33, 34; "Coming In from the Cold," 174, 200, 202; "Crisis," 192–93; "Don't Cry Sufferer," 128; "Don't Rock My Boat," 176; "Don't Wake the Lion," 57, 151; "Double Tribute to the O.M., A," 170; "Duppy Conqueror," 179; "Easy to Catch," 119, 151, 163, 210; "Emmanuel Road," 122; "Fool Will Fall, A," 131; "400 Years," 179; "Frying Pan," 121; "Get Ready to Ride the Lion to Zion," 39; "Get Up Stand Up," 129, 178, 179; "Give Me What I Want," 118, 151, 221; "Guiltiness," 190, 191; "Hallelujah," 27, 150, 157, 161, 163; "Hand a Bowl," 132, 159; "Happen Before the Time," 151, 163, 165, 166; "Heathen, The," 133, 173, 190; "Heavy Heavy Load," 159, 160; "Herbs Pirate," 141, 142, 145, 219; "I Am the Toughest," 57; "I Shot the Sheriff," 174–75, 179, 183–84; "In This Time," 149; "Innocent Blood," 34; "Iron, Lion, Zion," 128; "Iron Sharpeneth Iron," 59, 127; "Is This Love," 178; "Israelites, The," 160; "Jah Calling," 153–54; "Jah Helps Those," 151; "Jah Jah Hear My Plea," 116; "Jah Live," 173; "Jamming," 190, 212; "Kill Crime," 153–55, 222; "Kill Them with Music," 50, 53; "Lay it on the Line," 150; "Make Merry," 154, 223; "Midnight Ravers," 179; "Modern Age," 163; "My Religion," 32; "Nanny Goat," 159, 160; "Natty Dread Taking Over," 39; "Never Say Never," 151, 163; "O Carolina," 7, 160; "Oh Jah Jah," 116; "Old Broom," 150; "One Foundation," 130, 179, 182; "Outcast," 34; "Pass It On," 179, 182; "Put It On," 179, 230; "Rastafari Chariot," 141, 146, 151; "Rat Race," 150, 188; "Real Situation," 173, 201; "Redemption Song," 201–02; "Reggae Physician," 49; "Reincarnated Souls," 38; "Revolution," 185; "Ride Natty Ride," 174, 196; "Roll Rastafari Chariot," 142; "Run Baldhead," 151; "Run Dem Down," 131; "Running Away," 192–93; "Satisfy My Soul," 119, 192; "See Them a Come," 39; "Seeing is Believing," 151; "She's Gone," 192, 231; "Simmer Down," 35, 160, 175–76, 179; "Small Axe," 150, 176, 179–83; "Smile Knotty Dread," 151; "Smile Out of Style," 161; "So Much Things to Say," 41, 134, 190; "So Much Trouble in the World," 174, 195; "Steppin Razor," 57; "Stiff Necked Fools," 173; "Stir It Up" 179; "Stop Red Eye," 52, 53, 121; "Stop That Train," 179; "Survival," 197; "Them Belly Full," 150; "Things and Time," 150; "Time (Take No Share)," 151, 158; "Time Will Tell," 150–51, 192, 194, 212; "Titanic," 116, 163; "Together Forever," 163; "Top Rankin'," 65; "Trenchtown Rock," 31; "Truth Must Reveal," 143, 151, 219; "Wake Up and Live," 98, 196; "Wanti Wanti," 106, 151, 161, 163; "Weeping and Wailing," 138, 150; "Who Feels It," 176; "Who Lives it," 151; "Who No Waan Come," 150; "Who the Cap Fit," 150, 174, 175, 186; "Zion Train," 96, 202